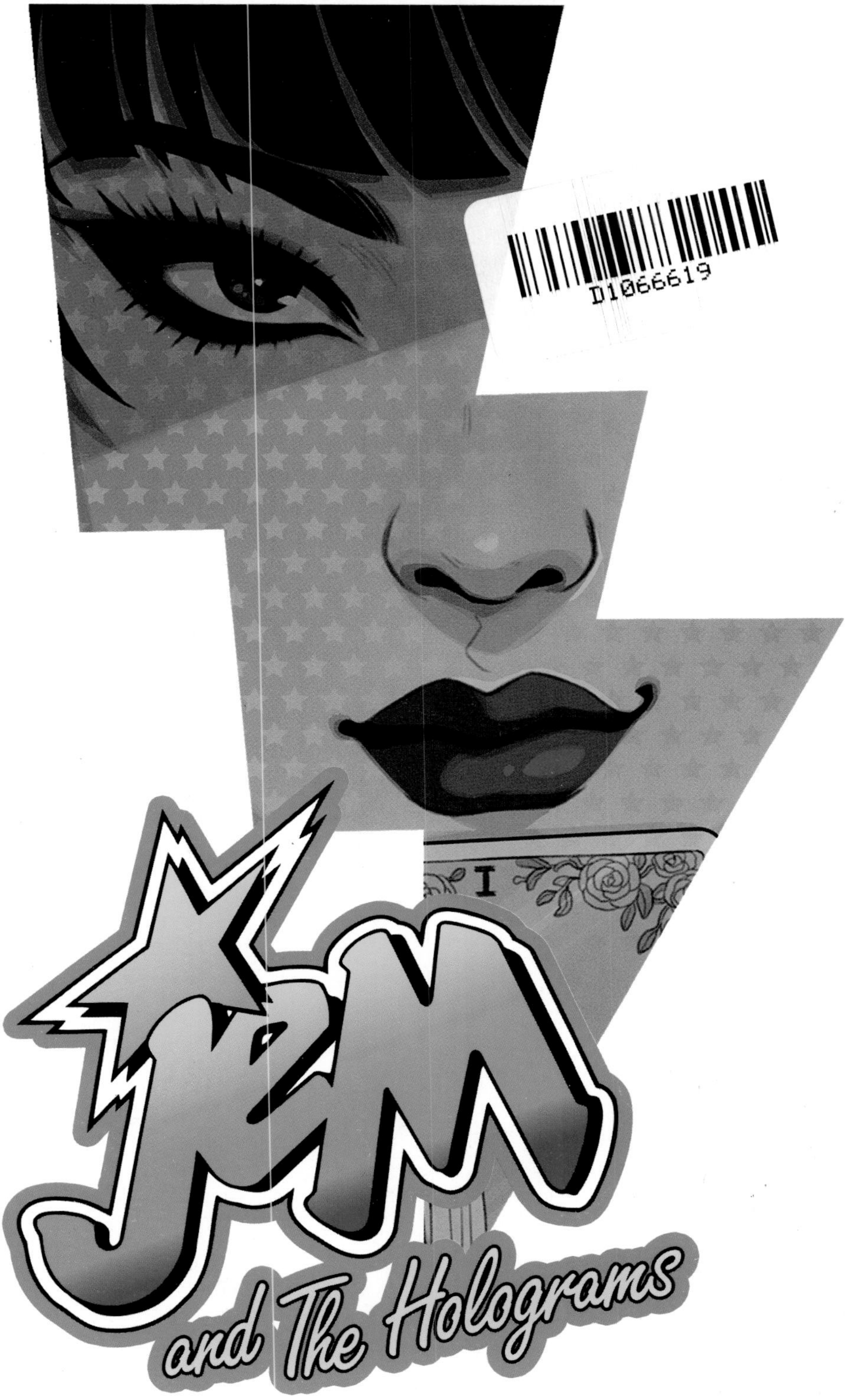
JEM
and The Holograms

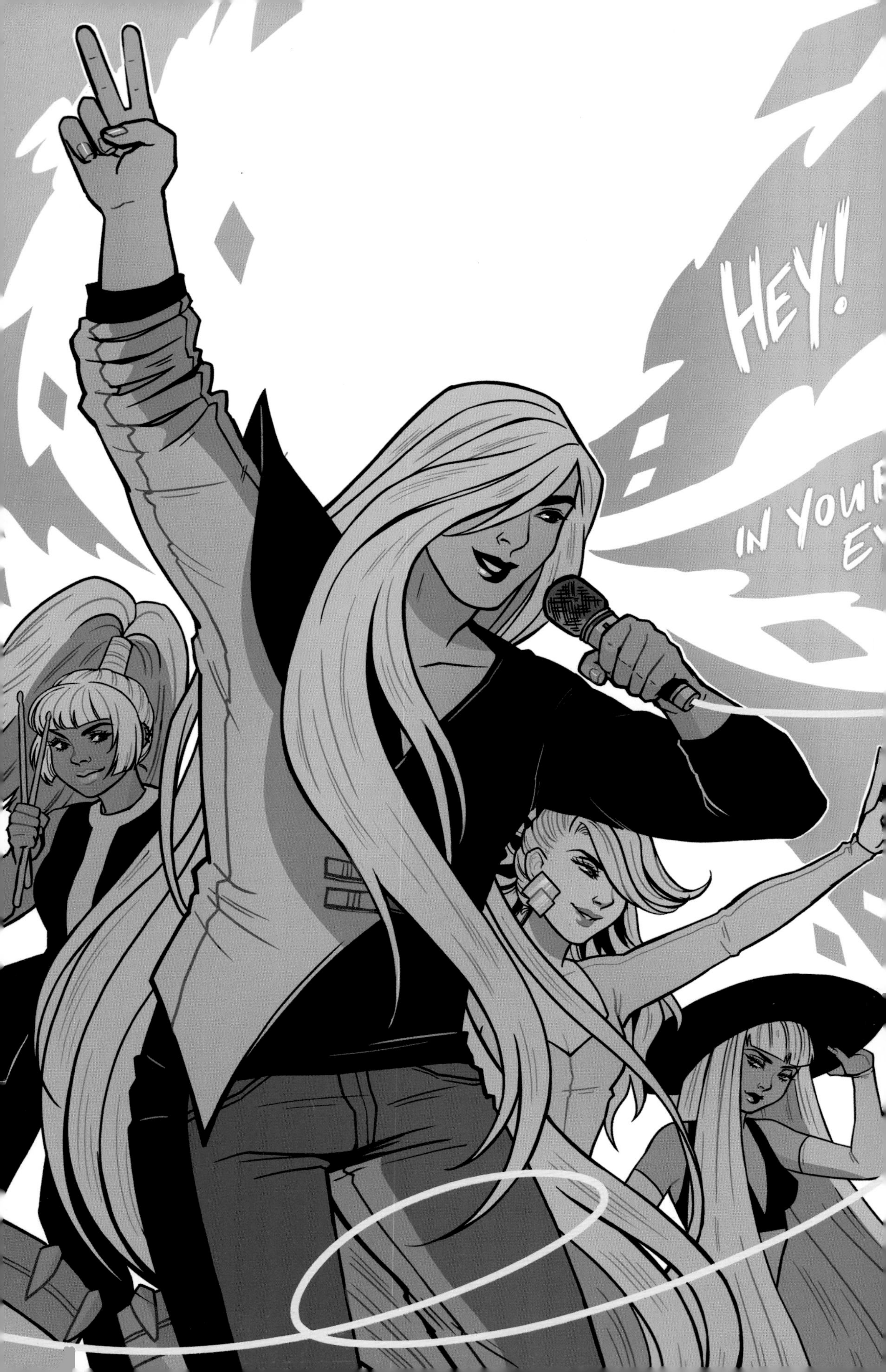
HEY!

WRITTEN BY **KELLY THOMPSON**

CH-CH-CHANGES
ART BY **JEN BARTEL**
COLORS BY **M. VICTORIA ROBADO**
LETTERS BY **SHAWN LEE**

ENTER THE STINGERS
ART BY **MEREDITH MCCLAREN**
COLORS BY **M. VICTORIA ROBADO**
LETTERS BY **SHAWN LEE**

COVER ART BY **MEREDITH MCCLAREN**
BACK COVER ART BY **JEN BARTEL**
SERIES EDITS BY **JOHN BARBER** AND **SARAH GAYDOS**
SERIES EDITORIAL ASSIST BY **CHRIS CERASI**
COLLECTION EDITS BY **JUSTIN EISINGER** AND **ALONZO SIMON**
COLLECTION DESIGN BY **CLAUDIA CHONG**
PUBLISHER: **TED ADAMS**

Special thanks to Hasbro's Andrea Hopelain, Elizabeth Malkin, Ed Lane, Beth Artale, and Michael Kelly for their invaluable assistance.   For international rights, contact licensing@idwpublishing.com

ISBN: 978-1-63140-837-3   20 19 18 17   1 2 3 4

Ted Adams, CEO & Publisher • Greg Goldstein, President & COO • Robbie Robbins, EVP/Sr. Graphic Artist • Chris Ryall, Chief Creative Officer • David Hedgecock, Editor-in-Chief • Laurie Windrow, Senior Vice President of Sales & Marketing • Matthew Ruzicka, CPA, Chief Financial Officer • Dirk Wood, VP of Marketing • Lorelei Bunjes, VP of Digital Services • Jeff Webber, VP of Licensing, Digital and Subsidiary Rights • Jerry Bennington, VP of New Product Development

Facebook: facebook.com/idwpublishing • Twitter: @idwpublishing •
YouTube: youtube.com/idwpublishing Tumblr: tumblr.idwpublishing.com
• Instagram: instagram.com/idwpublishing

  You Tube

www.IDWPUBLISHING.com

JEM AND THE HOLOGRAMS, VOLUME 4: ENTER THE STINGERS. APRIL 2017. FIRST PRINTING. HASBRO and its logo, JEM & THE HOLOGRAMS, and all related characters are trademarks of Hasbro and are used with permission. © 2017 Hasbro. All Rights Reserved. The IDW logo is registered in the U.S. Patent and Trademark Office. IDW Publishing, a division of Idea and Design Works, LLC. Editorial offices: 2765 Truxtun Road, San Diego, CA 92106. Any similarities to persons living or dead are purely coincidental. With the exception of artwork used for review purposes, none of the contents of this publication may be reprinted without the permission of Idea and Design Works, LLC. Printed in Korea.
IDW Publishing does not read or accept unsolicited submissions of ideas, stories, or artwork.

Originally published as JEM AND THE HOLOGRAMS issues #17–23.

3 1907 00370 9267

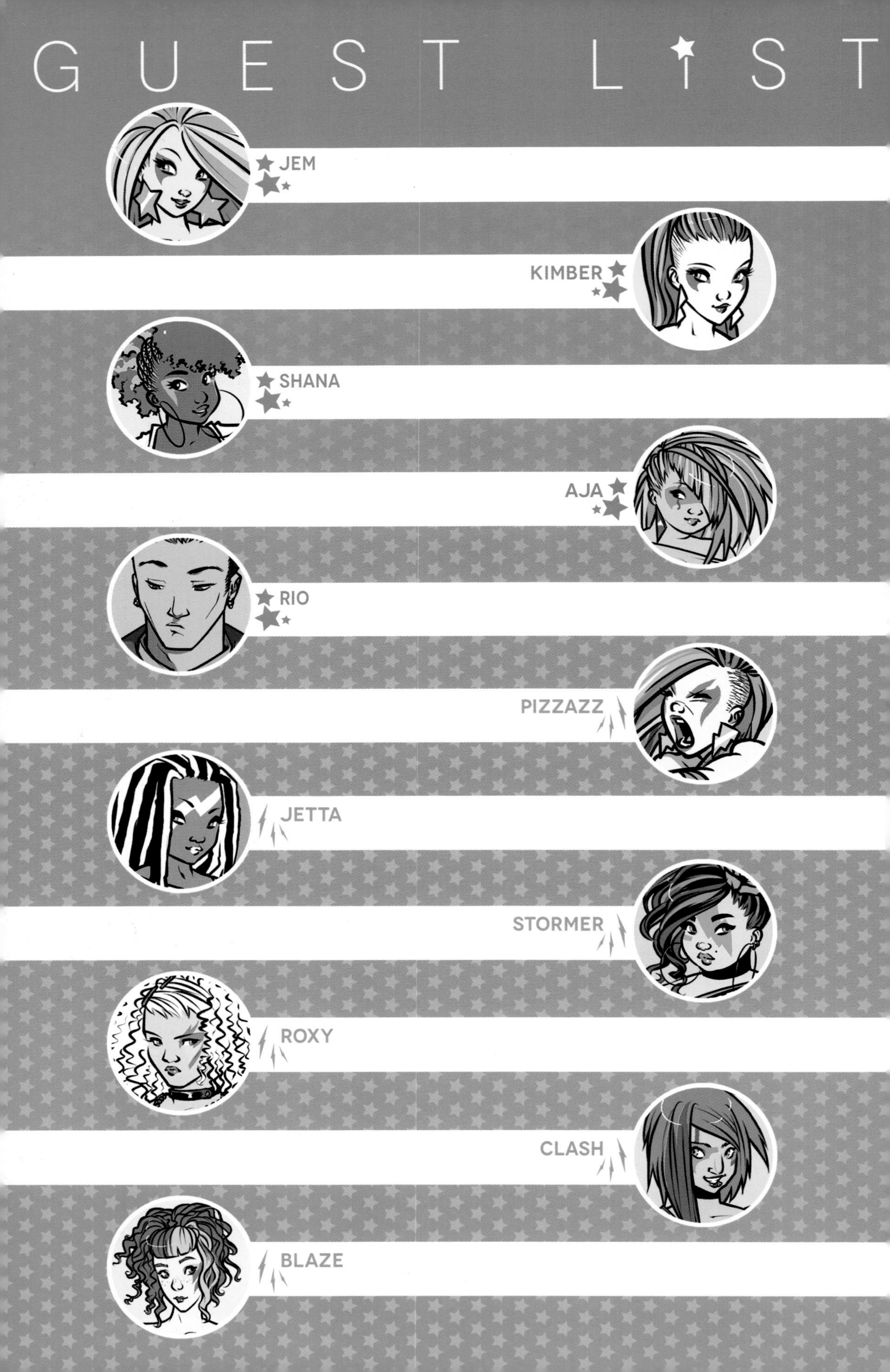
GUEST LIST
JEM
KIMBER
SHANA
AJA
RIO
PIZZAZZ
JETTA
STORMER
ROXY
CLASH
BLAZE

PREVIOUSLY

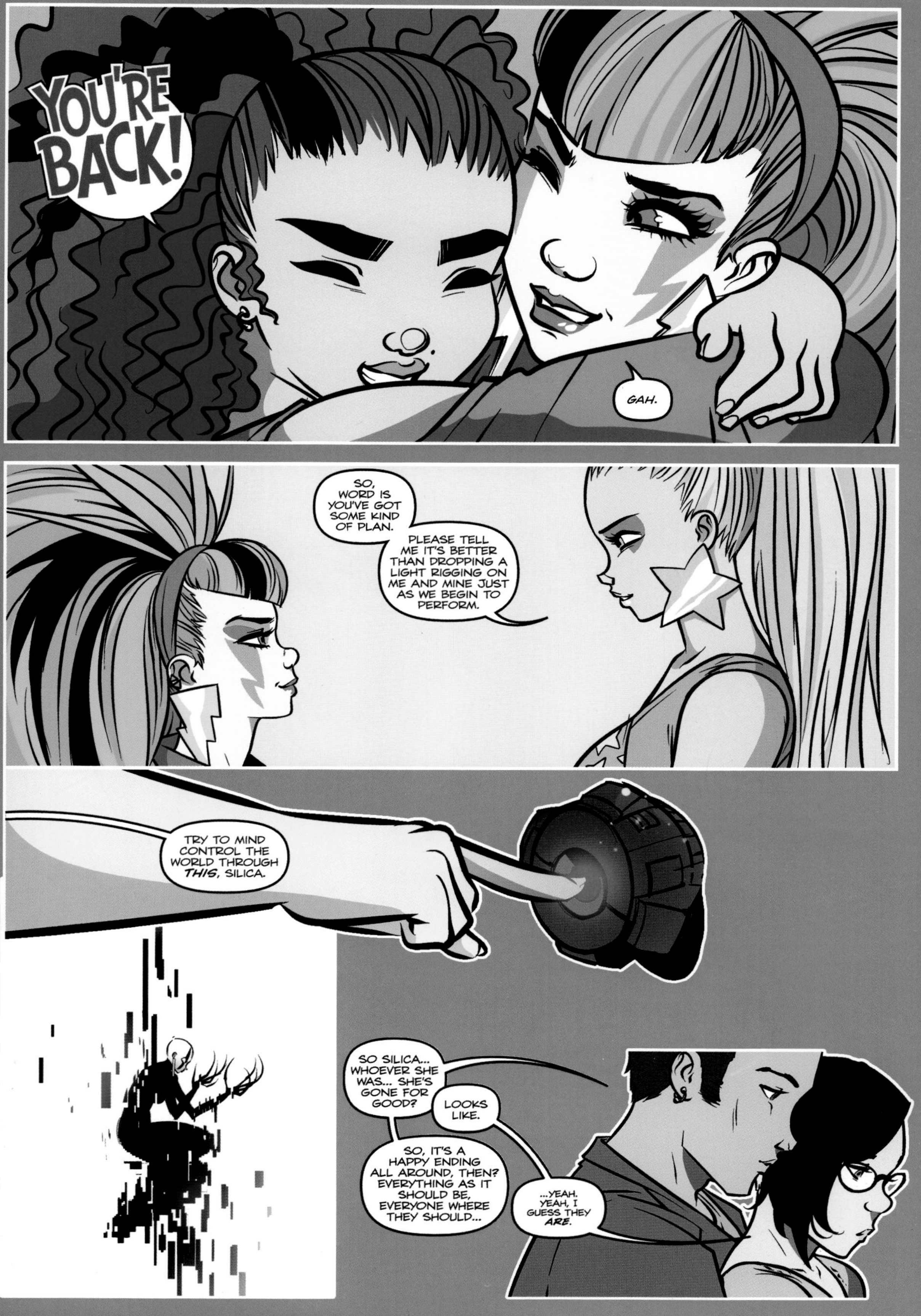

YOU'RE BACK!
GAH.
SO, WORD IS YOU'VE GOT SOME KIND OF PLAN.
PLEASE TELL ME IT'S BETTER THAN DROPPING A LIGHT RIGGING ON ME AND MINE JUST AS WE BEGIN TO PERFORM.
TRY TO MIND CONTROL THE WORLD THROUGH *THIS*, SILICA.
SO SILICA... WHOEVER SHE WAS... SHE'S GONE FOR GOOD?
LOOKS LIKE.
SO, IT'S A HAPPY ENDING ALL AROUND, THEN? EVERYTHING AS IT SHOULD BE, EVERYONE WHERE THEY SHOULD...
...YEAH. YEAH, I GUESS THEY *ARE*.

CH-CH-CHANGES PART 1

COVER ART BY **JEN BARTEL**

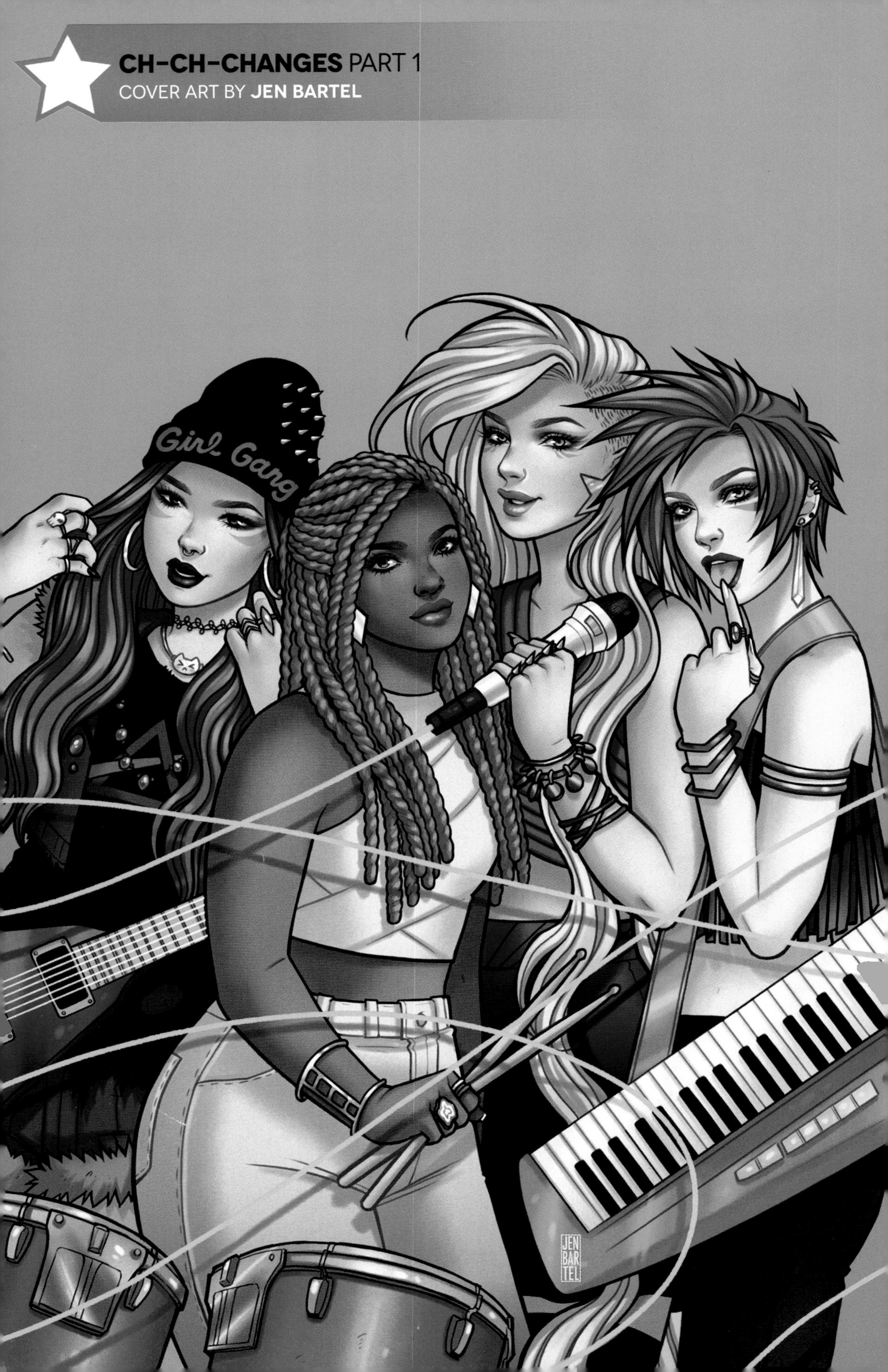
Girl Gang
JEN BAR TEL

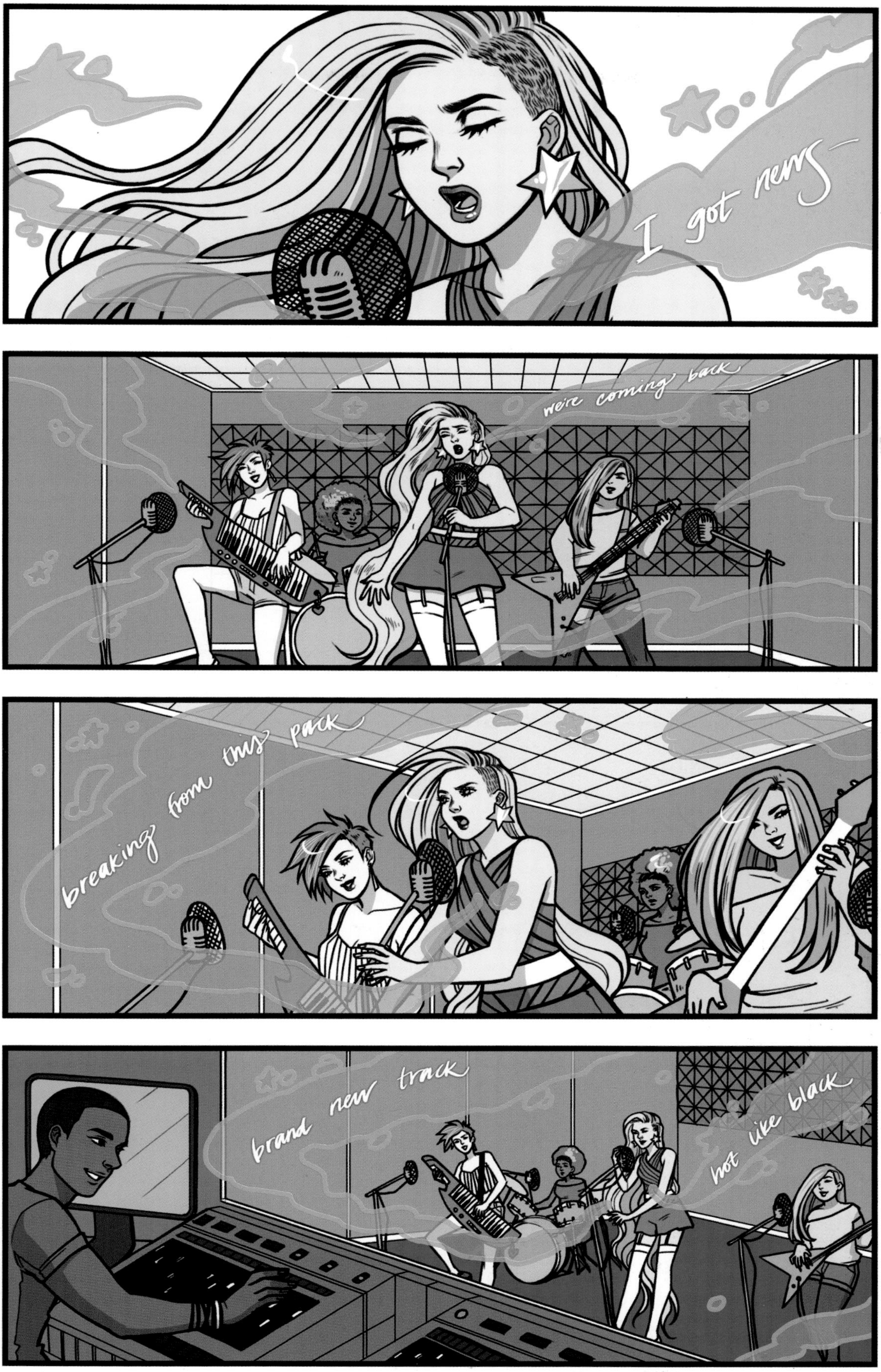
I got news—
we're coming back
breaking from this pack
brand new track
hot like black

you can disappear

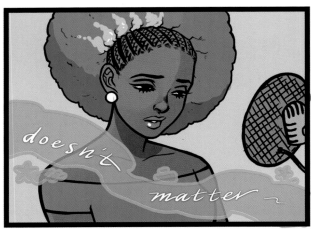

doesn't matter

We'll still be he—

SHANA? WHY'D YOU STOP?

YEAH, THAT SOUNDED AWESOME. BEST TAKE YET.

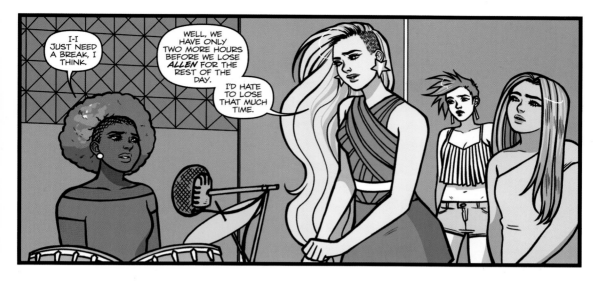

I-I JUST NEED A BREAK, I THINK.

WELL, WE HAVE ONLY TWO MORE HOURS BEFORE WE LOSE *ALLEN* FOR THE REST OF THE DAY.

I'D HATE TO LOSE THAT MUCH TIME.

FIVE BY FIVE WANTS THIS ALBUM WAY SOONER THAN I'M COMFORTABLE WITH...

...CAN YOU HANG IN THERE?

...NO.

NO, I'M SORRY, I CAN'T.

MY BLOOD SUGAR IS LOW OR SOMETHING. I NEED TO BE DONE.

WHAAAT IS GOING ON. SINCE WHEN DOES SHANA GET LOW BLOOD SUGAR?

I DON'T KNOW. SHE'S BEEN QUIET ALL DAY.

HEY, ALLEN. LOOKS LIKE THAT'S GONNA BE IT FOR TODAY.

SEE YOU TOMORROW AT TEN?

YOU GOT IT, JEM.

MAYBE SHE REALLY DOES JUST NEED A BREAK?

ALL RIGHT. LET'S GET SOMETHING TO EAT, MAYBE DECOMPRESS IN THE LAKE.

FINALLY A PLAN I CAN GET BEHIND.

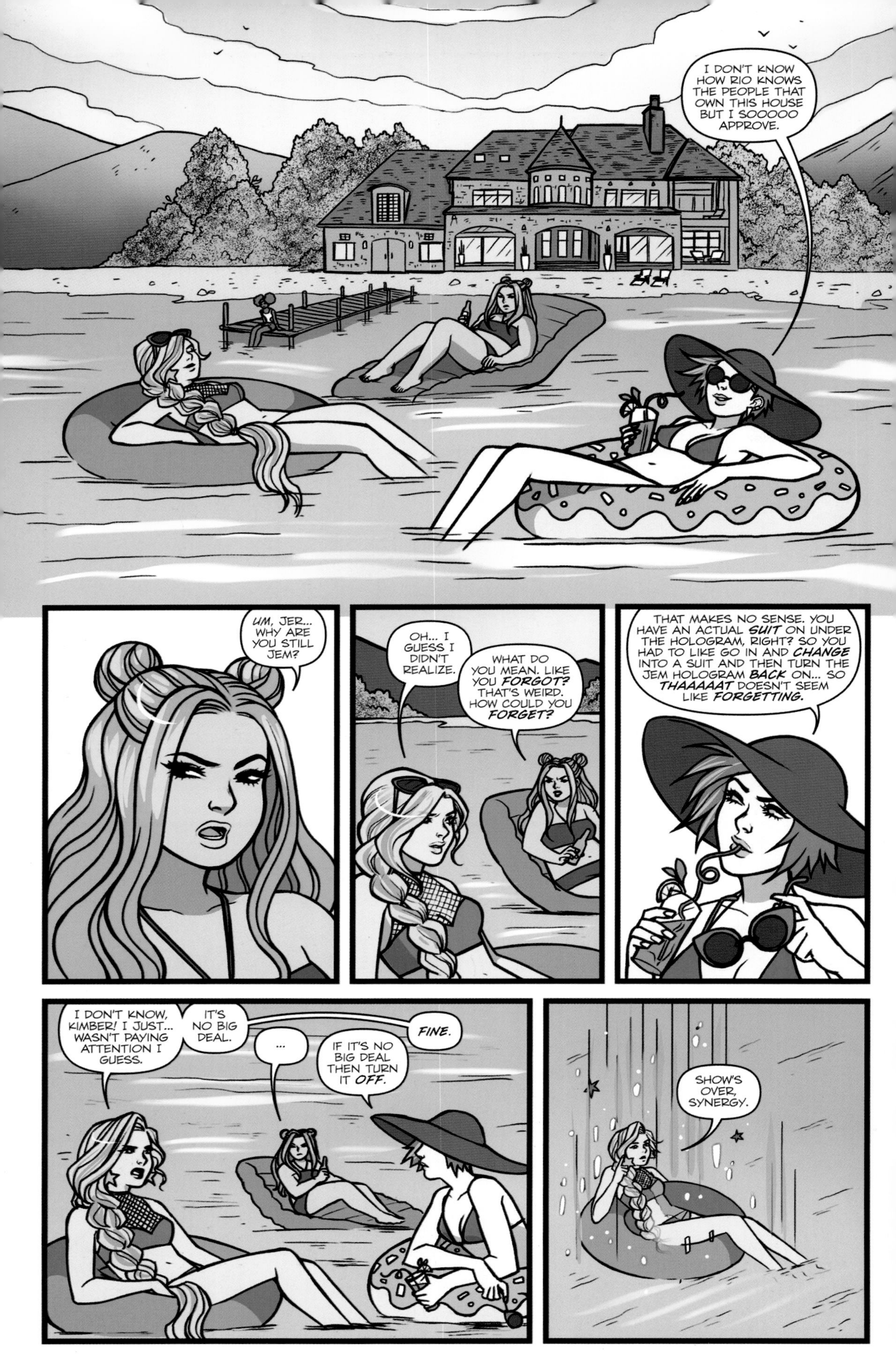
I DON'T KNOW HOW RIO KNOWS THE PEOPLE THAT OWN THIS HOUSE BUT I SOOOOOO APPROVE.
UM, JER... WHY ARE YOU STILL JEM?
OH... I GUESS I DIDN'T REALIZE.
WHAT DO YOU MEAN. LIKE YOU FORGOT? THAT'S WEIRD. HOW COULD YOU FORGET?
THAT MAKES NO SENSE. YOU HAVE AN ACTUAL SUIT ON UNDER THE HOLOGRAM, RIGHT? SO YOU HAD TO LIKE GO IN AND CHANGE INTO A SUIT AND THEN TURN THE JEM HOLOGRAM BACK ON... SO THAAAAAT DOESN'T SEEM LIKE FORGETTING.
I DON'T KNOW, KIMBER! I JUST... WASN'T PAYING ATTENTION I GUESS.
IT'S NO BIG DEAL.
...
IF IT'S NO BIG DEAL THEN TURN IT OFF.
FINE.
SHOW'S OVER, SYNERGY.

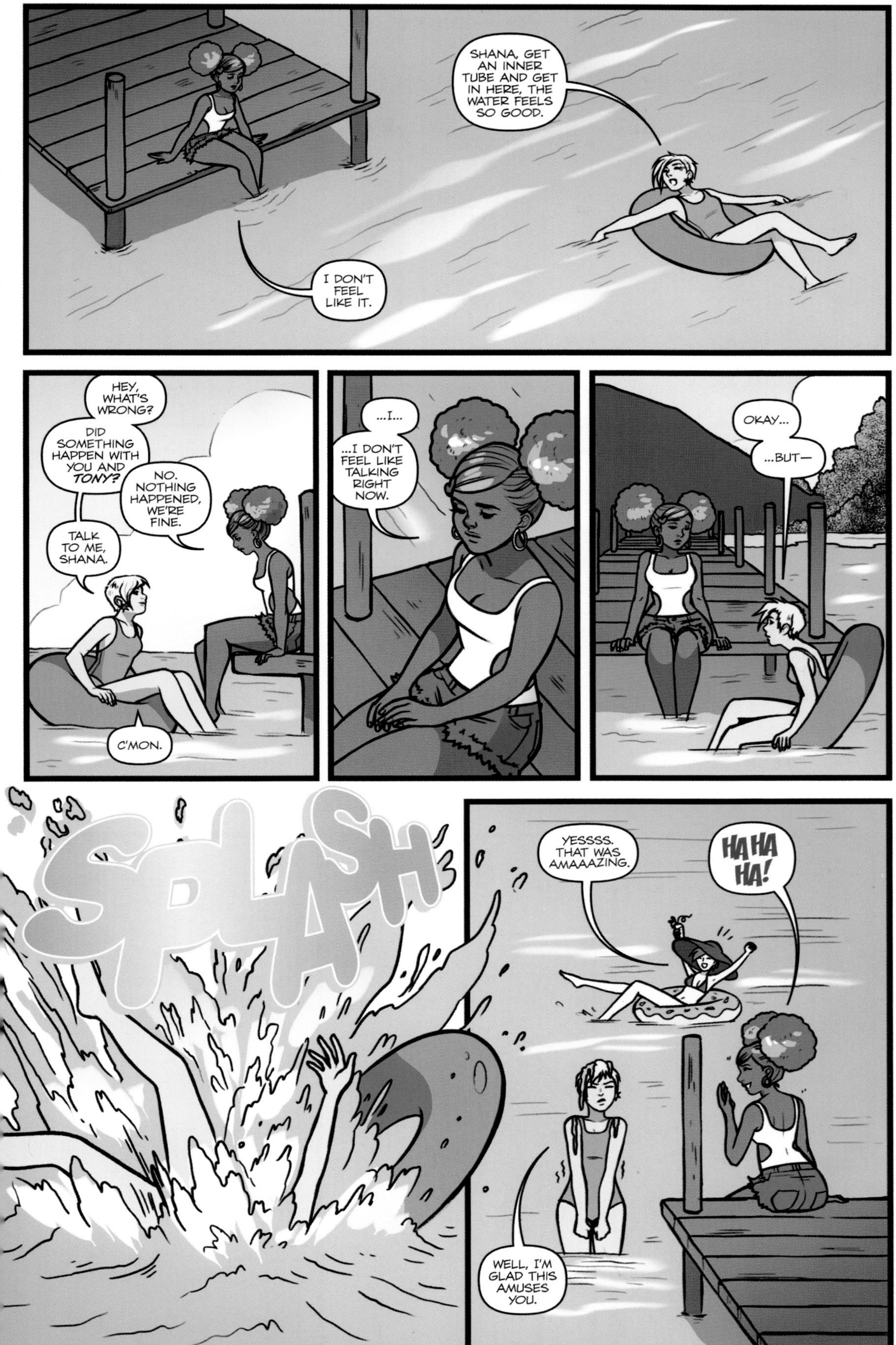
SHANA, GET AN INNER TUBE AND GET IN HERE, THE WATER FEELS SO GOOD.
I DON'T FEEL LIKE IT.
HEY, WHAT'S WRONG?
DID SOMETHING HAPPEN WITH YOU AND *TONY?*
NO. NOTHING HAPPENED, WE'RE FINE.
TALK TO ME, SHANA.
C'MON.
...I...
...I DON'T FEEL LIKE TALKING RIGHT NOW.
OKAY...
...BUT—
SPLASH
YESSSS. THAT WAS AMAAAZING.
HA HA HA!
WELL, I'M GLAD THIS AMUSES YOU.

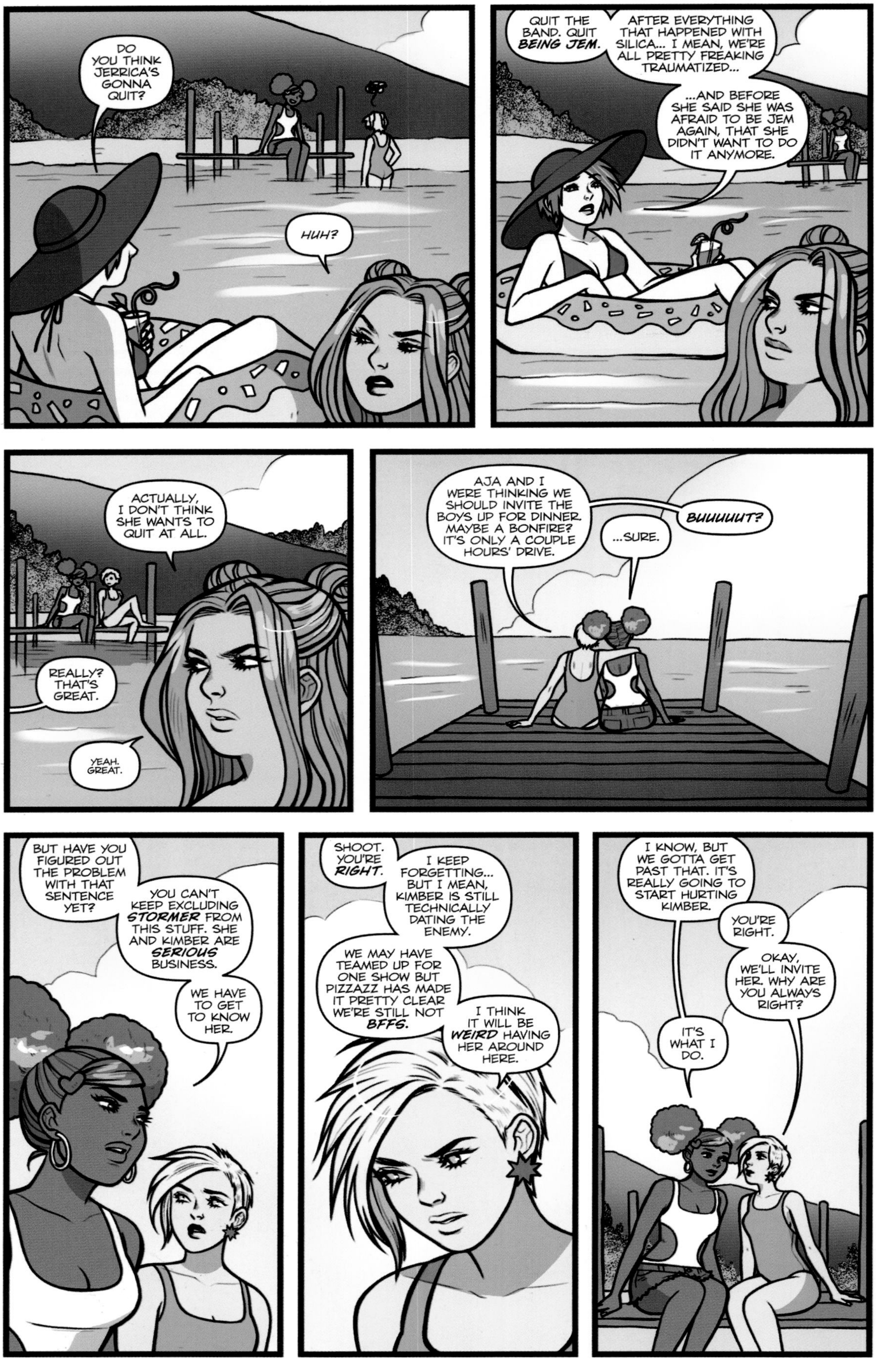
DO YOU THINK JERRICA'S GONNA QUIT?
HUH?
QUIT THE BAND. QUIT BEING JEM.
AFTER EVERYTHING THAT HAPPENED WITH SILICA... I MEAN, WE'RE ALL PRETTY FREAKING TRAUMATIZED...
...AND BEFORE SHE SAID SHE WAS AFRAID TO BE JEM AGAIN, THAT SHE DIDN'T WANT TO DO IT ANYMORE.
ACTUALLY, I DON'T THINK SHE WANTS TO QUIT AT ALL.
REALLY? THAT'S GREAT.
YEAH. GREAT.
AJA AND I WERE THINKING WE SHOULD INVITE THE BOYS UP FOR DINNER. MAYBE A BONFIRE? IT'S ONLY A COUPLE HOURS' DRIVE.
...SURE.
BUUUUUT?
BUT HAVE YOU FIGURED OUT THE PROBLEM WITH THAT SENTENCE YET?
YOU CAN'T KEEP EXCLUDING STORMER FROM THIS STUFF. SHE AND KIMBER ARE SERIOUS BUSINESS.
WE HAVE TO GET TO KNOW HER.
SHOOT. YOU'RE RIGHT.
I KEEP FORGETTING... BUT I MEAN, KIMBER IS STILL TECHNICALLY DATING THE ENEMY.
WE MAY HAVE TEAMED UP FOR ONE SHOW BUT PIZZAZZ HAS MADE IT PRETTY CLEAR WE'RE STILL NOT BFFS.
I THINK IT WILL BE WEIRD HAVING HER AROUND HERE.
I KNOW, BUT WE GOTTA GET PAST THAT. IT'S REALLY GOING TO START HURTING KIMBER.
YOU'RE RIGHT.
OKAY, WE'LL INVITE HER. WHY ARE YOU ALWAYS RIGHT?
IT'S WHAT I DO.

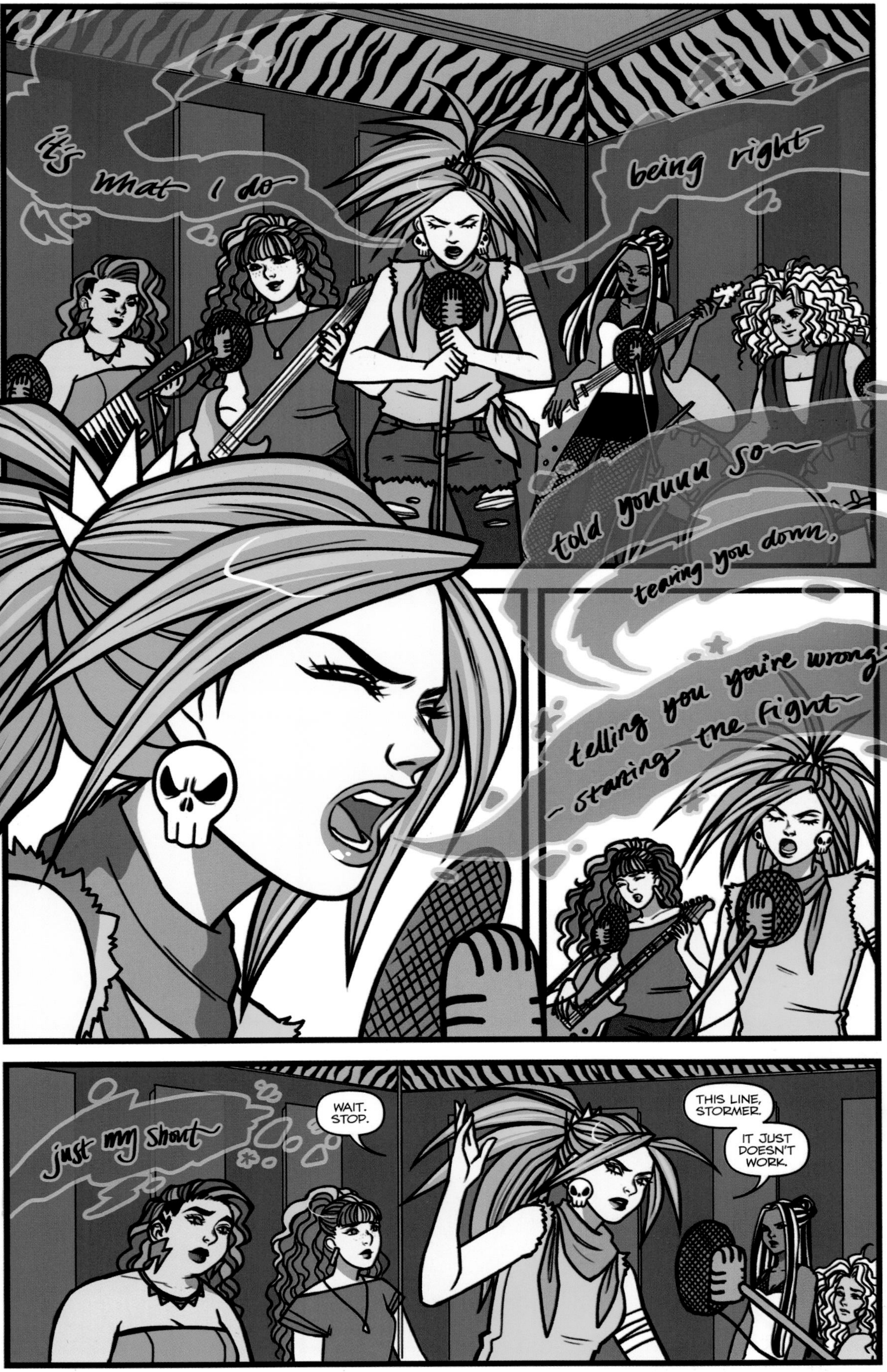

is what I do
being right
told youuuu so~
tearing you down,
telling you you're wrong~
~starting the fight~
just my shout~
WAIT. STOP.
THIS LINE, STORMER.
IT JUST DOESN'T WORK.

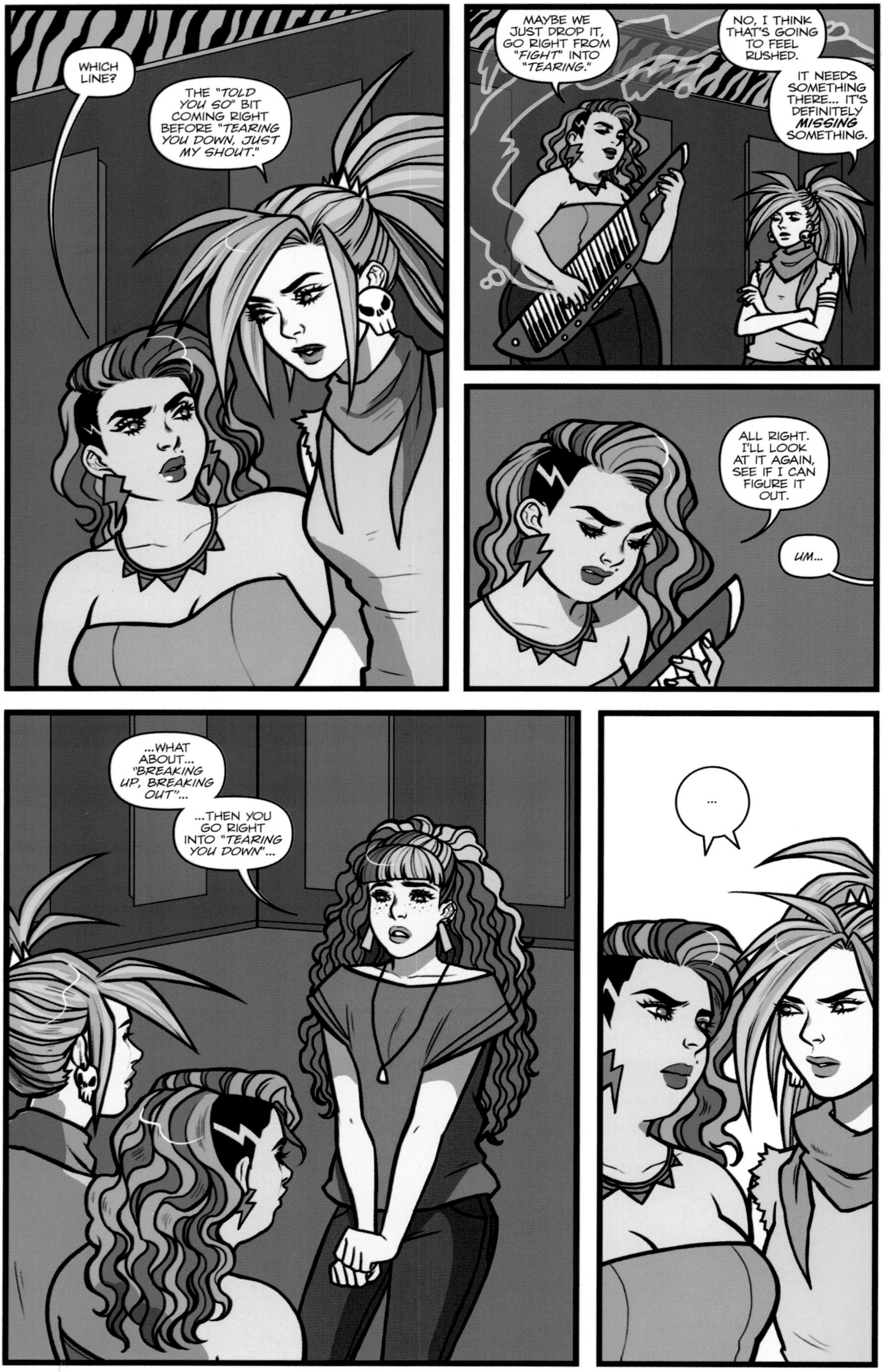
WHICH LINE?
THE "TOLD YOU SO" BIT COMING RIGHT BEFORE "TEARING YOU DOWN, JUST MY SHOUT."
MAYBE WE JUST DROP IT, GO RIGHT FROM "FIGHT" INTO "TEARING."
NO, I THINK THAT'S GOING TO FEEL RUSHED.
IT NEEDS SOMETHING THERE... IT'S DEFINITELY MISSING SOMETHING.
ALL RIGHT. I'LL LOOK AT IT AGAIN, SEE IF I CAN FIGURE IT OUT.
UM...
...WHAT ABOUT... "BREAKING UP, BREAKING OUT"...
...THEN YOU GO RIGHT INTO "TEARING YOU DOWN"...
...

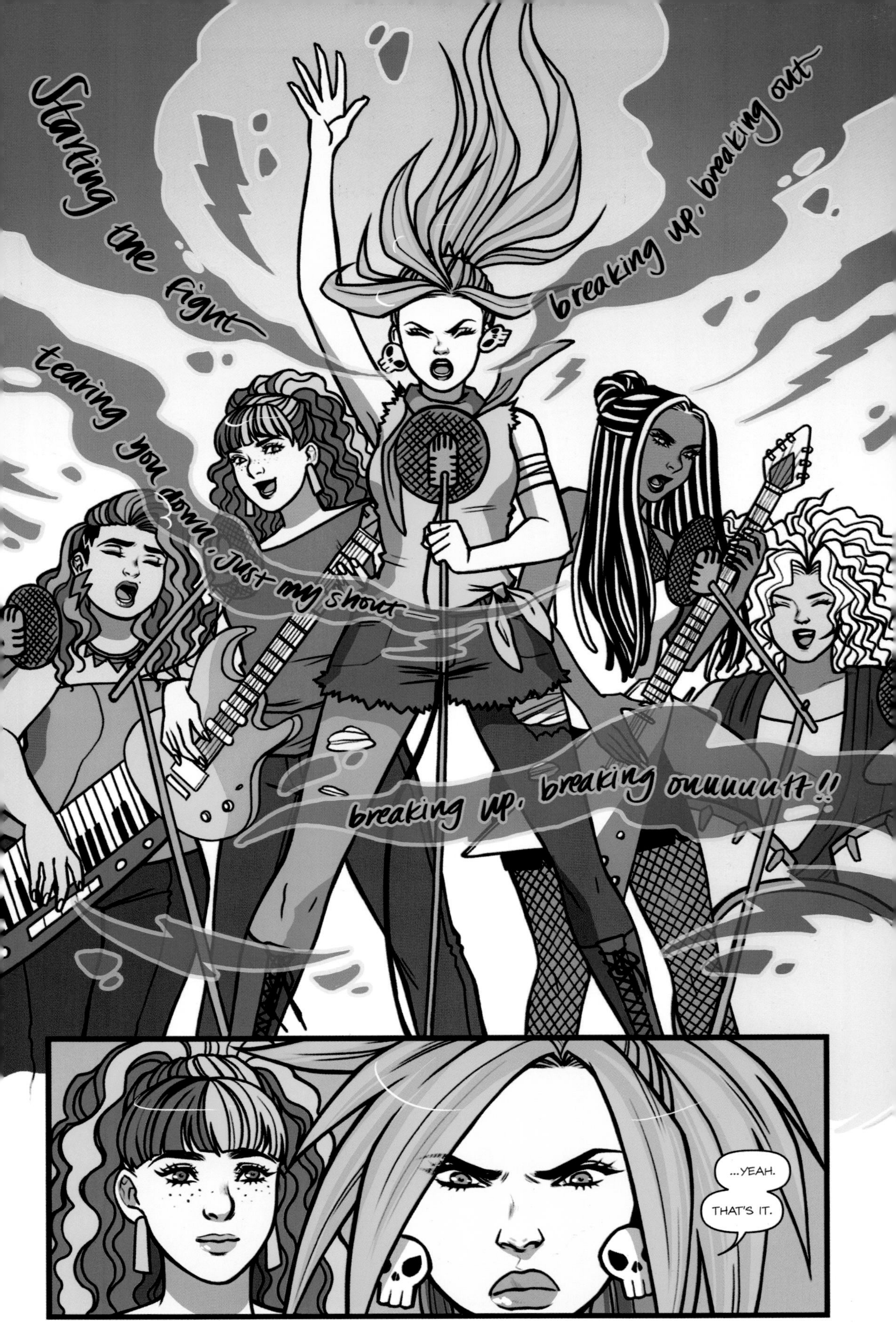
Starting the fight
breaking up, breaking out—
tearing you down, just my shout—
breaking up, breaking ouuuuut!!
...YEAH.
THAT'S IT.

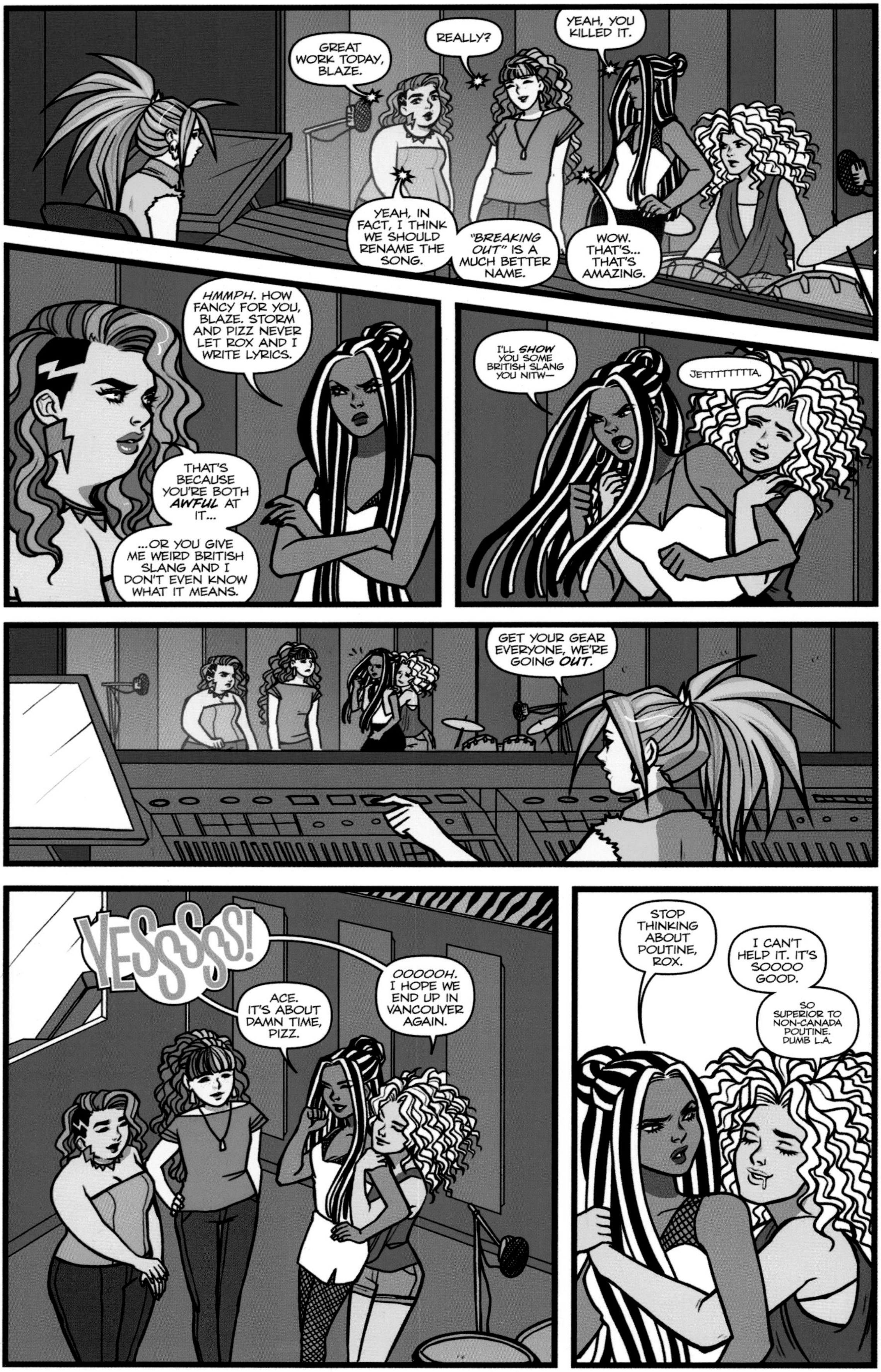
GREAT WORK TODAY, BLAZE.
REALLY?
YEAH, YOU KILLED IT.
YEAH, IN FACT, I THINK WE SHOULD RENAME THE SONG.
"BREAKING OUT" IS A MUCH BETTER NAME.
WOW. THAT'S... THAT'S AMAZING.
HMMPH. HOW FANCY FOR YOU, BLAZE. STORM AND PIZZ NEVER LET ROX AND I WRITE LYRICS.
THAT'S BECAUSE YOU'RE BOTH AWFUL AT IT...
...OR YOU GIVE ME WEIRD BRITISH SLANG AND I DON'T EVEN KNOW WHAT IT MEANS.
I'LL SHOW YOU SOME BRITISH SLANG YOU NITW—
JETTTTTTTTA.
GET YOUR GEAR EVERYONE, WE'RE GOING OUT.
YESSSSS!
ACE. IT'S ABOUT DAMN TIME, PIZZ.
OOOOOH. I HOPE WE END UP IN VANCOUVER AGAIN.
STOP THINKING ABOUT POUTINE, ROX.
I CAN'T HELP IT. IT'S SOOOO GOOD.
SO SUPERIOR TO NON-CANADA POUTINE. DUMB L.A.

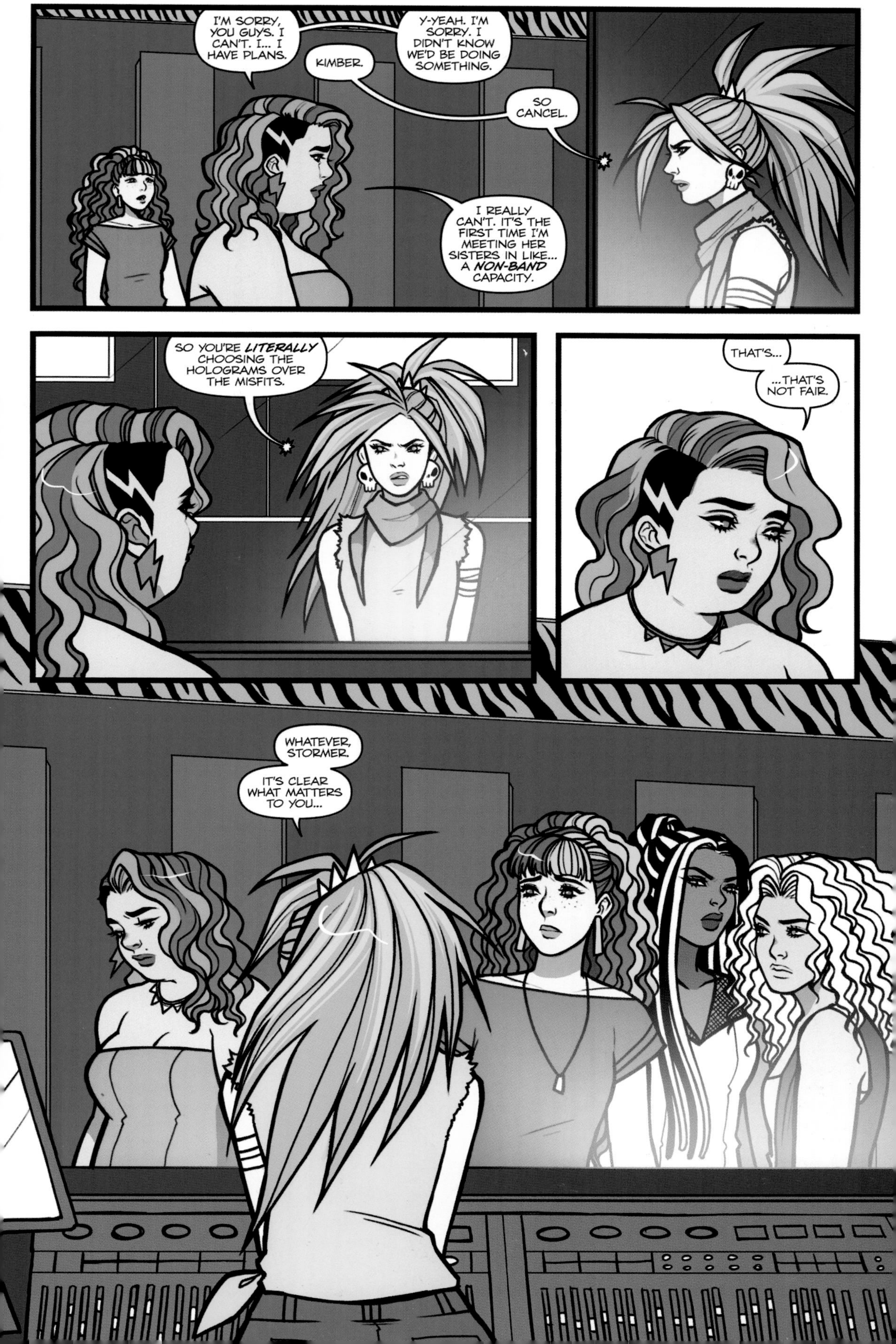
I'M SORRY, YOU GUYS. I CAN'T. I... I HAVE PLANS.
Y-YEAH. I'M SORRY. I DIDN'T KNOW WE'D BE DOING SOMETHING.
KIMBER.
SO CANCEL.
I REALLY CAN'T. IT'S THE FIRST TIME I'M MEETING HER SISTERS IN LIKE... A NON-BAND CAPACITY.
SO YOU'RE LITERALLY CHOOSING THE HOLOGRAMS OVER THE MISFITS.
THAT'S...
...THAT'S NOT FAIR.
WHATEVER, STORMER.
IT'S CLEAR WHAT MATTERS TO YOU...

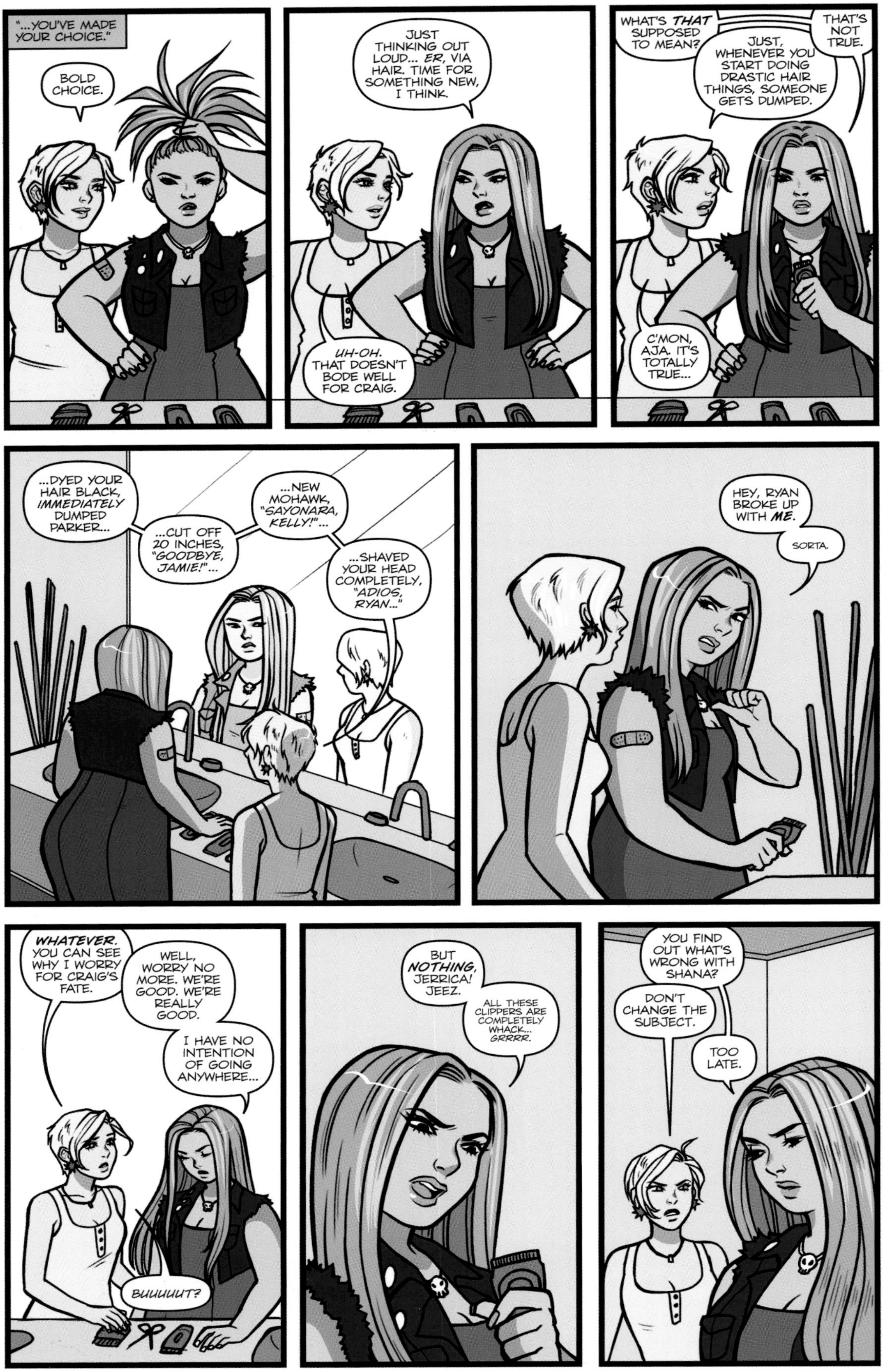
"...YOU'VE MADE YOUR CHOICE."
BOLD CHOICE.
JUST THINKING OUT LOUD... ER, VIA HAIR. TIME FOR SOMETHING NEW, I THINK.
UH-OH. THAT DOESN'T BODE WELL FOR CRAIG.
WHAT'S THAT SUPPOSED TO MEAN?
JUST, WHENEVER YOU START DOING DRASTIC HAIR THINGS, SOMEONE GETS DUMPED.
THAT'S NOT TRUE.
C'MON, AJA. IT'S TOTALLY TRUE...
...DYED YOUR HAIR BLACK, IMMEDIATELY DUMPED PARKER...
...CUT OFF 20 INCHES, "GOODBYE, JAMIE!"...
...NEW MOHAWK, "SAYONARA, KELLY!"...
...SHAVED YOUR HEAD COMPLETELY, "ADIOS, RYAN..."
HEY, RYAN BROKE UP WITH ME.
SORTA.
WHATEVER. YOU CAN SEE WHY I WORRY FOR CRAIG'S FATE.
WELL, WORRY NO MORE. WE'RE GOOD. WE'RE REALLY GOOD.
I HAVE NO INTENTION OF GOING ANYWHERE...
BUUUUUT?
BUT NOTHING, JERRICA! JEEZ.
ALL THESE CLIPPERS ARE COMPLETELY WHACK... GRRRR.
YOU FIND OUT WHAT'S WRONG WITH SHANA?
DON'T CHANGE THE SUBJECT.
TOO LATE.

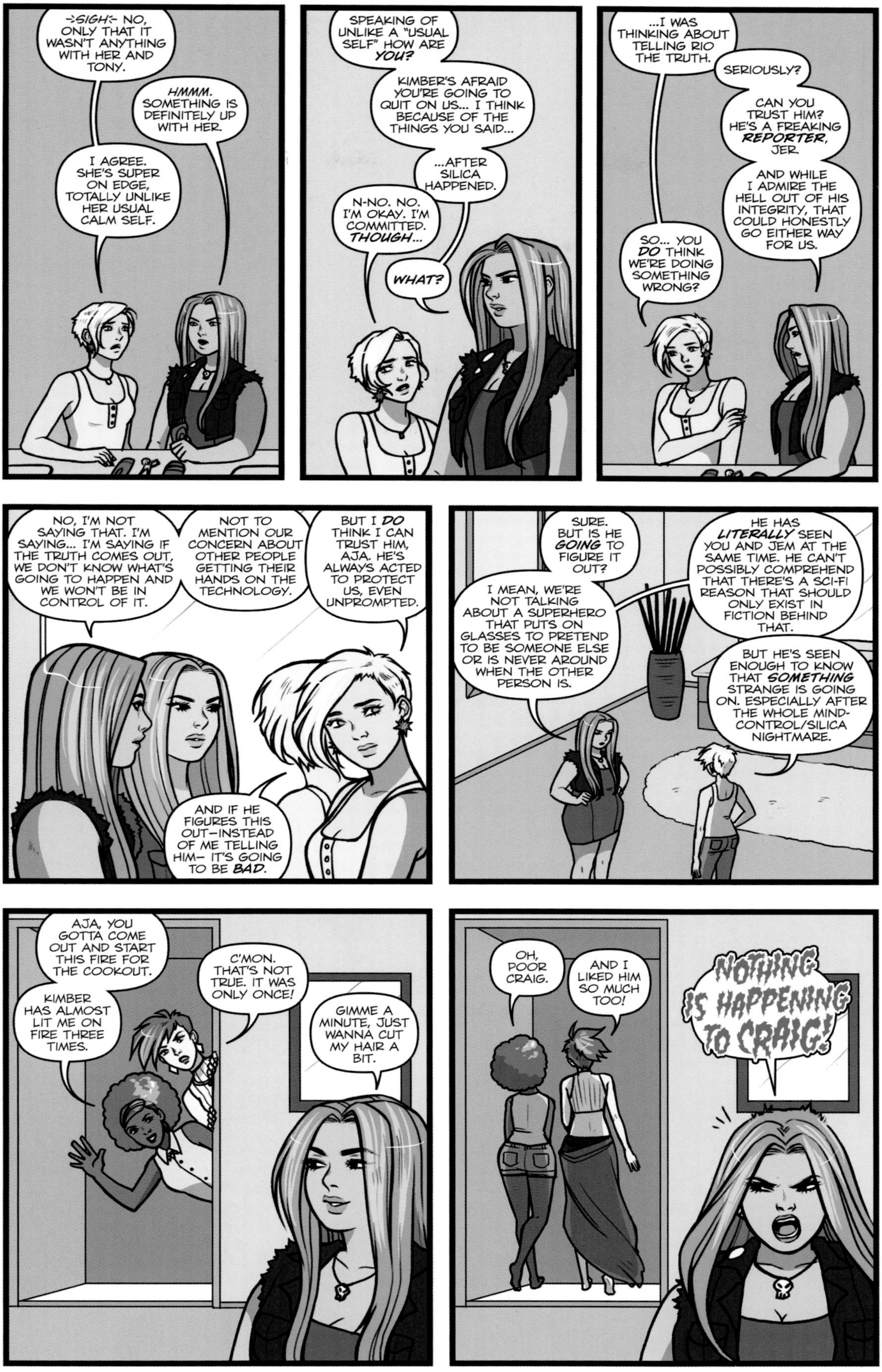

-SIGH- NO, ONLY THAT IT WASN'T ANYTHING WITH HER AND TONY.
HMMM. SOMETHING IS DEFINITELY UP WITH HER.
I AGREE. SHE'S SUPER ON EDGE, TOTALLY UNLIKE HER USUAL CALM SELF.
SPEAKING OF UNLIKE A "USUAL SELF" HOW ARE YOU?
KIMBER'S AFRAID YOU'RE GOING TO QUIT ON US... I THINK BECAUSE OF THE THINGS YOU SAID...
...AFTER SILICA HAPPENED.
N-NO. NO. I'M OKAY. I'M COMMITTED. THOUGH...
WHAT?
...I WAS THINKING ABOUT TELLING RIO THE TRUTH.
SERIOUSLY?
CAN YOU TRUST HIM? HE'S A FREAKING REPORTER, JER.
AND WHILE I ADMIRE THE HELL OUT OF HIS INTEGRITY, THAT COULD HONESTLY GO EITHER WAY FOR US.
SO... YOU DO THINK WE'RE DOING SOMETHING WRONG?
NO, I'M NOT SAYING THAT. I'M SAYING... I'M SAYING IF THE TRUTH COMES OUT, WE DON'T KNOW WHAT'S GOING TO HAPPEN AND WE WON'T BE IN CONTROL OF IT.
NOT TO MENTION OUR CONCERN ABOUT OTHER PEOPLE GETTING THEIR HANDS ON THE TECHNOLOGY.
BUT I DO THINK I CAN TRUST HIM, AJA. HE'S ALWAYS ACTED TO PROTECT US, EVEN UNPROMPTED.
AND IF HE FIGURES THIS OUT—INSTEAD OF ME TELLING HIM— IT'S GOING TO BE BAD.
SURE. BUT IS HE GOING TO FIGURE IT OUT?
I MEAN, WE'RE NOT TALKING ABOUT A SUPERHERO THAT PUTS ON GLASSES TO PRETEND TO BE SOMEONE ELSE OR IS NEVER AROUND WHEN THE OTHER PERSON IS.
HE HAS LITERALLY SEEN YOU AND JEM AT THE SAME TIME. HE CAN'T POSSIBLY COMPREHEND THAT THERE'S A SCI-FI REASON THAT SHOULD ONLY EXIST IN FICTION BEHIND THAT.
BUT HE'S SEEN ENOUGH TO KNOW THAT SOMETHING STRANGE IS GOING ON. ESPECIALLY AFTER THE WHOLE MIND-CONTROL/SILICA NIGHTMARE.
AJA, YOU GOTTA COME OUT AND START THIS FIRE FOR THE COOKOUT.
KIMBER HAS ALMOST LIT ME ON FIRE THREE TIMES.
C'MON. THAT'S NOT TRUE. IT WAS ONLY ONCE!
GIMME A MINUTE, JUST WANNA CUT MY HAIR A BIT.
OH, POOR CRAIG.
AND I LIKED HIM SO MUCH TOO!
NOTHING IS HAPPENING TO CRAIG!

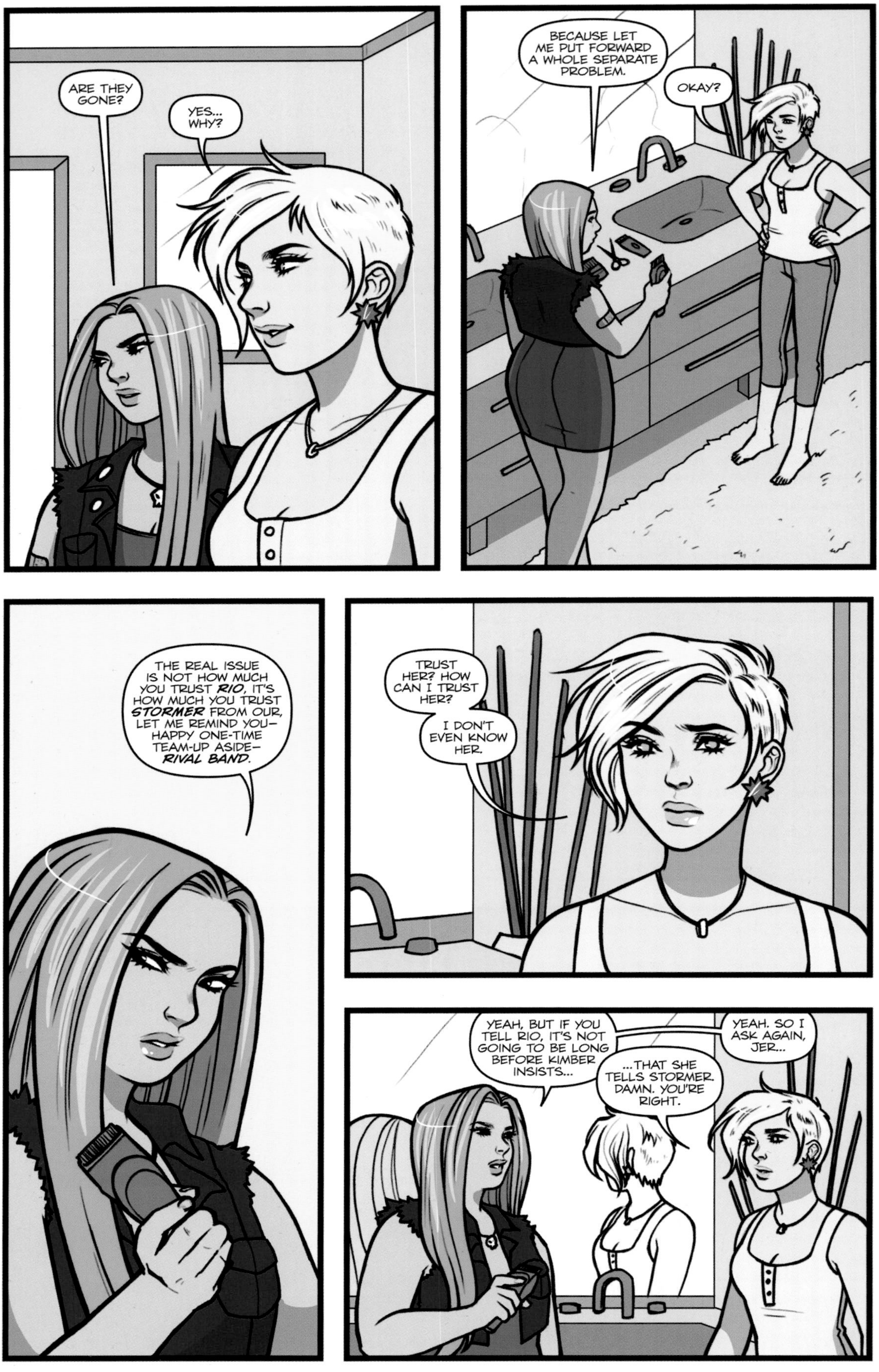
ARE THEY GONE?
YES... WHY?
BECAUSE LET ME PUT FORWARD A WHOLE SEPARATE PROBLEM.
OKAY?
THE REAL ISSUE IS NOT HOW MUCH YOU TRUST RIO, IT'S HOW MUCH YOU TRUST STORMER FROM OUR, LET ME REMIND YOU— HAPPY ONE-TIME TEAM-UP ASIDE— RIVAL BAND.
TRUST HER? HOW CAN I TRUST HER?
I DON'T EVEN KNOW HER.
YEAH, BUT IF YOU TELL RIO, IT'S NOT GOING TO BE LONG BEFORE KIMBER INSISTS...
...THAT SHE TELLS STORMER. DAMN. YOU'RE RIGHT.
YEAH. SO I ASK AGAIN, JER...

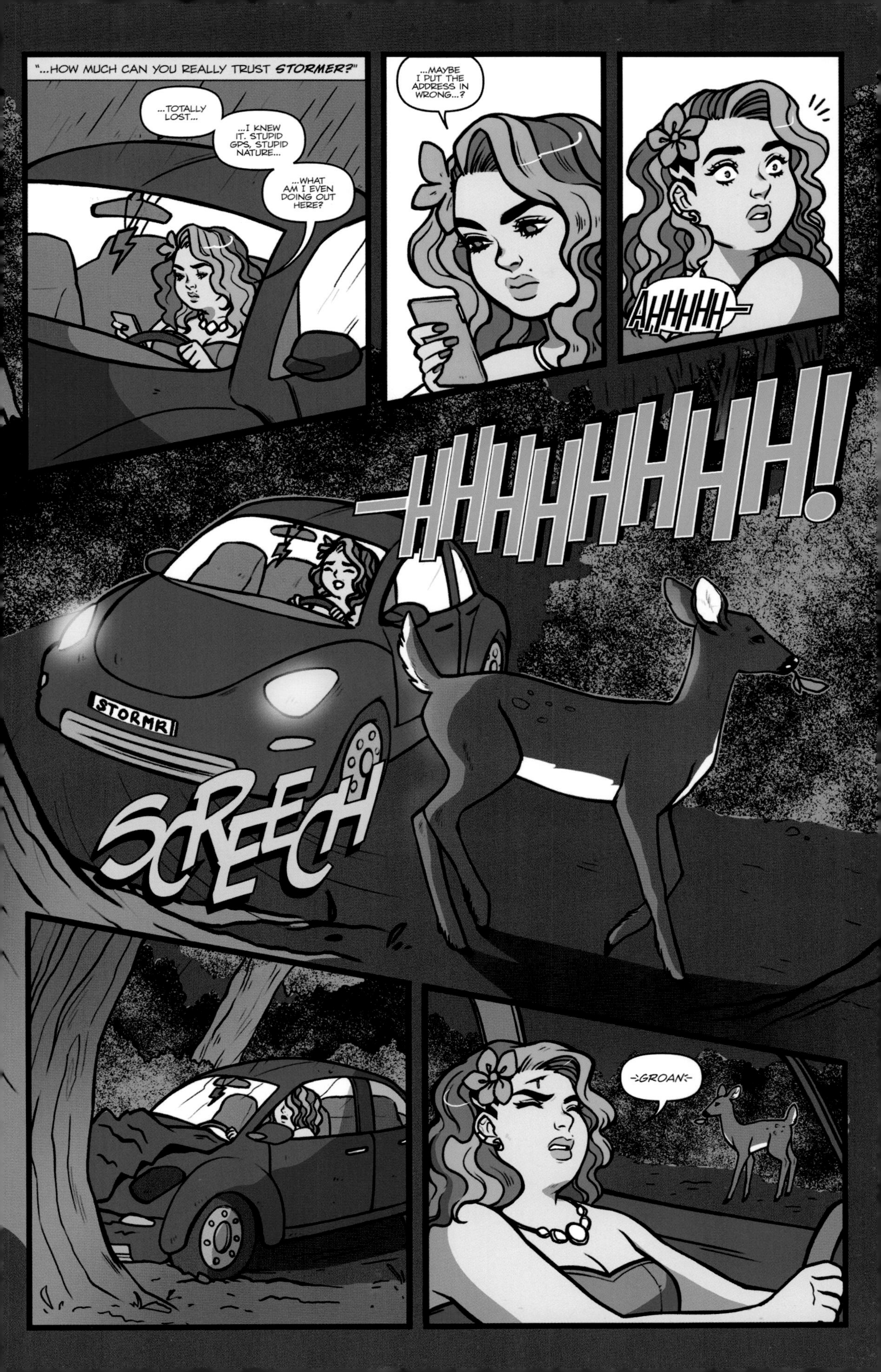
"...HOW MUCH CAN YOU REALLY TRUST STORMER?"
...TOTALLY LOST...
...I KNEW IT. STUPID GPS, STUPID NATURE...
...WHAT AM I EVEN DOING OUT HERE?
...MAYBE I PUT THE ADDRESS IN WRONG...?
AHHHHH—
—HHHHHHHHH!
STORMR
SCREECH
-GROAN-

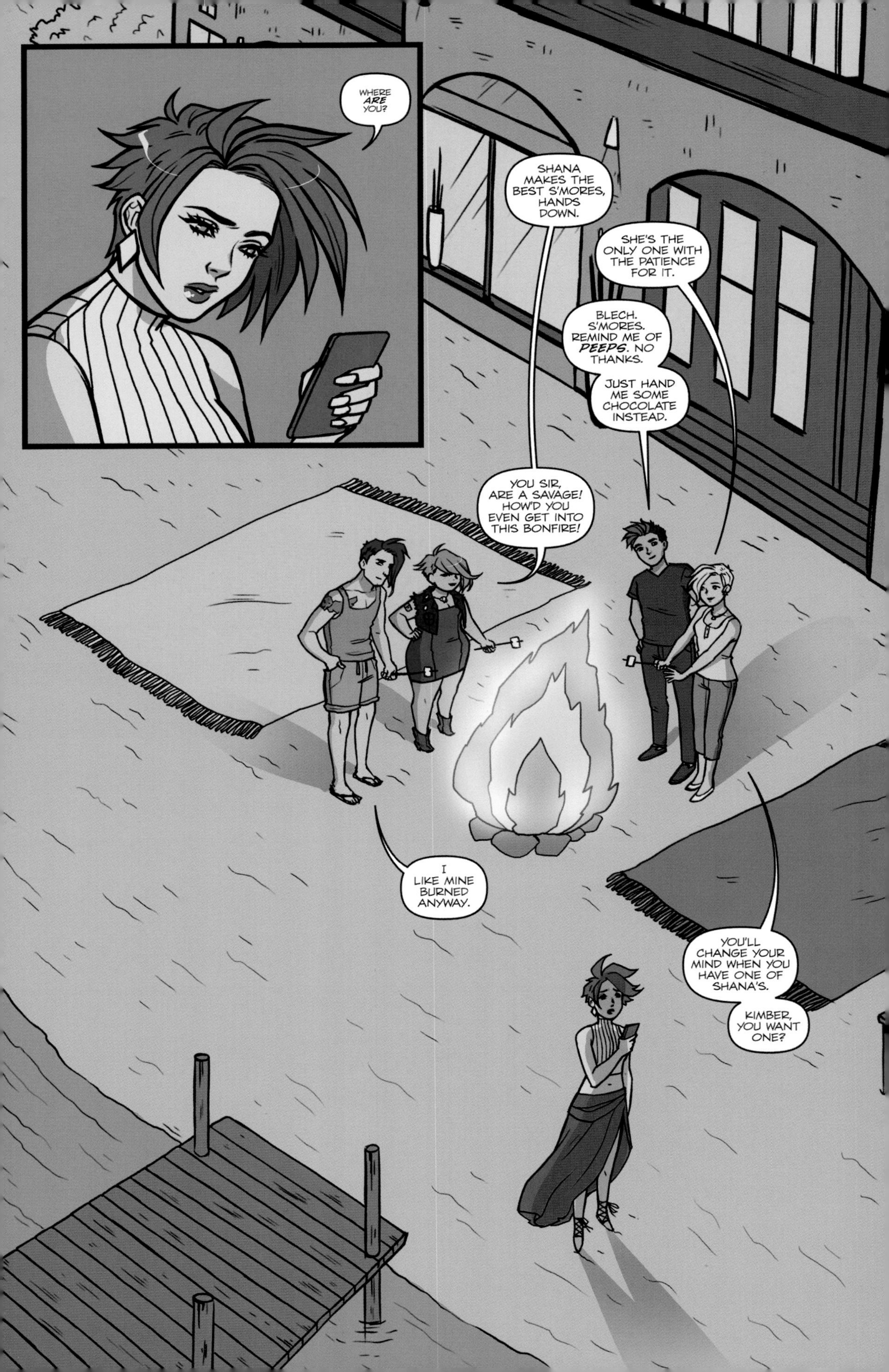
WHERE *ARE* YOU?
SHANA MAKES THE BEST S'MORES, HANDS DOWN.
SHE'S THE ONLY ONE WITH THE PATIENCE FOR IT.
BLECH. S'MORES. REMIND ME OF *PEEPS*. NO THANKS.
JUST HAND ME SOME CHOCOLATE INSTEAD.
YOU SIR, ARE A SAVAGE! HOW'D YOU EVEN GET INTO THIS BONFIRE!
I LIKE MINE BURNED ANYWAY.
YOU'LL CHANGE YOUR MIND WHEN YOU HAVE ONE OF SHANA'S.
KIMBER, YOU WANT ONE?

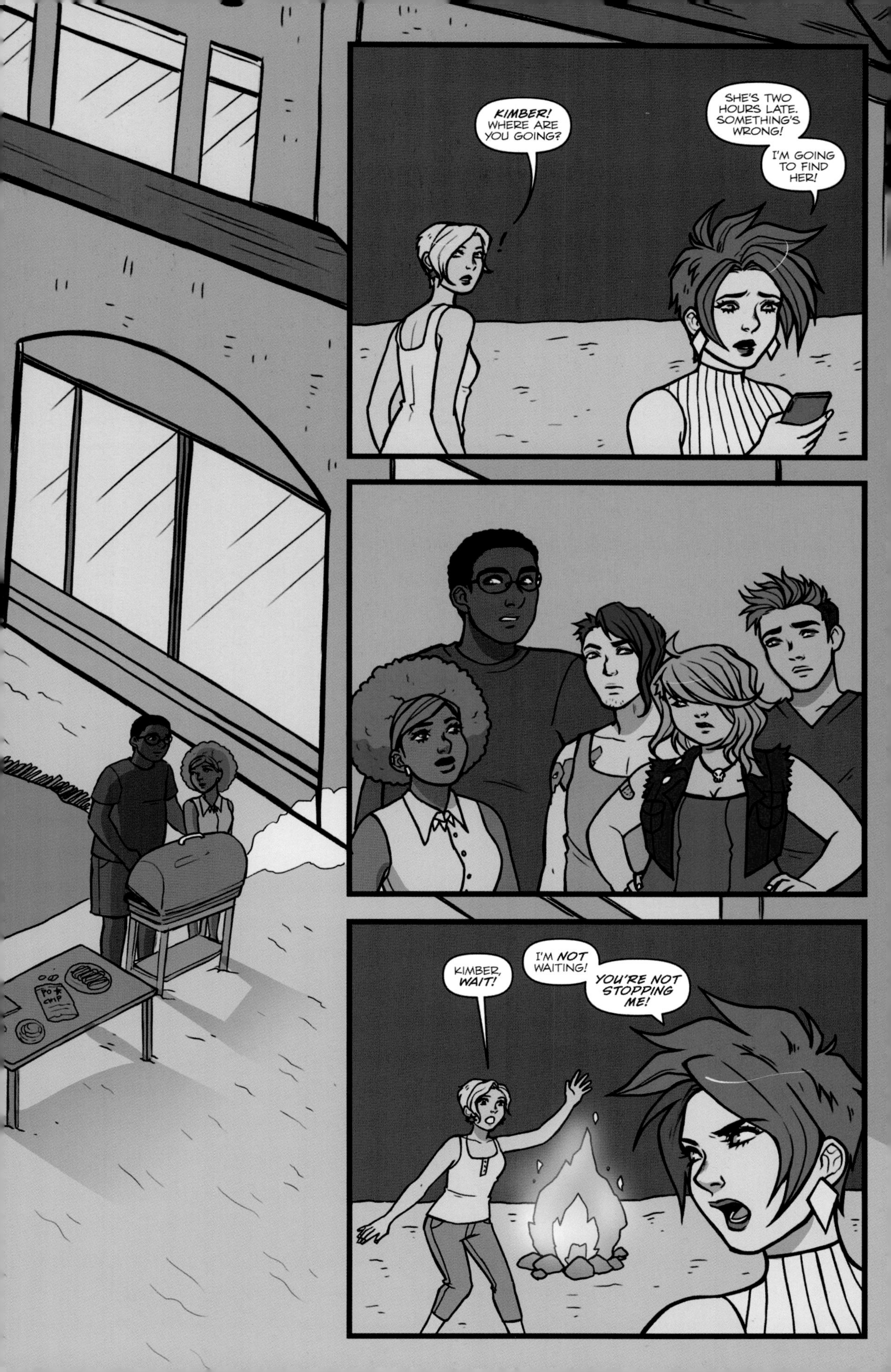
KIMBER! WHERE ARE YOU GOING?
SHE'S TWO HOURS LATE. SOMETHING'S WRONG!
I'M GOING TO FIND HER!
KIMBER, WAIT!
I'M NOT WAITING!
YOU'RE NOT STOPPING ME!

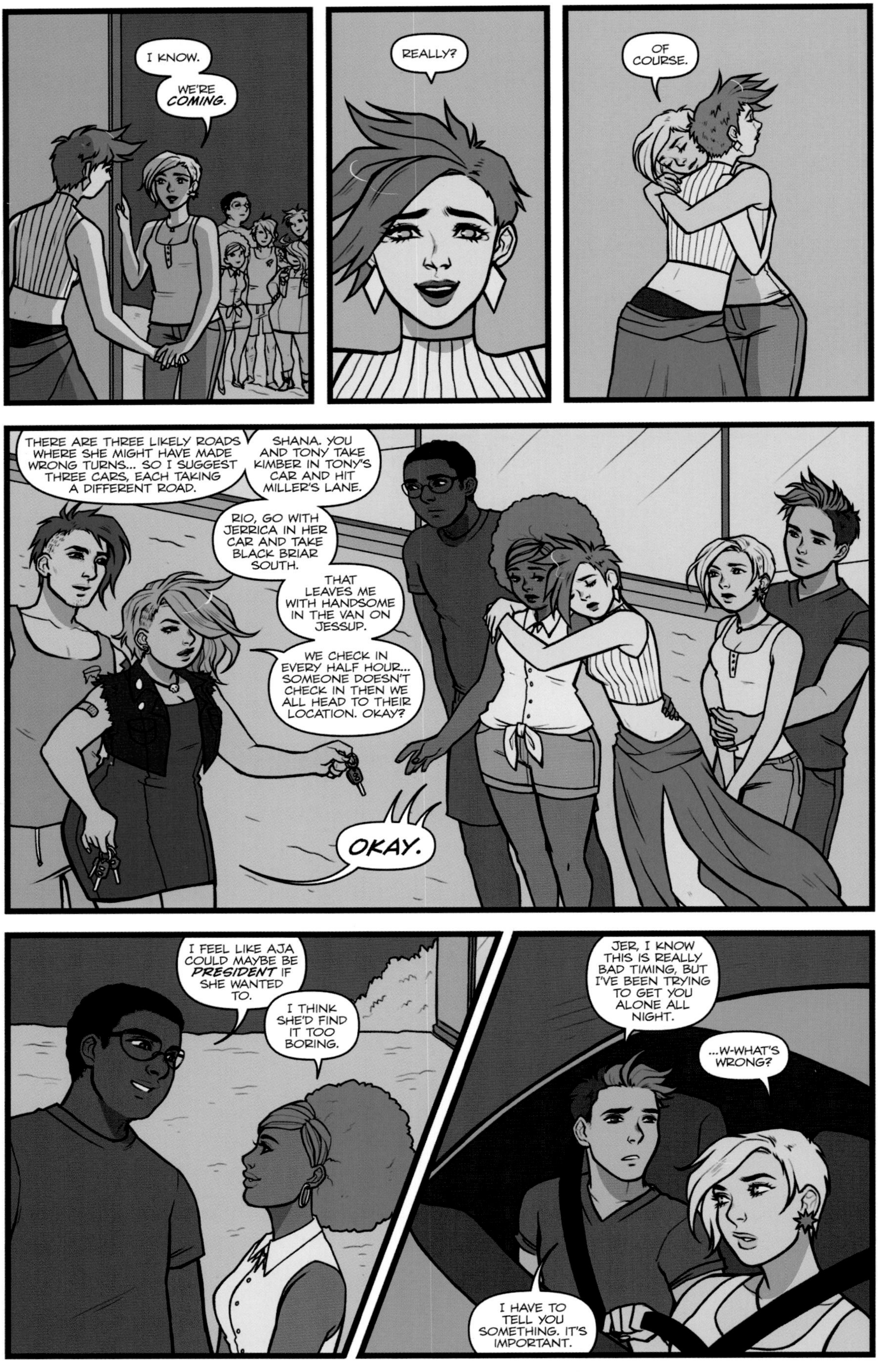
I KNOW.
WE'RE *COMING*.
REALLY?
OF COURSE.
THERE ARE THREE LIKELY ROADS WHERE SHE MIGHT HAVE MADE WRONG TURNS... SO I SUGGEST THREE CARS, EACH TAKING A DIFFERENT ROAD.
SHANA. YOU AND TONY TAKE KIMBER IN TONY'S CAR AND HIT MILLER'S LANE.
RIO, GO WITH JERRICA IN HER CAR AND TAKE BLACK BRIAR SOUTH.
THAT LEAVES ME WITH HANDSOME IN THE VAN ON JESSUP.
WE CHECK IN EVERY HALF HOUR... SOMEONE DOESN'T CHECK IN THEN WE ALL HEAD TO THEIR LOCATION. OKAY?
OKAY.
I FEEL LIKE AJA COULD MAYBE BE *PRESIDENT* IF SHE WANTED TO.
I THINK SHE'D FIND IT TOO BORING.
JER, I KNOW THIS IS REALLY BAD TIMING, BUT I'VE BEEN TRYING TO GET YOU ALONE ALL NIGHT.
...W-WHAT'S WRONG?
I HAVE TO TELL YOU SOMETHING. IT'S IMPORTANT.

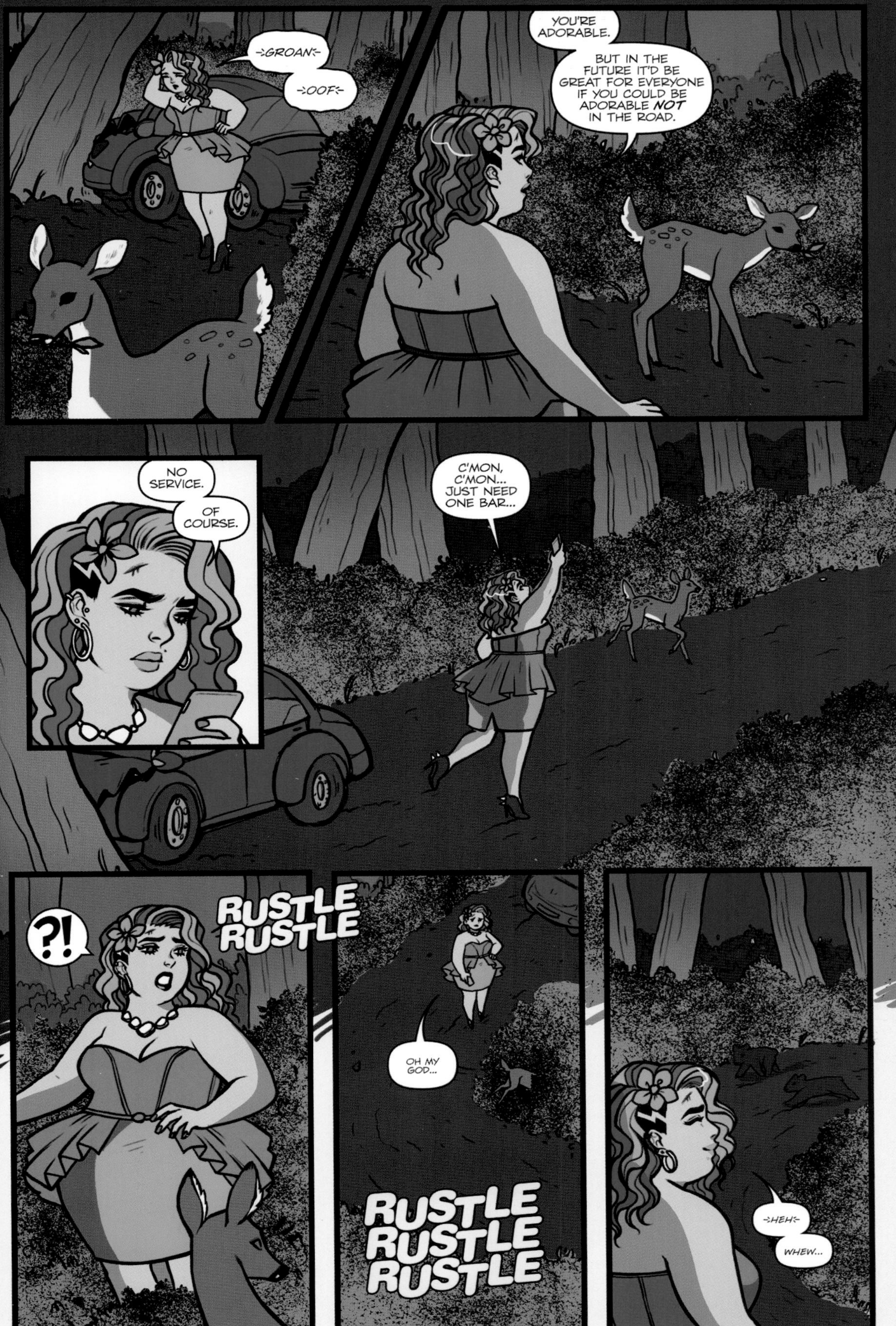
~GROAN~
~OOF~
YOU'RE ADORABLE.
BUT IN THE FUTURE IT'D BE GREAT FOR EVERYONE IF YOU COULD BE ADORABLE NOT IN THE ROAD.
NO SERVICE.
OF COURSE.
C'MON, C'MON... JUST NEED ONE BAR...
?!
RUSTLE RUSTLE
OH MY GOD...
RUSTLE RUSTLE RUSTLE
~HEH~
WHEW...

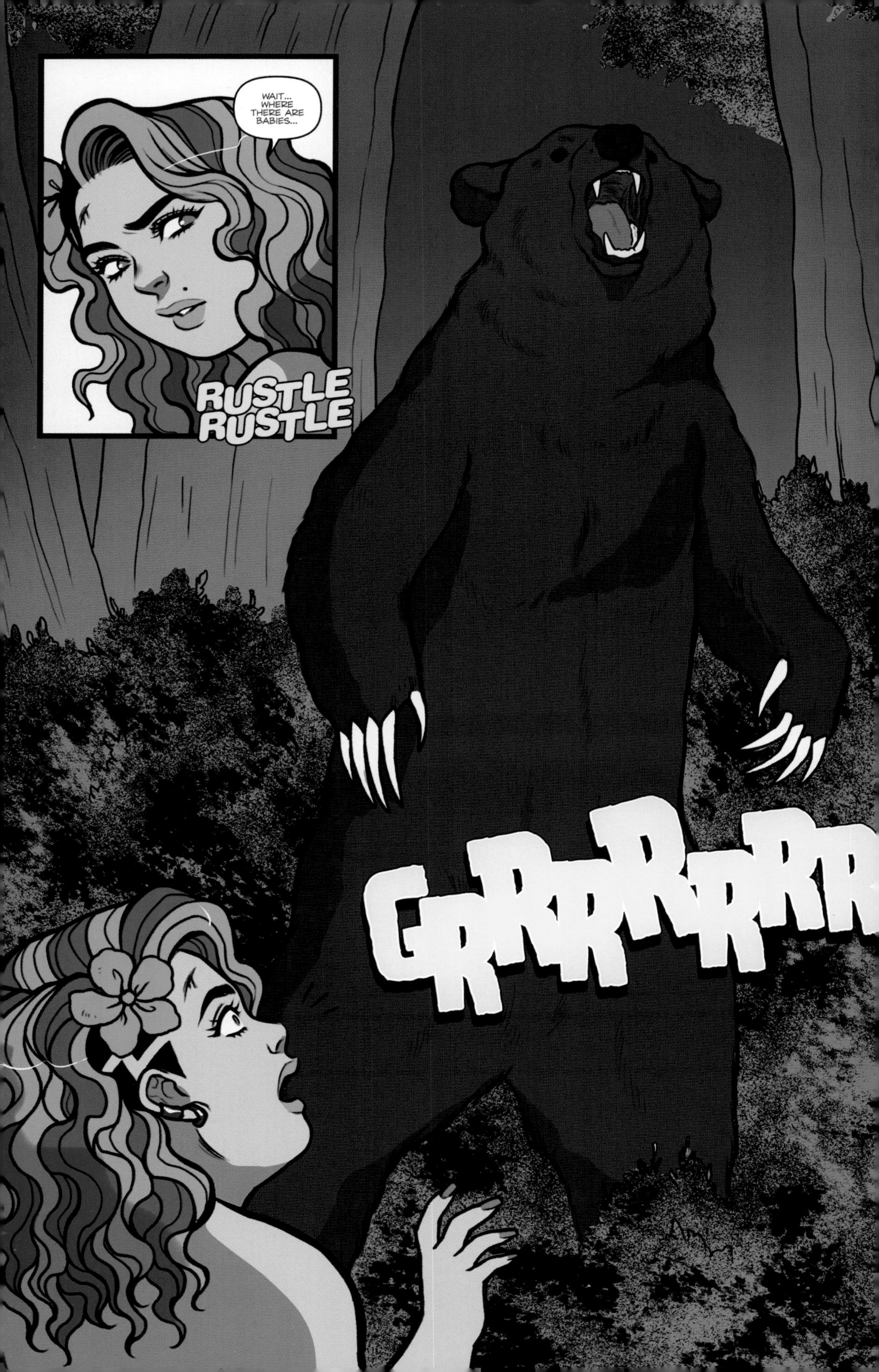
WAIT... WHERE THERE ARE BABIES...
RUSTLE RUSTLE
GRRRRRRRR

COVER ART BY **M. VICTORIA ROBADO**

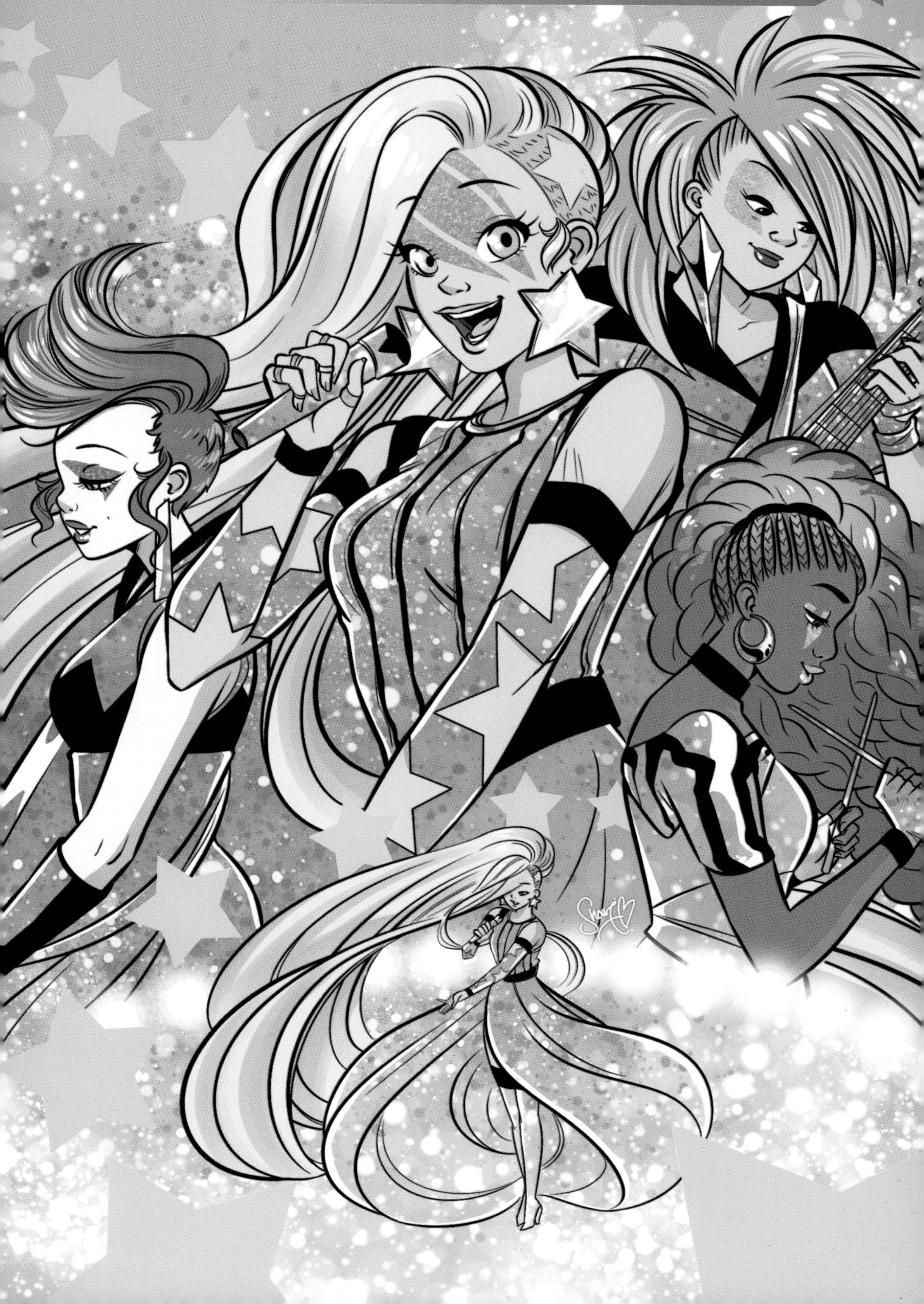

CH-CH-CHANGES PART 2

COVER ART BY **JEN BARTEL**

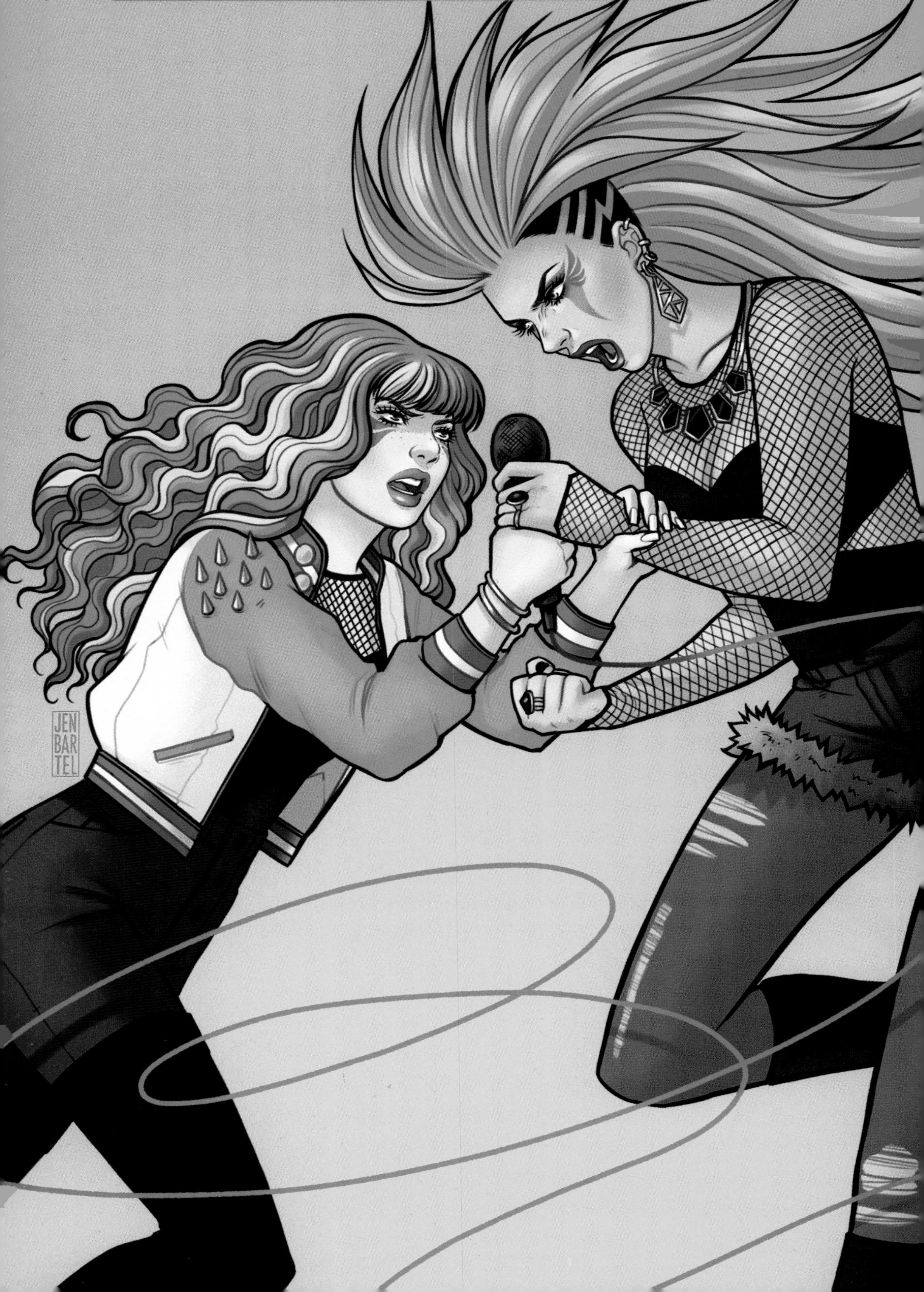
JEN
BAR
TEL

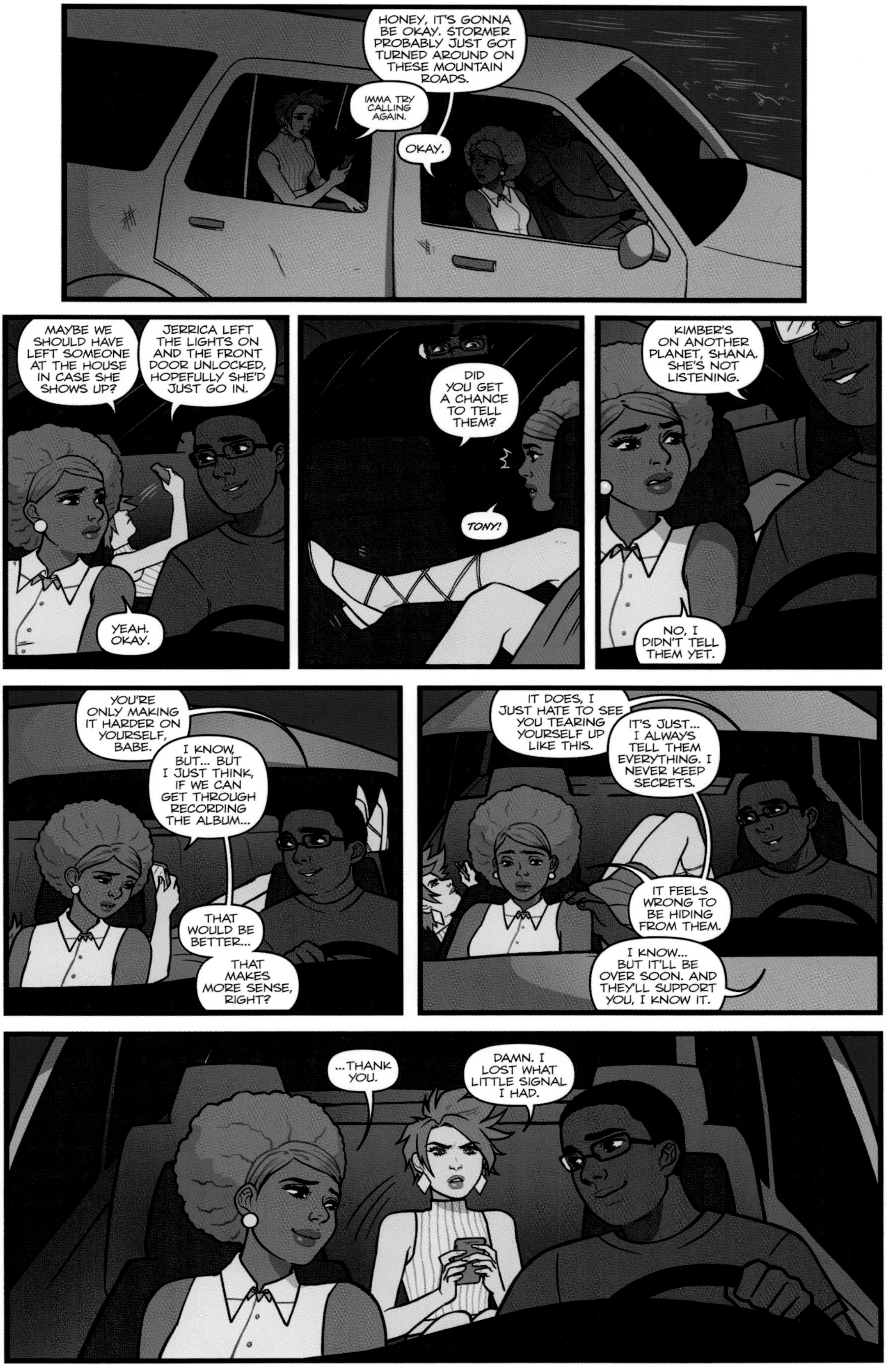
HONEY, IT'S GONNA BE OKAY. STORMER PROBABLY JUST GOT TURNED AROUND ON THESE MOUNTAIN ROADS.
IMMA TRY CALLING AGAIN.
OKAY.
MAYBE WE SHOULD HAVE LEFT SOMEONE AT THE HOUSE IN CASE SHE SHOWS UP?
JERRICA LEFT THE LIGHTS ON AND THE FRONT DOOR UNLOCKED, HOPEFULLY SHE'D JUST GO IN.
YEAH. OKAY.
DID YOU GET A CHANCE TO TELL THEM?
TONY!
KIMBER'S ON ANOTHER PLANET, SHANA. SHE'S NOT LISTENING.
NO, I DIDN'T TELL THEM YET.
YOU'RE ONLY MAKING IT HARDER ON YOURSELF, BABE.
I KNOW, BUT... BUT I JUST THINK, IF WE CAN GET THROUGH RECORDING THE ALBUM...
THAT WOULD BE BETTER...
THAT MAKES MORE SENSE, RIGHT?
IT DOES, I JUST HATE TO SEE YOU TEARING YOURSELF UP LIKE THIS.
IT'S JUST... I ALWAYS TELL THEM EVERYTHING. I NEVER KEEP SECRETS.
IT FEELS WRONG TO BE HIDING FROM THEM.
I KNOW... BUT IT'LL BE OVER SOON. AND THEY'LL SUPPORT YOU, I KNOW IT.
...THANK YOU.
DAMN. I LOST WHAT LITTLE SIGNAL I HAD.

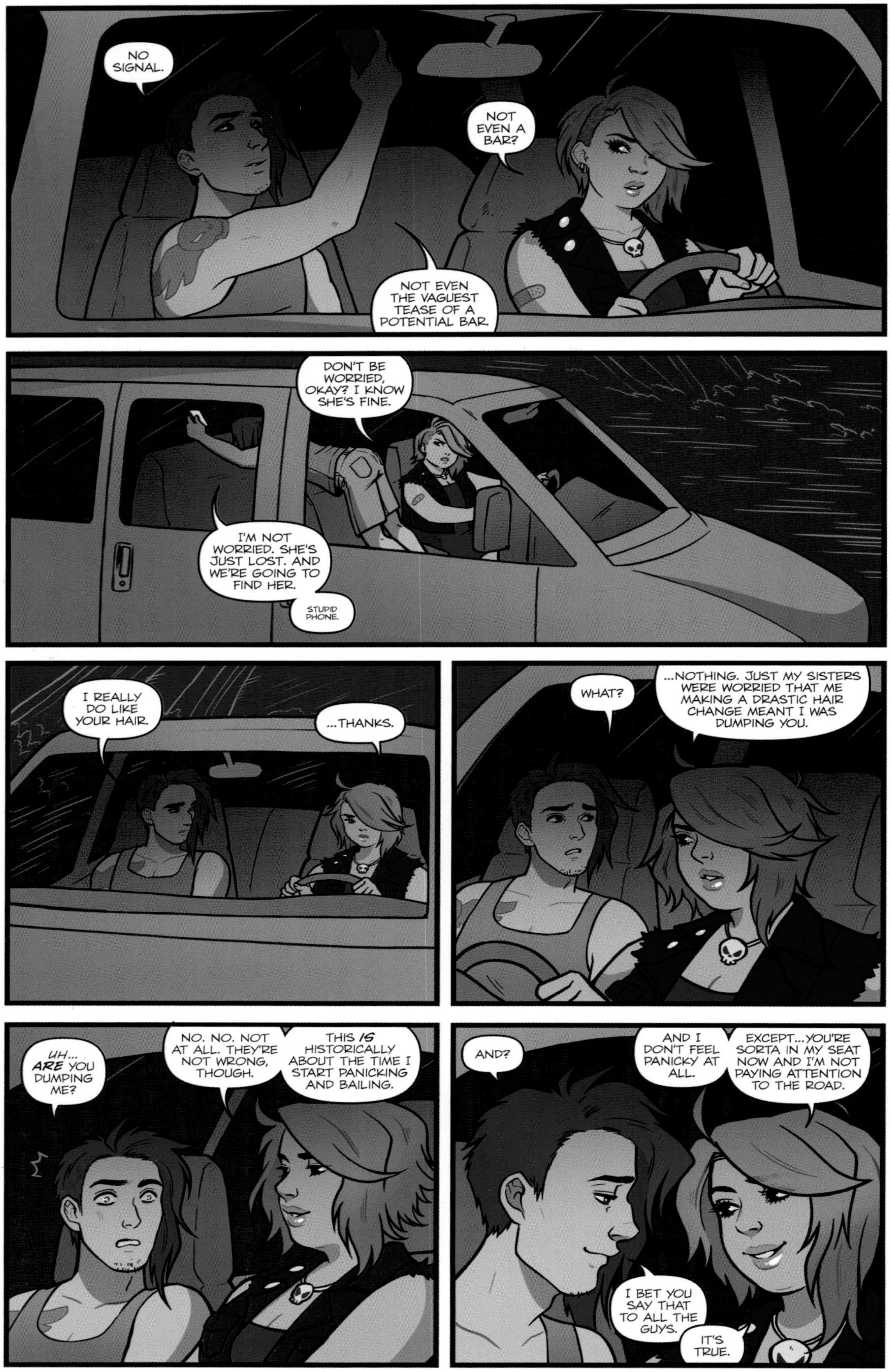
NO SIGNAL.
NOT EVEN A BAR?
NOT EVEN THE VAGUEST TEASE OF A POTENTIAL BAR.
DON'T BE WORRIED, OKAY? I KNOW SHE'S FINE.
I'M NOT WORRIED. SHE'S JUST LOST. AND WE'RE GOING TO FIND HER.
STUPID PHONE.
I REALLY DO LIKE YOUR HAIR.
...THANKS.
WHAT?
...NOTHING. JUST MY SISTERS WERE WORRIED THAT ME MAKING A DRASTIC HAIR CHANGE MEANT I WAS DUMPING YOU.
UH... ARE YOU DUMPING ME?
NO. NO. NOT AT ALL. THEY'RE NOT WRONG, THOUGH.
THIS IS HISTORICALLY ABOUT THE TIME I START PANICKING AND BAILING.
AND?
AND I DON'T FEEL PANICKY AT ALL.
EXCEPT...YOU'RE SORTA IN MY SEAT NOW AND I'M NOT PAYING ATTENTION TO THE ROAD.
I BET YOU SAY THAT TO ALL THE GUYS.
IT'S TRUE.

YOU'RE REALLY FREAKING ME OUT, RIO, WHAT DO YOU NEED TO SAY?

I'M SORRY. I... MAYBE WE SHOULDN'T TALK ABOUT THIS WHILE YOU'RE DRIVING.

YOU CAN'T SAY THAT *NOW!*

NOW YOU HAVE TO TELL ME OR I'M JUST GONNA WORRY ABOUT WHAT IT IS UNTIL IT DRIVES ME INSANE!

OKAY, OKAY, I'LL TELL YOU, JUST... WATCH THE ROAD.

SO, BEFORE, ON THE TOUR, THE DAY THAT YOU CAME TO THE HOTEL, THE DAY WE KIDNAPPED YOUR SISTERS FOR THE *SECOND* TIME?

WELL, I HAD BEEN LOOKING FOR YOU FOR DAYS... AND I TRIED TO TALK TO JEM ABOUT IT AND... WELL, SHE *KISSED ME.*

OH. ÷HEH÷ IS THAT ALL? THANK GOD.

THANK GOD? YOU DON'T CARE?

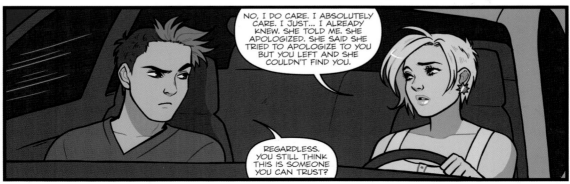

NO, I DO CARE. I ABSOLUTELY CARE. I JUST... I ALREADY KNEW. SHE TOLD ME. SHE APOLOGIZED. SHE SAID SHE TRIED TO APOLOGIZE TO YOU BUT YOU LEFT AND SHE COULDN'T FIND YOU.

REGARDLESS. YOU STILL THINK THIS IS SOMEONE YOU CAN TRUST?

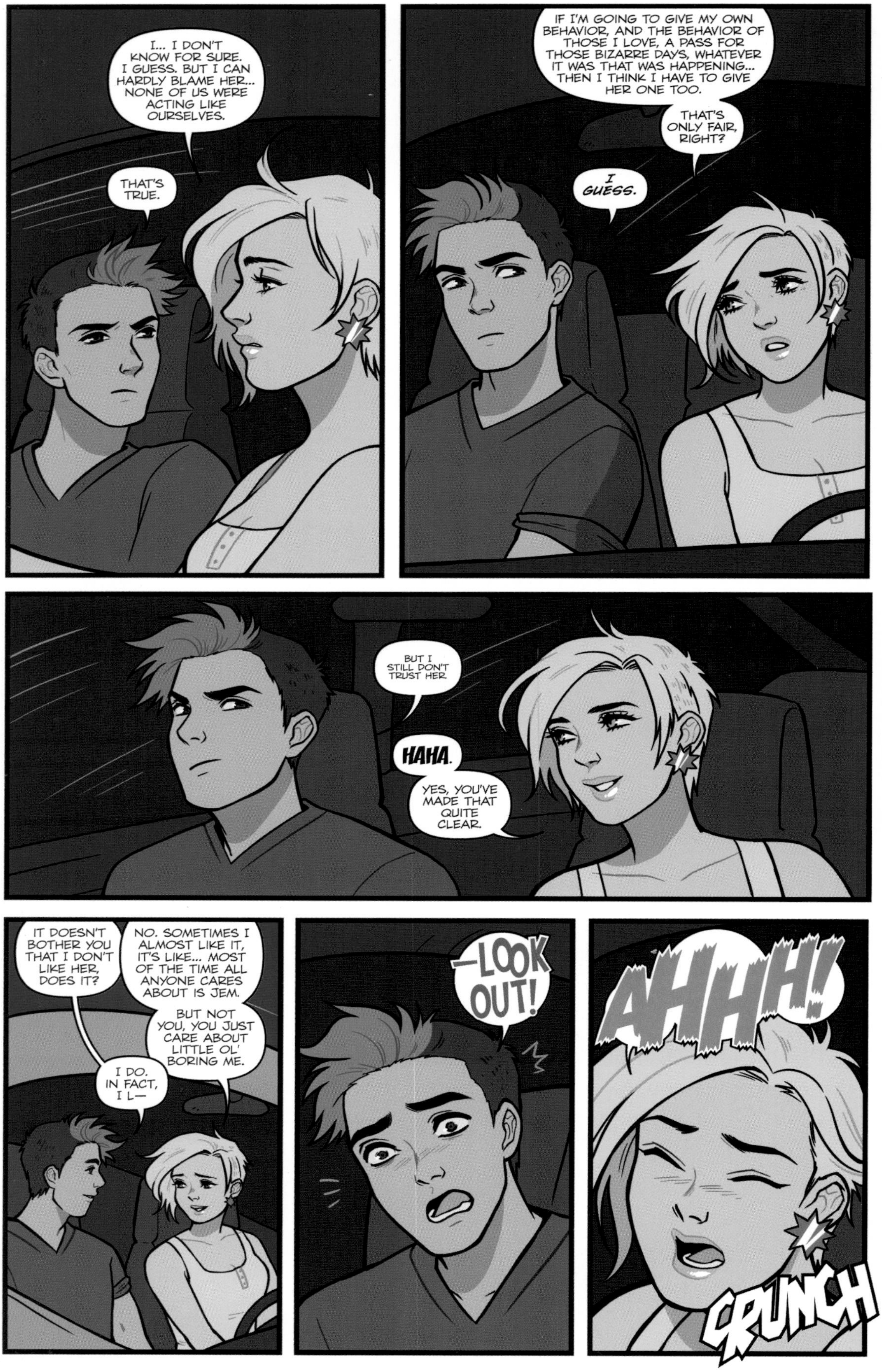
I... I DON'T KNOW FOR SURE. I GUESS. BUT I CAN HARDLY BLAME HER... NONE OF US WERE ACTING LIKE OURSELVES.
THAT'S TRUE.
IF I'M GOING TO GIVE MY OWN BEHAVIOR, AND THE BEHAVIOR OF THOSE I LOVE, A PASS FOR THOSE BIZARRE DAYS, WHATEVER IT WAS THAT WAS HAPPENING... THEN I THINK I HAVE TO GIVE HER ONE TOO.
THAT'S ONLY FAIR, RIGHT?
I GUESS.
BUT I STILL DON'T TRUST HER.
HAHA.
YES, YOU'VE MADE THAT QUITE CLEAR.
IT DOESN'T BOTHER YOU THAT I DON'T LIKE HER, DOES IT?
NO. SOMETIMES I ALMOST LIKE IT, IT'S LIKE... MOST OF THE TIME ALL ANYONE CARES ABOUT IS JEM.
BUT NOT YOU, YOU JUST CARE ABOUT LITTLE OL' BORING ME.
I DO. IN FACT, I L—
—LOOK OUT!
AHHH!
CRUNCH

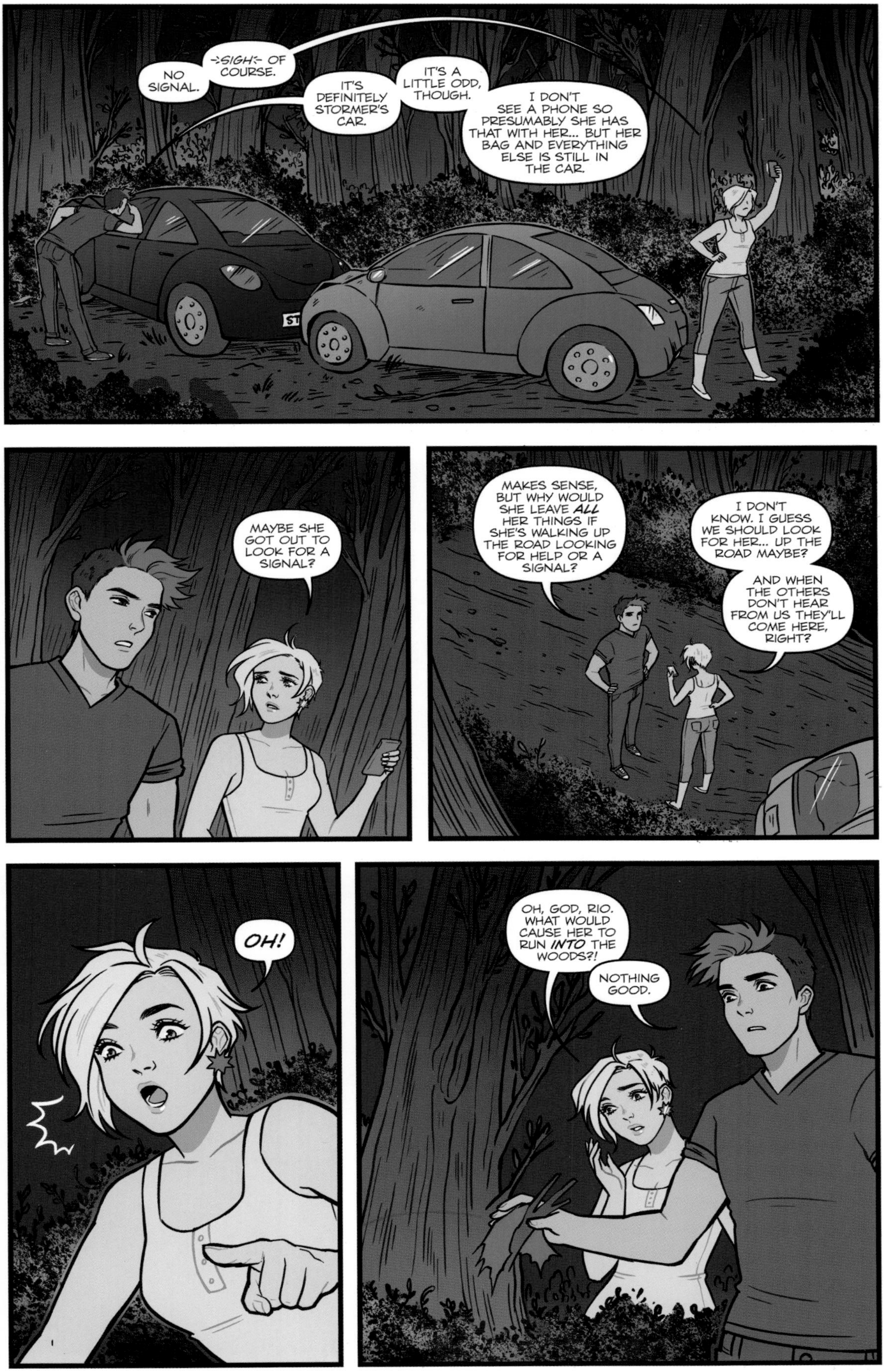
NO SIGNAL.
-SIGH- OF COURSE.
IT'S DEFINITELY STORMER'S CAR.
IT'S A LITTLE ODD, THOUGH.
I DON'T SEE A PHONE SO PRESUMABLY SHE HAS THAT WITH HER... BUT HER BAG AND EVERYTHING ELSE IS STILL IN THE CAR.
MAYBE SHE GOT OUT TO LOOK FOR A SIGNAL?
MAKES SENSE, BUT WHY WOULD SHE LEAVE ALL HER THINGS IF SHE'S WALKING UP THE ROAD LOOKING FOR HELP OR A SIGNAL?
I DON'T KNOW. I GUESS WE SHOULD LOOK FOR HER... UP THE ROAD MAYBE?
AND WHEN THE OTHERS DON'T HEAR FROM US THEY'LL COME HERE, RIGHT?
OH!
OH, GOD, RIO. WHAT WOULD CAUSE HER TO RUN INTO THE WOODS?!
NOTHING GOOD.

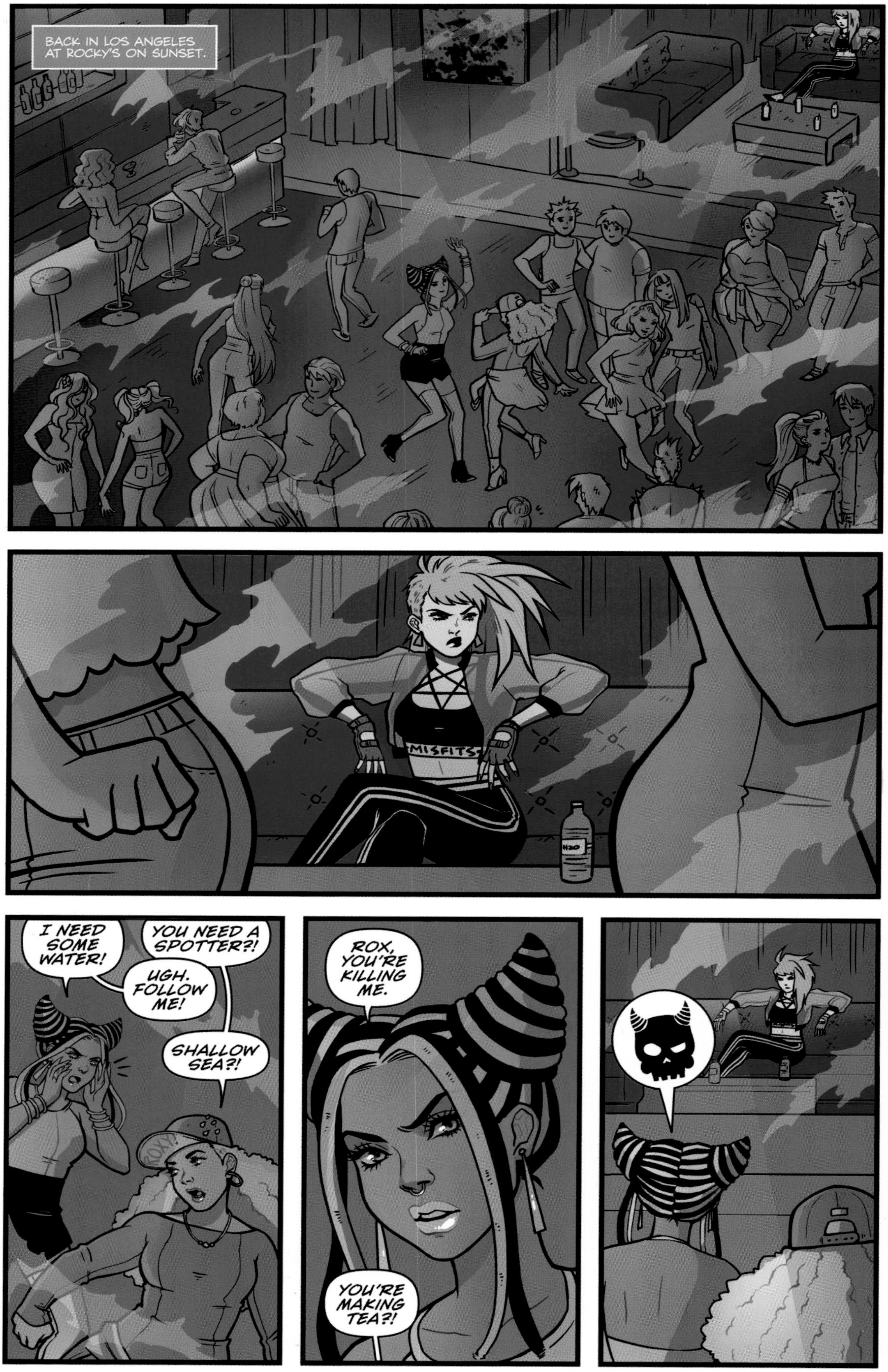
BACK IN LOS ANGELES AT ROCKY'S ON SUNSET.
MISFITS
H2O
I NEED SOME WATER!
YOU NEED A SPOTTER?!
UGH. FOLLOW ME!
SHALLOW SEA?!
ROXY!
ROX, YOU'RE KILLING ME.
YOU'RE MAKING TEA?!

WHERE'S BLAZE?!

IN THE BATHROOM.

IN THE **WOMB?!**

BATHROOM!

OH, YEAH. THAT MAKES MORE SENSE.

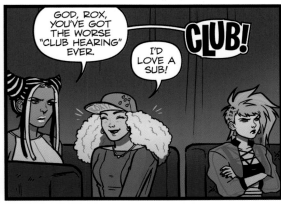

GOD, ROX, YOU'VE GOT THE WORSE "CLUB HEARING" EVER.

I'D LOVE A SUB!

CLUB!

I'M THINKING WE SHOULD PLAY AFTER THIS SET.

NOW? HERE? JUST GET UP AND PLAY?

ROCKY SAID SHE DOESN'T MIND, WE CAN USE THEIR INSTRUMENTS.

CROWD WILL LOVE IT. SUPER SECRET MISFITS POP-UP SHOW.

BUT STORMER ISN'T HERE.

WE DON'T NEED HER.

UMMMM...

BLAZE IS HERE, HER GUITAR CAN MORE THAN COVER FOR THE LOSS OF STORMER'S KEYTAR... AND GOD KNOWS STORMER'S VOCALS WON'T BE MISSED.

HEY. DON'T SAY THAT.

SHE'S A TRAITOR, GUYS.

YEAH.

I DON'T KNOW WHEN YOU'RE GONNA WAKE UP TO THIS.

YOU KNOW, WHILE YOU WERE OUT SHE WAS YOUR BIGGEST SUPPORTER DEFENDING YOU AND TRYING TO PROTECT YOU, FIGHTING ELISE HARDER THAN ANYONE TO KEEP US TOGETHER.

WELL, SHE DIDN'T DO TOO GREAT A JOB OF IT, NOW DID SHE?

WASN'T HER FAULT, PIZZ.

SHE DID EVERYTHING SHE COULD. WE WERE IN A CORNER 'CAUSE OF THAT BLOODY CONTRACT.

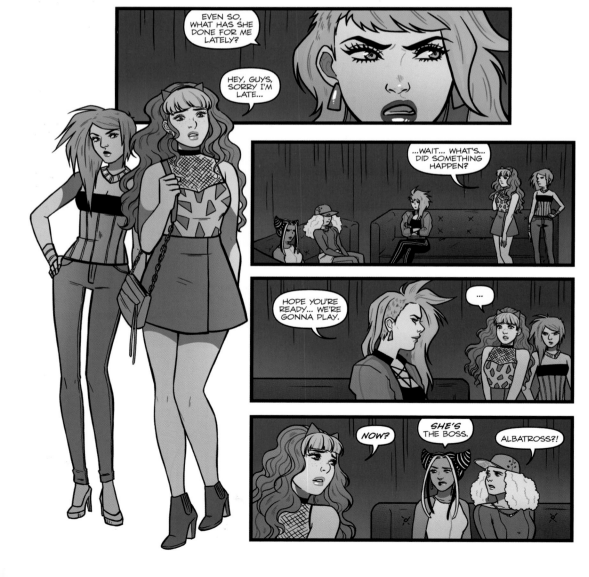

EVEN SO, WHAT HAS SHE DONE FOR ME LATELY?

HEY, GUYS, SORRY I'M LATE...

...WAIT... WHAT'S... DID SOMETHING HAPPEN?

HOPE YOU'RE READY... WE'RE GONNA PLAY.

...

NOW?

SHE'S THE BOSS.

ALBATROSS?!

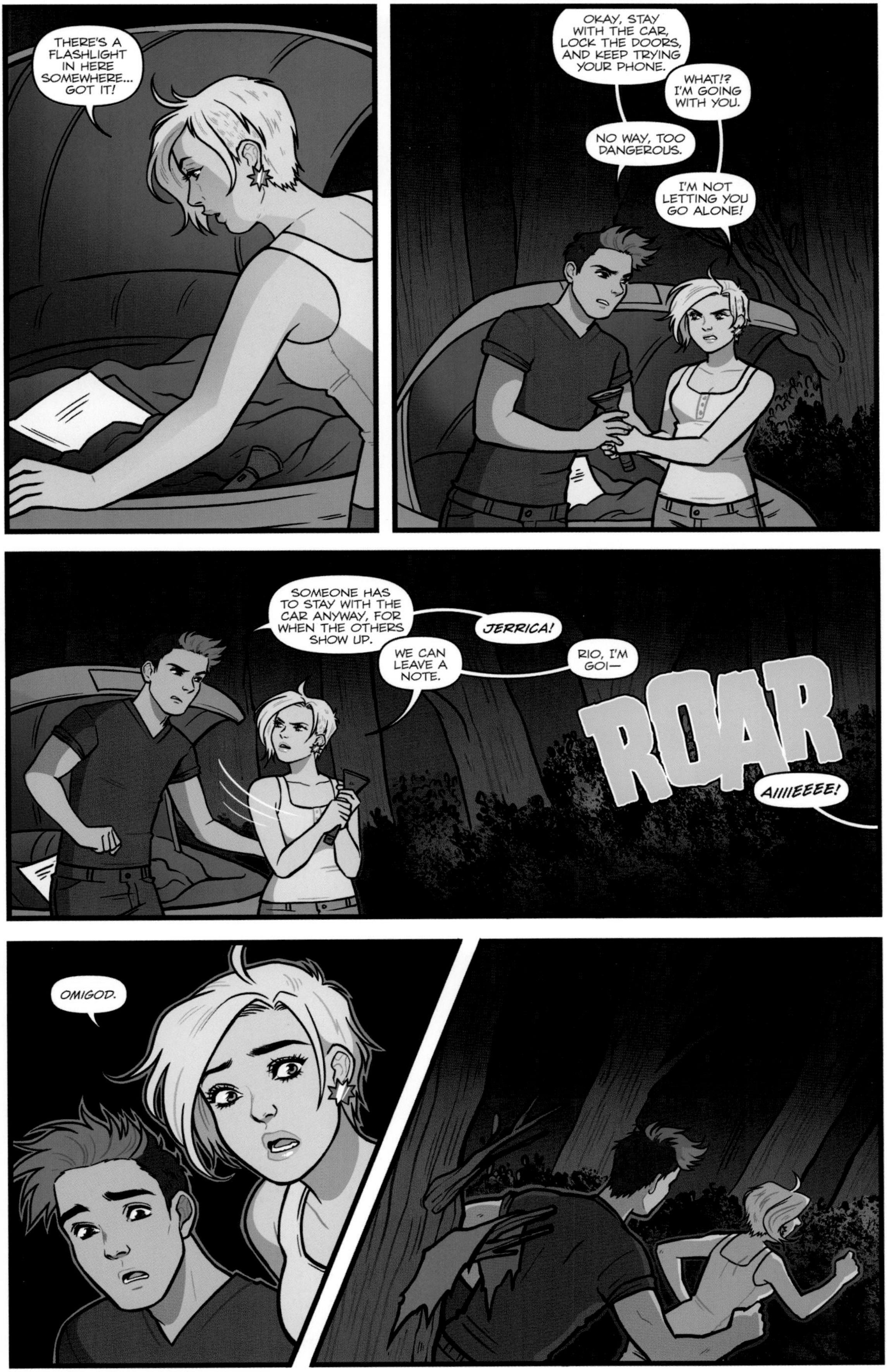
THERE'S A FLASHLIGHT IN HERE SOMEWHERE... GOT IT!
OKAY, STAY WITH THE CAR, LOCK THE DOORS, AND KEEP TRYING YOUR PHONE.
WHAT!? I'M GOING WITH YOU.
NO WAY, TOO DANGEROUS.
I'M NOT LETTING YOU GO ALONE!
SOMEONE HAS TO STAY WITH THE CAR ANYWAY, FOR WHEN THE OTHERS SHOW UP.
JERRICA!
WE CAN LEAVE A NOTE.
RIO, I'M GOI—
ROAR
AIIIIEEEE!
OMIGOD.

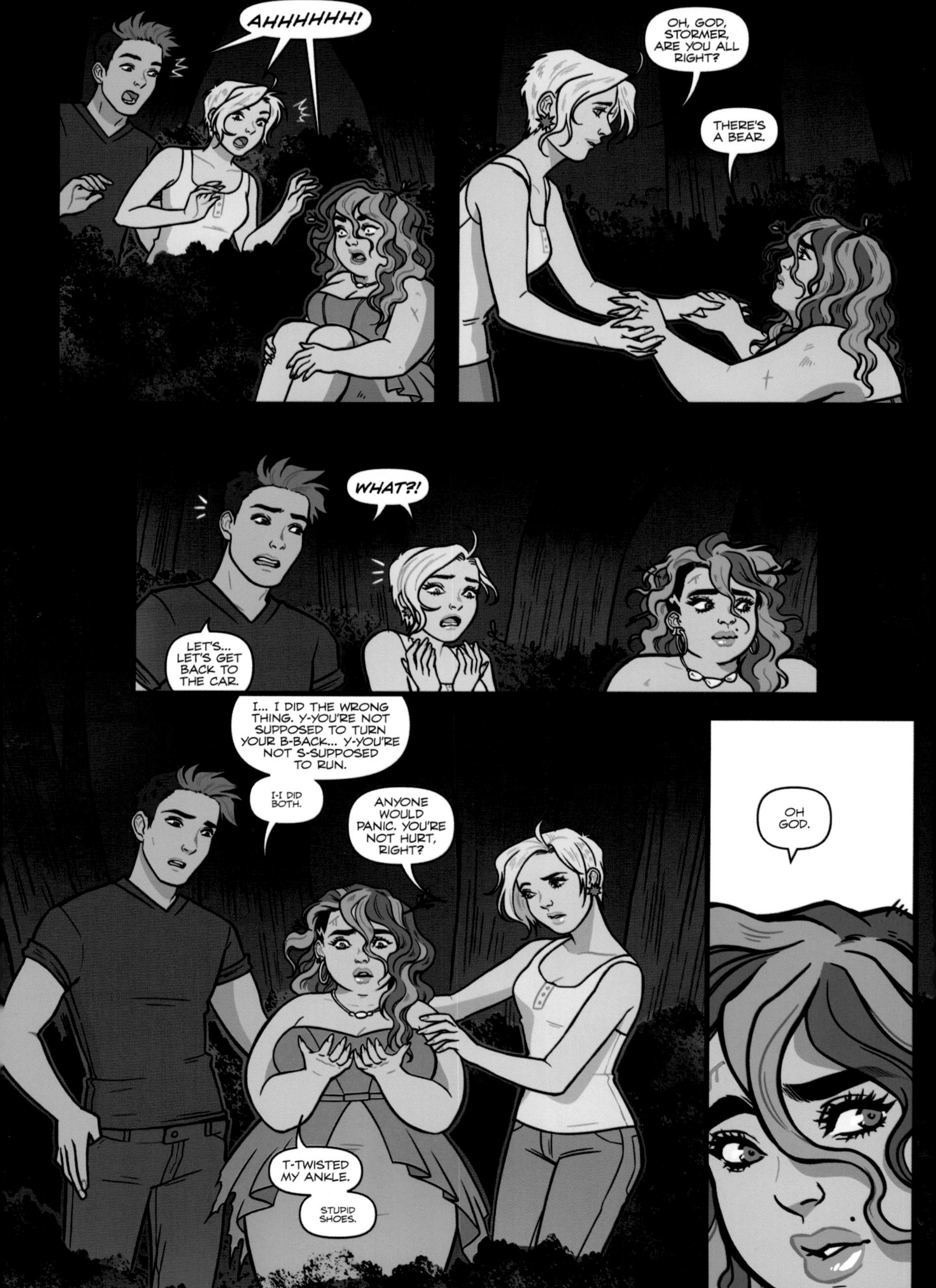
AHHHHHH!
OH, GOD, STORMER, ARE YOU ALL RIGHT?
THERE'S A BEAR.
WHAT?!
LET'S... LET'S GET BACK TO THE CAR.
I... I DID THE WRONG THING. Y-YOU'RE NOT SUPPOSED TO TURN YOUR B-BACK... Y-YOU'RE NOT S-SUPPOSED TO RUN.
I-I DID BOTH.
ANYONE WOULD PANIC. YOU'RE NOT HURT, RIGHT?
T-TWISTED MY ANKLE.
STUPID SHOES.
OH GOD.

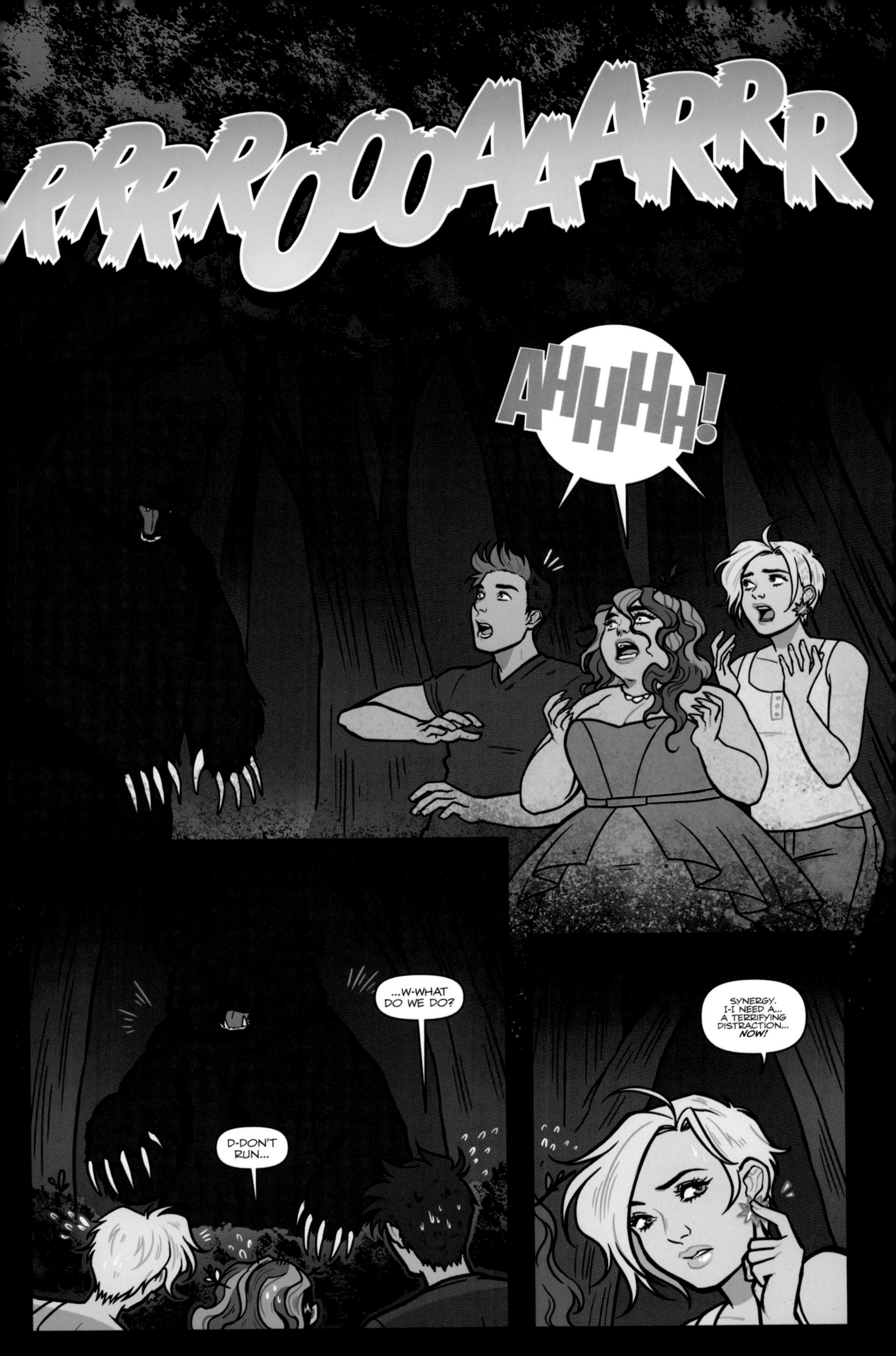
RRRROOOOAAARRR
AHHHH!
...W-WHAT DO WE DO?
D-DON'T RUN...
SYNERGY. I-I NEED A... A TERRIFYING DISTRACTION... *NOW!*

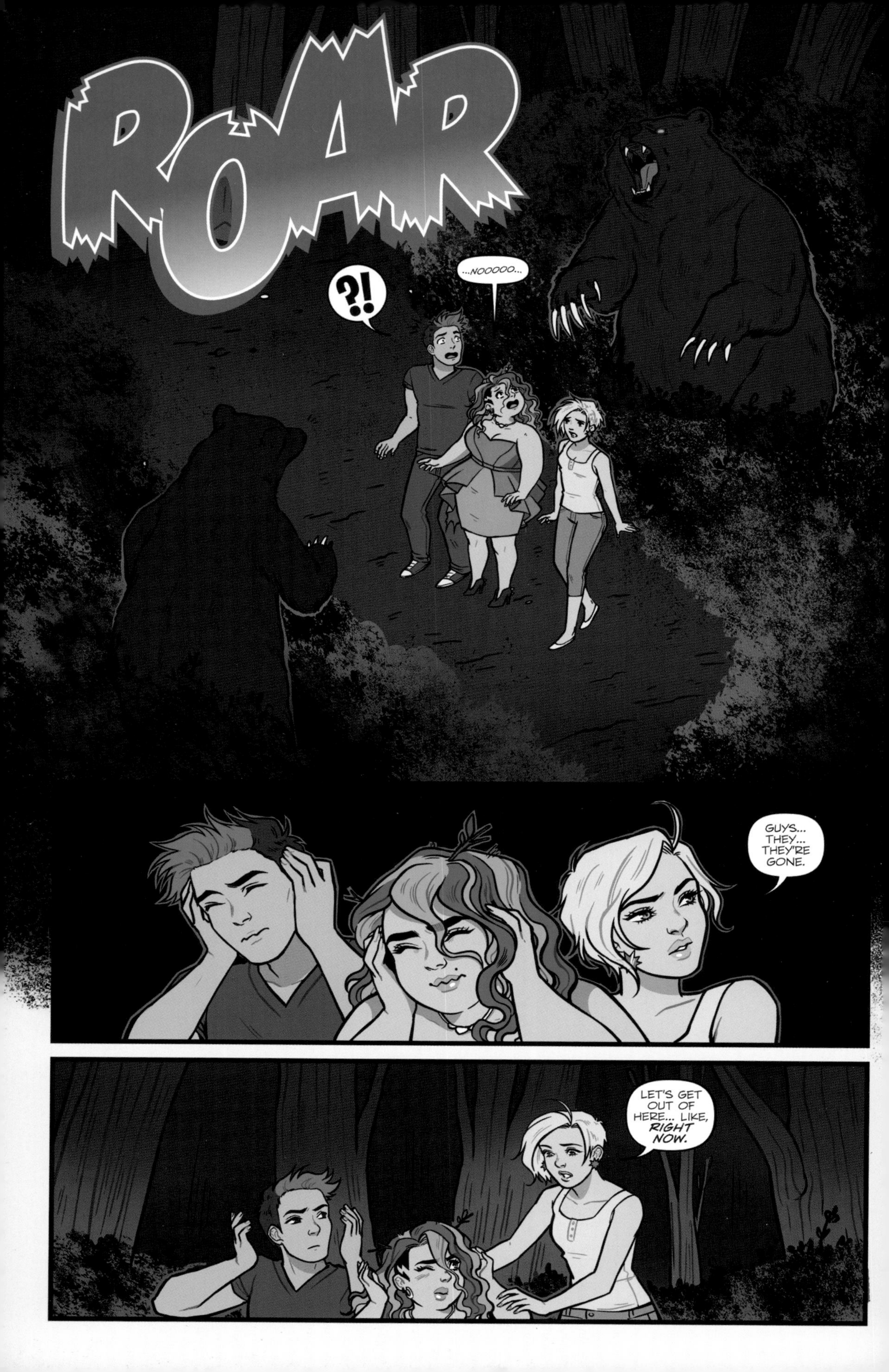
ROAR
?!
...NOOOOO...
GUYS... THEY... THEY'RE GONE.
LET'S GET OUT OF HERE... LIKE, *RIGHT NOW.*

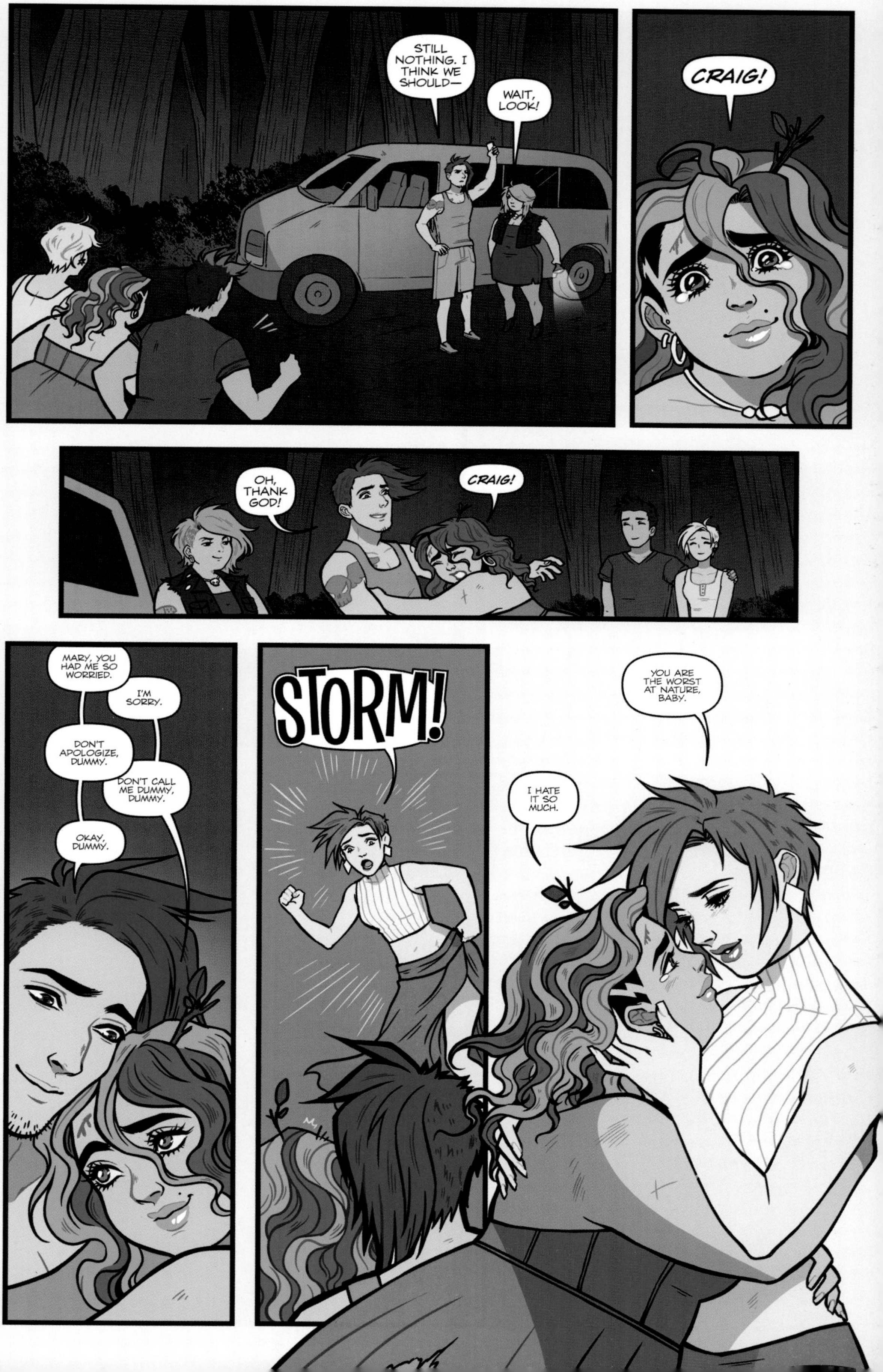
STILL NOTHING. I THINK WE SHOULD—
WAIT, LOOK!
CRAIG!
OH, THANK GOD!
CRAIG!
MARY, YOU HAD ME SO WORRIED.
I'M SORRY.
DON'T APOLOGIZE, DUMMY.
DON'T CALL ME DUMMY, DUMMY.
OKAY, DUMMY.
STORM!
YOU ARE THE WORST AT NATURE, BABY.
I HATE IT SO MUCH.

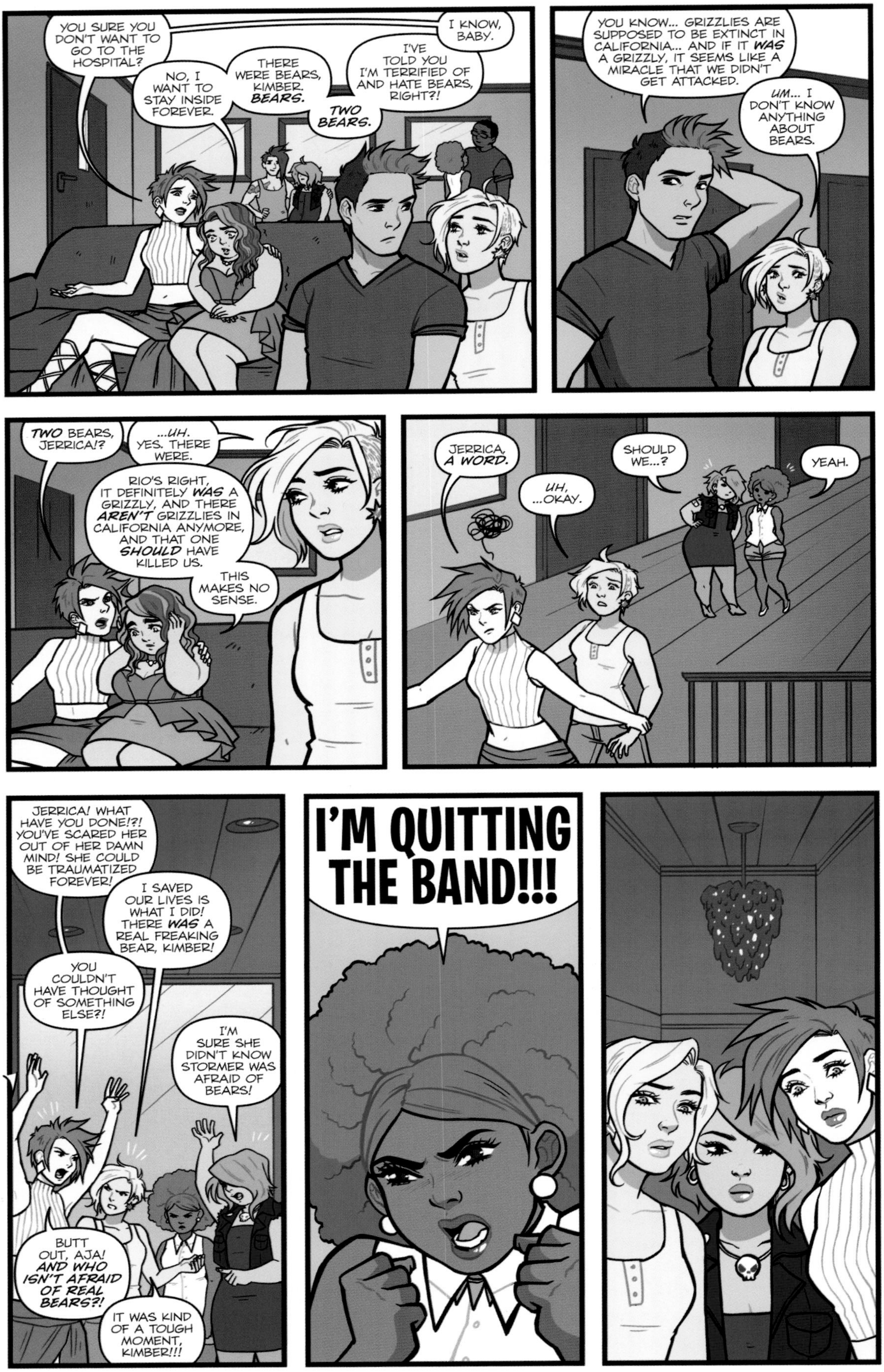
YOU SURE YOU DON'T WANT TO GO TO THE HOSPITAL?
NO, I WANT TO STAY INSIDE FOREVER.
THERE WERE BEARS, KIMBER. *BEARS.*
TWO BEARS.
I KNOW, BABY.
I'VE TOLD YOU I'M TERRIFIED OF AND HATE BEARS, RIGHT?!
YOU KNOW... GRIZZLIES ARE SUPPOSED TO BE EXTINCT IN CALIFORNIA... AND IF IT *WAS* A GRIZZLY, IT SEEMS LIKE A MIRACLE THAT WE DIDN'T GET ATTACKED.
UM... I DON'T KNOW ANYTHING ABOUT BEARS.
TWO BEARS, JERRICA!?
...UH. YES. THERE WERE.
RIO'S RIGHT, IT DEFINITELY *WAS* A GRIZZLY, AND THERE *AREN'T* GRIZZLIES IN CALIFORNIA ANYMORE, AND THAT ONE *SHOULD* HAVE KILLED US.
THIS MAKES NO SENSE.
JERRICA, *A WORD.*
UH, ...OKAY.
SHOULD WE...?
YEAH.
JERRICA! WHAT HAVE YOU DONE!?! YOU'VE SCARED HER OUT OF HER DAMN MIND! SHE COULD BE TRAUMATIZED FOREVER!
I SAVED OUR LIVES IS WHAT I DID! THERE *WAS* A REAL FREAKING BEAR, KIMBER!
YOU COULDN'T HAVE THOUGHT OF SOMETHING ELSE?!
I'M SURE SHE DIDN'T KNOW STORMER WAS AFRAID OF BEARS!
BUTT OUT, AJA! ***AND WHO ISN'T AFRAID OF REAL BEARS?!***
IT WAS KIND OF A TOUGH MOMENT, KIMBER!!!
I'M QUITTING THE BAND!!!

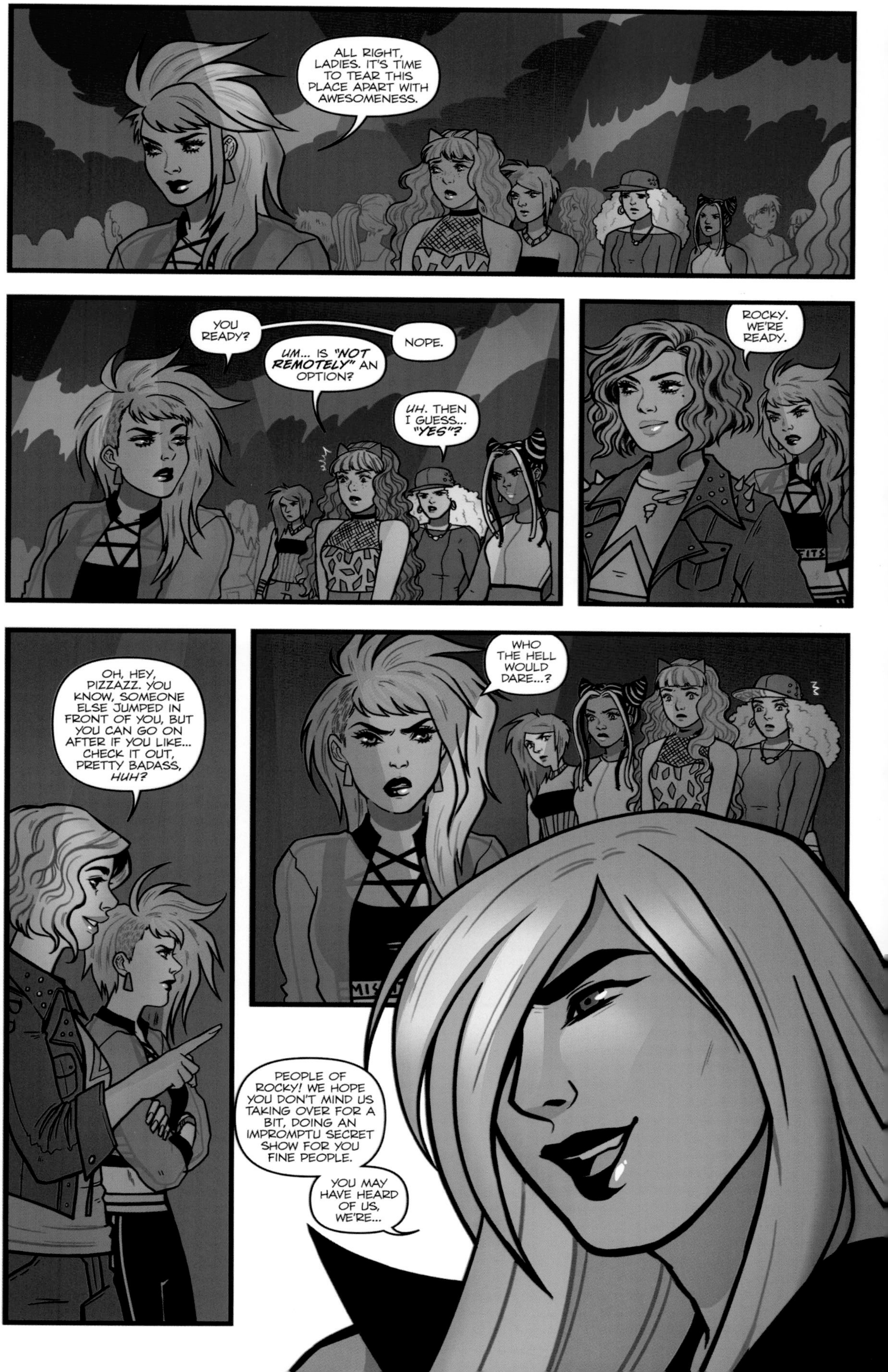

ALL RIGHT, LADIES. IT'S TIME TO TEAR THIS PLACE APART WITH AWESOMENESS.
YOU READY?
NOPE.
UM... IS "NOT REMOTELY" AN OPTION?
UH. THEN I GUESS... "YES"?
ROCKY. WE'RE READY.
OH, HEY, PIZZAZZ. YOU KNOW, SOMEONE ELSE JUMPED IN FRONT OF YOU, BUT YOU CAN GO ON AFTER IF YOU LIKE... CHECK IT OUT, PRETTY BADASS, HUH?
WHO THE HELL WOULD DARE...?
PEOPLE OF ROCKY! WE HOPE YOU DON'T MIND US TAKING OVER FOR A BIT, DOING AN IMPROMPTU SECRET SHOW FOR YOU FINE PEOPLE.
YOU MAY HAVE HEARD OF US, WE'RE...

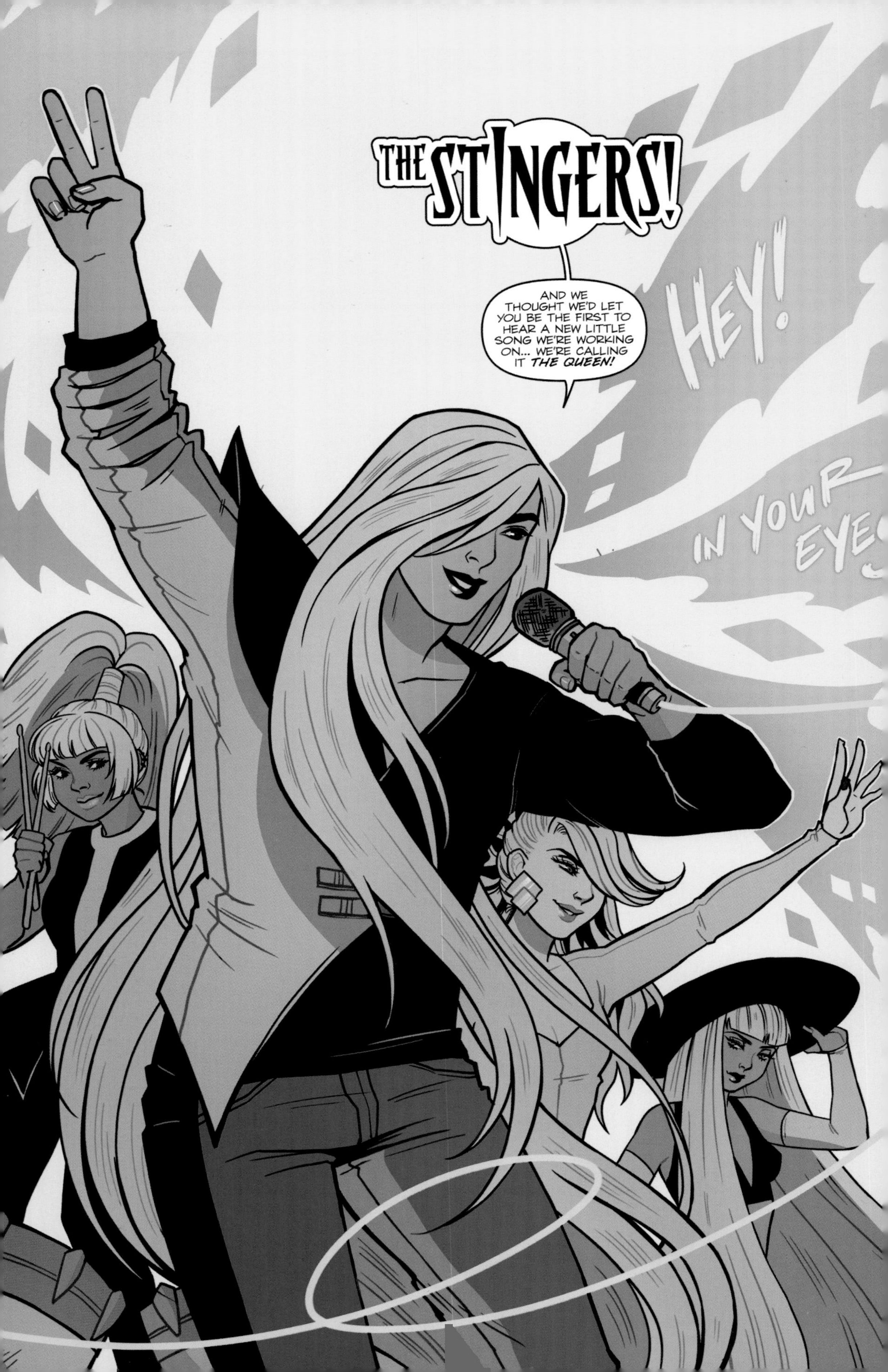
THE STINGERS!
AND WE THOUGHT WE'D LET YOU BE THE FIRST TO HEAR A NEW LITTLE SONG WE'RE WORKING ON... WE'RE CALLING IT THE QUEEN!
HEY!
IN YOUR

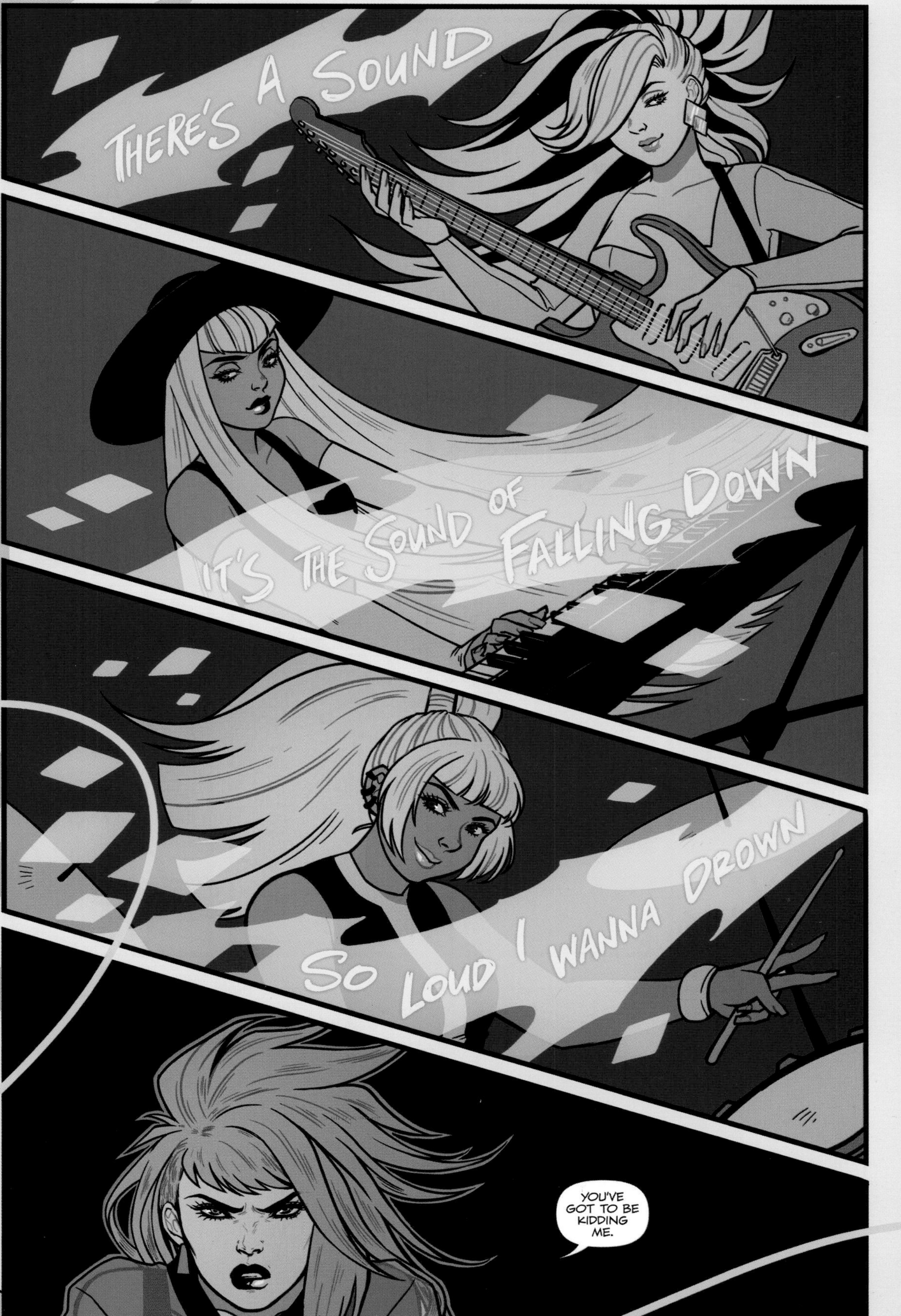
THERE'S A SOUND
IT'S THE SOUND OF FALLING DOWN
SO LOUD I WANNA DROWN
YOU'VE GOT TO BE KIDDING ME.

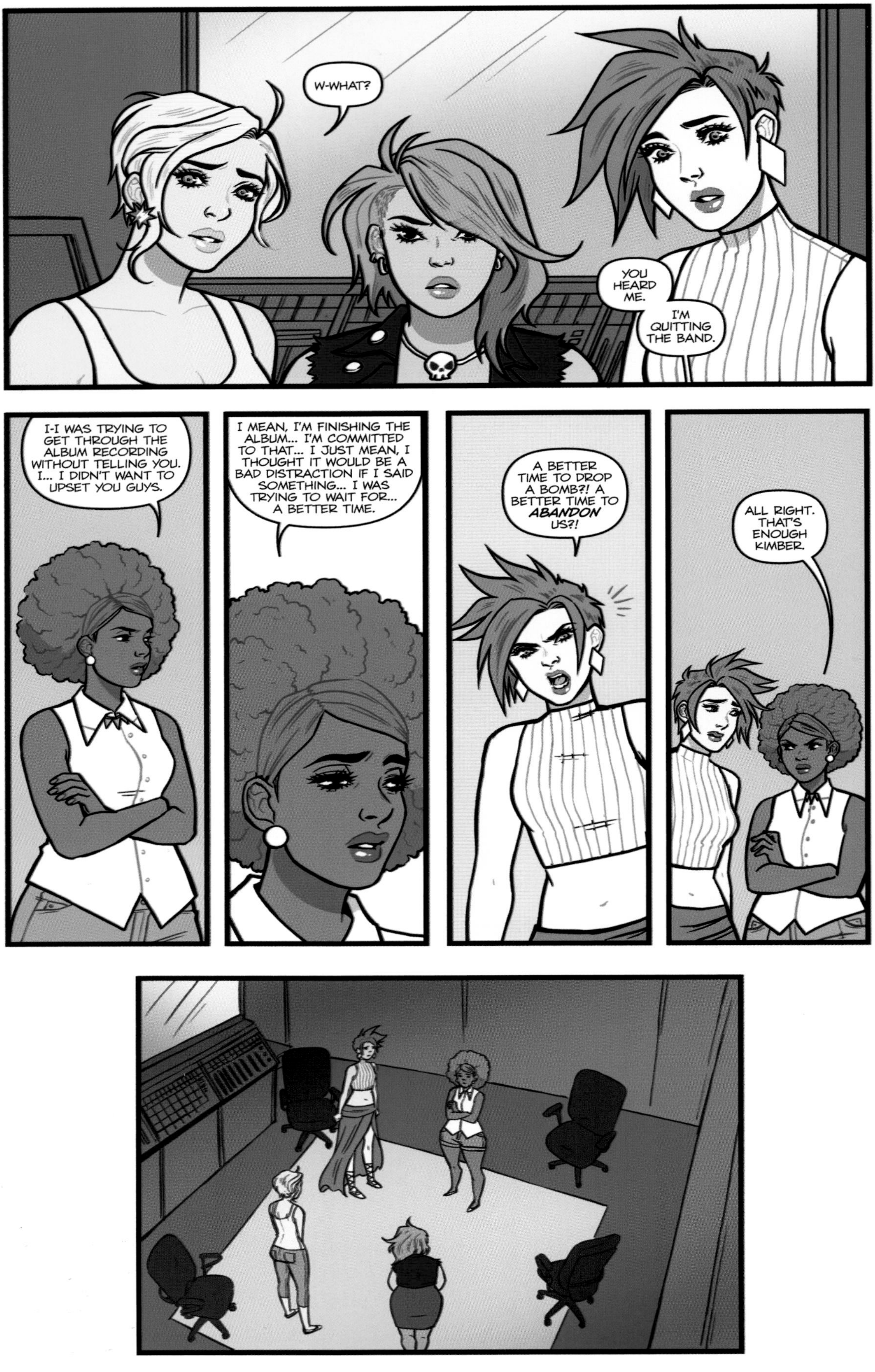
W-WHAT?
YOU HEARD ME.
I'M QUITTING THE BAND.
I-I WAS TRYING TO GET THROUGH THE ALBUM RECORDING WITHOUT TELLING YOU. I... I DIDN'T WANT TO UPSET YOU GUYS.
I MEAN, I'M FINISHING THE ALBUM... I'M COMMITTED TO THAT... I JUST MEAN, I THOUGHT IT WOULD BE A BAD DISTRACTION IF I SAID SOMETHING... I WAS TRYING TO WAIT FOR... A BETTER TIME.
A BETTER TIME TO DROP A BOMB?! A BETTER TIME TO *ABANDON* US?!
ALL RIGHT. THAT'S ENOUGH KIMBER.

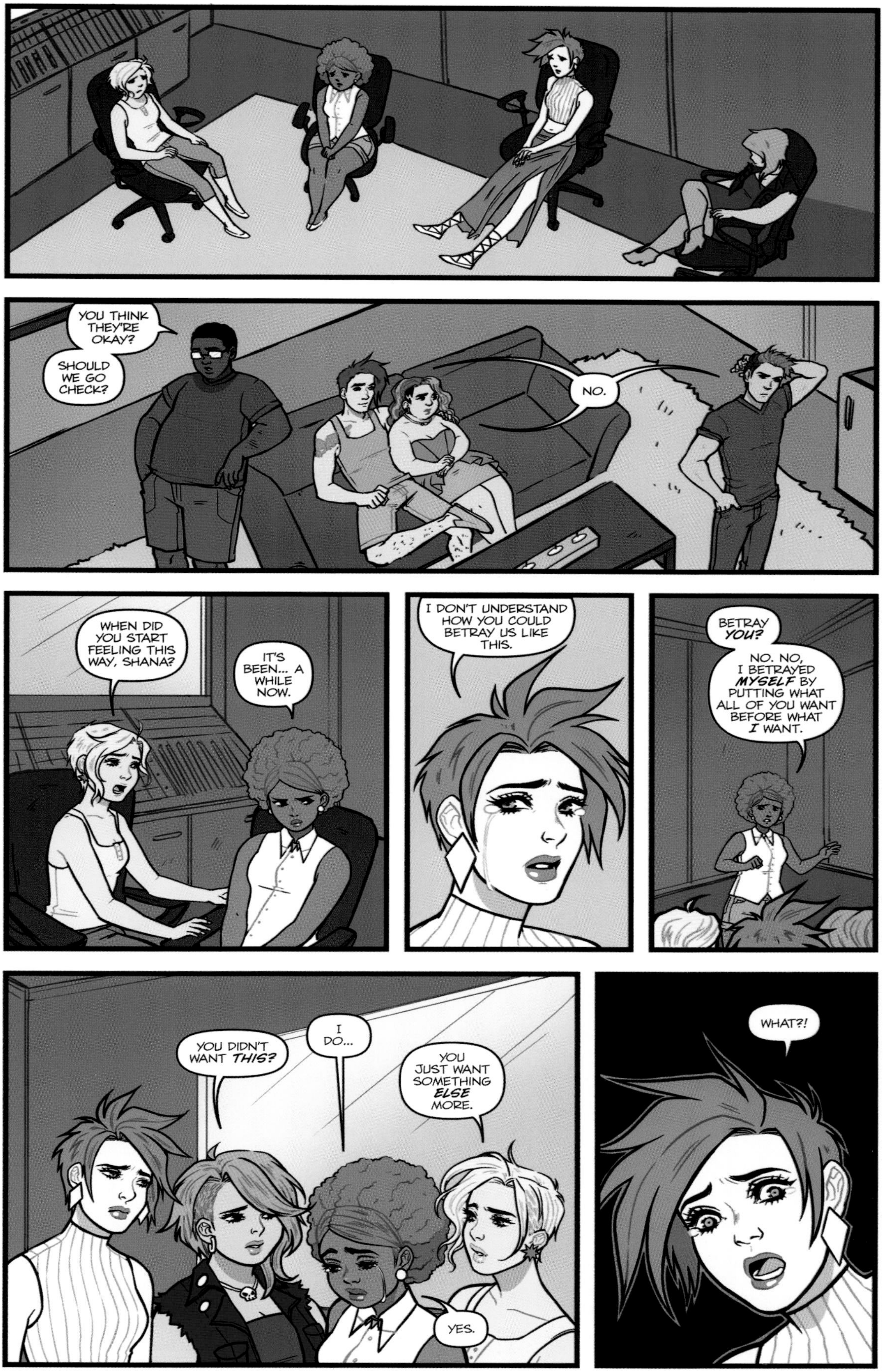
YOU THINK THEY'RE OKAY?
SHOULD WE GO CHECK?
NO.
WHEN DID YOU START FEELING THIS WAY, SHANA?
IT'S BEEN... A WHILE NOW.
I DON'T UNDERSTAND HOW YOU COULD BETRAY US LIKE THIS.
BETRAY YOU?
NO. NO, I BETRAYED MYSELF BY PUTTING WHAT ALL OF YOU WANT BEFORE WHAT I WANT.
YOU DIDN'T WANT THIS?
I DO...
YOU JUST WANT SOMETHING ELSE MORE.
YES.
WHAT?!

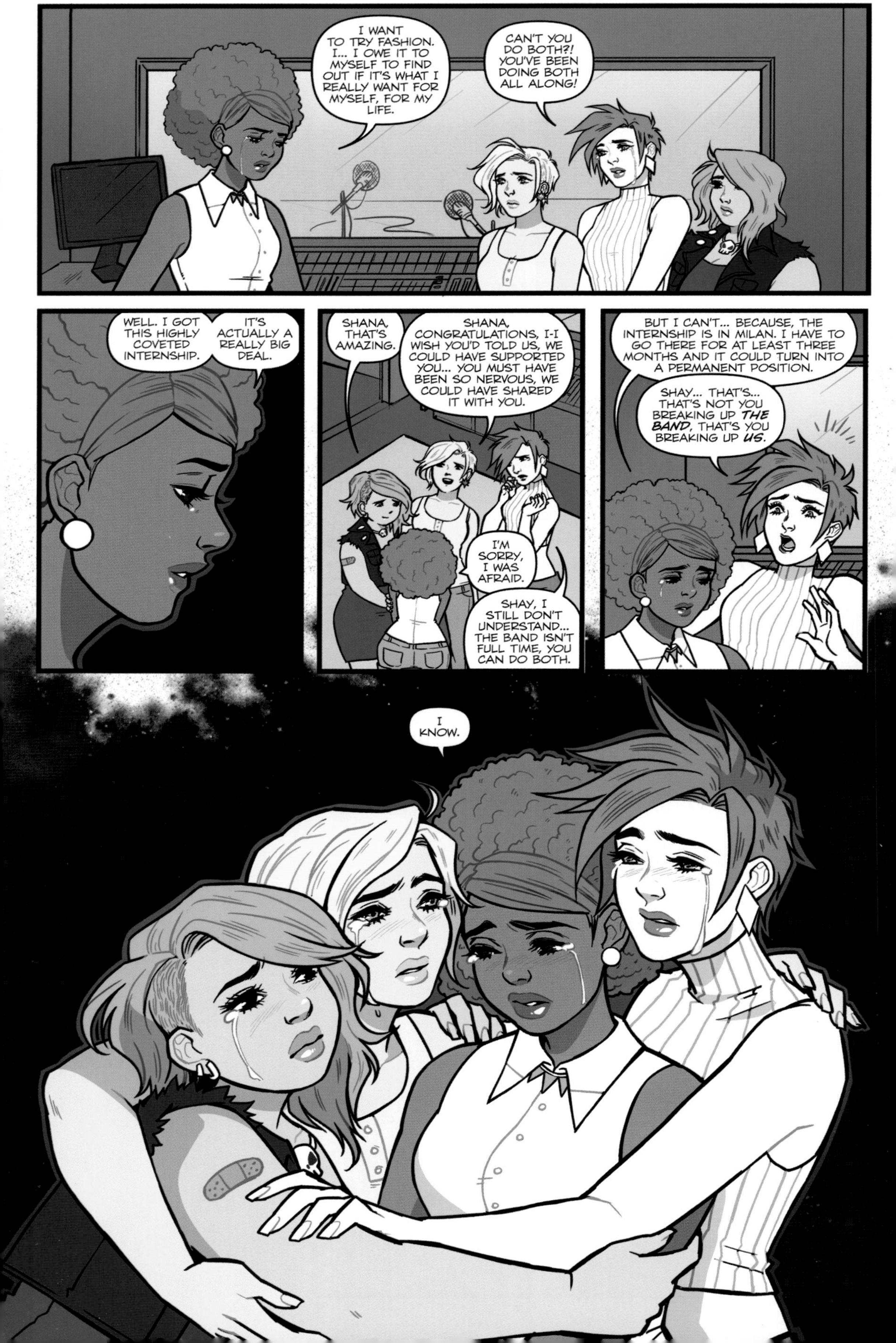
I WANT TO TRY FASHION. I... I OWE IT TO MYSELF TO FIND OUT IF IT'S WHAT I REALLY WANT FOR MYSELF, FOR MY LIFE.
CAN'T YOU DO BOTH?! YOU'VE BEEN DOING BOTH ALL ALONG!
WELL. I GOT THIS HIGHLY COVETED INTERNSHIP.
IT'S ACTUALLY A REALLY BIG DEAL.
SHANA, THAT'S AMAZING.
SHANA, CONGRATULATIONS, I-I WISH YOU'D TOLD US, WE COULD HAVE SUPPORTED YOU... YOU MUST HAVE BEEN SO NERVOUS, WE COULD HAVE SHARED IT WITH YOU.
I'M SORRY, I WAS AFRAID.
SHAY, I STILL DON'T UNDERSTAND... THE BAND ISN'T FULL TIME, YOU CAN DO BOTH.
BUT I CAN'T... BECAUSE, THE INTERNSHIP IS IN MILAN. I HAVE TO GO THERE FOR AT LEAST THREE MONTHS AND IT COULD TURN INTO A PERMANENT POSITION.
SHAY... THAT'S... THAT'S NOT YOU BREAKING UP *THE BAND*, THAT'S YOU BREAKING UP *US*.
I KNOW.

COVER ART BY **M. VICTORIA ROBADO**

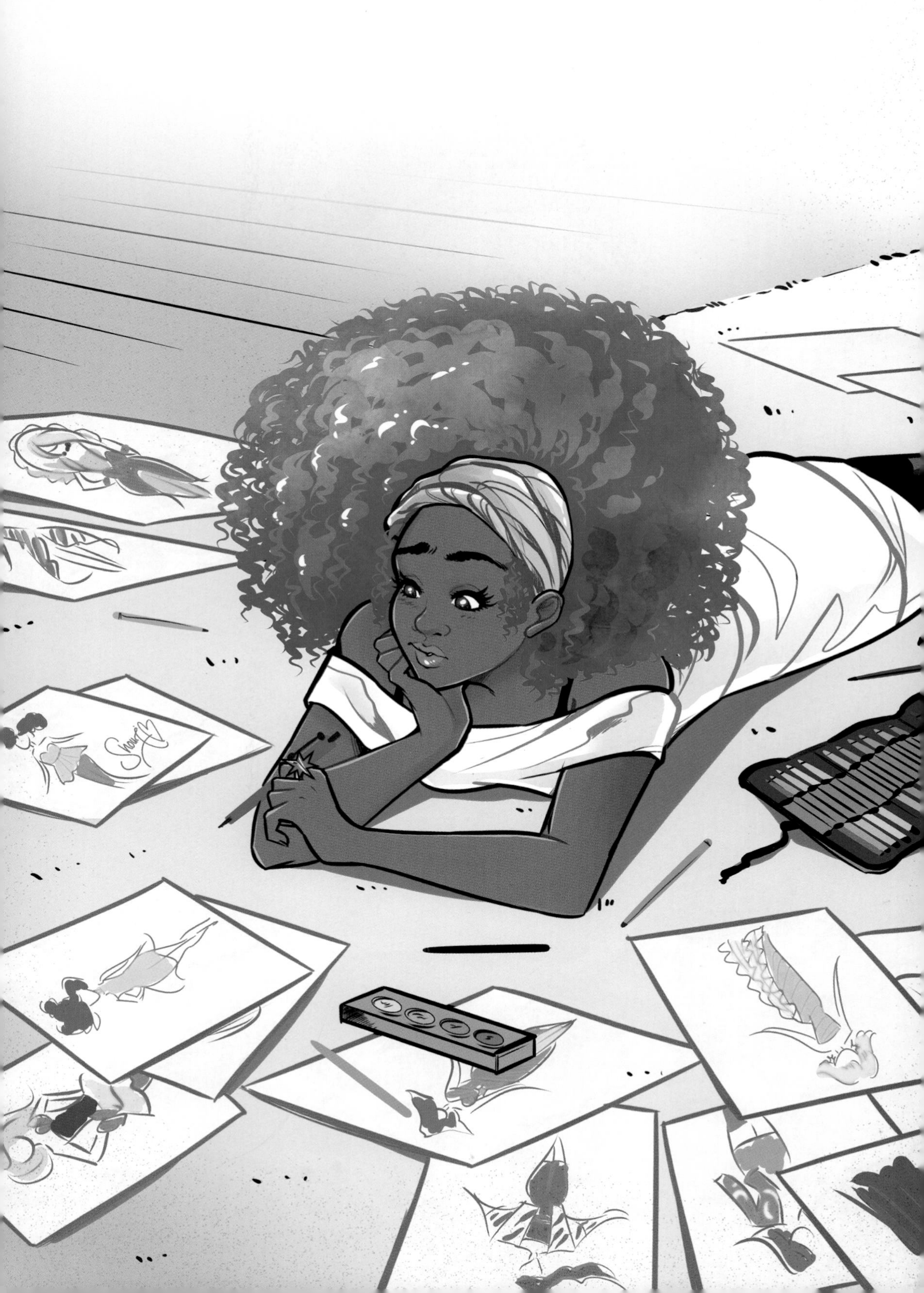

ENTER THE STINGERS PART 1

COVER ART BY **MEREDITH MCCLAREN**

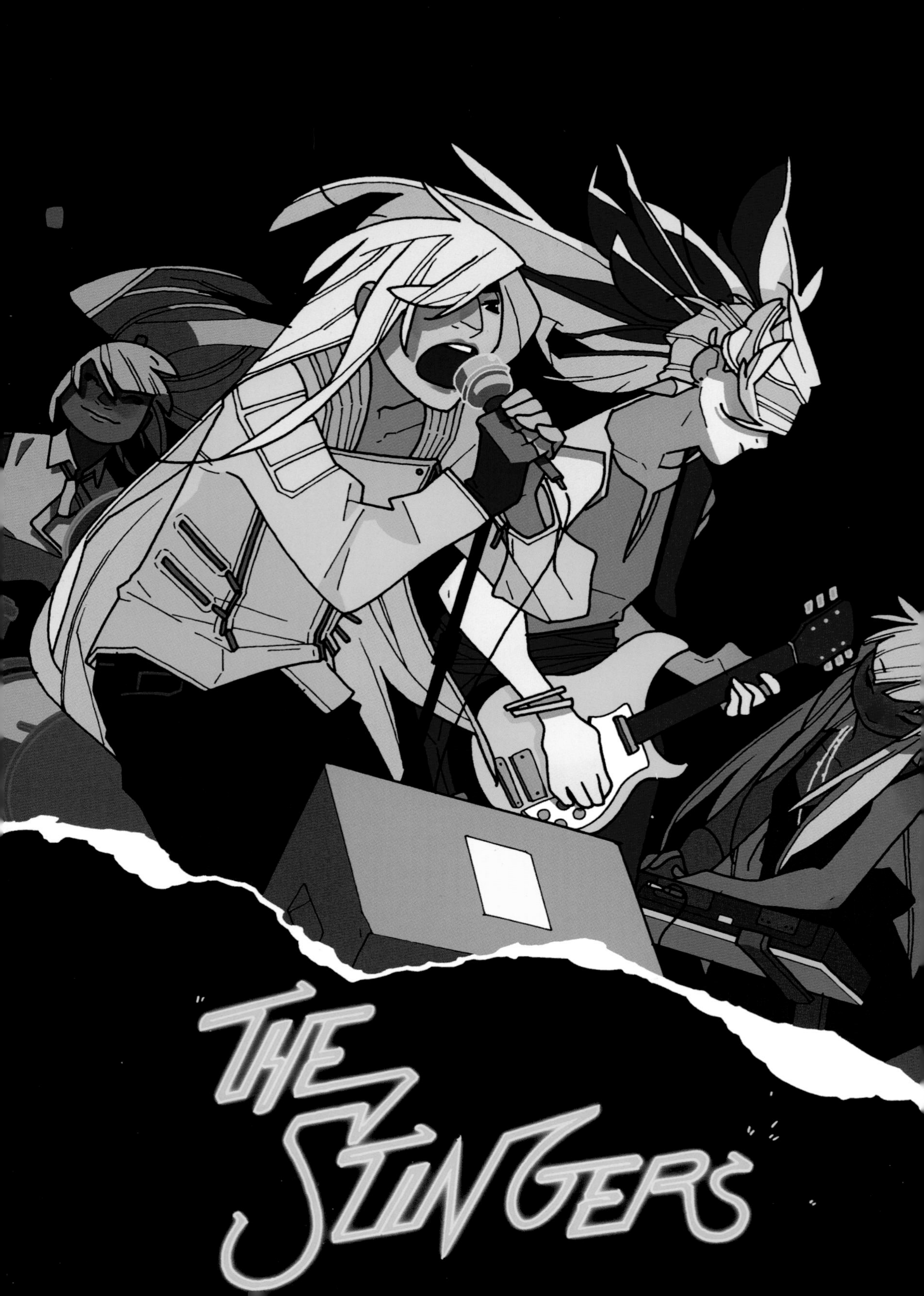
THE STINGERS

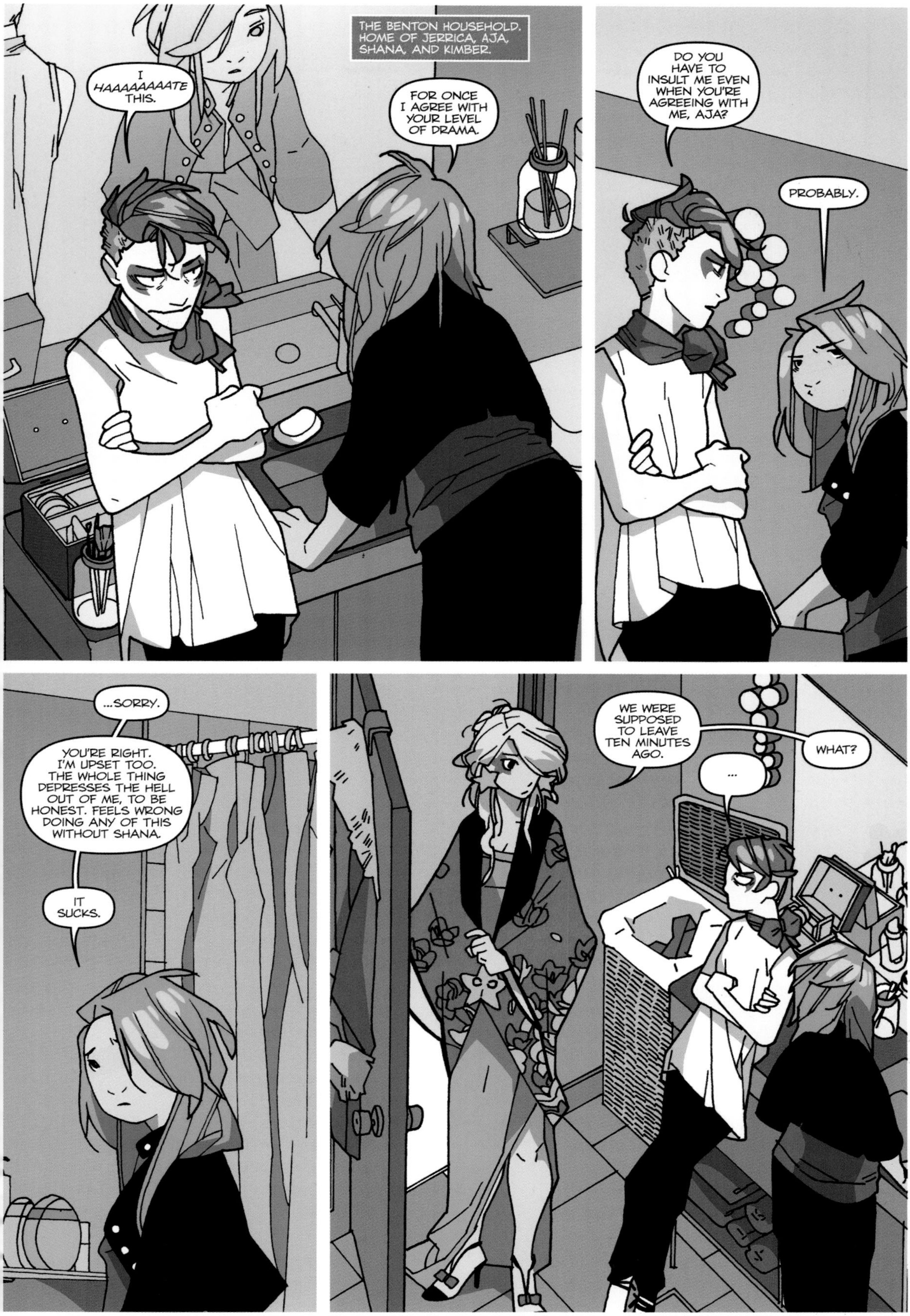
THE BENTON HOUSEHOLD. HOME OF JERRICA, AJA, SHANA, AND KIMBER.
I *HAAAAAAAATE* THIS.
FOR ONCE I AGREE WITH YOUR LEVEL OF DRAMA.
DO YOU HAVE TO INSULT ME EVEN WHEN YOU'RE AGREEING WITH ME, AJA?
PROBABLY.
...SORRY.
YOU'RE RIGHT. I'M UPSET TOO. THE WHOLE THING DEPRESSES THE HELL OUT OF ME, TO BE HONEST. FEELS WRONG DOING ANY OF THIS WITHOUT SHANA.
IT SUCKS.
WE WERE SUPPOSED TO LEAVE TEN MINUTES AGO.
WHAT?
...

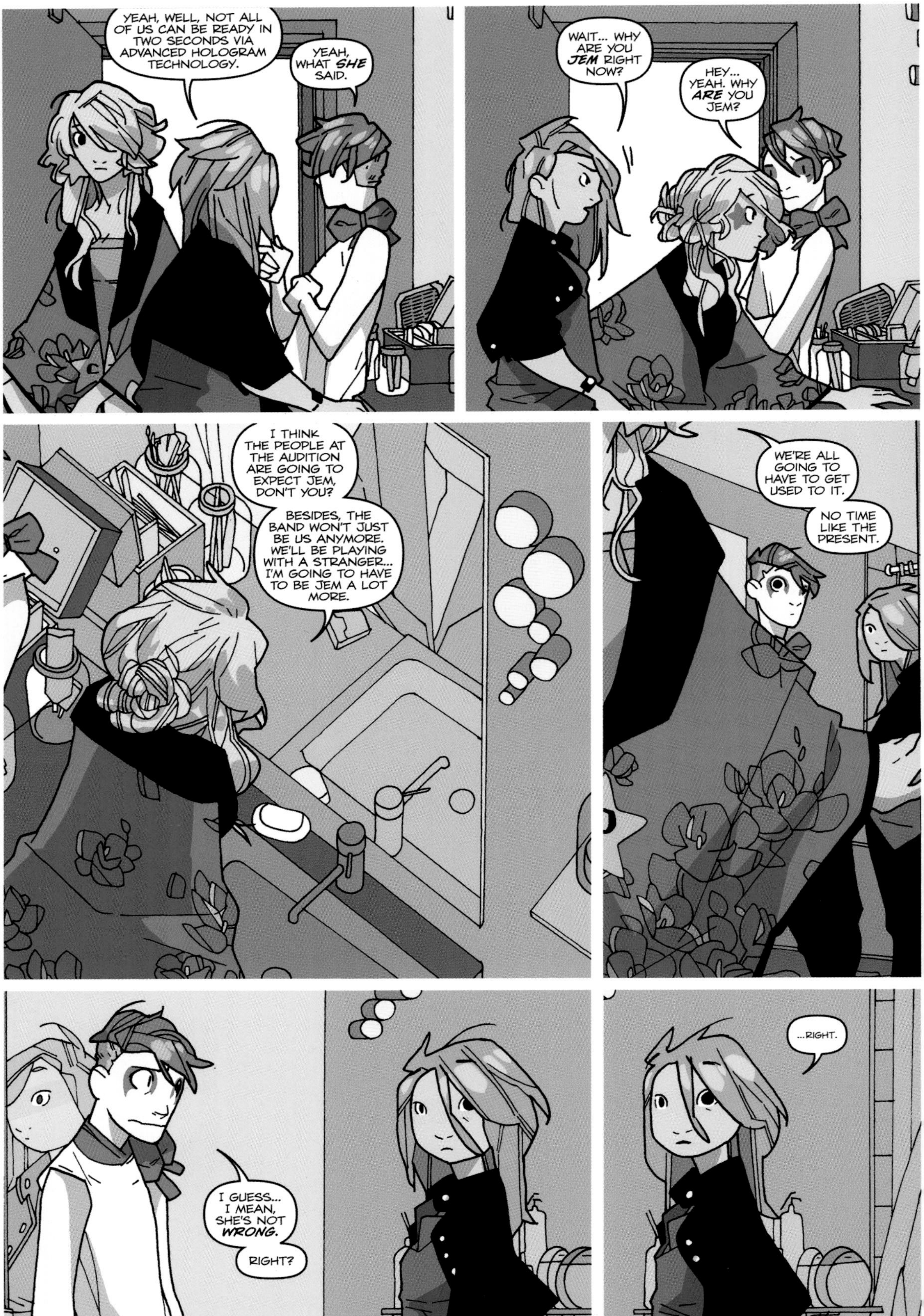
YEAH, WELL, NOT ALL OF US CAN BE READY IN TWO SECONDS VIA ADVANCED HOLOGRAM TECHNOLOGY.
YEAH, WHAT SHE SAID.
WAIT... WHY ARE YOU JEM RIGHT NOW?
HEY... YEAH. WHY ARE YOU JEM?
I THINK THE PEOPLE AT THE AUDITION ARE GOING TO EXPECT JEM, DON'T YOU?
BESIDES, THE BAND WON'T JUST BE US ANYMORE. WE'LL BE PLAYING WITH A STRANGER... I'M GOING TO HAVE TO BE JEM A LOT MORE.
WE'RE ALL GOING TO HAVE TO GET USED TO IT.
NO TIME LIKE THE PRESENT.
I GUESS... I MEAN, SHE'S NOT WRONG.
RIGHT?
...RIGHT.

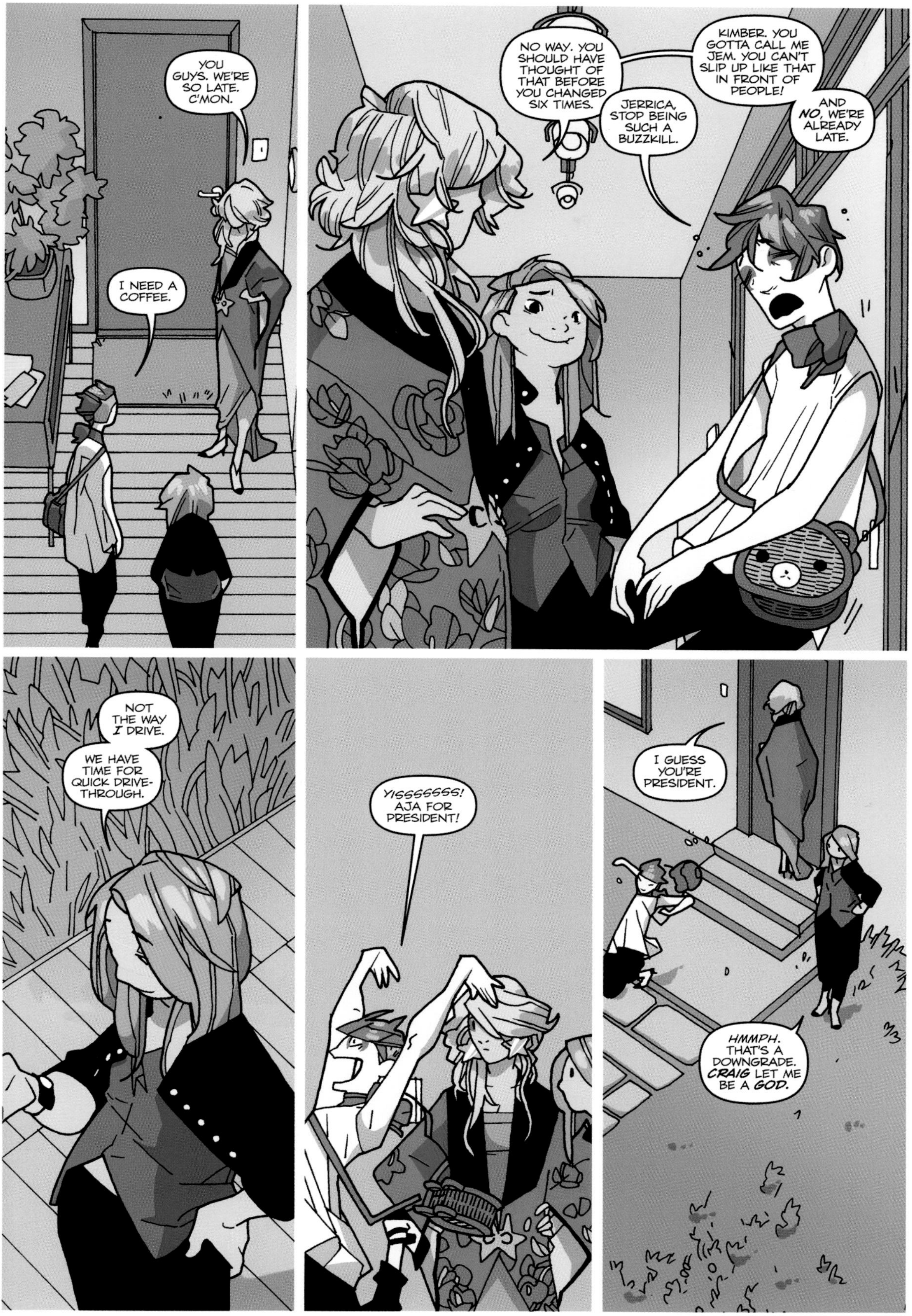
YOU GUYS. WE'RE SO LATE. C'MON.
I NEED A COFFEE.
NO WAY. YOU SHOULD HAVE THOUGHT OF THAT BEFORE YOU CHANGED SIX TIMES.
JERRICA, STOP BEING SUCH A BUZZKILL.
KIMBER. YOU GOTTA CALL ME JEM. YOU CAN'T SLIP UP LIKE THAT IN FRONT OF PEOPLE!
AND NO, WE'RE ALREADY LATE.
NOT THE WAY I DRIVE.
WE HAVE TIME FOR QUICK DRIVE-THROUGH.
YISSSSSSS! AJA FOR PRESIDENT!
I GUESS YOU'RE PRESIDENT.
HMMPH. THAT'S A DOWNGRADE. CRAIG LET ME BE A GOD.

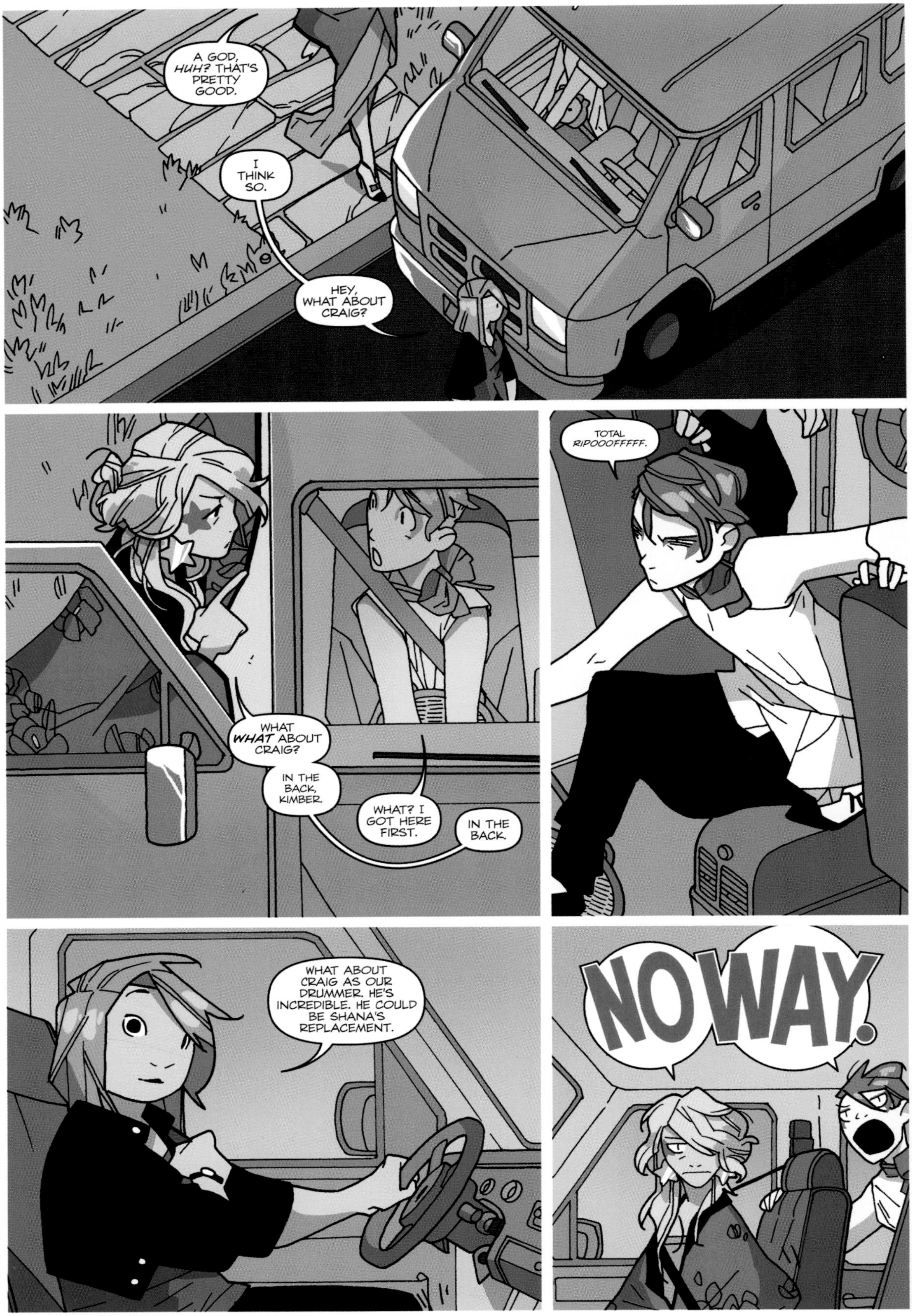
A GOD, *HUH*? THAT'S PRETTY GOOD.
I THINK SO.
HEY, WHAT ABOUT CRAIG?
WHAT ***WHAT*** ABOUT CRAIG?
IN THE BACK, KIMBER.
WHAT? I GOT HERE FIRST.
IN THE BACK.
TOTAL *RIPOOOFFFFF.*
WHAT ABOUT CRAIG AS OUR DRUMMER. HE'S INCREDIBLE. HE COULD BE SHANA'S REPLACEMENT.
NO WAY.

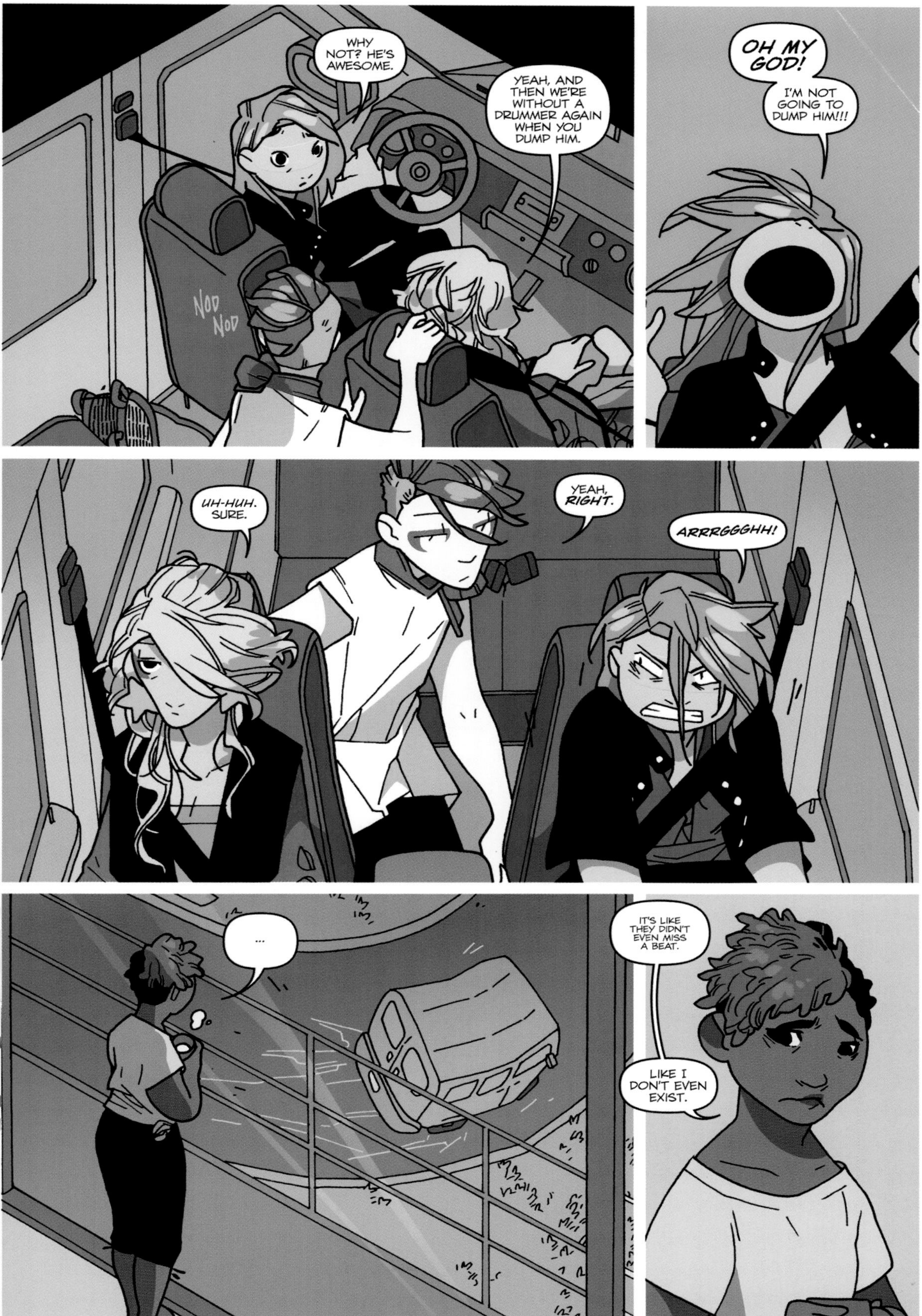
WHY NOT? HE'S AWESOME.
YEAH, AND THEN WE'RE WITHOUT A DRUMMER AGAIN WHEN YOU DUMP HIM.
NOD NOD
OH MY GOD!
I'M NOT GOING TO DUMP HIM!!!
UH-HUH. SURE.
YEAH, RIGHT.
ARRRGGGHH!
...
IT'S LIKE THEY DIDN'T EVEN MISS A BEAT.
LIKE I DON'T EVEN EXIST.

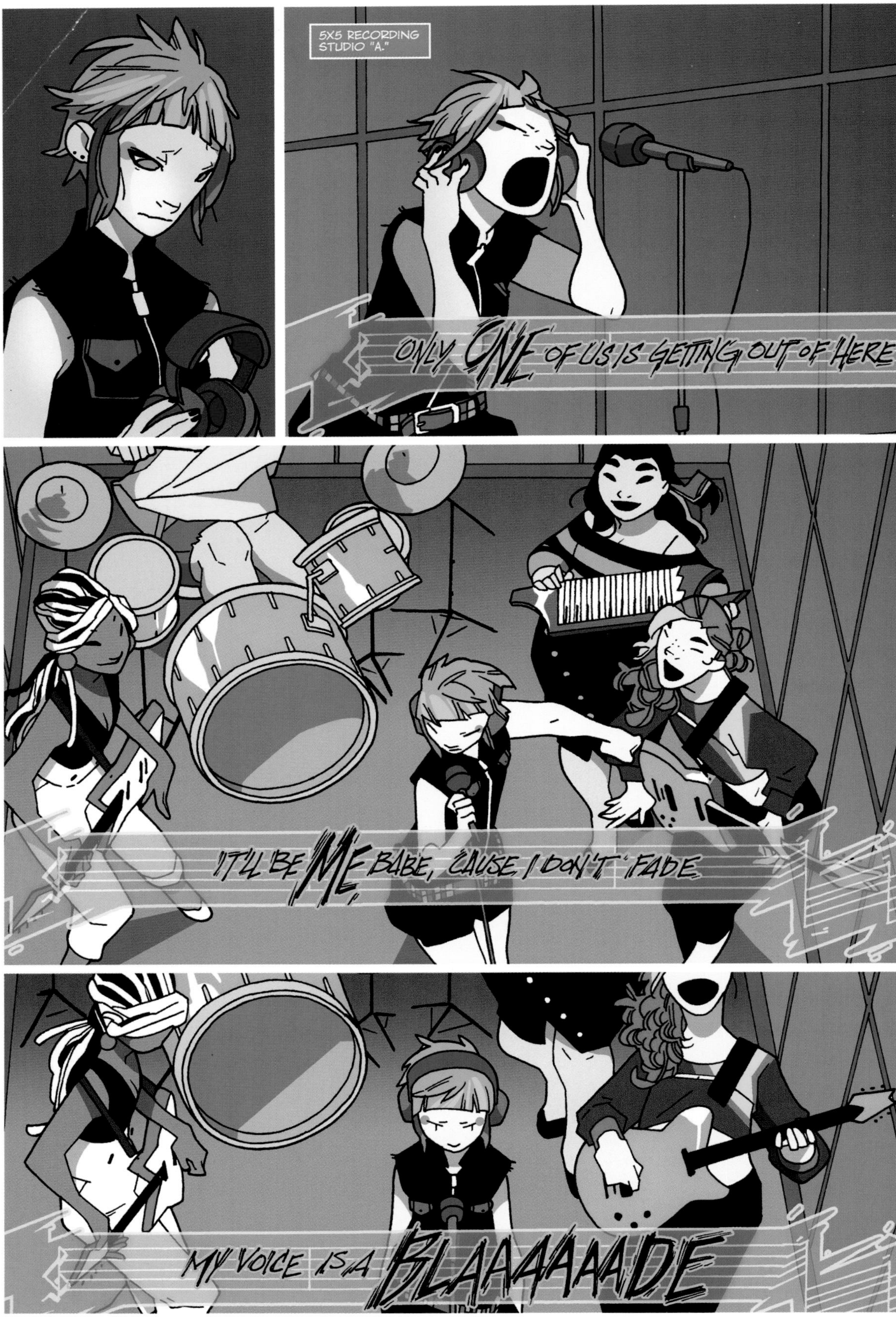
5X5 RECORDING STUDIO "A."
ONLY ONE OF US IS GETTING OUT OF HERE
IT'LL BE ME, BABE, CAUSE I DON'T FADE
MY VOICE IS A BLAAAAAADE

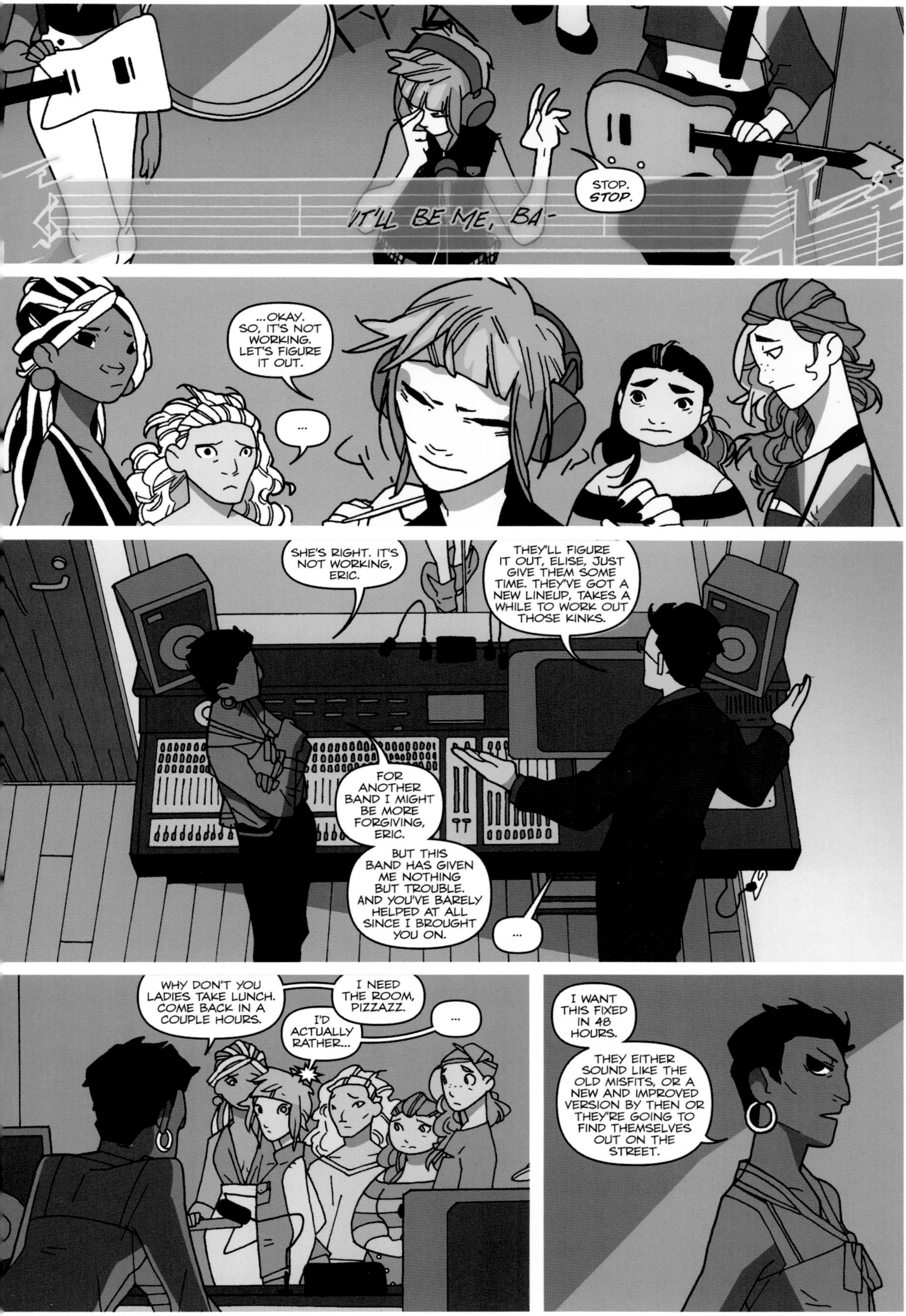
IT'LL BE ME, BA-
STOP. STOP.
...OKAY. SO, IT'S NOT WORKING. LET'S FIGURE IT OUT.
...
SHE'S RIGHT. IT'S NOT WORKING, ERIC.
THEY'LL FIGURE IT OUT, ELISE, JUST GIVE THEM SOME TIME. THEY'VE GOT A NEW LINEUP, TAKES A WHILE TO WORK OUT THOSE KINKS.
FOR ANOTHER BAND I MIGHT BE MORE FORGIVING, ERIC.
BUT THIS BAND HAS GIVEN ME NOTHING BUT TROUBLE. AND YOU'VE BARELY HELPED AT ALL SINCE I BROUGHT YOU ON.
...
WHY DON'T YOU LADIES TAKE LUNCH. COME BACK IN A COUPLE HOURS.
I NEED THE ROOM, PIZZAZZ.
I'D ACTUALLY RATHER...
...
I WANT THIS FIXED IN 48 HOURS.
THEY EITHER SOUND LIKE THE OLD MISFITS, OR A NEW AND IMPROVED VERSION BY THEN OR THEY'RE GOING TO FIND THEMSELVES OUT ON THE STREET.

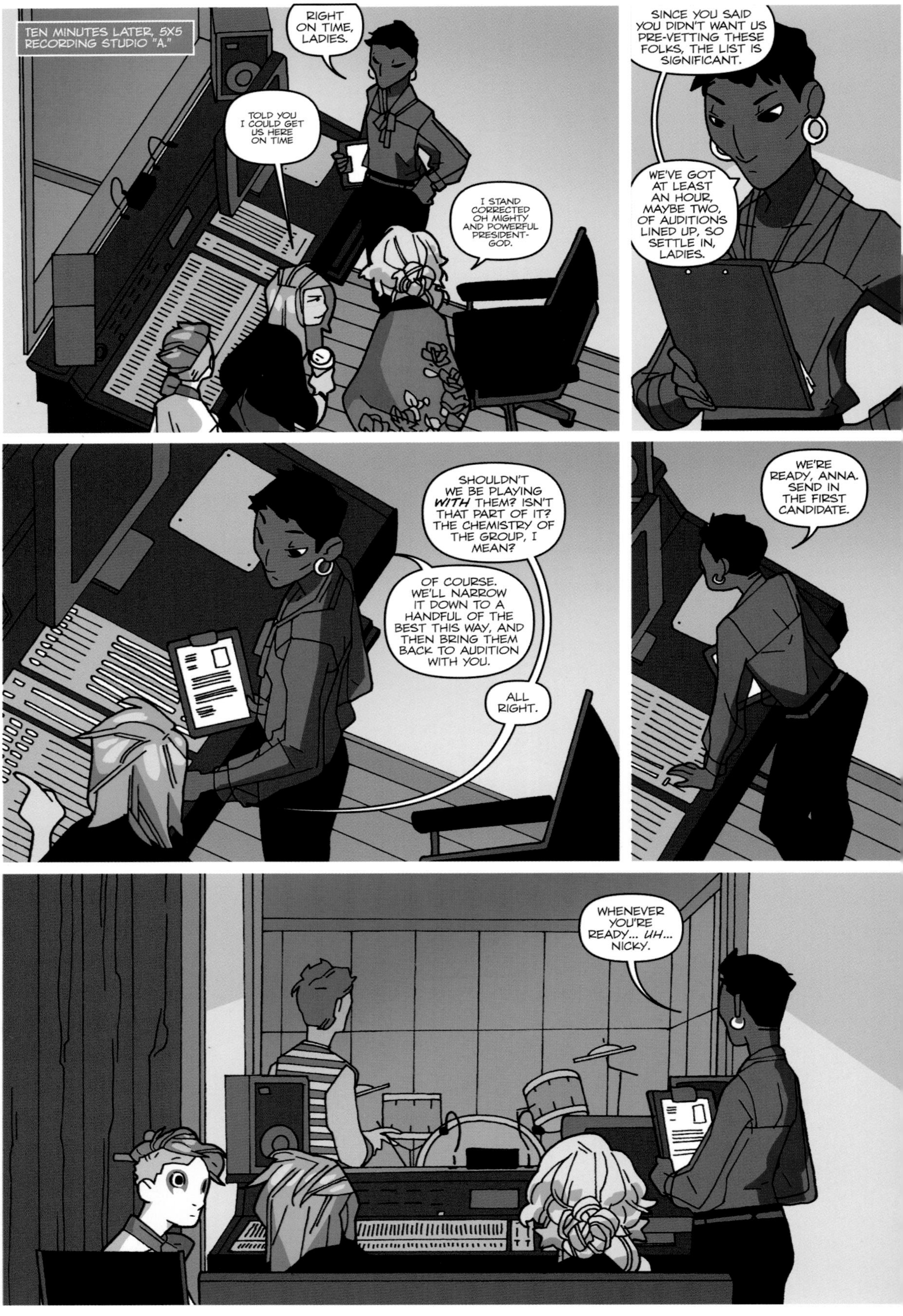
TEN MINUTES LATER, 5X5 RECORDING STUDIO "A."
RIGHT ON TIME, LADIES.
TOLD YOU I COULD GET US HERE ON TIME
I STAND CORRECTED OH MIGHTY AND POWERFUL PRESIDENT-GOD.
SINCE YOU SAID YOU DIDN'T WANT US PRE-VETTING THESE FOLKS, THE LIST IS SIGNIFICANT.
WE'VE GOT AT LEAST AN HOUR, MAYBE TWO, OF AUDITIONS LINED UP, SO SETTLE IN, LADIES.
SHOULDN'T WE BE PLAYING *WITH* THEM? ISN'T THAT PART OF IT? THE CHEMISTRY OF THE GROUP, I MEAN?
OF COURSE. WE'LL NARROW IT DOWN TO A HANDFUL OF THE BEST THIS WAY, AND THEN BRING THEM BACK TO AUDITION WITH YOU.
ALL RIGHT.
WE'RE READY, ANNA. SEND IN THE FIRST CANDIDATE.
WHENEVER YOU'RE READY... *UH*... NICKY.

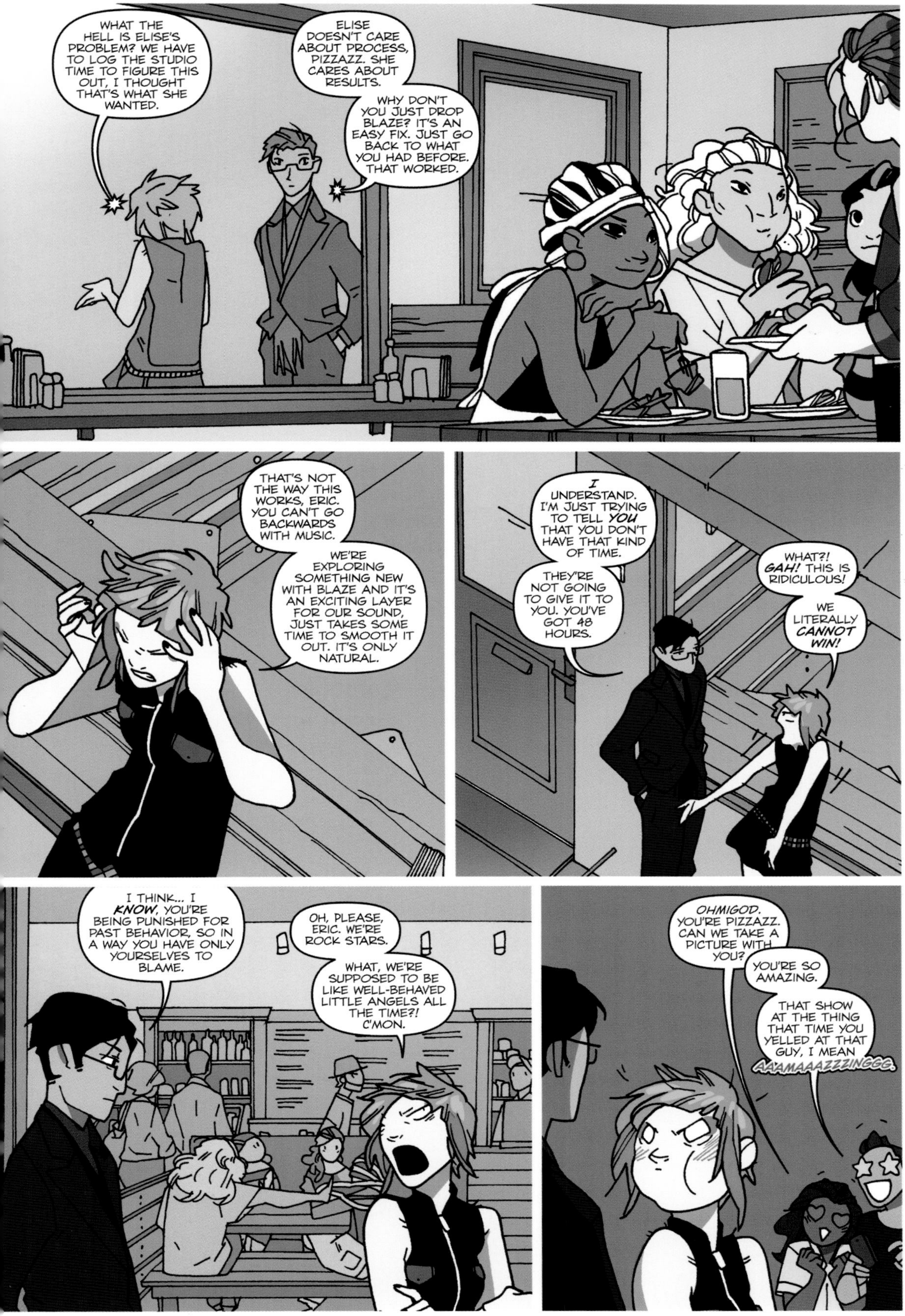
WHAT THE HELL IS ELISE'S PROBLEM? WE HAVE TO LOG THE STUDIO TIME TO FIGURE THIS OUT, I THOUGHT THAT'S WHAT SHE WANTED.
ELISE DOESN'T CARE ABOUT PROCESS, PIZZAZZ. SHE CARES ABOUT RESULTS.
WHY DON'T YOU JUST DROP BLAZE? IT'S AN EASY FIX. JUST GO BACK TO WHAT YOU HAD BEFORE. THAT WORKED.
THAT'S NOT THE WAY THIS WORKS, ERIC. YOU CAN'T GO BACKWARDS WITH MUSIC.
WE'RE EXPLORING SOMETHING NEW WITH BLAZE AND IT'S AN EXCITING LAYER FOR OUR SOUND, JUST TAKES SOME TIME TO SMOOTH IT OUT. IT'S ONLY NATURAL.
I UNDERSTAND. I'M JUST TRYING TO TELL ***YOU*** THAT YOU DON'T HAVE THAT KIND OF TIME.
THEY'RE NOT GOING TO GIVE IT TO YOU. YOU'VE GOT 48 HOURS.
WHAT?! ***GAH!*** THIS IS RIDICULOUS!
WE LITERALLY ***CANNOT WIN!***
I THINK... I ***KNOW***, YOU'RE BEING PUNISHED FOR PAST BEHAVIOR, SO IN A WAY YOU HAVE ONLY YOURSELVES TO BLAME.
OH, PLEASE, ERIC. WE'RE ROCK STARS.
WHAT, WE'RE SUPPOSED TO BE LIKE WELL-BEHAVED LITTLE ANGELS ALL THE TIME?! C'MON.
OHMIGOD. YOU'RE PIZZAZZ. CAN WE TAKE A PICTURE WITH YOU?
YOU'RE SO AMAZING.
THAT SHOW AT THE THING THAT TIME YOU YELLED AT THAT GUY, I MEAN AAAMAAAZZZINGGG.

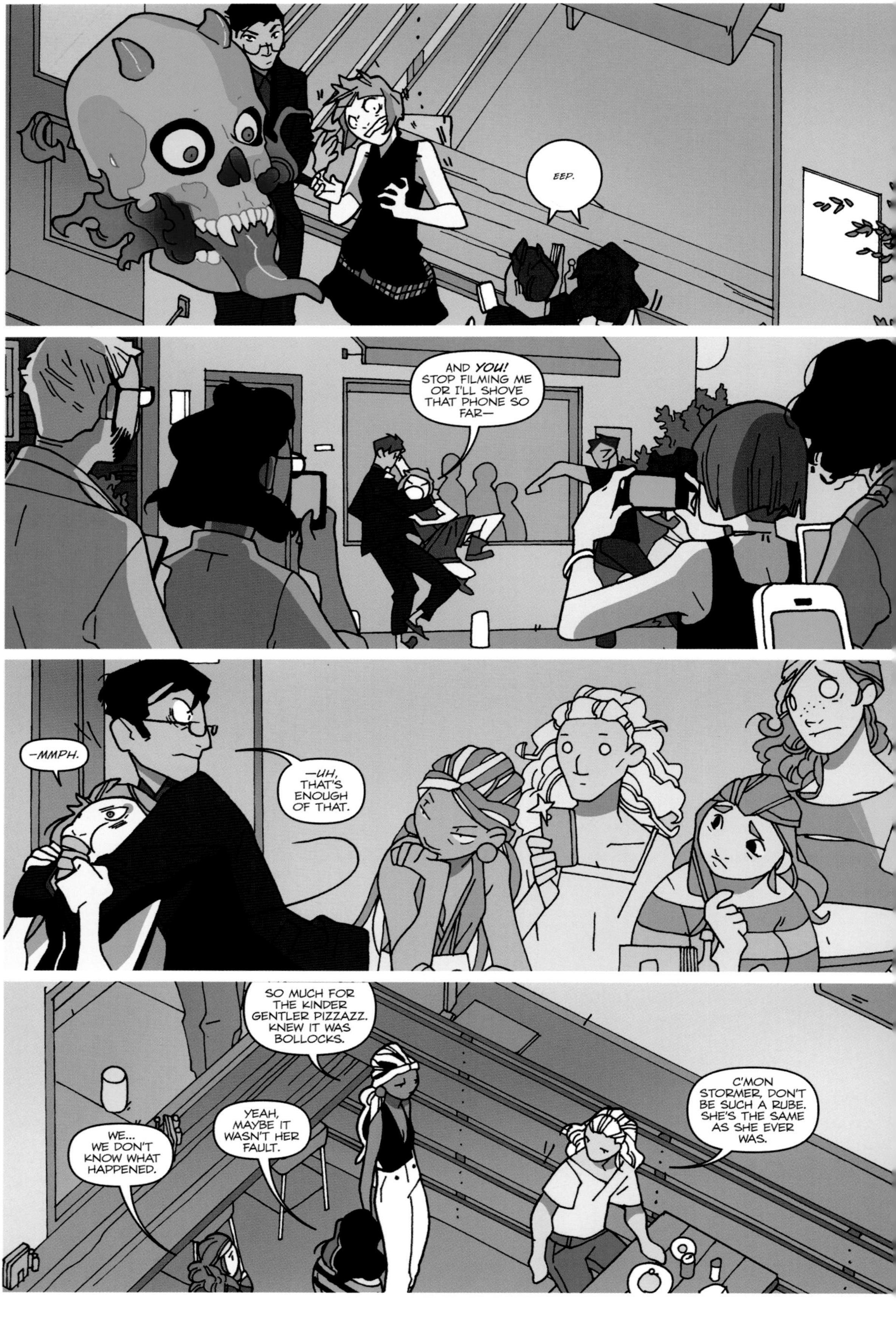
EEP.
AND YOU! STOP FILMING ME OR I'LL SHOVE THAT PHONE SO FAR—
—MMPH.
—UH, THAT'S ENOUGH OF THAT.
SO MUCH FOR THE KINDER GENTLER PIZZAZZ. KNEW IT WAS BOLLOCKS.
C'MON STORMER, DON'T BE SUCH A RUBE. SHE'S THE SAME AS SHE EVER WAS.
YEAH, MAYBE IT WASN'T HER FAULT.
WE... WE DON'T KNOW WHAT HAPPENED.

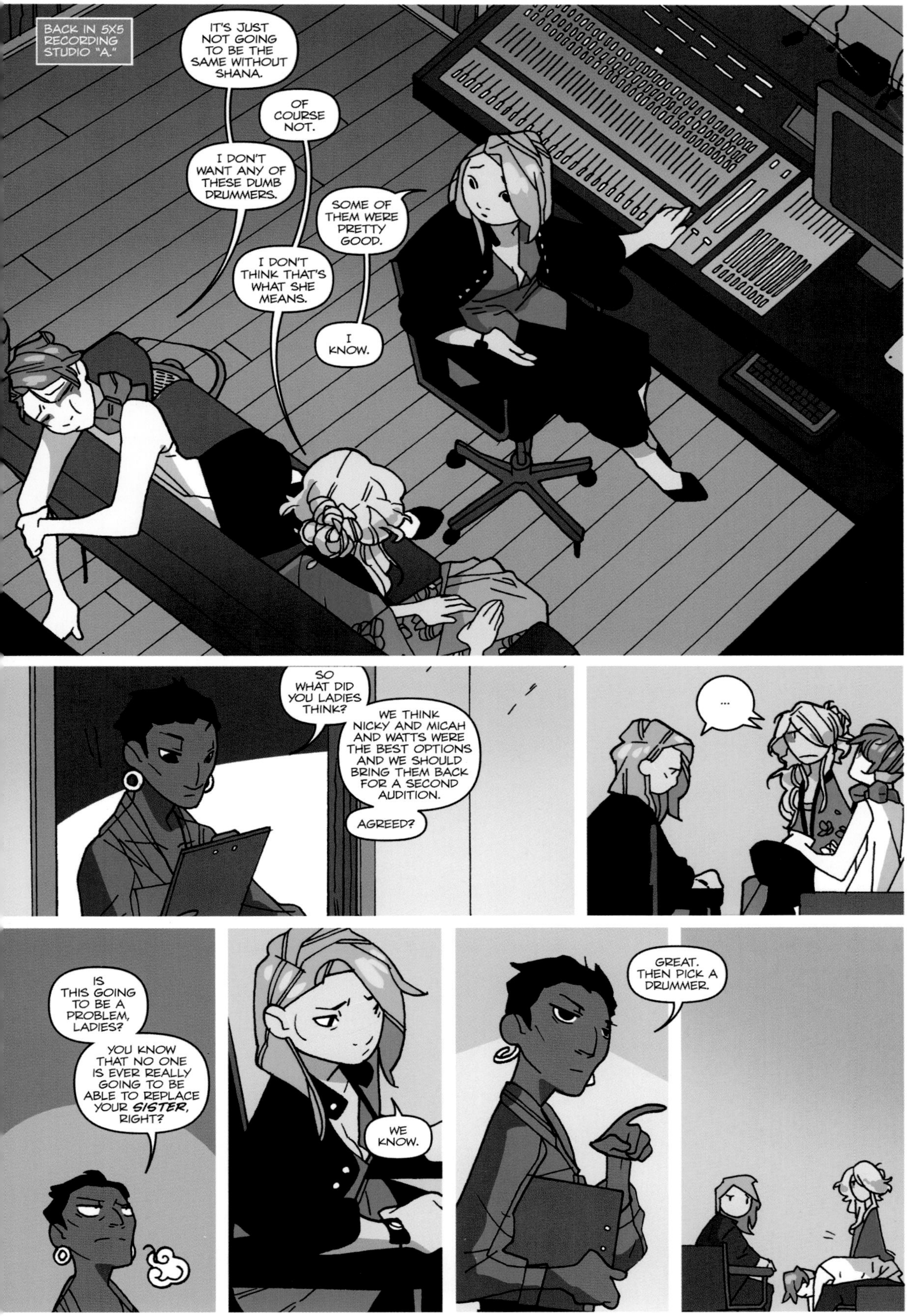
BACK IN 5X5 RECORDING STUDIO "A."
IT'S JUST NOT GOING TO BE THE SAME WITHOUT SHANA.
OF COURSE NOT.
I DON'T WANT ANY OF THESE DUMB DRUMMERS.
SOME OF THEM WERE PRETTY GOOD.
I DON'T THINK THAT'S WHAT SHE MEANS.
I KNOW.
SO WHAT DID YOU LADIES THINK?
WE THINK NICKY AND MICAH AND WATTS WERE THE BEST OPTIONS AND WE SHOULD BRING THEM BACK FOR A SECOND AUDITION.
AGREED?
...
IS THIS GOING TO BE A PROBLEM, LADIES?
YOU KNOW THAT NO ONE IS EVER REALLY GOING TO BE ABLE TO REPLACE YOUR *SISTER*, RIGHT?
WE KNOW.
GREAT. THEN PICK A DRUMMER.

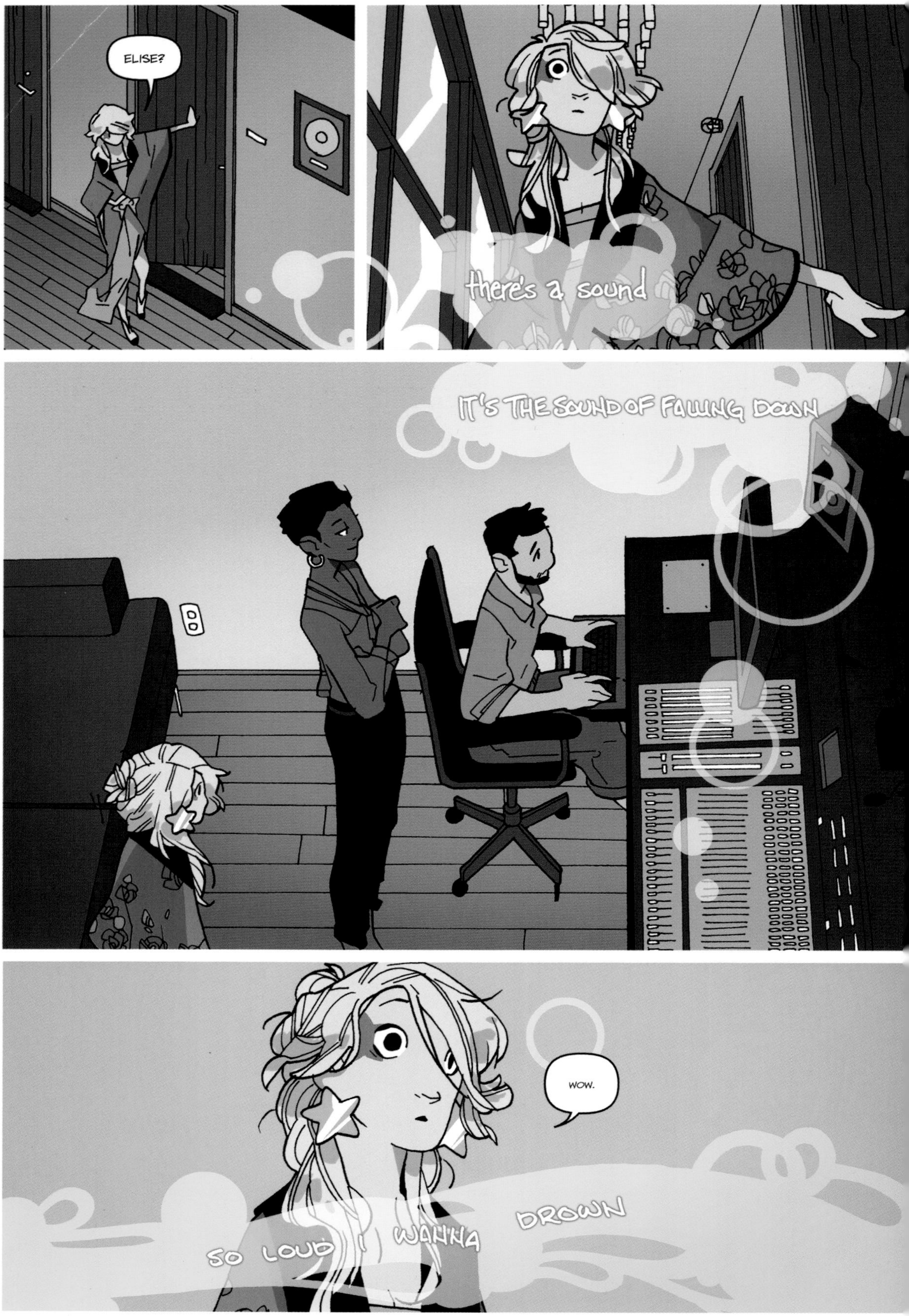
ELISE?
there's a sound
IT'S THE SOUND OF FALLING DOWN
WOW.
SO LOUD I WANNA DROWN

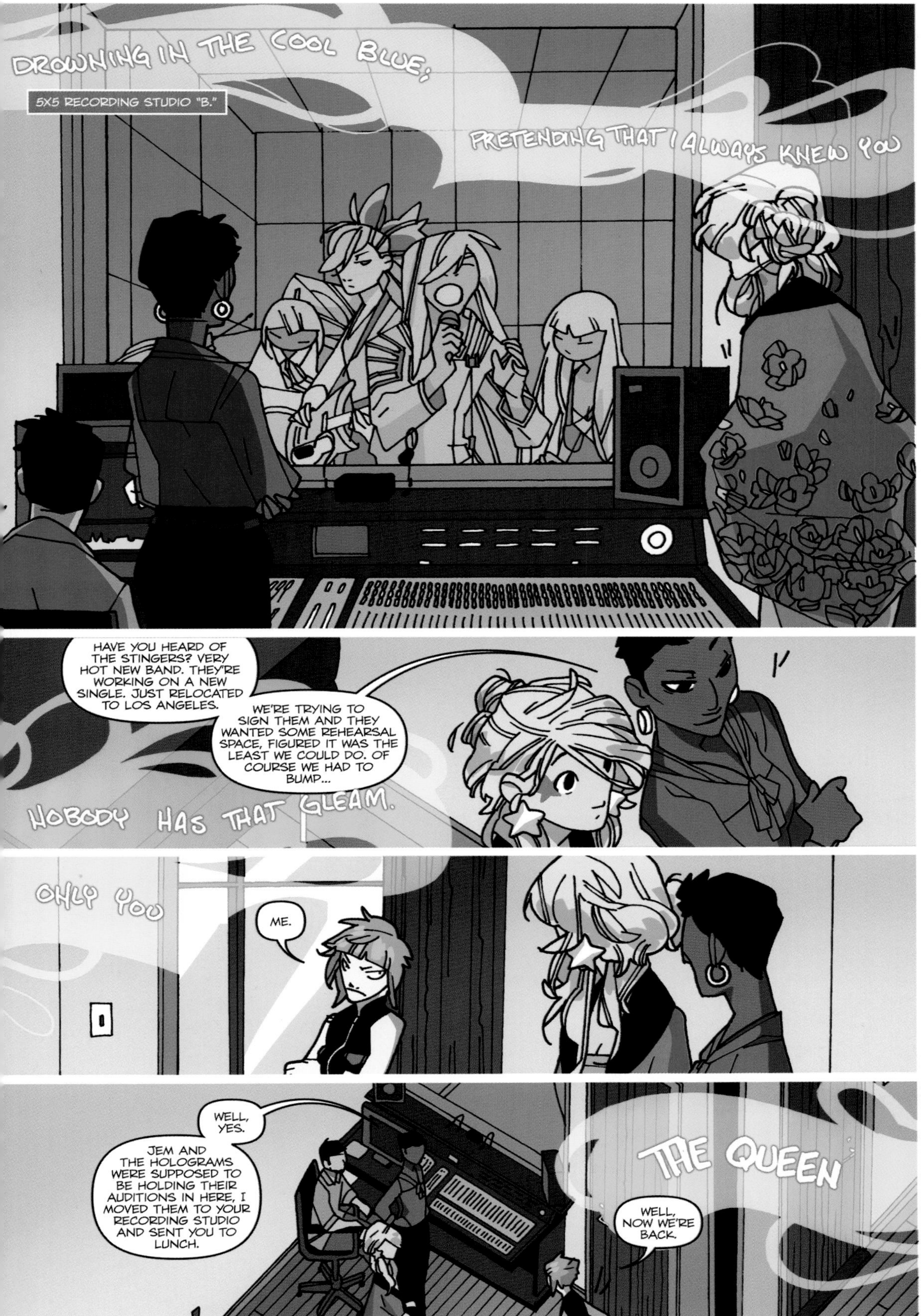
DROWNING IN THE COOL BLUE;
5X5 RECORDING STUDIO "B."
PRETENDING THAT I ALWAYS KNEW YOU
HAVE YOU HEARD OF THE STINGERS? VERY HOT NEW BAND. THEY'RE WORKING ON A NEW SINGLE. JUST RELOCATED TO LOS ANGELES.
WE'RE TRYING TO SIGN THEM AND THEY WANTED SOME REHEARSAL SPACE, FIGURED IT WAS THE LEAST WE COULD DO. OF COURSE WE HAD TO BUMP...
NOBODY HAS THAT GLEAM.
ONLY YOU
ME.
WELL, YES.
JEM AND THE HOLOGRAMS WERE SUPPOSED TO BE HOLDING THEIR AUDITIONS IN HERE, I MOVED THEM TO YOUR RECORDING STUDIO AND SENT YOU TO LUNCH.
THE QUEEN
WELL, NOW WE'RE BACK.

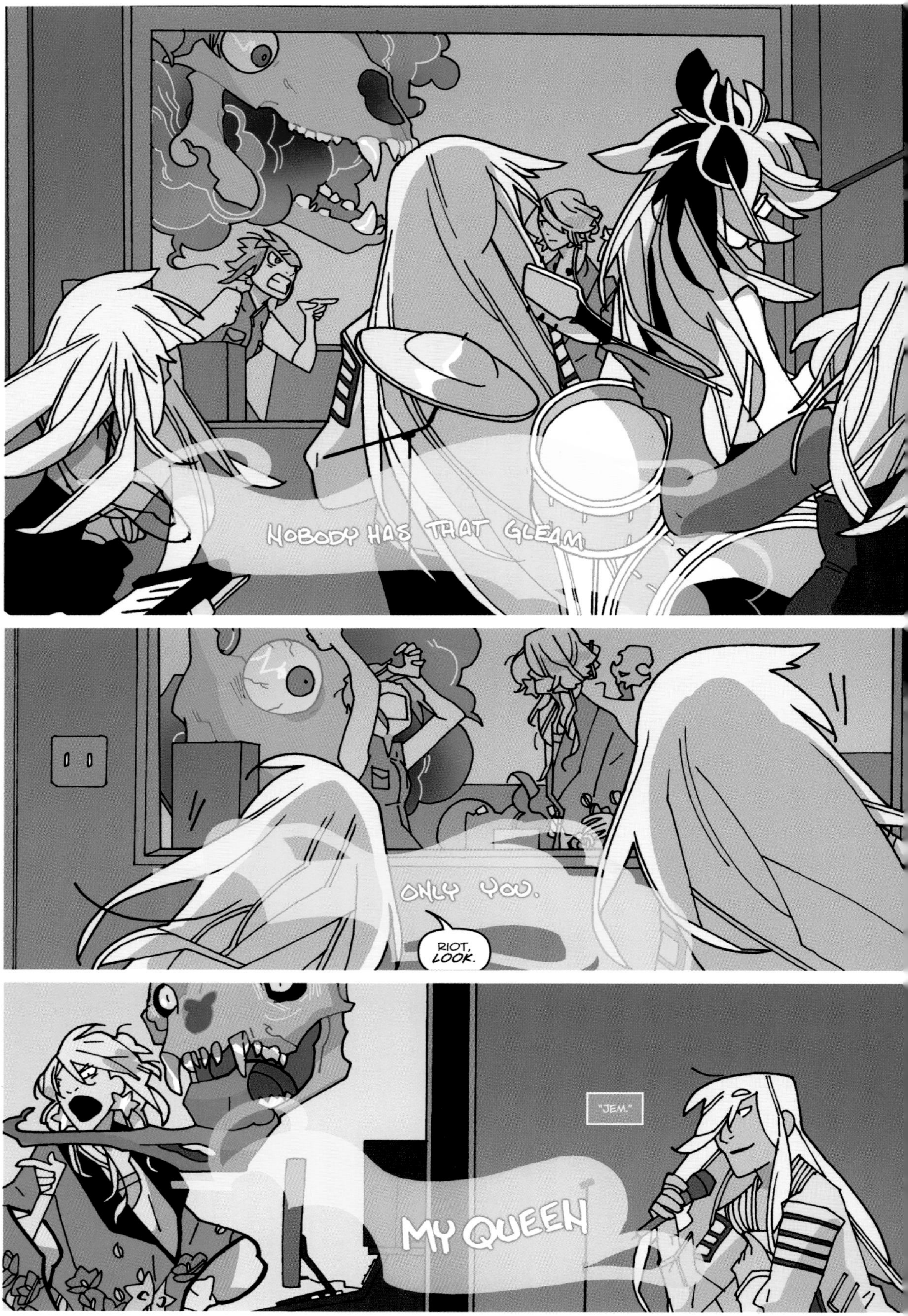
NOBODY HAS THAT GLEAM
ONLY YOU.
RIOT, LOOK.
"JEM."
MY QUEEN

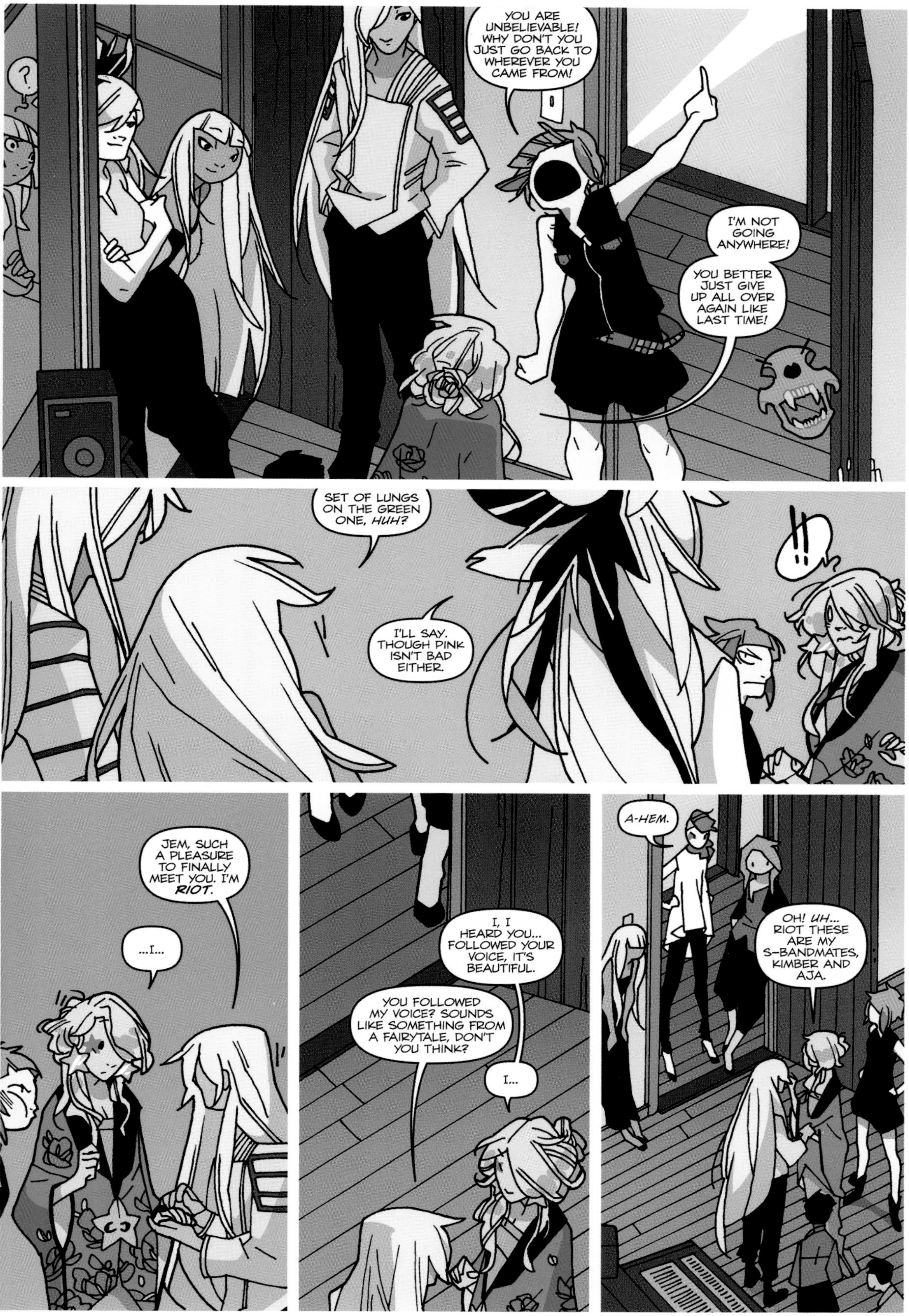
?
YOU ARE UNBELIEVABLE! WHY DON'T YOU JUST GO BACK TO WHEREVER YOU CAME FROM!
I'M NOT GOING ANYWHERE!
YOU BETTER JUST GIVE UP ALL OVER AGAIN LIKE LAST TIME!
SET OF LUNGS ON THE GREEN ONE, *HUH?*
I'LL SAY. THOUGH PINK ISN'T BAD EITHER.
!!
JEM, SUCH A PLEASURE TO FINALLY MEET YOU. I'M *RIOT*.
...I...
I, I HEARD YOU... FOLLOWED YOUR VOICE, IT'S BEAUTIFUL.
YOU FOLLOWED MY VOICE? SOUNDS LIKE SOMETHING FROM A FAIRYTALE, DON'T YOU THINK?
I...
A-HEM.
OH! UH... RIOT THESE ARE MY S-BANDMATES, KIMBER AND AJA.

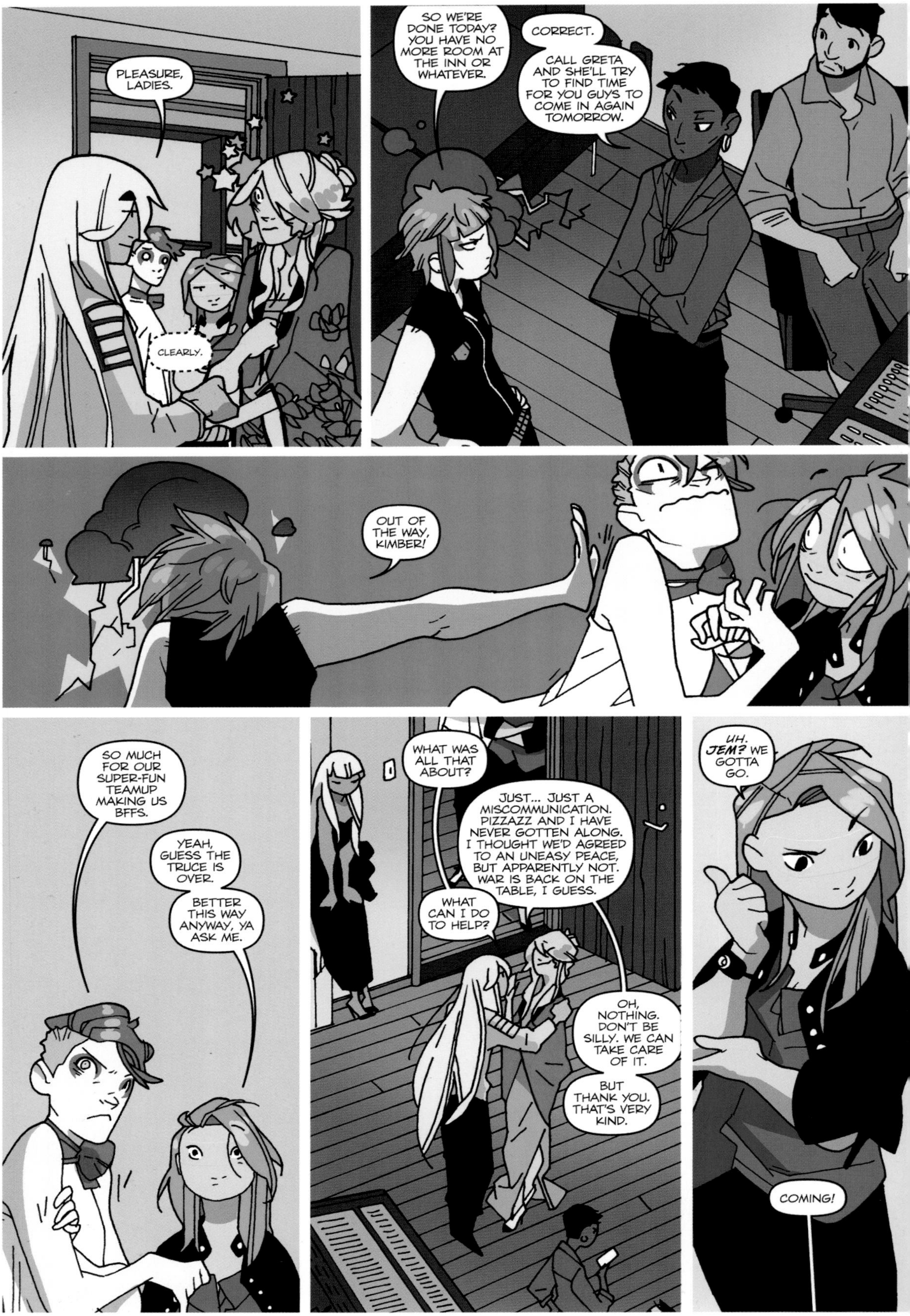
PLEASURE, LADIES.
CLEARLY.
SO WE'RE DONE TODAY? YOU HAVE NO MORE ROOM AT THE INN OR WHATEVER.
CORRECT.
CALL GRETA AND SHE'LL TRY TO FIND TIME FOR YOU GUYS TO COME IN AGAIN TOMORROW.
OUT OF THE WAY, KIMBER!
SO MUCH FOR OUR SUPER-FUN TEAMUP MAKING US BFFS.
YEAH, GUESS THE TRUCE IS OVER.
BETTER THIS WAY ANYWAY, YA ASK ME.
WHAT WAS ALL THAT ABOUT?
JUST... JUST A MISCOMMUNICATION. PIZZAZZ AND I HAVE NEVER GOTTEN ALONG. I THOUGHT WE'D AGREED TO AN UNEASY PEACE, BUT APPARENTLY NOT. WAR IS BACK ON THE TABLE, I GUESS.
WHAT CAN I DO TO HELP?
OH, NOTHING. DON'T BE SILLY. WE CAN TAKE CARE OF IT.
BUT THANK YOU. THAT'S VERY KIND.
UH. JEM? WE GOTTA GO.
COMING!

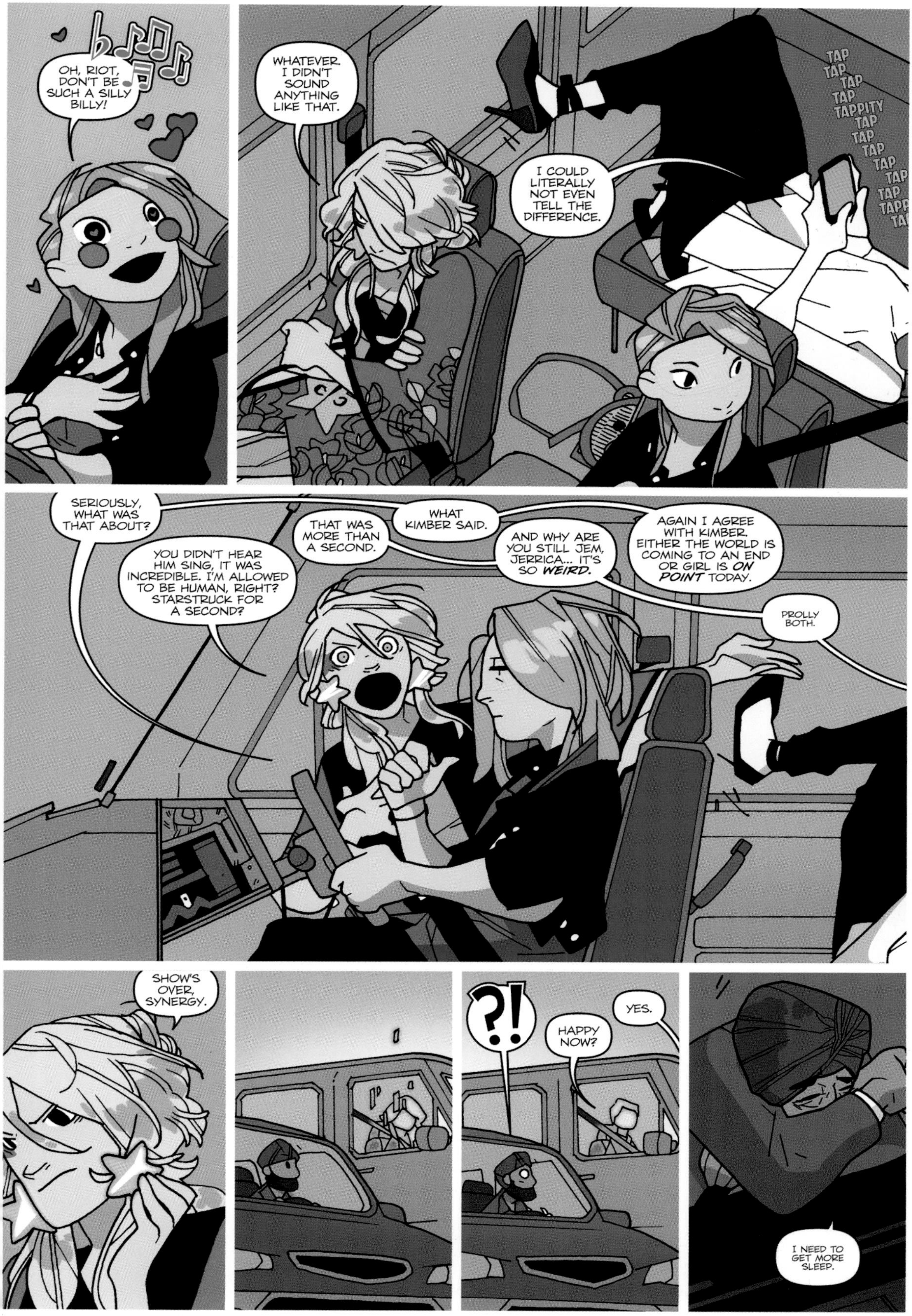

OH, RIOT, DON'T BE SUCH A SILLY BILLY!
WHATEVER. I DIDN'T SOUND ANYTHING LIKE THAT.
I COULD LITERALLY NOT EVEN TELL THE DIFFERENCE.
TAP TAP TAP TAP TAPPITY TAP TAP TAP TAP TAP TAP TAPP
SERIOUSLY, WHAT WAS THAT ABOUT?
YOU DIDN'T HEAR HIM SING, IT WAS INCREDIBLE. I'M ALLOWED TO BE HUMAN, RIGHT? STARSTRUCK FOR A SECOND?
THAT WAS MORE THAN A SECOND.
WHAT KIMBER SAID.
AND WHY ARE YOU STILL JEM, JERRICA... IT'S SO *WEIRD.*
AGAIN I AGREE WITH KIMBER. EITHER THE WORLD IS COMING TO AN END OR GIRL IS ***ON POINT*** TODAY.
PROLLY BOTH.
SHOW'S OVER, SYNERGY.
?!
HAPPY NOW?
YES.
I NEED TO GET MORE SLEEP.

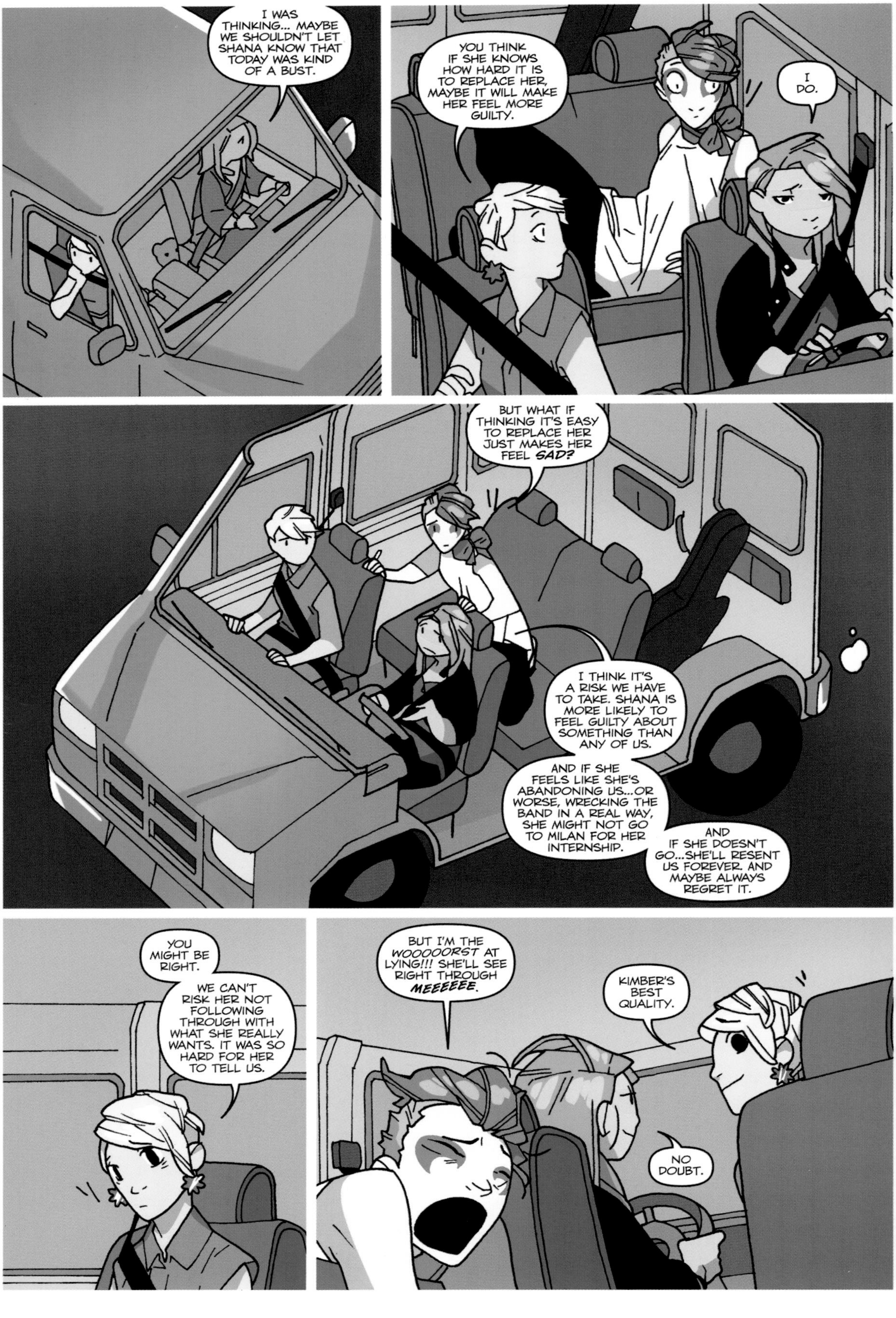
I WAS THINKING... MAYBE WE SHOULDN'T LET SHANA KNOW THAT TODAY WAS KIND OF A BUST.
YOU THINK IF SHE KNOWS HOW HARD IT IS TO REPLACE HER, MAYBE IT WILL MAKE HER FEEL MORE GUILTY.
I DO.
BUT WHAT IF THINKING IT'S EASY TO REPLACE HER JUST MAKES HER FEEL SAD?
I THINK IT'S A RISK WE HAVE TO TAKE. SHANA IS MORE LIKELY TO FEEL GUILTY ABOUT SOMETHING THAN ANY OF US.
AND IF SHE FEELS LIKE SHE'S ABANDONING US...OR WORSE, WRECKING THE BAND IN A REAL WAY, SHE MIGHT NOT GO TO MILAN FOR HER INTERNSHIP.
AND IF SHE DOESN'T GO...SHE'LL RESENT US FOREVER. AND MAYBE ALWAYS REGRET IT.
YOU MIGHT BE RIGHT.
WE CAN'T RISK HER NOT FOLLOWING THROUGH WITH WHAT SHE REALLY WANTS. IT WAS SO HARD FOR HER TO TELL US.
BUT I'M THE WOOOOORST AT LYING!!! SHE'LL SEE RIGHT THROUGH MEEEEEE.
KIMBER'S BEST QUALITY.
NO DOUBT.

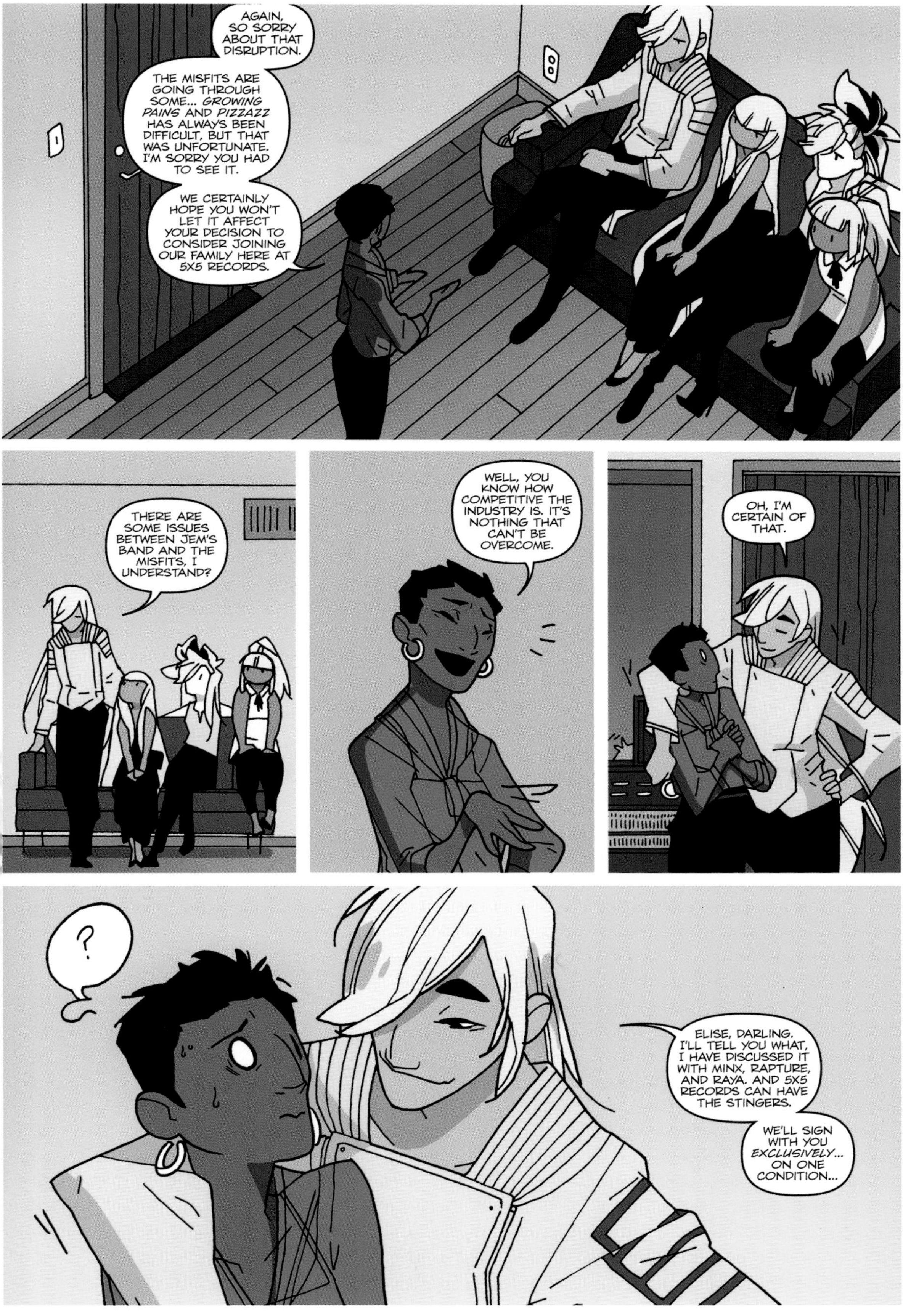
AGAIN, SO SORRY ABOUT THAT DISRUPTION.
THE MISFITS ARE GOING THROUGH SOME... *GROWING PAINS* AND *PIZZAZZ* HAS ALWAYS BEEN DIFFICULT, BUT THAT WAS UNFORTUNATE. I'M SORRY YOU HAD TO SEE IT.
WE CERTAINLY HOPE YOU WON'T LET IT AFFECT YOUR DECISION TO CONSIDER JOINING OUR FAMILY HERE AT 5X5 RECORDS.
THERE ARE SOME ISSUES BETWEEN JEM'S BAND AND THE MISFITS, I UNDERSTAND?
WELL, YOU KNOW HOW COMPETITIVE THE INDUSTRY IS. IT'S NOTHING THAT CAN'T BE OVERCOME.
OH, I'M CERTAIN OF THAT.
?
ELISE, DARLING. I'LL TELL YOU WHAT, I HAVE DISCUSSED IT WITH MINX, RAPTURE, AND RAYA. AND 5X5 RECORDS CAN HAVE THE STINGERS.
WE'LL SIGN WITH YOU *EXCLUSIVELY*... ON ONE CONDITION...

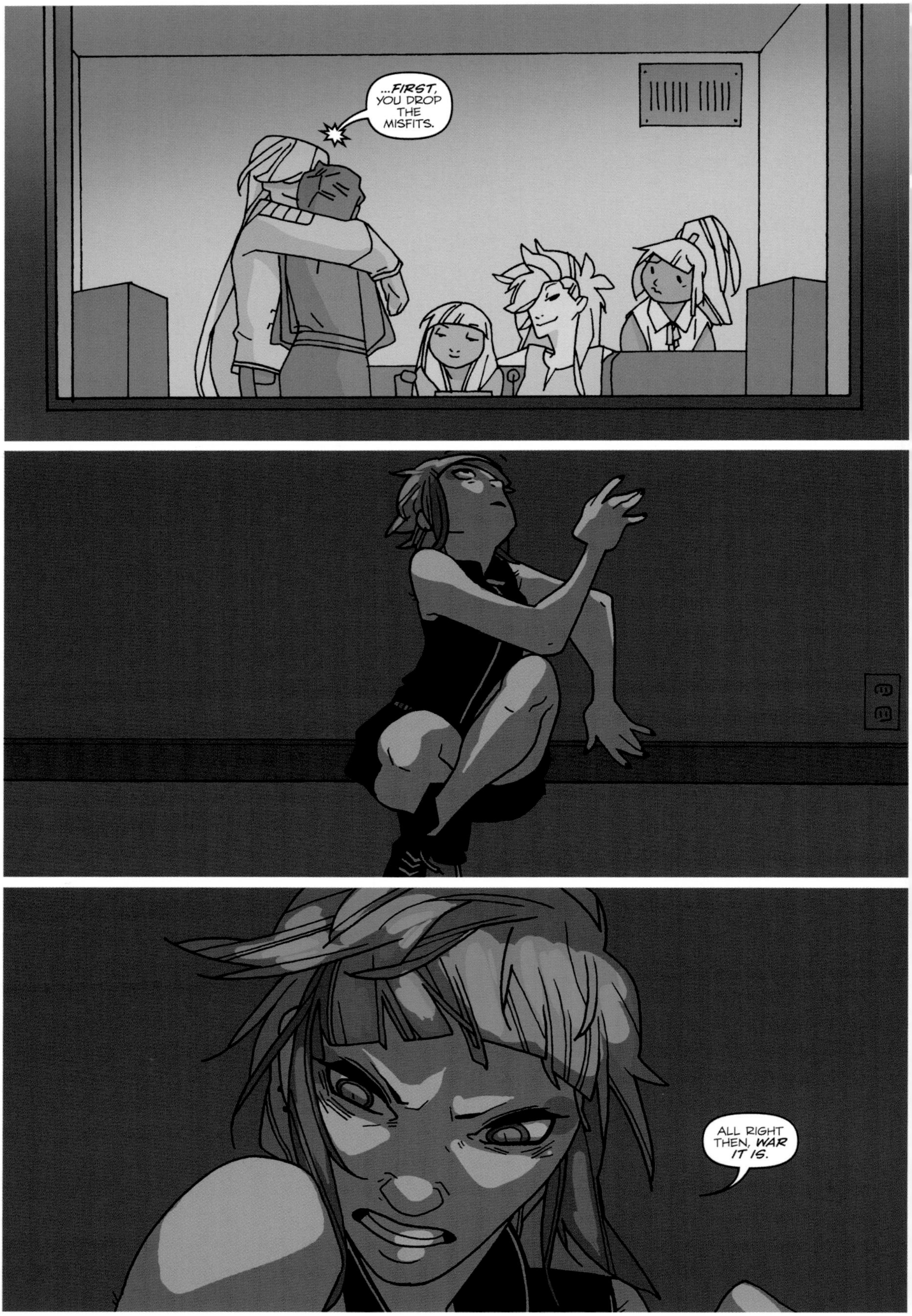
...FIRST, YOU DROP THE MISFITS.
ALL RIGHT THEN, WAR IT IS.

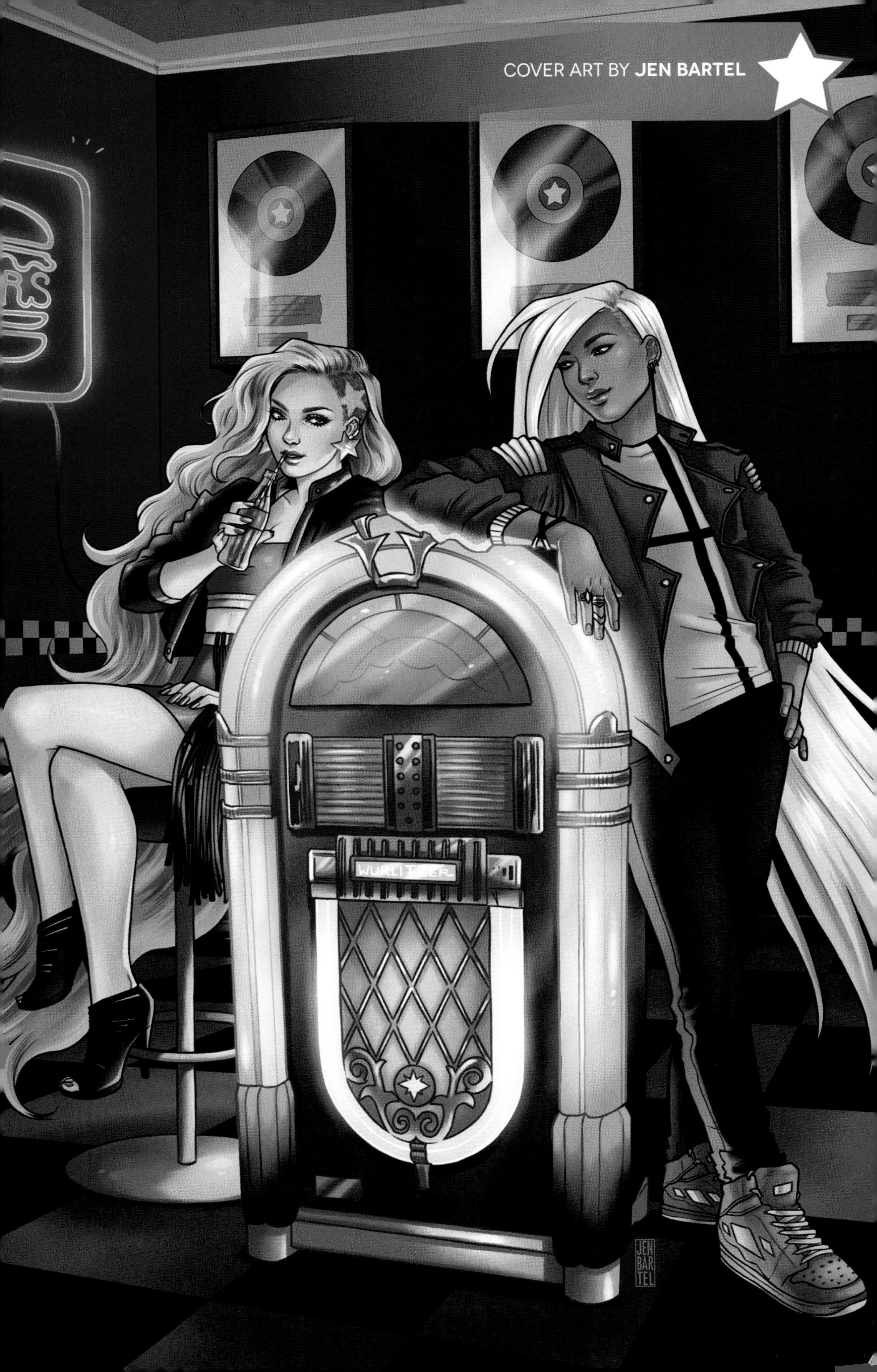
COVER ART BY **JEN BARTEL**
WURLITZER
JEN BAR TEL

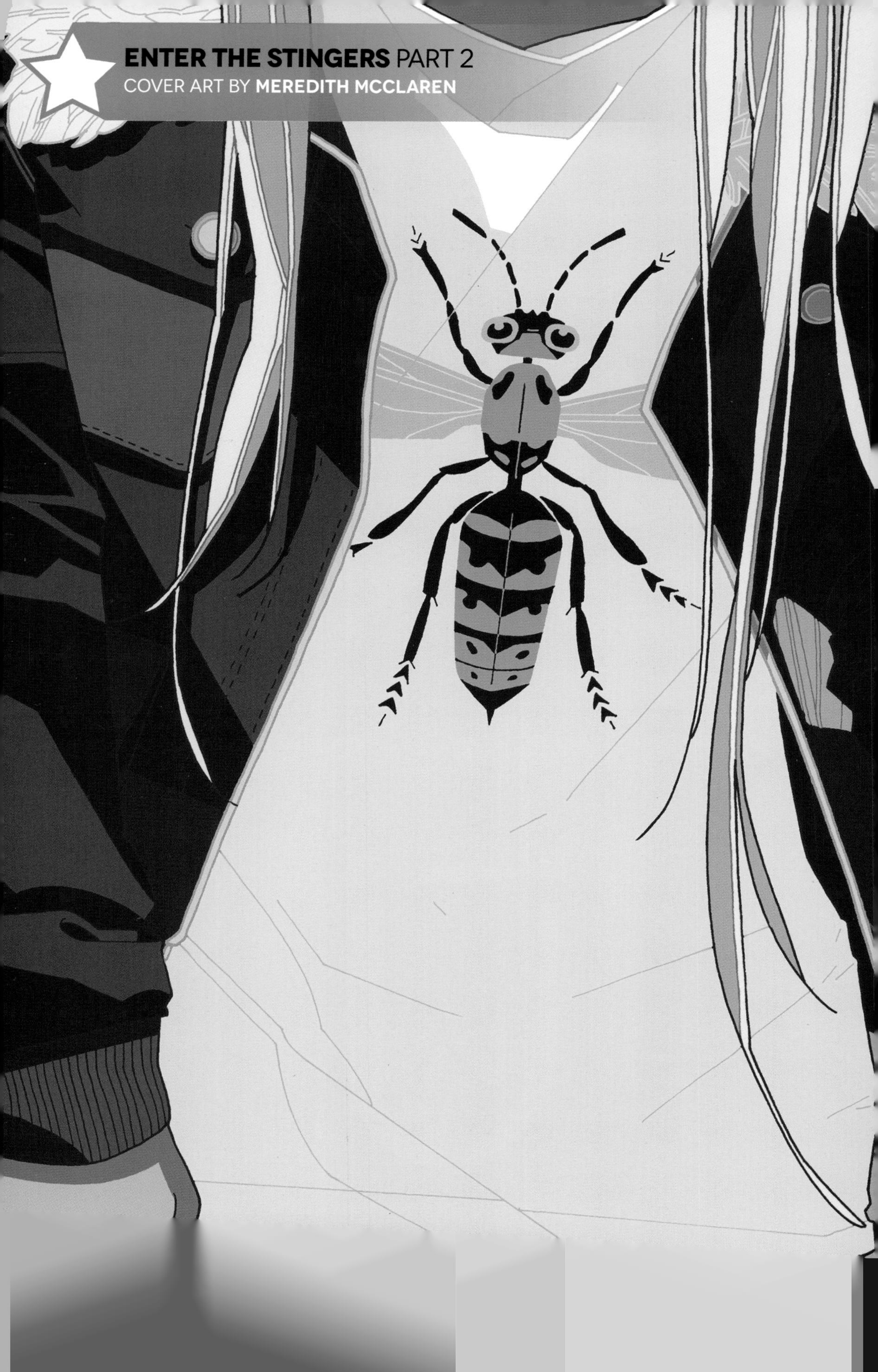
ENTER THE STINGERS PART 2
COVER ART BY MEREDITH MCCLAREN

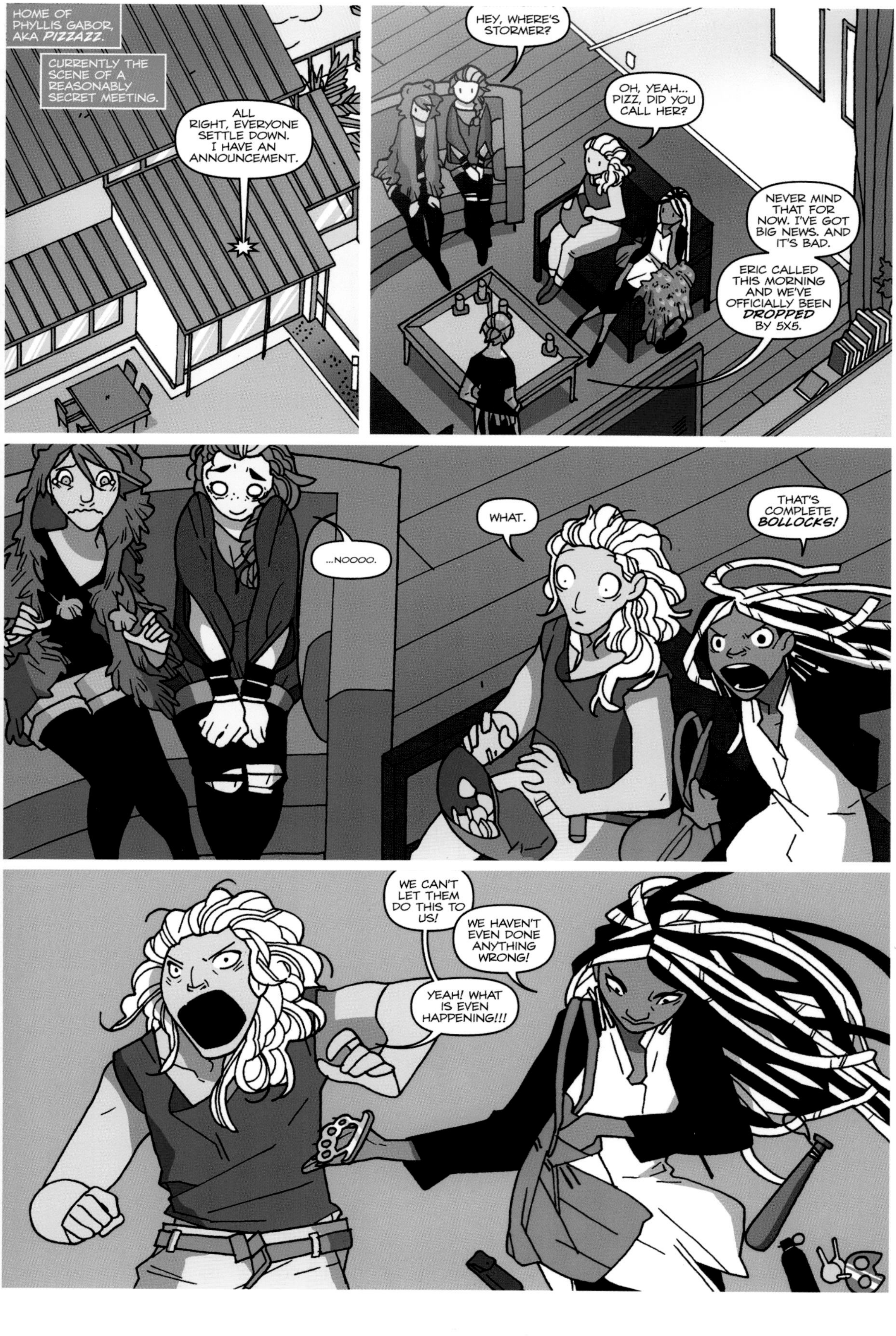
HOME OF PHYLLIS GABOR, AKA *PIZZAZZ*.
CURRENTLY THE SCENE OF A REASONABLY SECRET MEETING.
ALL RIGHT, EVERYONE SETTLE DOWN. I HAVE AN ANNOUNCEMENT.
HEY, WHERE'S STORMER?
OH, YEAH... PIZZ, DID YOU CALL HER?
NEVER MIND THAT FOR NOW. I'VE GOT BIG NEWS. AND IT'S BAD.
ERIC CALLED THIS MORNING AND WE'VE OFFICIALLY BEEN ***DROPPED*** BY 5X5.
...NOOOO.
WHAT.
THAT'S COMPLETE ***BOLLOCKS!***
WE CAN'T LET THEM DO THIS TO US!
WE HAVEN'T EVEN DONE ANYTHING WRONG!
YEAH! WHAT IS EVEN HAPPENING!!!

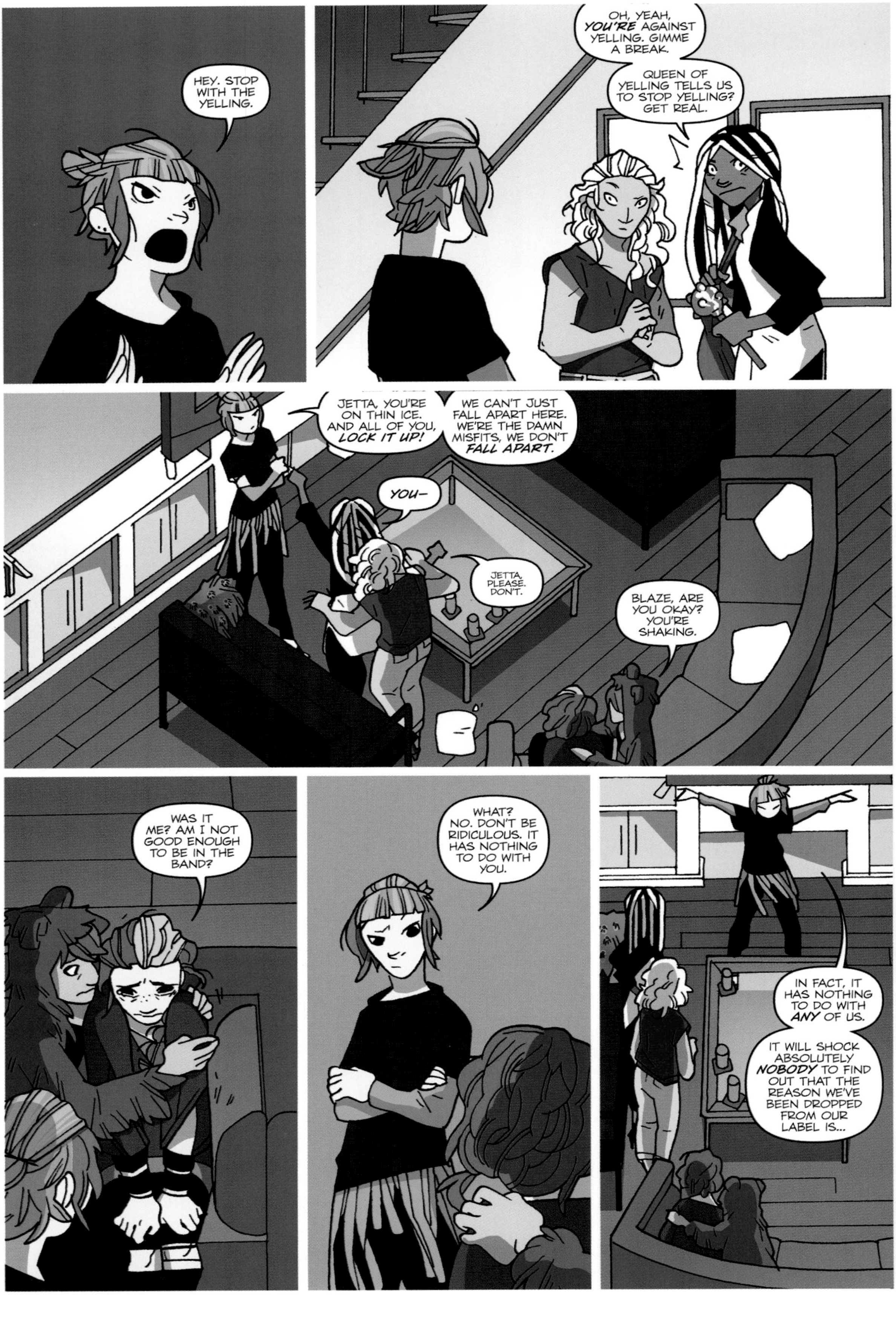

HEY. STOP WITH THE YELLING.
OH, YEAH, *YOU'RE* AGAINST YELLING. GIMME A BREAK.
QUEEN OF YELLING TELLS US TO STOP YELLING? GET REAL.
JETTA, YOU'RE ON THIN ICE. AND ALL OF YOU, *LOCK IT UP!*
WE CAN'T JUST FALL APART HERE. WE'RE THE DAMN MISFITS, WE DON'T *FALL APART*.
YOU–
JETTA, PLEASE. DON'T.
BLAZE, ARE YOU OKAY? YOU'RE SHAKING.
WAS IT ME? AM I NOT GOOD ENOUGH TO BE IN THE BAND?
WHAT? NO. DON'T BE RIDICULOUS. IT HAS NOTHING TO DO WITH YOU.
IN FACT, IT HAS NOTHING TO DO WITH *ANY* OF US.
IT WILL SHOCK ABSOLUTELY *NOBODY* TO FIND OUT THAT THE REASON WE'VE BEEN DROPPED FROM OUR LABEL IS...

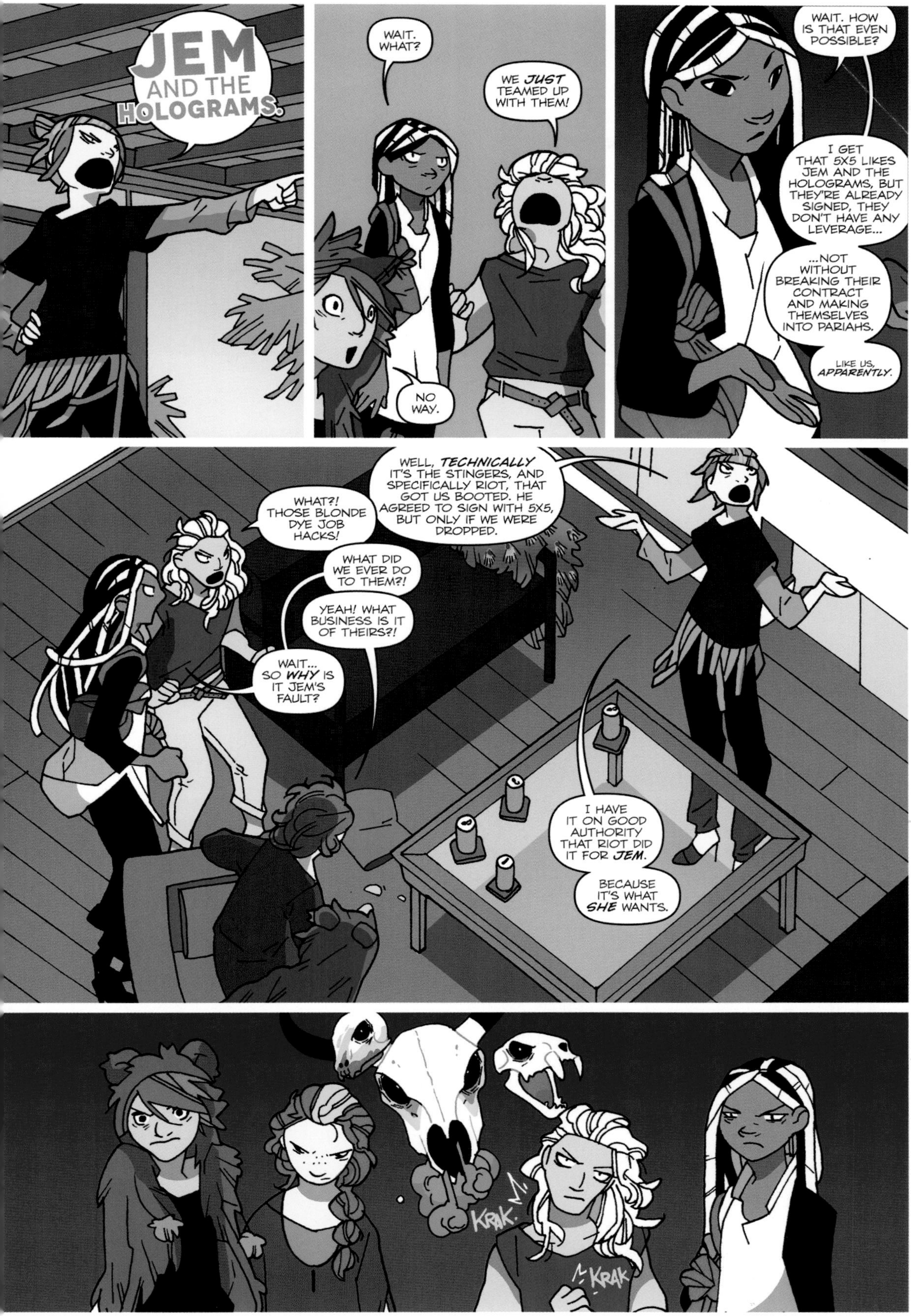
JEM AND THE HOLOGRAMS.
WAIT. WHAT?
WE JUST TEAMED UP WITH THEM!
NO WAY.
WAIT. HOW IS THAT EVEN POSSIBLE?
I GET THAT 5X5 LIKES JEM AND THE HOLOGRAMS, BUT THEY'RE ALREADY SIGNED, THEY DON'T HAVE ANY LEVERAGE...
...NOT WITHOUT BREAKING THEIR CONTRACT AND MAKING THEMSELVES INTO PARIAHS.
LIKE US, APPARENTLY.
WELL, TECHNICALLY IT'S THE STINGERS, AND SPECIFICALLY RIOT, THAT GOT US BOOTED. HE AGREED TO SIGN WITH 5X5, BUT ONLY IF WE WERE DROPPED.
WHAT?! THOSE BLONDE DYE JOB HACKS!
WHAT DID WE EVER DO TO THEM?!
YEAH! WHAT BUSINESS IS IT OF THEIRS?!
WAIT... SO WHY IS IT JEM'S FAULT?
I HAVE IT ON GOOD AUTHORITY THAT RIOT DID IT FOR JEM.
BECAUSE IT'S WHAT SHE WANTS.
KRAK
KRAK

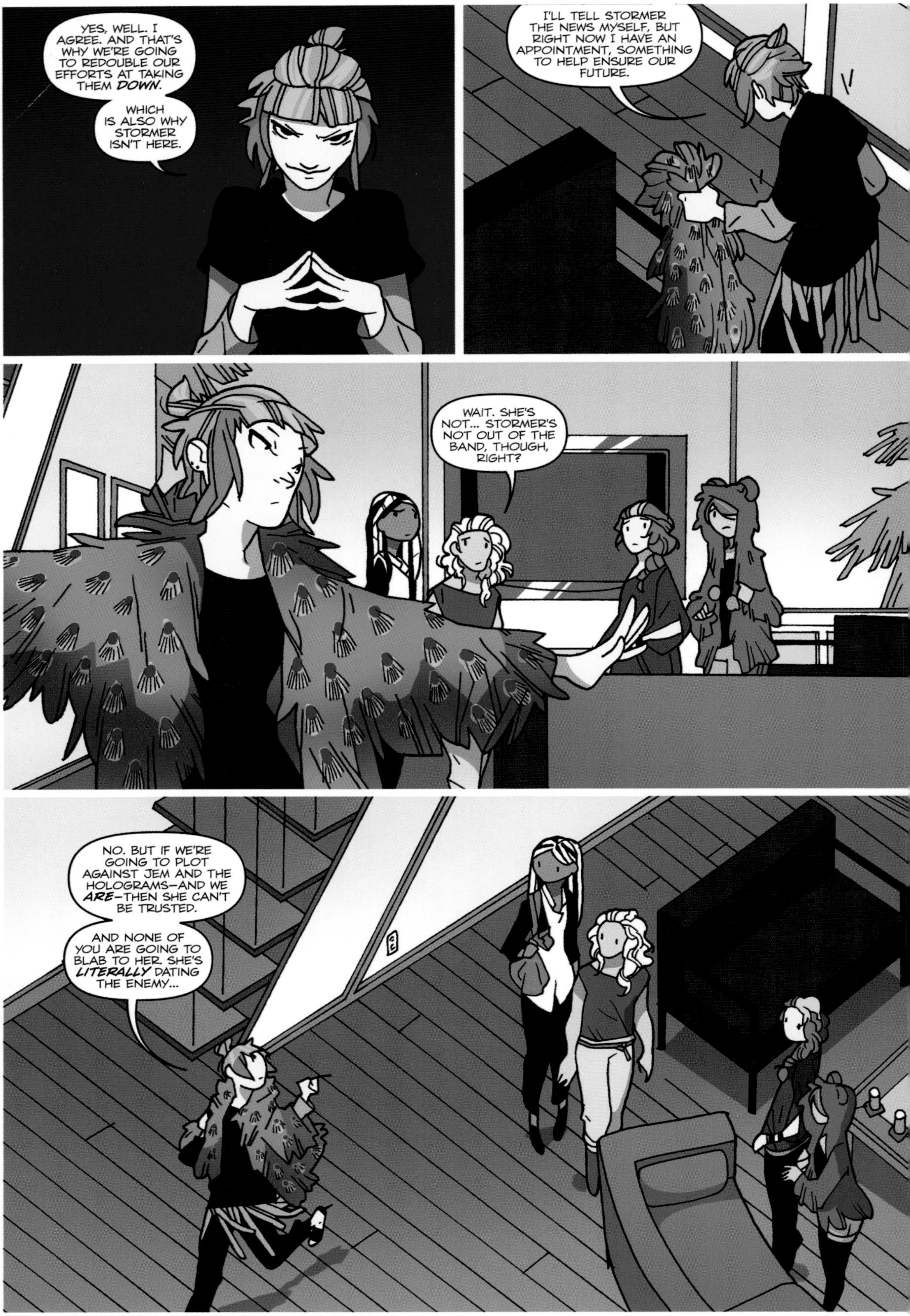
YES, WELL. I AGREE. AND THAT'S WHY WE'RE GOING TO REDOUBLE OUR EFFORTS AT TAKING THEM *DOWN*.
WHICH IS ALSO WHY STORMER ISN'T HERE.
I'LL TELL STORMER THE NEWS MYSELF, BUT RIGHT NOW I HAVE AN APPOINTMENT, SOMETHING TO HELP ENSURE OUR FUTURE.
WAIT. SHE'S NOT... STORMER'S NOT OUT OF THE BAND, THOUGH, RIGHT?
NO. BUT IF WE'RE GOING TO PLOT AGAINST JEM AND THE HOLOGRAMS—AND WE *ARE*—THEN SHE CAN'T BE TRUSTED.
AND NONE OF YOU ARE GOING TO BLAB TO HER. SHE'S *LITERALLY* DATING THE ENEMY...

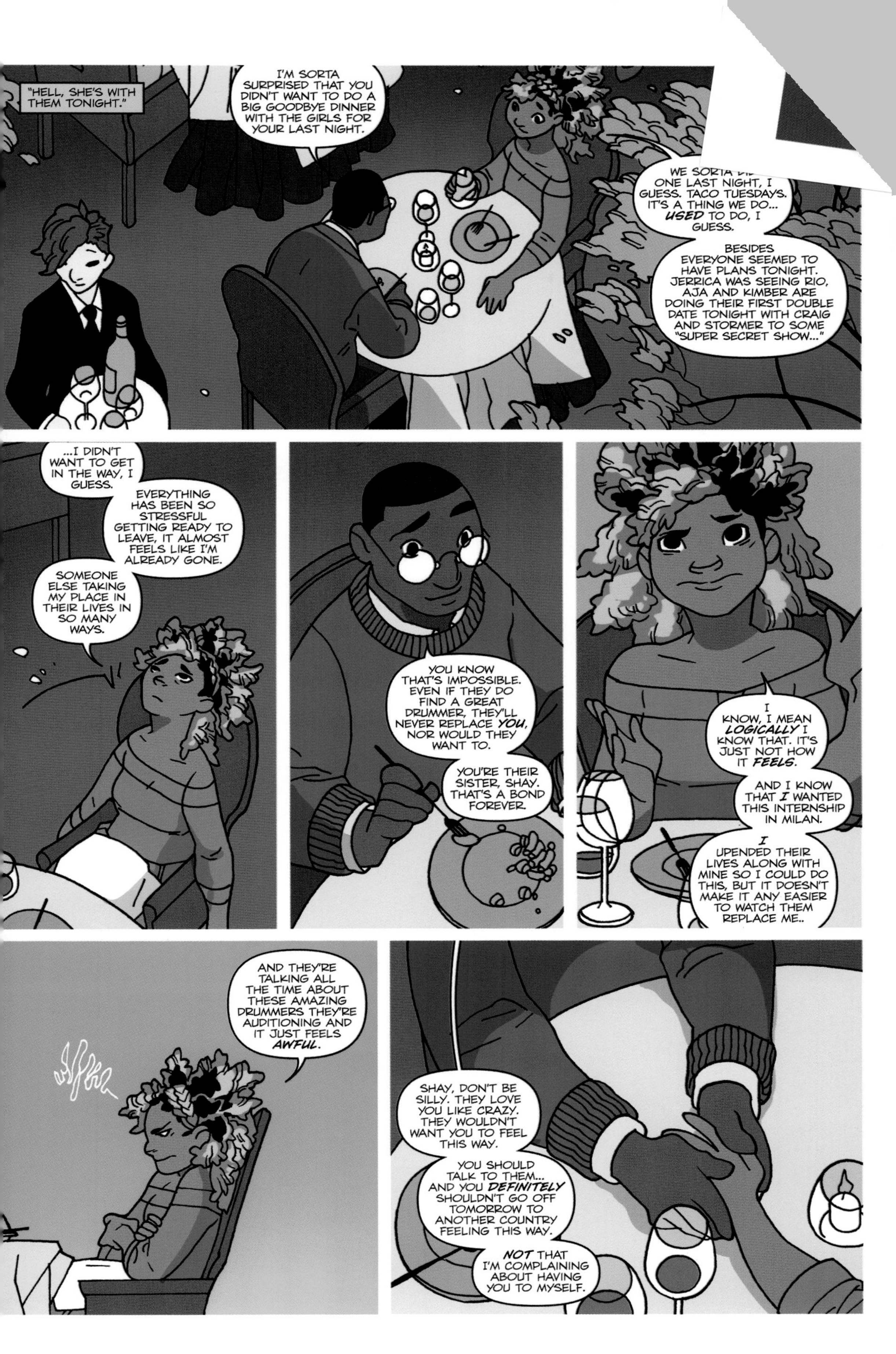
"HELL, SHE'S WITH THEM TONIGHT."
I'M SORTA SURPRISED THAT YOU DIDN'T WANT TO DO A BIG GOODBYE DINNER WITH THE GIRLS FOR YOUR LAST NIGHT.
WE SORTA DID ONE LAST NIGHT, I GUESS. TACO TUESDAYS. IT'S A THING WE DO... USED TO DO, I GUESS.
BESIDES EVERYONE SEEMED TO HAVE PLANS TONIGHT. JERRICA WAS SEEING RIO, AJA AND KIMBER ARE DOING THEIR FIRST DOUBLE DATE TONIGHT WITH CRAIG AND STORMER TO SOME "SUPER SECRET SHOW..."
...I DIDN'T WANT TO GET IN THE WAY, I GUESS.
EVERYTHING HAS BEEN SO STRESSFUL GETTING READY TO LEAVE, IT ALMOST FEELS LIKE I'M ALREADY GONE.
SOMEONE ELSE TAKING MY PLACE IN THEIR LIVES IN SO MANY WAYS.
YOU KNOW THAT'S IMPOSSIBLE. EVEN IF THEY DO FIND A GREAT DRUMMER, THEY'LL NEVER REPLACE YOU, NOR WOULD THEY WANT TO.
YOU'RE THEIR SISTER, SHAY. THAT'S A BOND FOREVER.
I KNOW, I MEAN LOGICALLY I KNOW THAT. IT'S JUST NOT HOW IT FEELS.
AND I KNOW THAT I WANTED THIS INTERNSHIP IN MILAN.
I UPENDED THEIR LIVES ALONG WITH MINE SO I COULD DO THIS, BUT IT DOESN'T MAKE IT ANY EASIER TO WATCH THEM REPLACE ME..
AND THEY'RE TALKING ALL THE TIME ABOUT THESE AMAZING DRUMMERS THEY'RE AUDITIONING AND IT JUST FEELS AWFUL.
SHAY, DON'T BE SILLY. THEY LOVE YOU LIKE CRAZY. THEY WOULDN'T WANT YOU TO FEEL THIS WAY.
YOU SHOULD TALK TO THEM... AND YOU DEFINITELY SHOULDN'T GO OFF TOMORROW TO ANOTHER COUNTRY FEELING THIS WAY.
NOT THAT I'M COMPLAINING ABOUT HAVING YOU TO MYSELF.

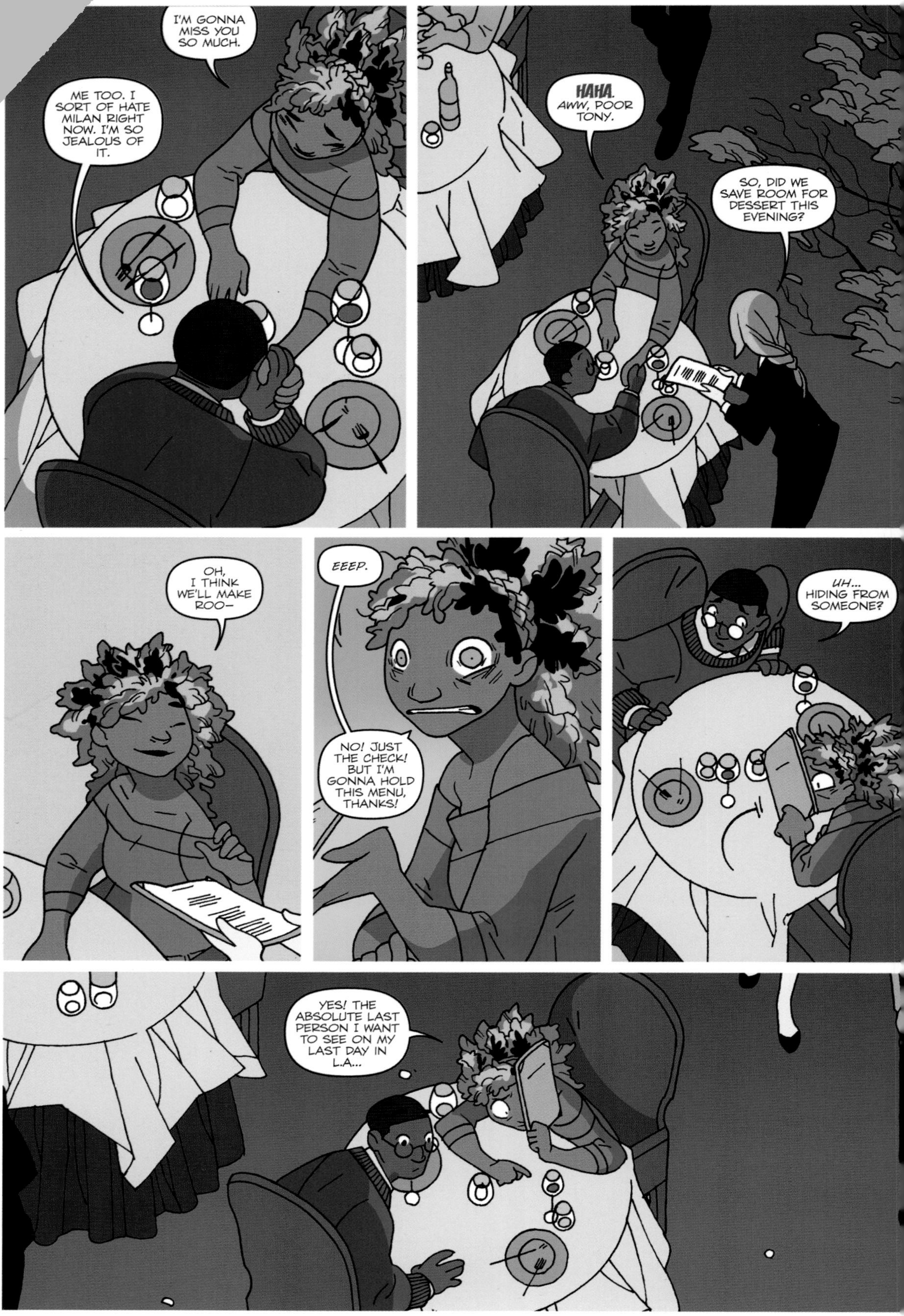
I'M GONNA MISS YOU SO MUCH.
ME TOO. I SORT OF HATE MILAN RIGHT NOW. I'M SO JEALOUS OF IT.
HAHA. AWW, POOR TONY.
SO, DID WE SAVE ROOM FOR DESSERT THIS EVENING?
OH, I THINK WE'LL MAKE ROO—
EEEP.
NO! JUST THE CHECK! BUT I'M GONNA HOLD THIS MENU, THANKS!
UH... HIDING FROM SOMEONE?
YES! THE ABSOLUTE LAST PERSON I WANT TO SEE ON MY LAST DAY IN L.A...

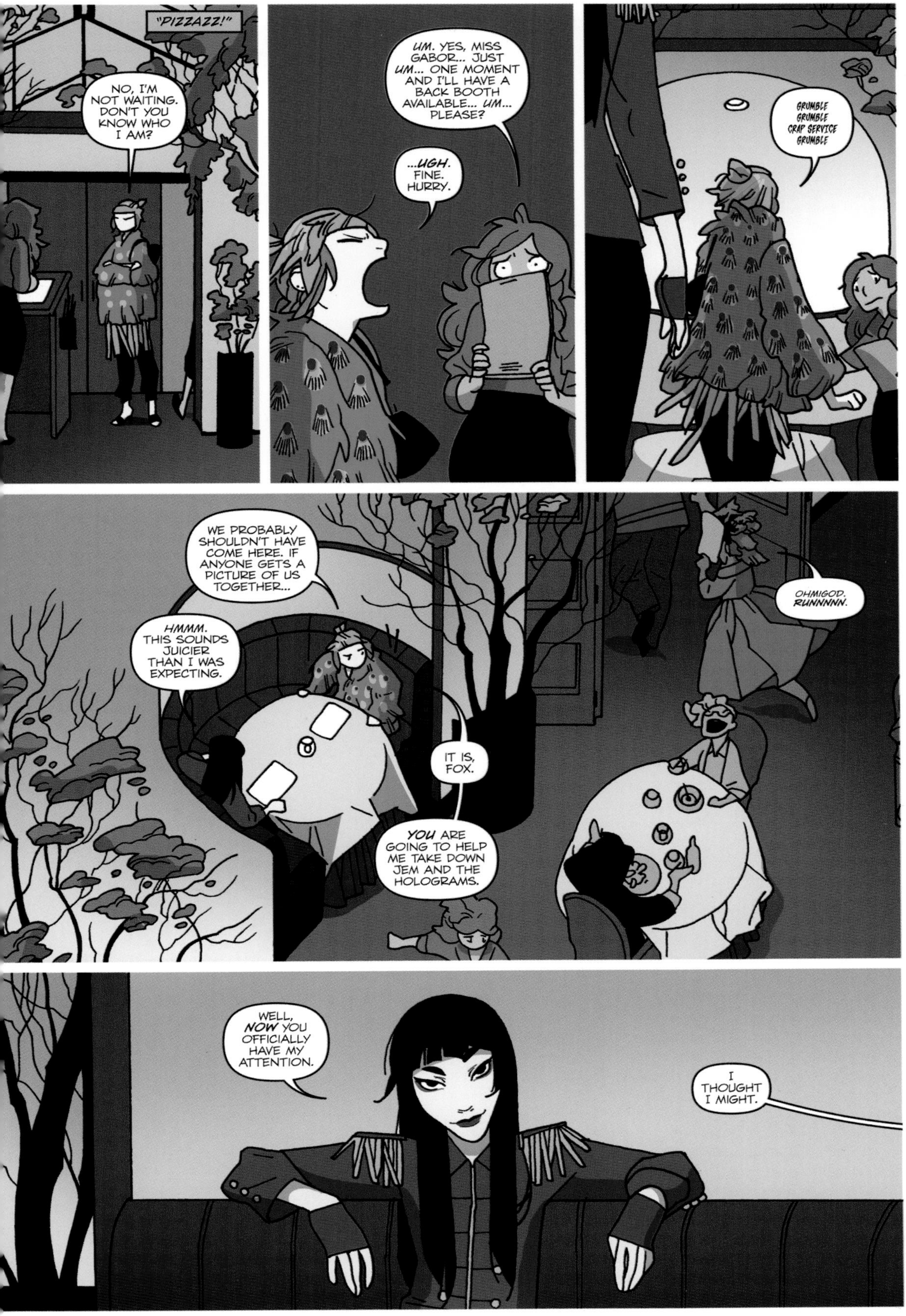
"PIZZAZZ!"
NO, I'M NOT WAITING. DON'T YOU KNOW WHO I AM?
UM. YES, MISS GABOR... JUST UM... ONE MOMENT AND I'LL HAVE A BACK BOOTH AVAILABLE... UM... PLEASE?
...UGH. FINE. HURRY.
GRUMBLE GRUMBLE CRAP SERVICE GRUMBLE
WE PROBABLY SHOULDN'T HAVE COME HERE. IF ANYONE GETS A PICTURE OF US TOGETHER...
HMMM. THIS SOUNDS JUICIER THAN I WAS EXPECTING.
OHMIGOD. RUNNNNN.
IT IS, FOX.
YOU ARE GOING TO HELP ME TAKE DOWN JEM AND THE HOLOGRAMS.
WELL, NOW YOU OFFICIALLY HAVE MY ATTENTION.
I THOUGHT I MIGHT.

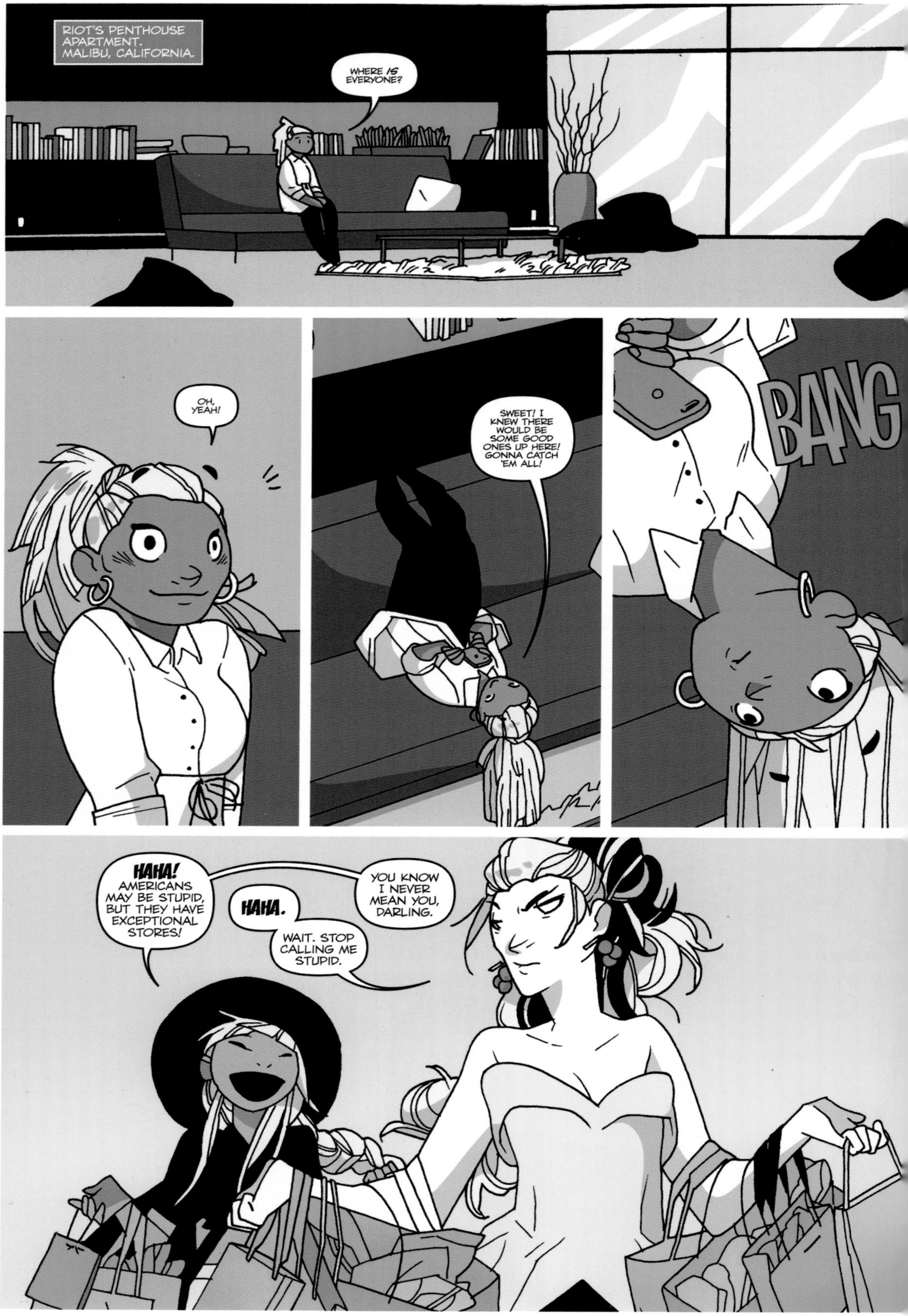
RIOT'S PENTHOUSE APARTMENT. MALIBU, CALIFORNIA.
WHERE *IS* EVERYONE?
OH, YEAH!
SWEET! I KNEW THERE WOULD BE SOME GOOD ONES UP HERE! GONNA CATCH 'EM ALL!
BANG
HAHA! AMERICANS MAY BE STUPID, BUT THEY HAVE EXCEPTIONAL STORES!
HAHA.
YOU KNOW I NEVER MEAN YOU, DARLING.
WAIT. STOP CALLING ME STUPID.

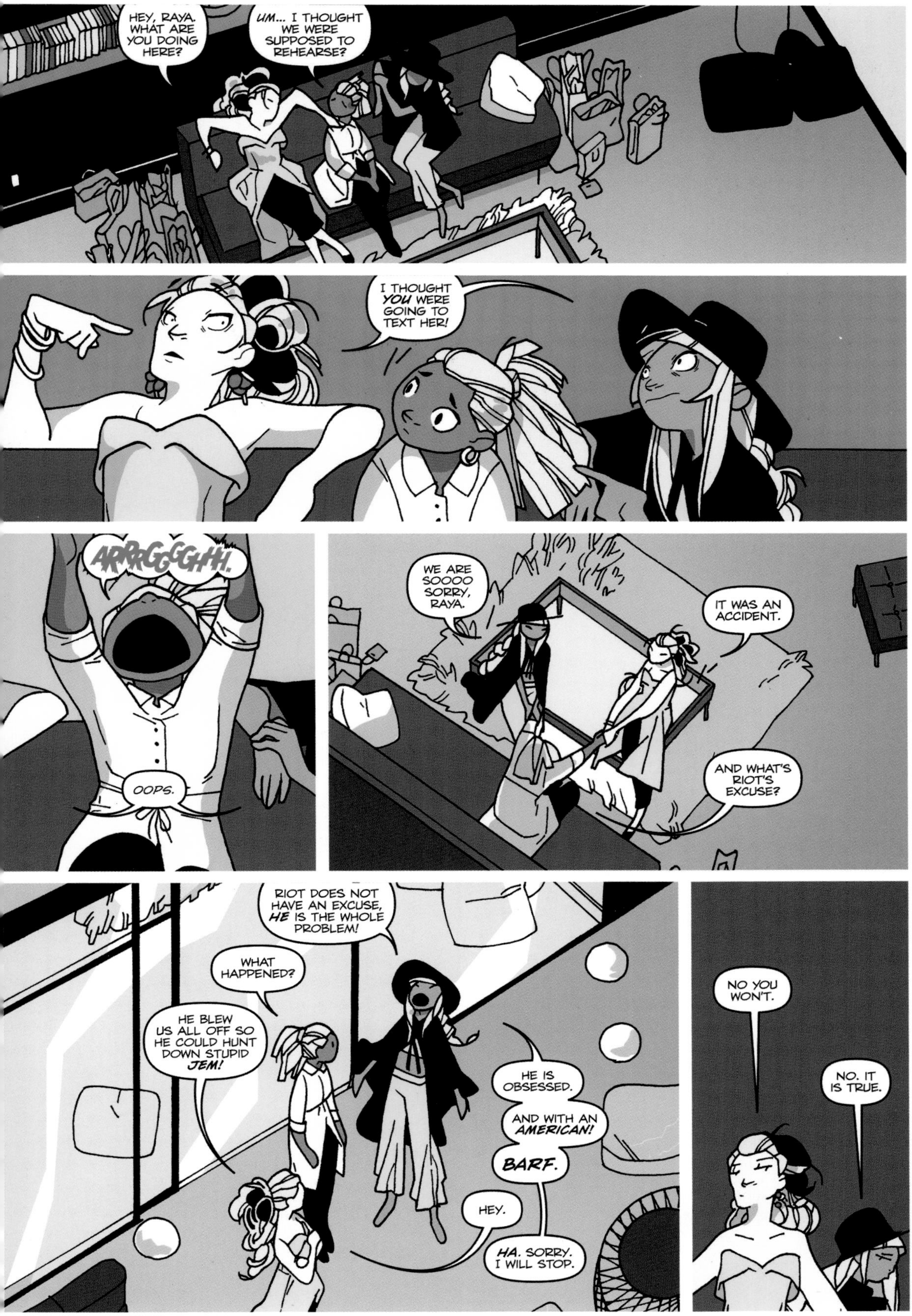
HEY, RAYA. WHAT ARE YOU DOING HERE?
UM... I THOUGHT WE WERE SUPPOSED TO REHEARSE?
I THOUGHT YOU WERE GOING TO TEXT HER!
ARRRGGGGHH.
OOPS.
WE ARE SOOOO SORRY, RAYA.
IT WAS AN ACCIDENT.
AND WHAT'S RIOT'S EXCUSE?
RIOT DOES NOT HAVE AN EXCUSE, HE IS THE WHOLE PROBLEM!
WHAT HAPPENED?
HE BLEW US ALL OFF SO HE COULD HUNT DOWN STUPID JEM!
HE IS OBSESSED.
AND WITH AN AMERICAN!
BARF.
HEY.
HA. SORRY. I WILL STOP.
NO YOU WON'T.
NO. IT IS TRUE.

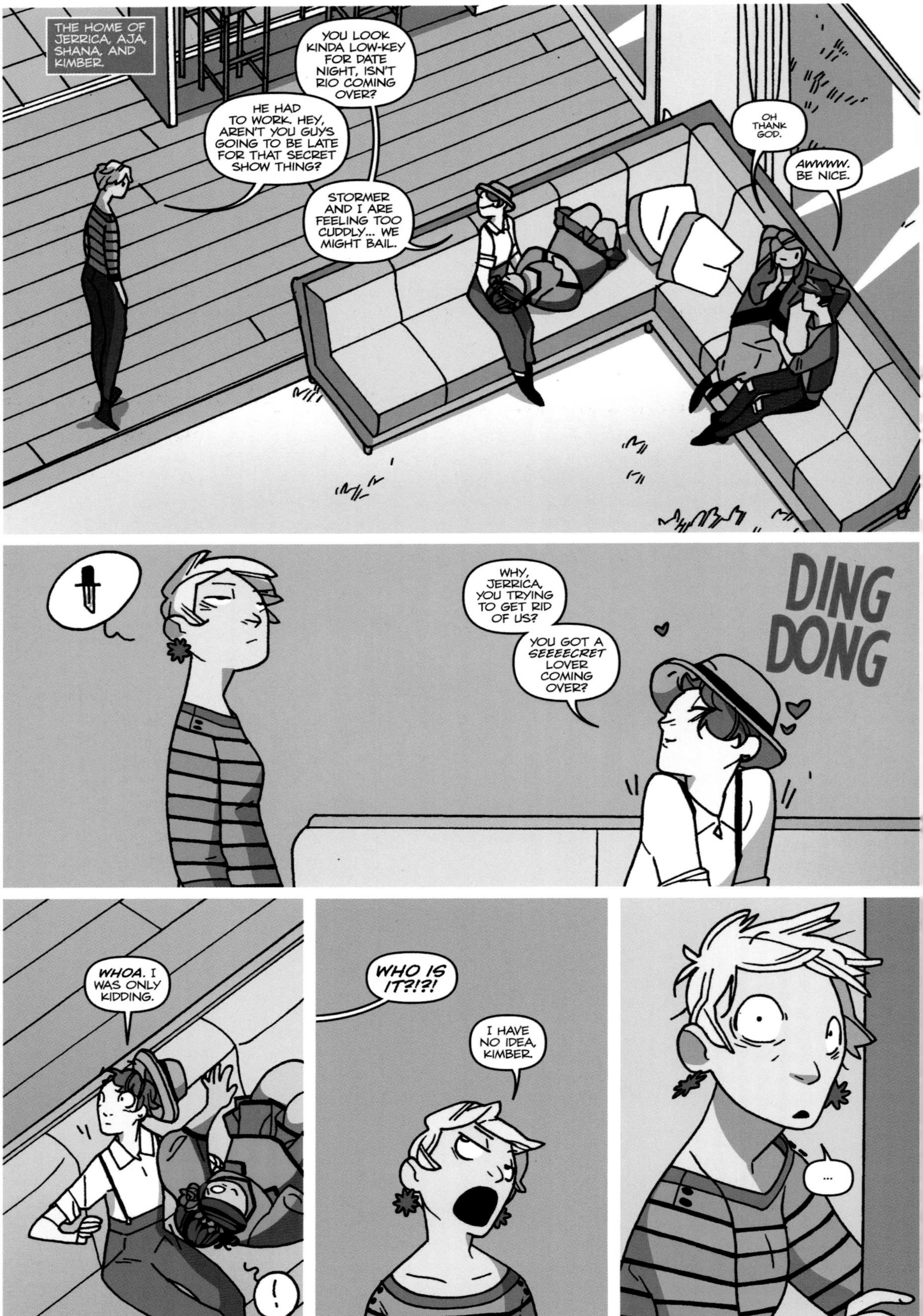
THE HOME OF JERRICA, AJA, SHANA, AND KIMBER.
YOU LOOK KINDA LOW-KEY FOR DATE NIGHT, ISN'T RIO COMING OVER?
HE HAD TO WORK. HEY, AREN'T YOU GUYS GOING TO BE LATE FOR THAT SECRET SHOW THING?
STORMER AND I ARE FEELING TOO CUDDLY... WE MIGHT BAIL.
OH THANK GOD.
AWWWW. BE NICE.
WHY, JERRICA, YOU TRYING TO GET RID OF US?
YOU GOT A SEEEECRET LOVER COMING OVER?
DING DONG
WHOA. I WAS ONLY KIDDING.
!
WHO IS IT?!?!
I HAVE NO IDEA, KIMBER.
...

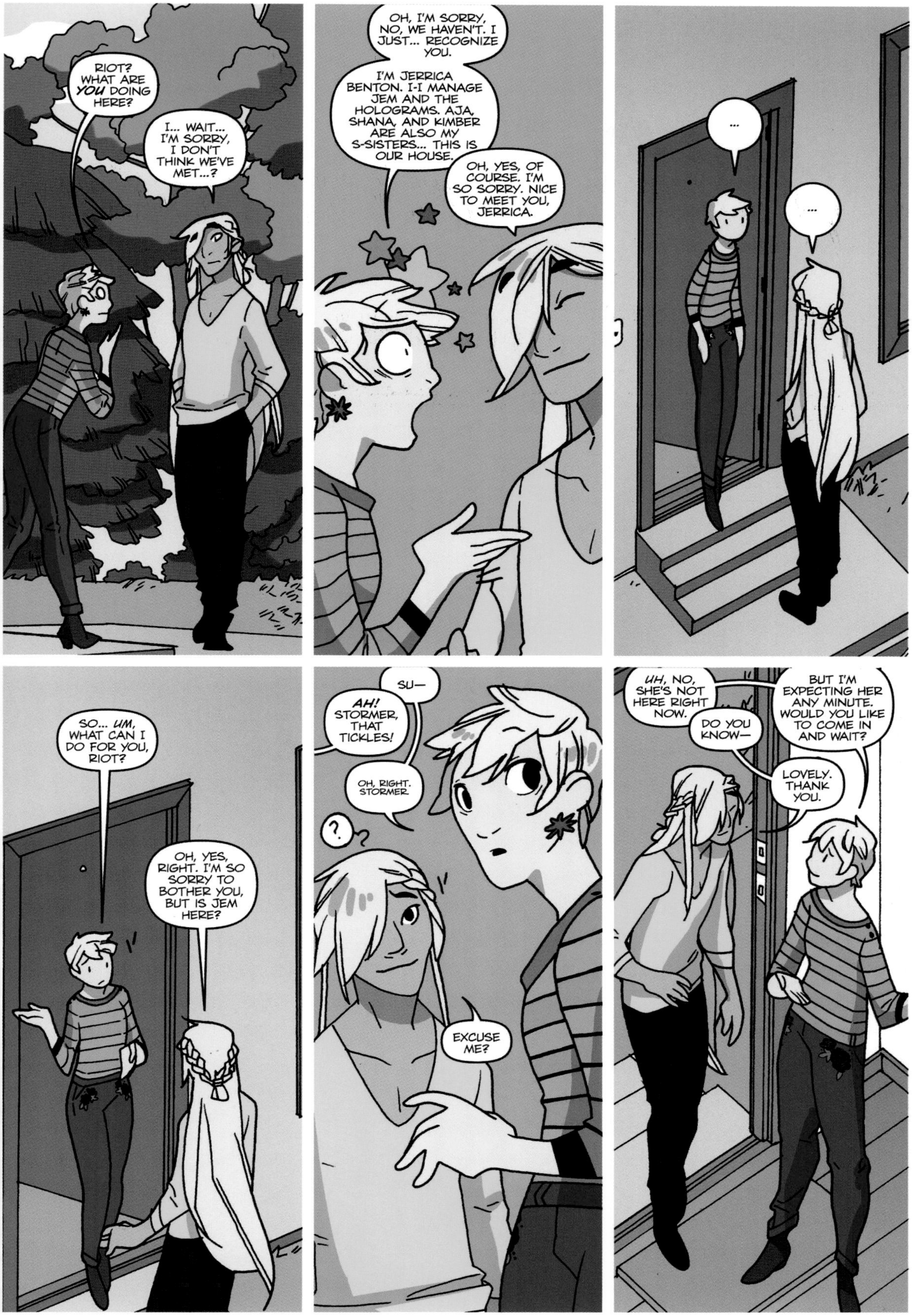
RIOT? WHAT ARE *YOU* DOING HERE?
I... WAIT... I'M SORRY, I DON'T THINK WE'VE MET...?
OH, I'M SORRY, NO, WE HAVEN'T. I JUST... RECOGNIZE YOU.
I'M JERRICA BENTON. I-I MANAGE JEM AND THE HOLOGRAMS. AJA, SHANA, AND KIMBER ARE ALSO MY S-SISTERS... THIS IS OUR HOUSE.
OH, YES, OF COURSE. I'M SO SORRY. NICE TO MEET YOU, JERRICA.
...
...
SO... *UM*, WHAT CAN I DO FOR YOU, RIOT?
OH, YES, RIGHT. I'M SO SORRY TO BOTHER YOU, BUT IS JEM HERE?
SU—
AH! STORMER, THAT TICKLES!
OH, RIGHT. STORMER
?
EXCUSE ME?
UH, NO, SHE'S NOT HERE RIGHT NOW.
BUT I'M EXPECTING HER ANY MINUTE. WOULD YOU LIKE TO COME IN AND WAIT?
DO YOU KNOW—
LOVELY. THANK YOU.

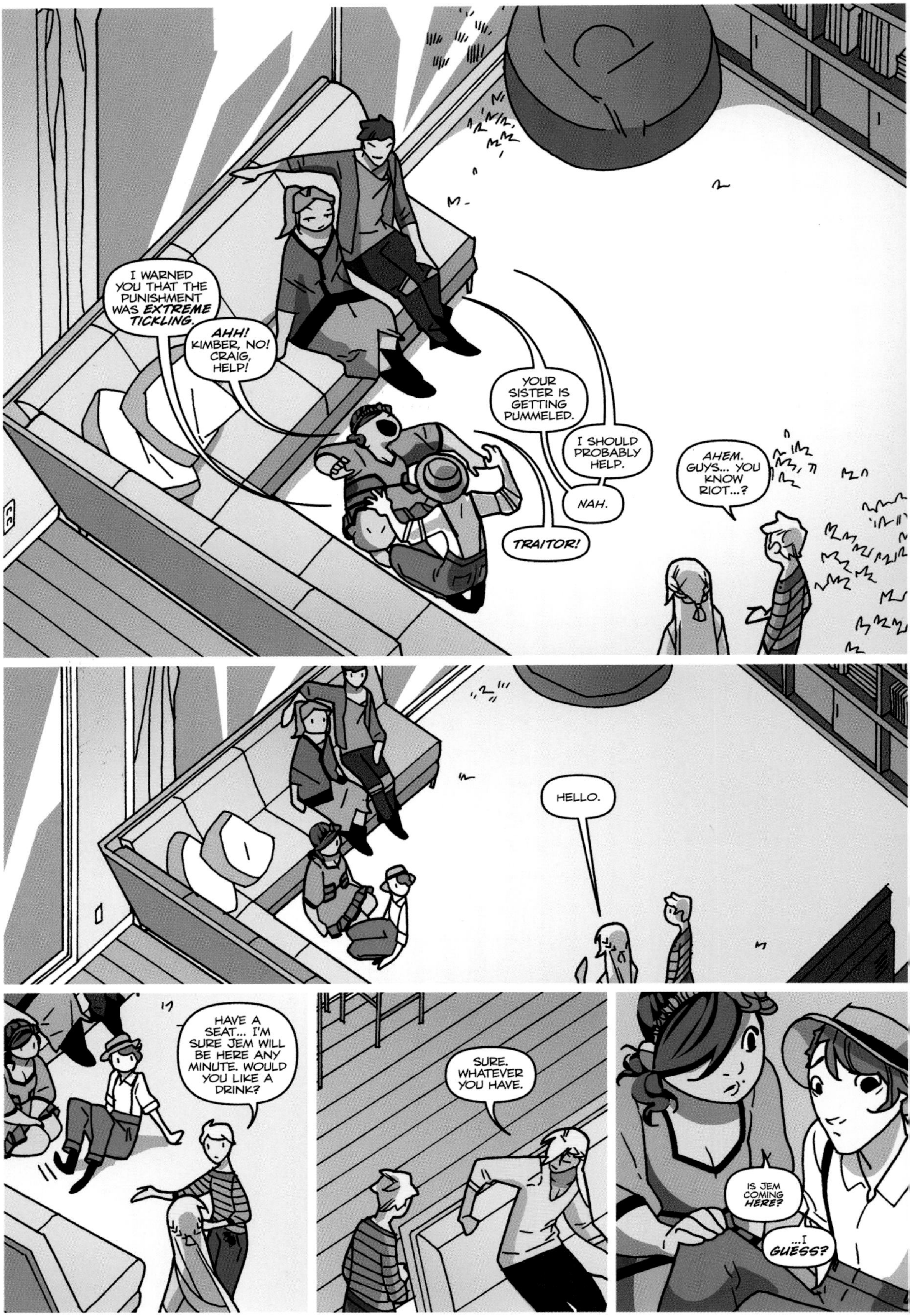

I WARNED YOU THAT THE PUNISHMENT WAS ***EXTREME TICKLING.***
AHH! KIMBER, NO! CRAIG, HELP!
YOUR SISTER IS GETTING PUMMELED.
I SHOULD PROBABLY HELP.
NAH.
TRAITOR!
AHEM. GUYS... YOU KNOW RIOT...?
HELLO.
HAVE A SEAT... I'M SURE JEM WILL BE HERE ANY MINUTE. WOULD YOU LIKE A DRINK?
SURE. WHATEVER YOU HAVE.
IS JEM COMING ***HERE?***
...I ***GUESS?***

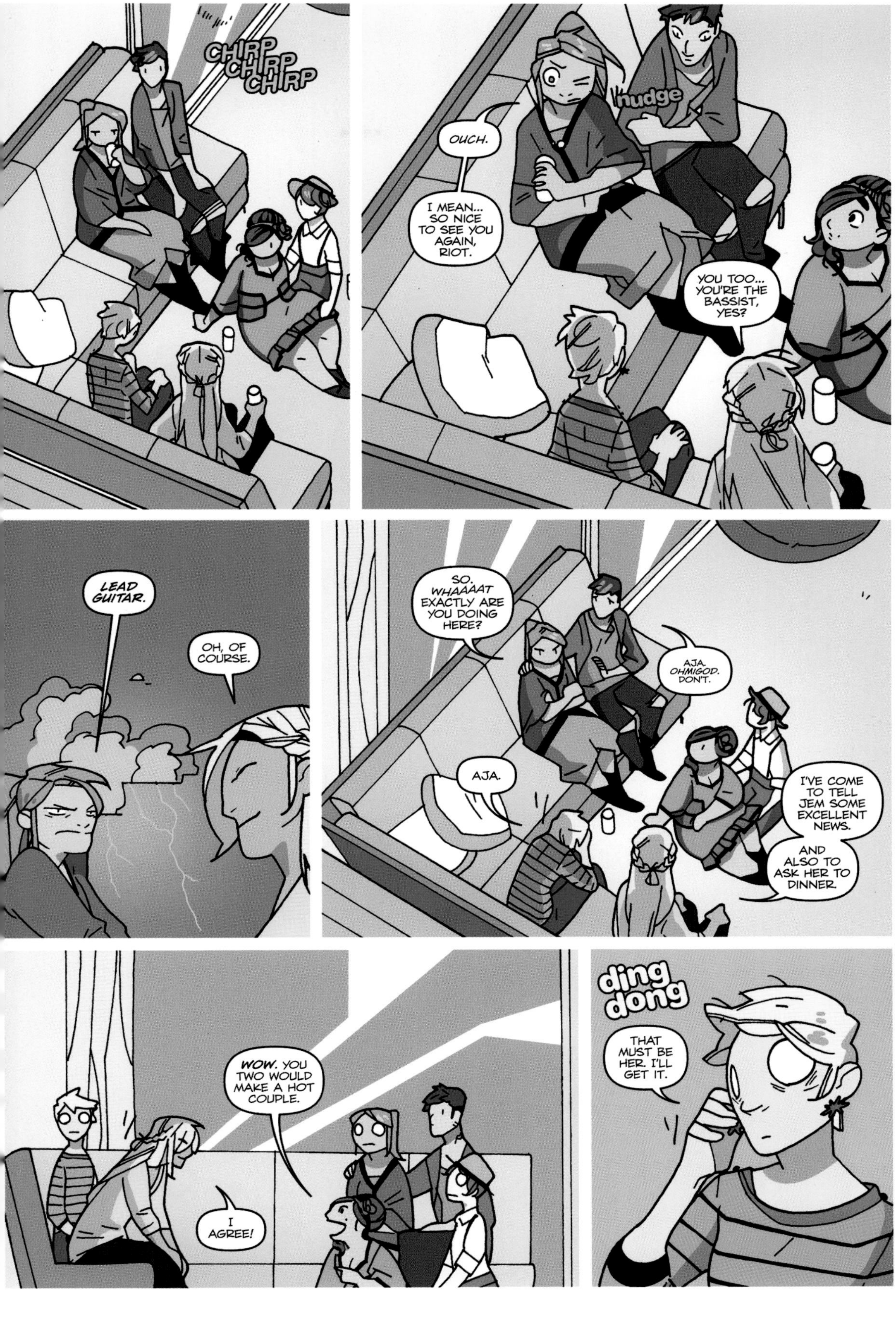
CHIRP
CHIRP
CHIRP
nudge
OUCH.
I MEAN... SO NICE TO SEE YOU AGAIN, RIOT.
YOU TOO... YOU'RE THE BASSIST, YES?
LEAD GUITAR.
OH, OF COURSE.
SO. WHAAAAT EXACTLY ARE YOU DOING HERE?
AJA. OHMIGOD. DON'T.
AJA.
I'VE COME TO TELL JEM SOME EXCELLENT NEWS.
AND ALSO TO ASK HER TO DINNER.
WOW. YOU TWO WOULD MAKE A HOT COUPLE.
I AGREE!
ding dong
THAT MUST BE HER. I'LL GET IT.

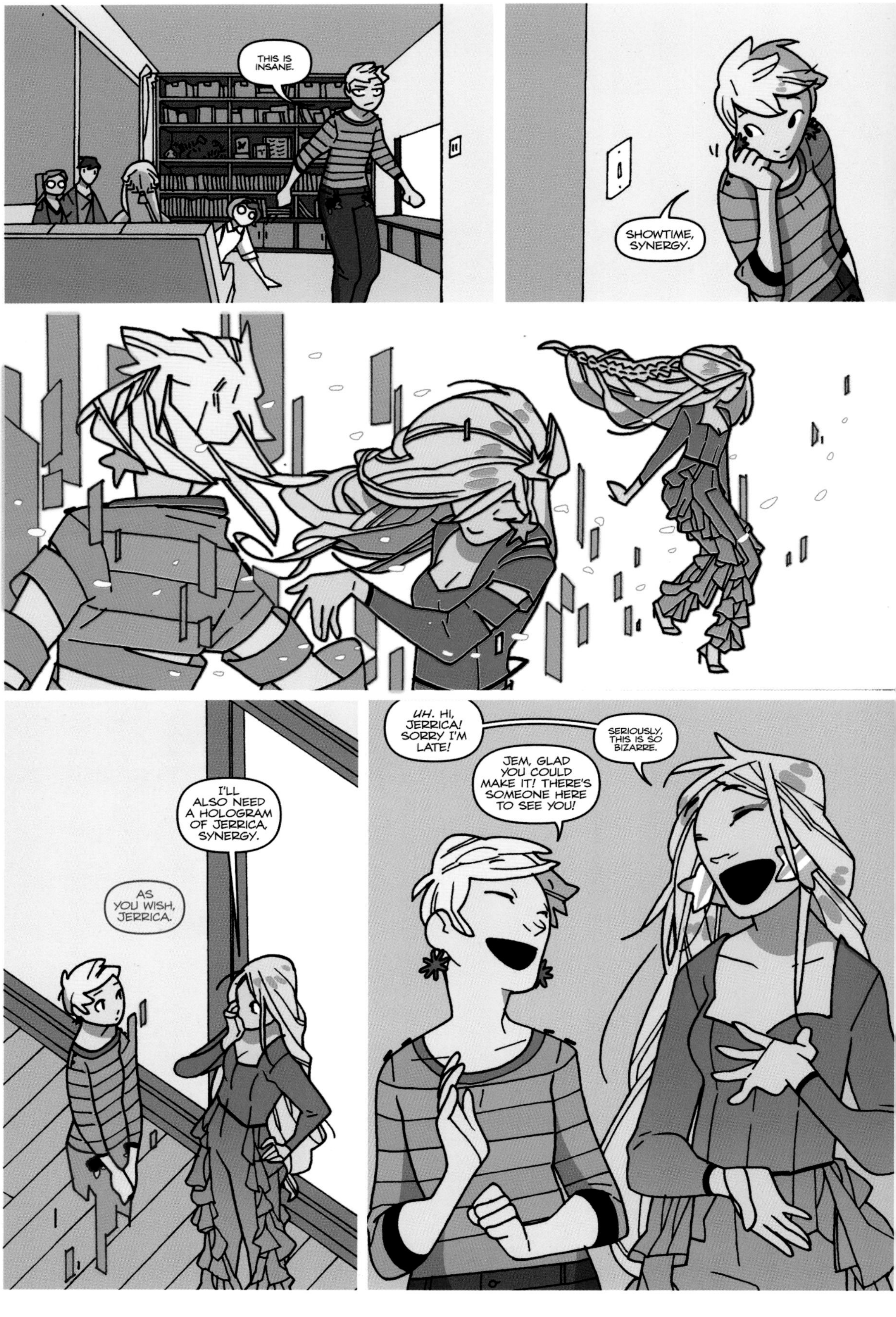
THIS IS INSANE.
SHOWTIME, SYNERGY.
I'LL ALSO NEED A HOLOGRAM OF JERRICA, SYNERGY.
AS YOU WISH, JERRICA.
UH. HI, JERRICA! SORRY I'M LATE!
SERIOUSLY, THIS IS SO BIZARRE.
JEM, GLAD YOU COULD MAKE IT! THERE'S SOMEONE HERE TO SEE YOU!

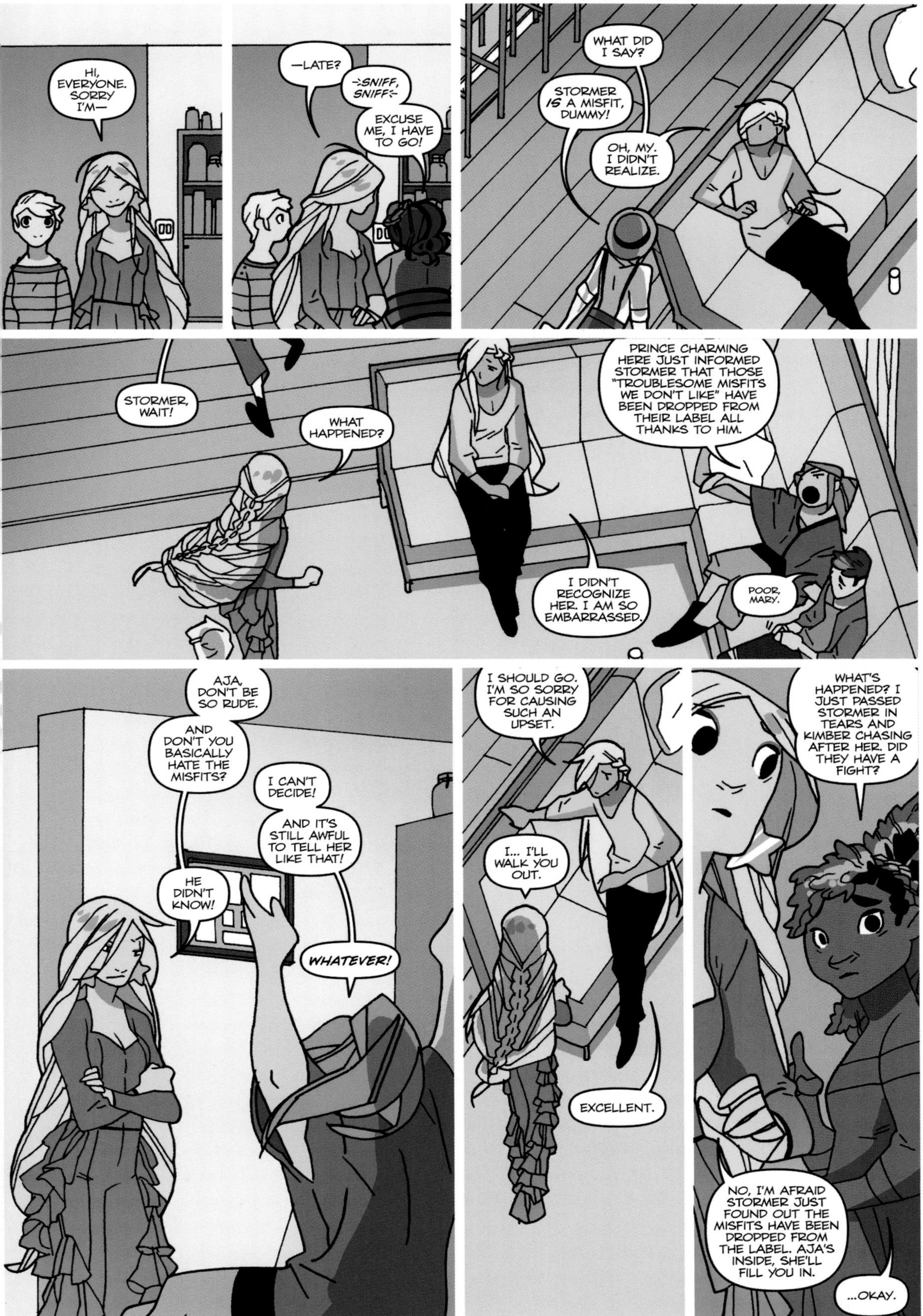
HI, EVERYONE. SORRY I'M—
—LATE?
~SNIFF, SNIFF~
EXCUSE ME, I HAVE TO GO!
WHAT DID I SAY?
STORMER *IS* A MISFIT, DUMMY!
OH, MY. I DIDN'T REALIZE.
STORMER, WAIT!
WHAT HAPPENED?
PRINCE CHARMING HERE JUST INFORMED STORMER THAT THOSE "TROUBLESOME MISFITS WE DON'T LIKE" HAVE BEEN DROPPED FROM THEIR LABEL ALL THANKS TO HIM.
I DIDN'T RECOGNIZE HER. I AM SO EMBARRASSED.
POOR, MARY.
AJA, DON'T BE SO RUDE.
AND DON'T YOU BASICALLY HATE THE MISFITS?
I CAN'T DECIDE!
AND IT'S STILL AWFUL TO TELL HER LIKE THAT!
HE DIDN'T KNOW!
WHATEVER!
I SHOULD GO. I'M SO SORRY FOR CAUSING SUCH AN UPSET.
I... I'LL WALK YOU OUT.
EXCELLENT.
WHAT'S HAPPENED? I JUST PASSED STORMER IN TEARS AND KIMBER CHASING AFTER HER. DID THEY HAVE A FIGHT?
NO, I'M AFRAID STORMER JUST FOUND OUT THE MISFITS HAVE BEEN DROPPED FROM THE LABEL. AJA'S INSIDE, SHE'LL FILL YOU IN.
...OKAY.

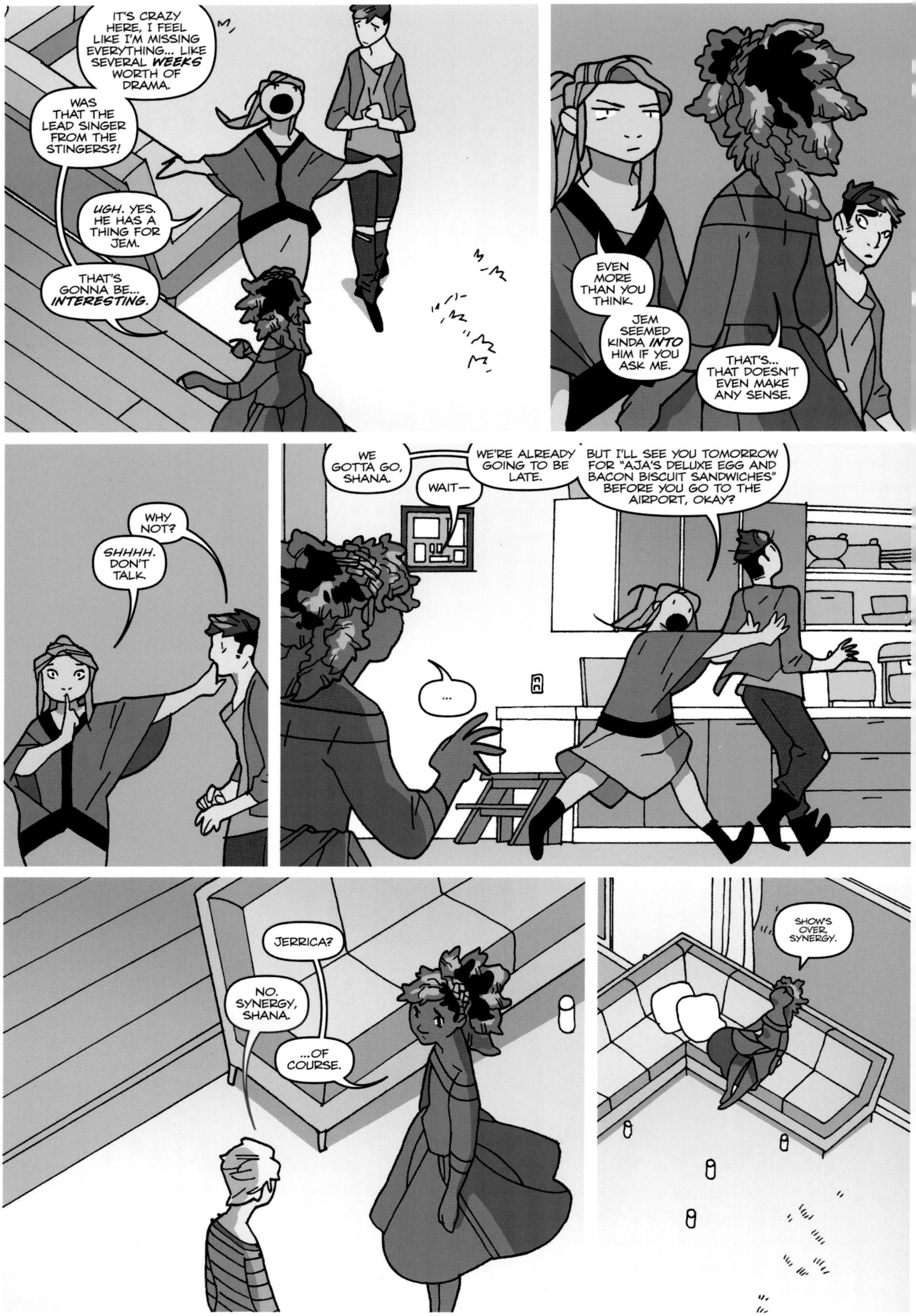

IT'S CRAZY HERE, I FEEL LIKE I'M MISSING EVERYTHING... LIKE SEVERAL WEEKS WORTH OF DRAMA.
WAS THAT THE LEAD SINGER FROM THE STINGERS?!
UGH. YES. HE HAS A THING FOR JEM.
THAT'S GONNA BE... INTERESTING.
EVEN MORE THAN YOU THINK.
JEM SEEMED KINDA INTO HIM IF YOU ASK ME.
THAT'S... THAT DOESN'T EVEN MAKE ANY SENSE.
WHY NOT?
SHHHH. DON'T TALK.
WE GOTTA GO, SHANA.
WE'RE ALREADY GOING TO BE LATE.
WAIT—
BUT I'LL SEE YOU TOMORROW FOR "AJA'S DELUXE EGG AND BACON BISCUIT SANDWICHES" BEFORE YOU GO TO THE AIRPORT, OKAY?
...
JERRICA?
NO. SYNERGY, SHANA.
...OF COURSE.
SHOW'S OVER, SYNERGY.

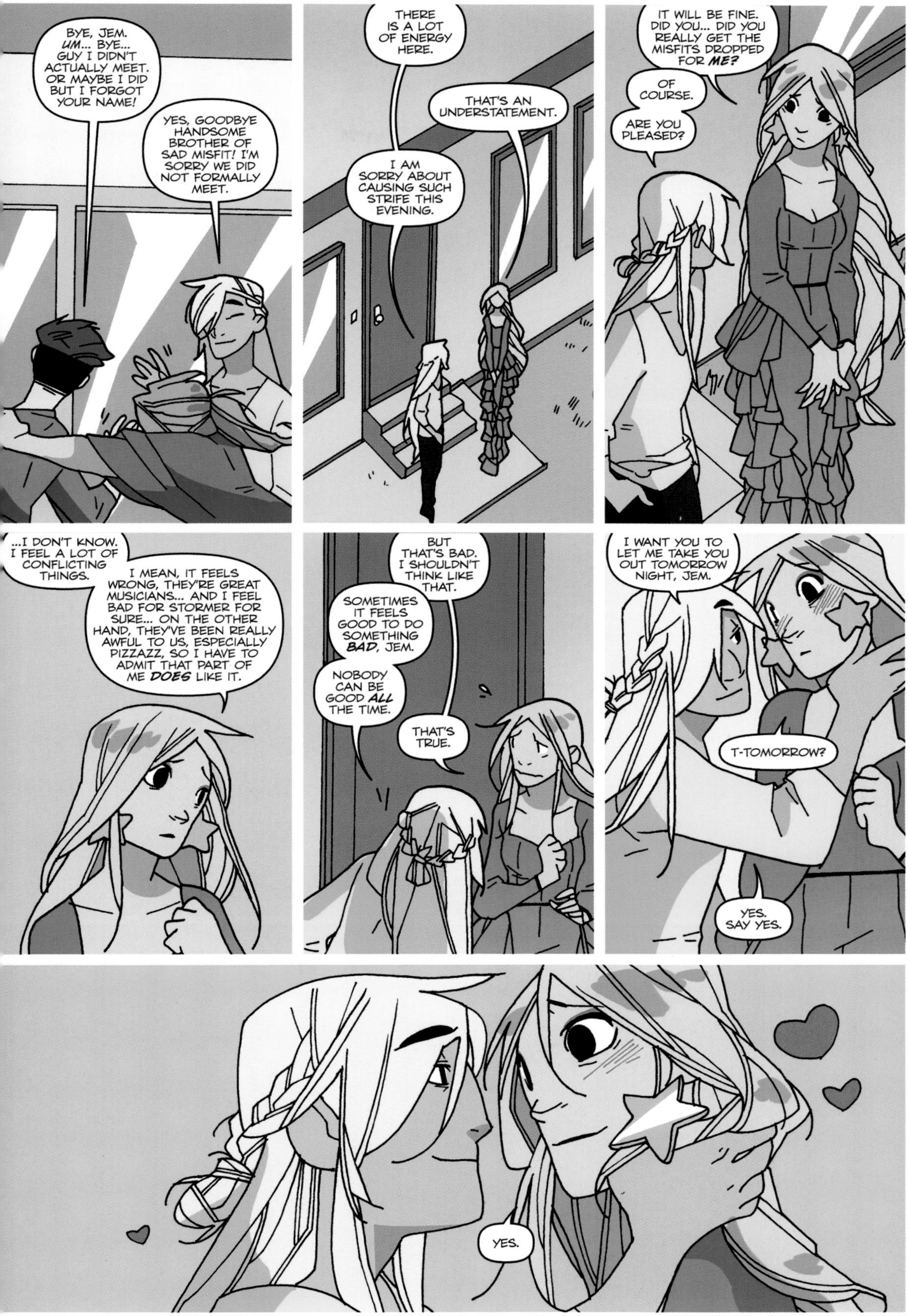
BYE, JEM. UM... BYE... GUY I DIDN'T ACTUALLY MEET. OR MAYBE I DID BUT I FORGOT YOUR NAME!
YES, GOODBYE HANDSOME BROTHER OF SAD MISFIT! I'M SORRY WE DID NOT FORMALLY MEET.
THERE IS A LOT OF ENERGY HERE.
THAT'S AN UNDERSTATEMENT.
I AM SORRY ABOUT CAUSING SUCH STRIFE THIS EVENING.
IT WILL BE FINE. DID YOU... DID YOU REALLY GET THE MISFITS DROPPED FOR ME?
OF COURSE.
ARE YOU PLEASED?
...I DON'T KNOW. I FEEL A LOT OF CONFLICTING THINGS.
I MEAN, IT FEELS WRONG, THEY'RE GREAT MUSICIANS... AND I FEEL BAD FOR STORMER FOR SURE... ON THE OTHER HAND, THEY'VE BEEN REALLY AWFUL TO US, ESPECIALLY PIZZAZZ, SO I HAVE TO ADMIT THAT PART OF ME DOES LIKE IT.
BUT THAT'S BAD. I SHOULDN'T THINK LIKE THAT.
SOMETIMES IT FEELS GOOD TO DO SOMETHING BAD, JEM.
NOBODY CAN BE GOOD ALL THE TIME.
THAT'S TRUE.
I WANT YOU TO LET ME TAKE YOU OUT TOMORROW NIGHT, JEM.
T-TOMORROW?
YES. SAY YES.
YES.

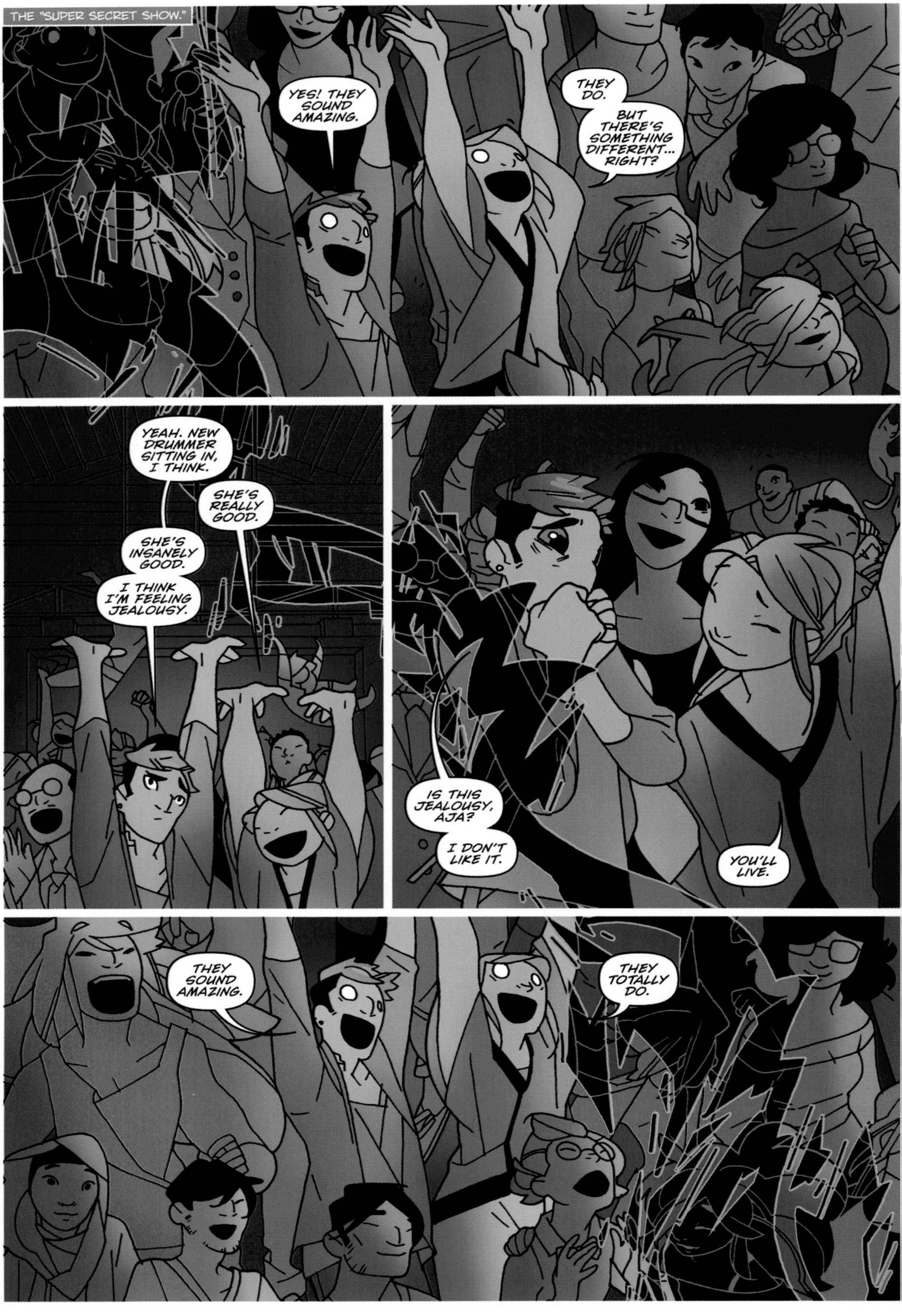
THE "SUPER SECRET SHOW."
YES! THEY SOUND AMAZING.
THEY DO.
BUT THERE'S SOMETHING DIFFERENT... RIGHT?
YEAH. NEW DRUMMER SITTING IN, I THINK.
SHE'S REALLY GOOD.
SHE'S INSANELY GOOD.
I THINK I'M FEELING JEALOUSY.
IS THIS JEALOUSY, AJA?
I DON'T LIKE IT.
YOU'LL LIVE.
THEY SOUND AMAZING.
THEY TOTALLY DO.

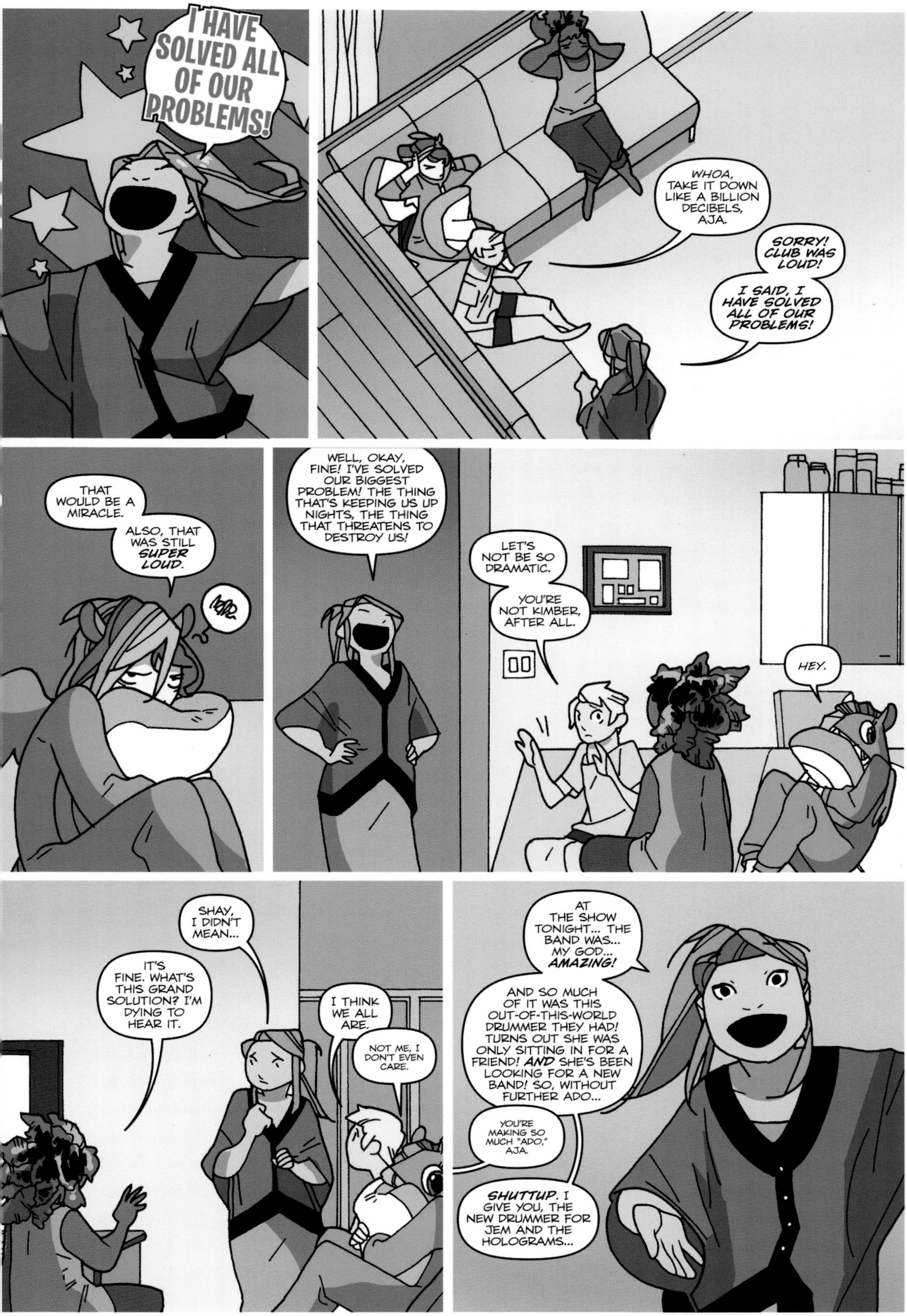

I HAVE SOLVED ALL OF OUR PROBLEMS!
WHOA, TAKE IT DOWN LIKE A BILLION DECIBELS, AJA.
SORRY! CLUB WAS LOUD!
I SAID, I HAVE SOLVED ALL OF OUR PROBLEMS!
THAT WOULD BE A MIRACLE.
ALSO, THAT WAS STILL SUPER LOUD.
WELL, OKAY, FINE! I'VE SOLVED OUR BIGGEST PROBLEM! THE THING THAT'S KEEPING US UP NIGHTS, THE THING THAT THREATENS TO DESTROY US!
LET'S NOT BE SO DRAMATIC.
YOU'RE NOT KIMBER, AFTER ALL.
HEY.
SHAY, I DIDN'T MEAN...
IT'S FINE. WHAT'S THIS GRAND SOLUTION? I'M DYING TO HEAR IT.
I THINK WE ALL ARE.
NOT ME, I DON'T EVEN CARE.
AT THE SHOW TONIGHT... THE BAND WAS... MY GOD... AMAZING!
AND SO MUCH OF IT WAS THIS OUT-OF-THIS-WORLD DRUMMER THEY HAD! TURNS OUT SHE WAS ONLY SITTING IN FOR A FRIEND! AND SHE'S BEEN LOOKING FOR A NEW BAND! SO, WITHOUT FURTHER ADO...
YOU'RE MAKING SO MUCH "ADO," AJA.
SHUTTUP. I GIVE YOU, THE NEW DRUMMER FOR JEM AND THE HOLOGRAMS...

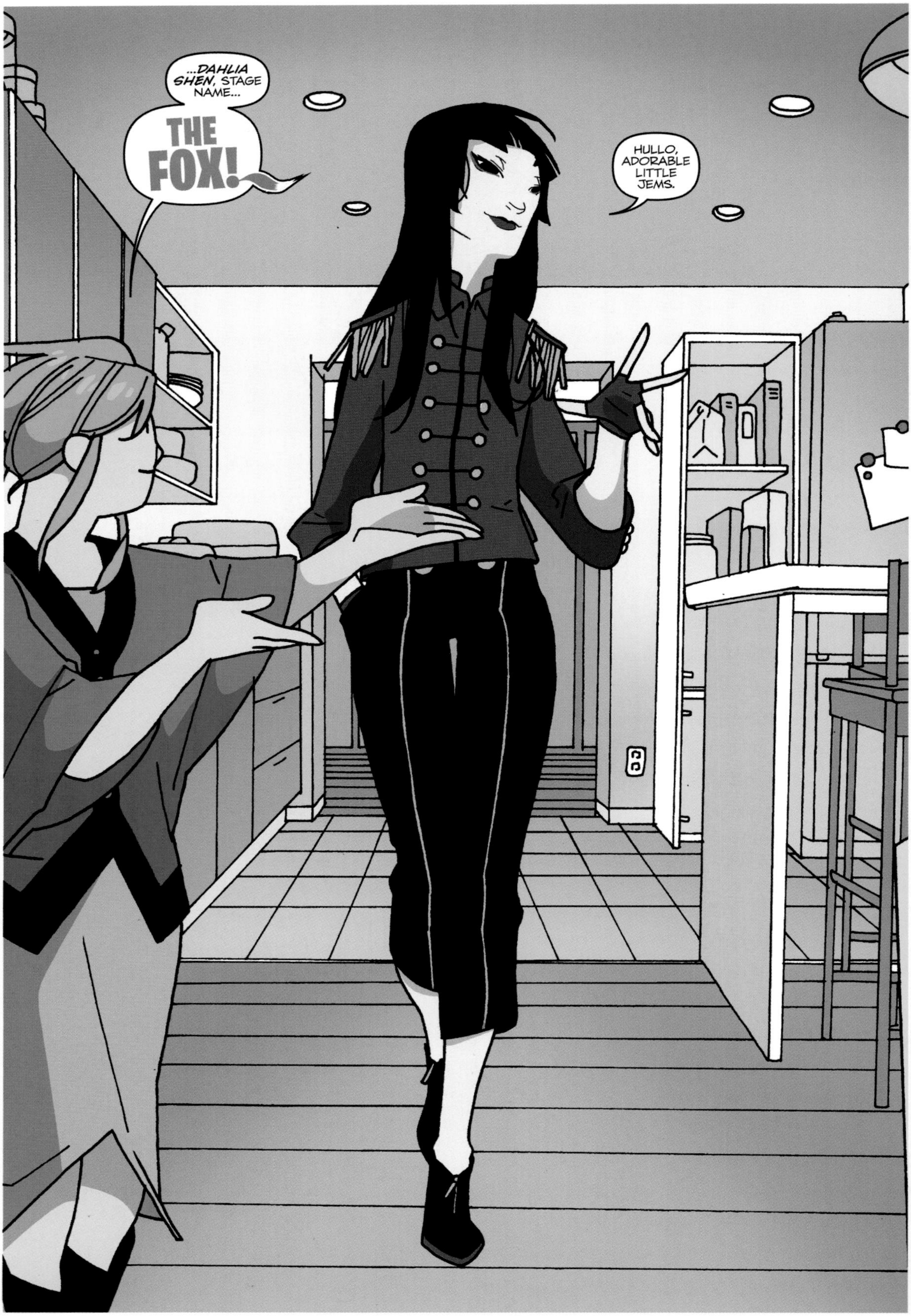
...DAHLIA SHEN, STAGE NAME...
THE FOX!
HULLO, ADORABLE LITTLE JEMS.

COVER ART BY **JEN BARTEL**

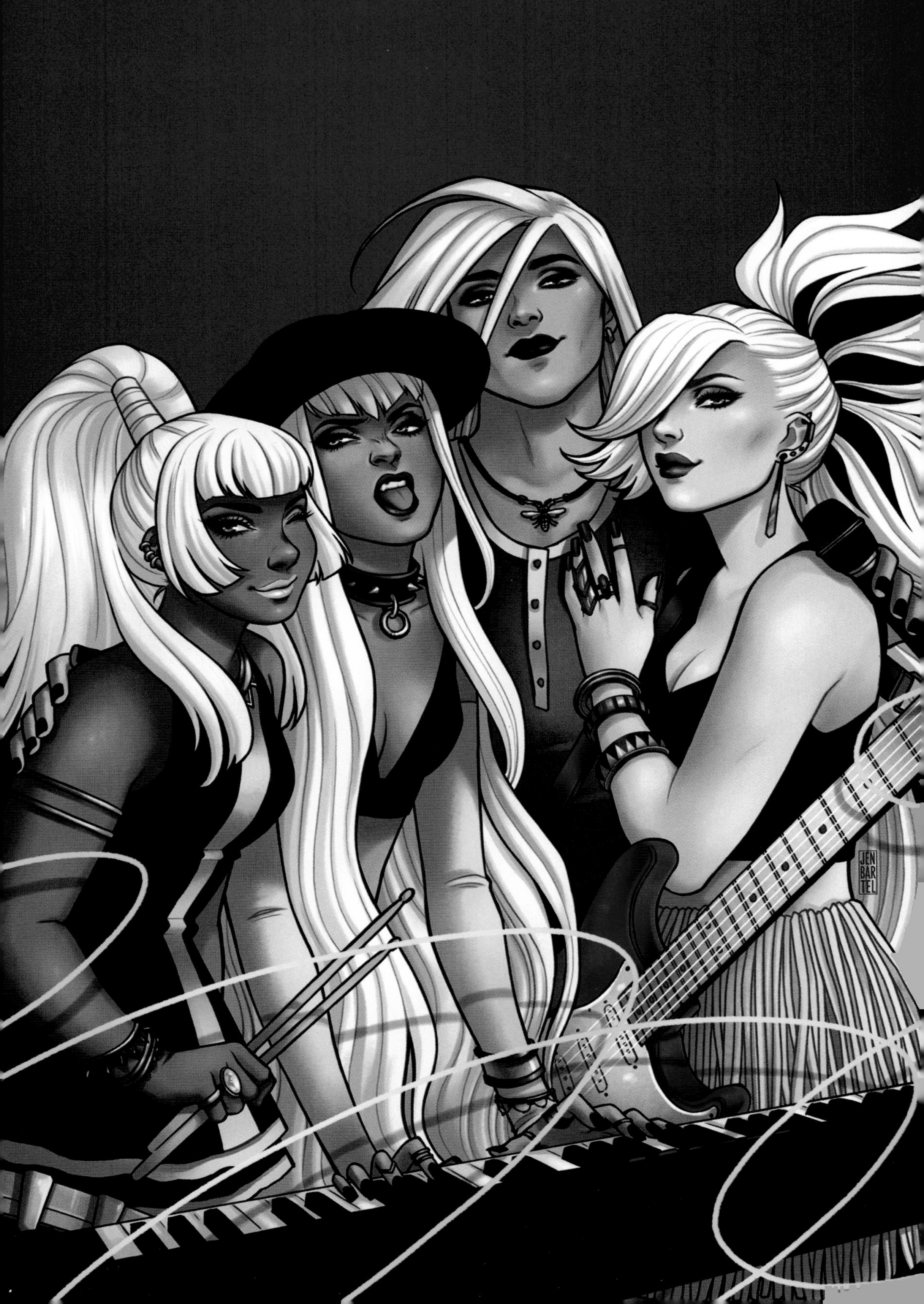

JEN BARTEL

ENTER THE STINGERS PART 3
COVER ART BY **MEREDITH MCCLAREN**

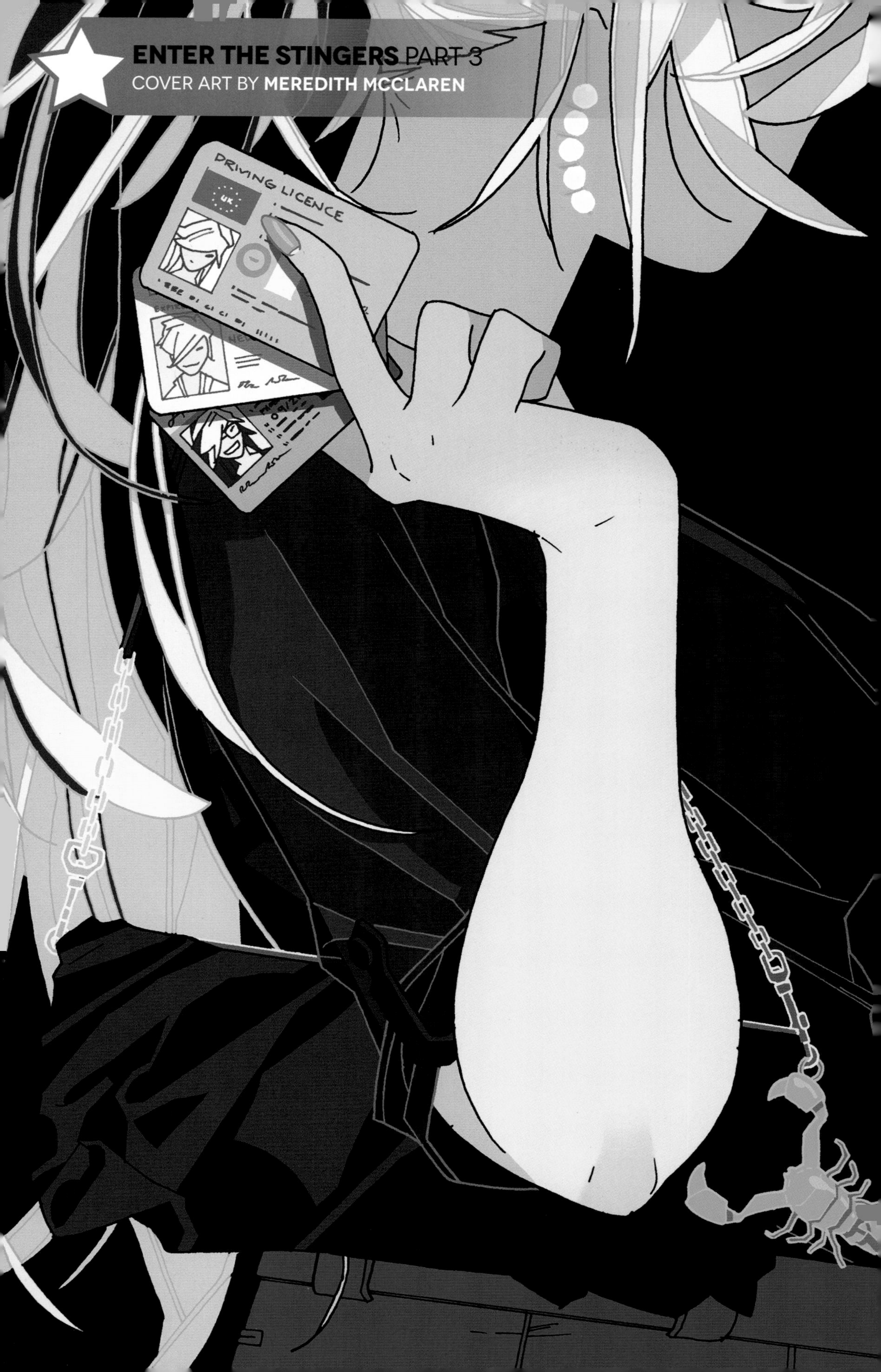
DRIVING LICENCE
UK

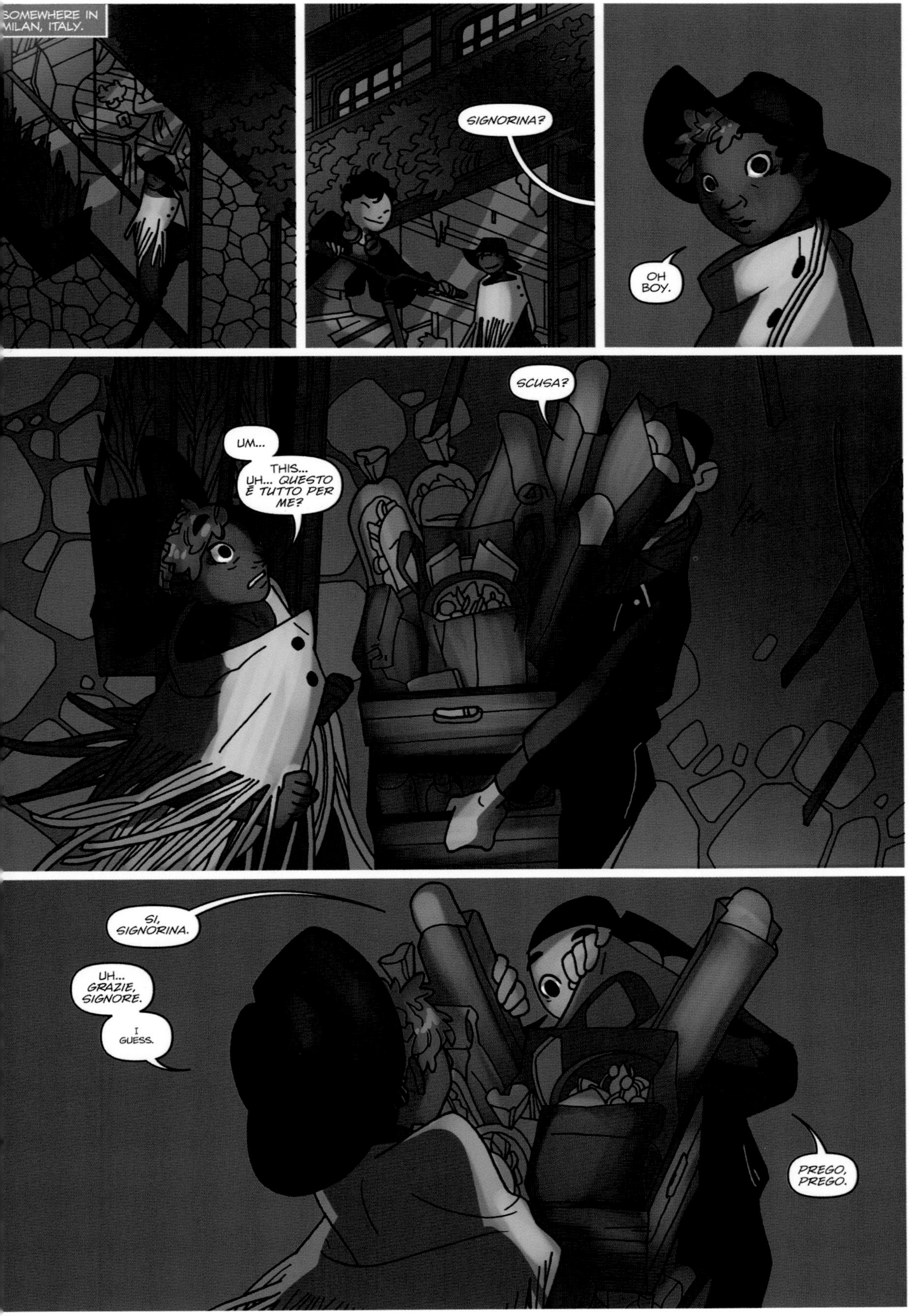
SOMEWHERE IN MILAN, ITALY.
SIGNORINA?
OH BOY.
SCUSA?
UM...
THIS... UH... QUESTO È TUTTO PER ME?
SI, SIGNORINA.
UH... GRAZIE, SIGNORE.
I GUESS.
PREGO, PREGO.

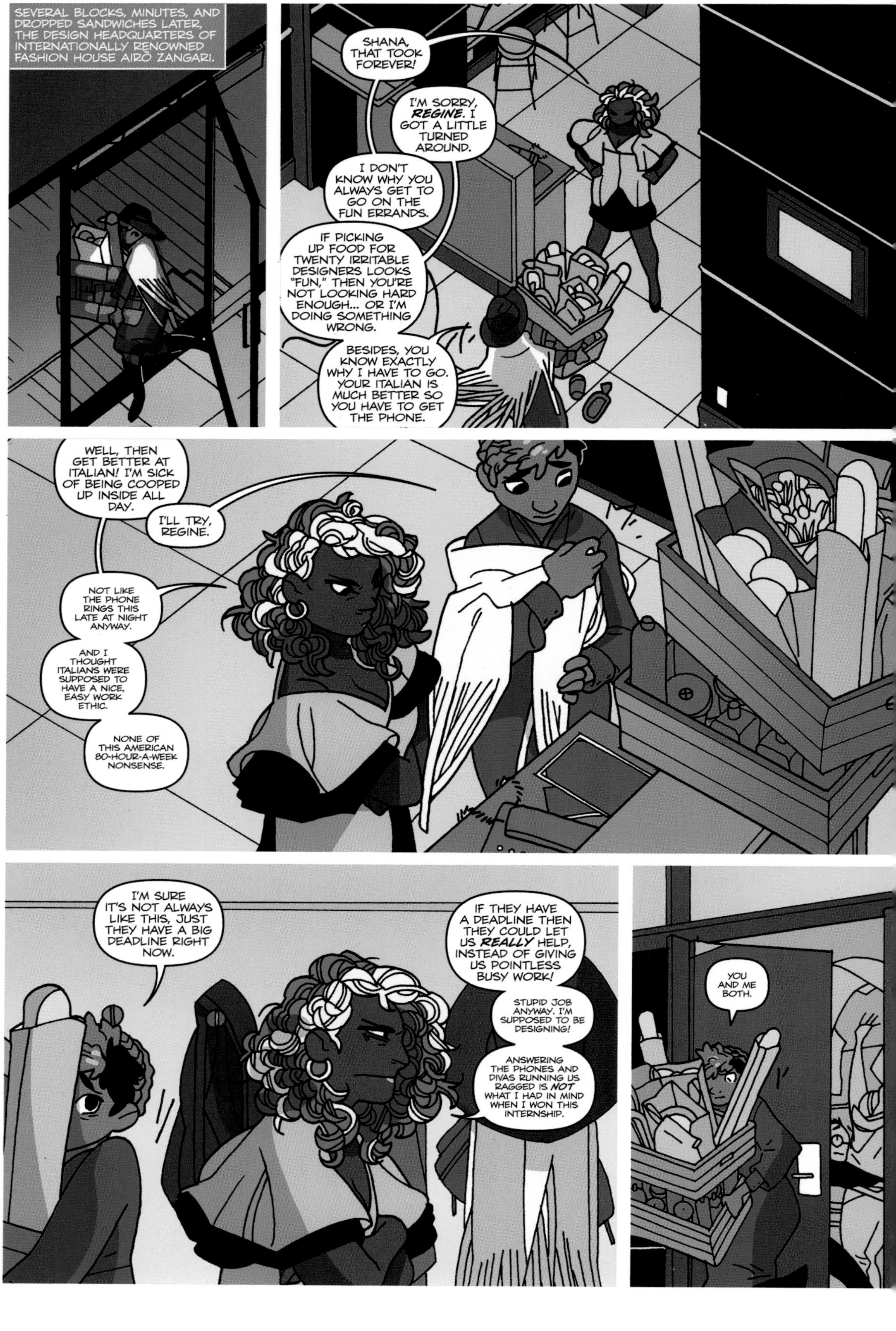
SEVERAL BLOCKS, MINUTES, AND DROPPED SANDWICHES LATER, THE DESIGN HEADQUARTERS OF INTERNATIONALLY RENOWNED FASHION HOUSE AIRÒ ZANGARI.
SHANA, THAT TOOK FOREVER!
I'M SORRY, REGINE. I GOT A LITTLE TURNED AROUND.
I DON'T KNOW WHY YOU ALWAYS GET TO GO ON THE FUN ERRANDS.
IF PICKING UP FOOD FOR TWENTY IRRITABLE DESIGNERS LOOKS "FUN," THEN YOU'RE NOT LOOKING HARD ENOUGH... OR I'M DOING SOMETHING WRONG.
BESIDES, YOU KNOW EXACTLY WHY I HAVE TO GO. YOUR ITALIAN IS MUCH BETTER SO YOU HAVE TO GET THE PHONE.
WELL, THEN GET BETTER AT ITALIAN! I'M SICK OF BEING COOPED UP INSIDE ALL DAY.
I'LL TRY, REGINE.
NOT LIKE THE PHONE RINGS THIS LATE AT NIGHT ANYWAY.
AND I THOUGHT ITALIANS WERE SUPPOSED TO HAVE A NICE, EASY WORK ETHIC.
NONE OF THIS AMERICAN 80-HOUR-A-WEEK NONSENSE.
I'M SURE IT'S NOT ALWAYS LIKE THIS, JUST THEY HAVE A BIG DEADLINE RIGHT NOW.
IF THEY HAVE A DEADLINE THEN THEY COULD LET US REALLY HELP, INSTEAD OF GIVING US POINTLESS BUSY WORK!
STUPID JOB ANYWAY. I'M SUPPOSED TO BE DESIGNING!
ANSWERING THE PHONES AND DIVAS RUNNING US RAGGED IS NOT WHAT I HAD IN MIND WHEN I WON THIS INTERNSHIP.
YOU AND ME BOTH.

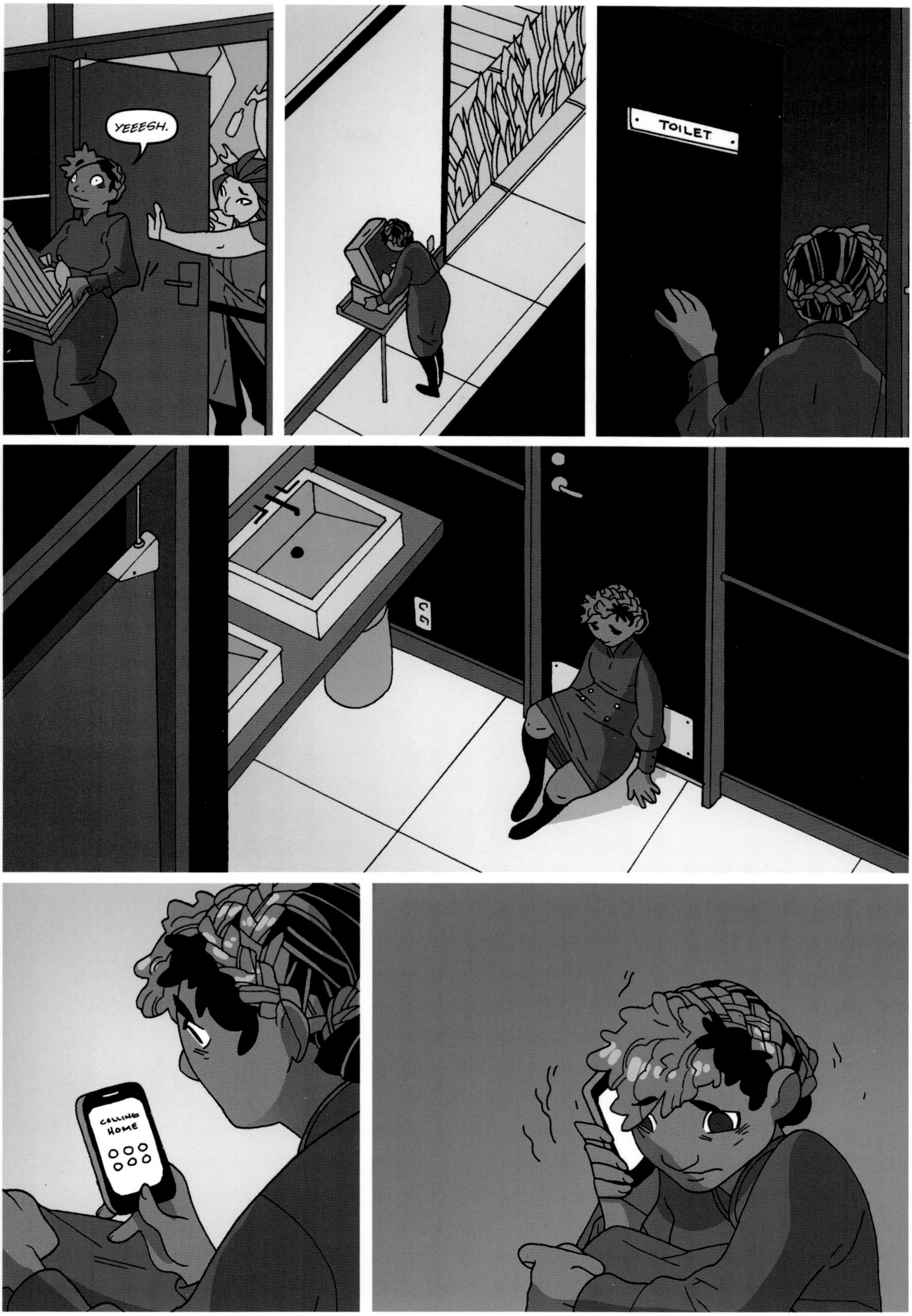
YEEESH.
TOILET
CALLING
HOME

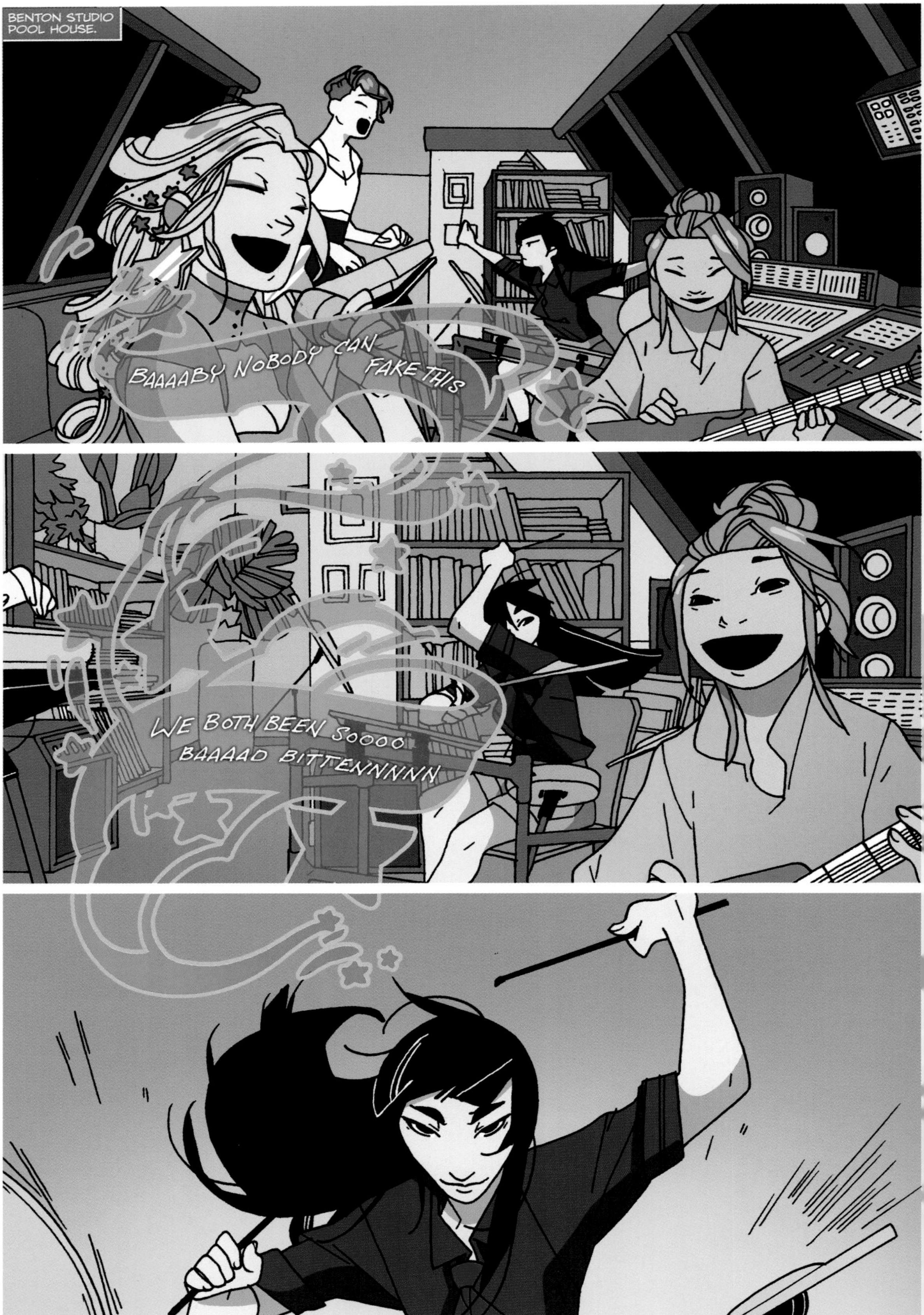
BENTON STUDIO POOL HOUSE.
BAAAABY NOBODY CAN FAKE THIS
WE BOTH BEEN SOOOO BAAAAD BITTENNNNN

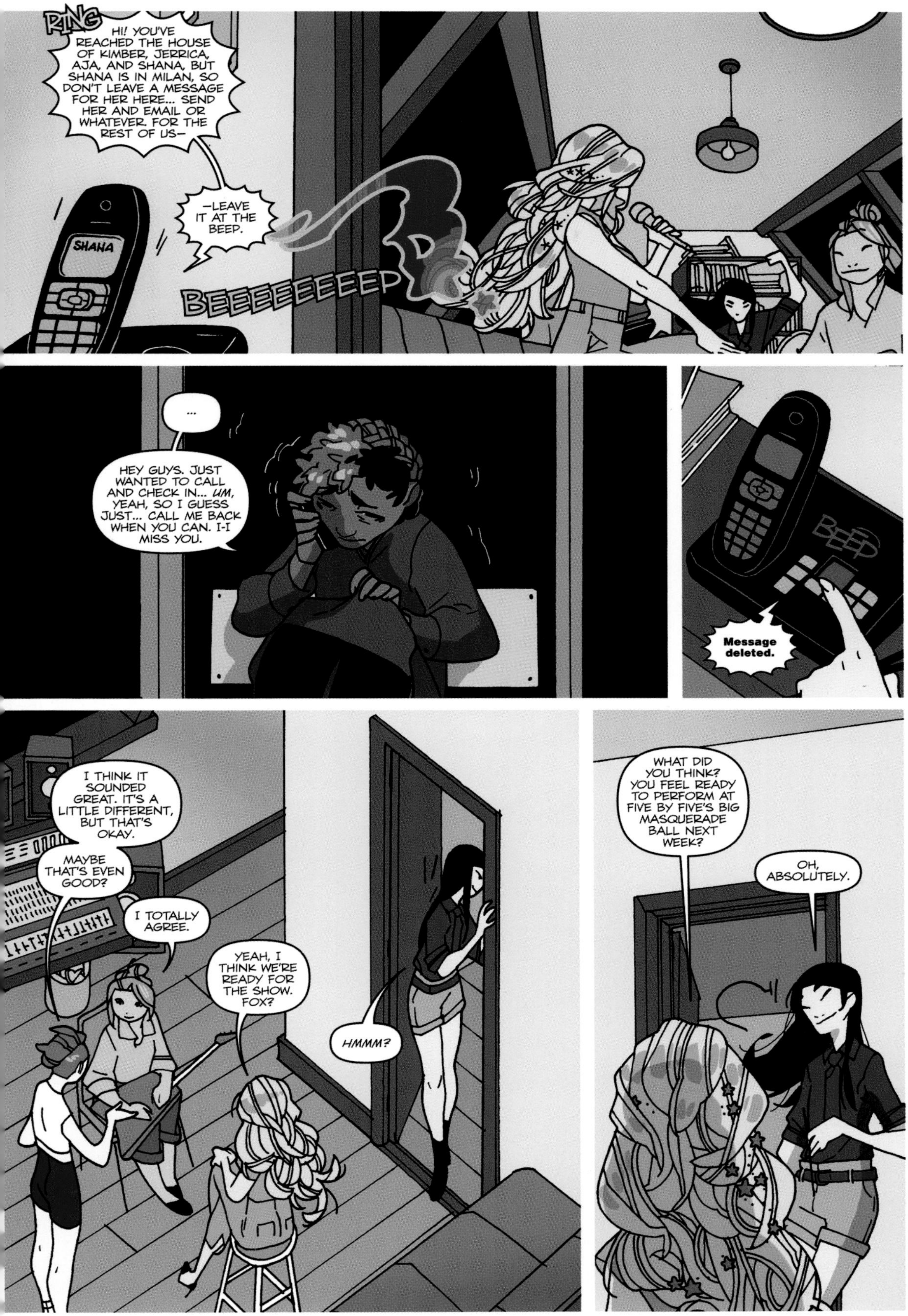
RING
HI! YOU'VE REACHED THE HOUSE OF KIMBER, JERRICA, AJA, AND SHANA, BUT SHANA IS IN MILAN, SO DON'T LEAVE A MESSAGE FOR HER HERE... SEND HER AND EMAIL OR WHATEVER. FOR THE REST OF US—
—LEAVE IT AT THE BEEP.
SHANA
BEEEEEEEEEP
...
HEY GUYS. JUST WANTED TO CALL AND CHECK IN... *UM*, YEAH, SO I GUESS JUST... CALL ME BACK WHEN YOU CAN. I-I MISS YOU.
BEEP
Message deleted.
I THINK IT SOUNDED GREAT. IT'S A LITTLE DIFFERENT, BUT THAT'S OKAY.
MAYBE THAT'S EVEN GOOD?
I TOTALLY AGREE.
YEAH, I THINK WE'RE READY FOR THE SHOW. FOX?
HMMM?
WHAT DID YOU THINK? YOU FEEL READY TO PERFORM AT FIVE BY FIVE'S BIG MASQUERADE BALL NEXT WEEK?
OH, ABSOLUTELY.

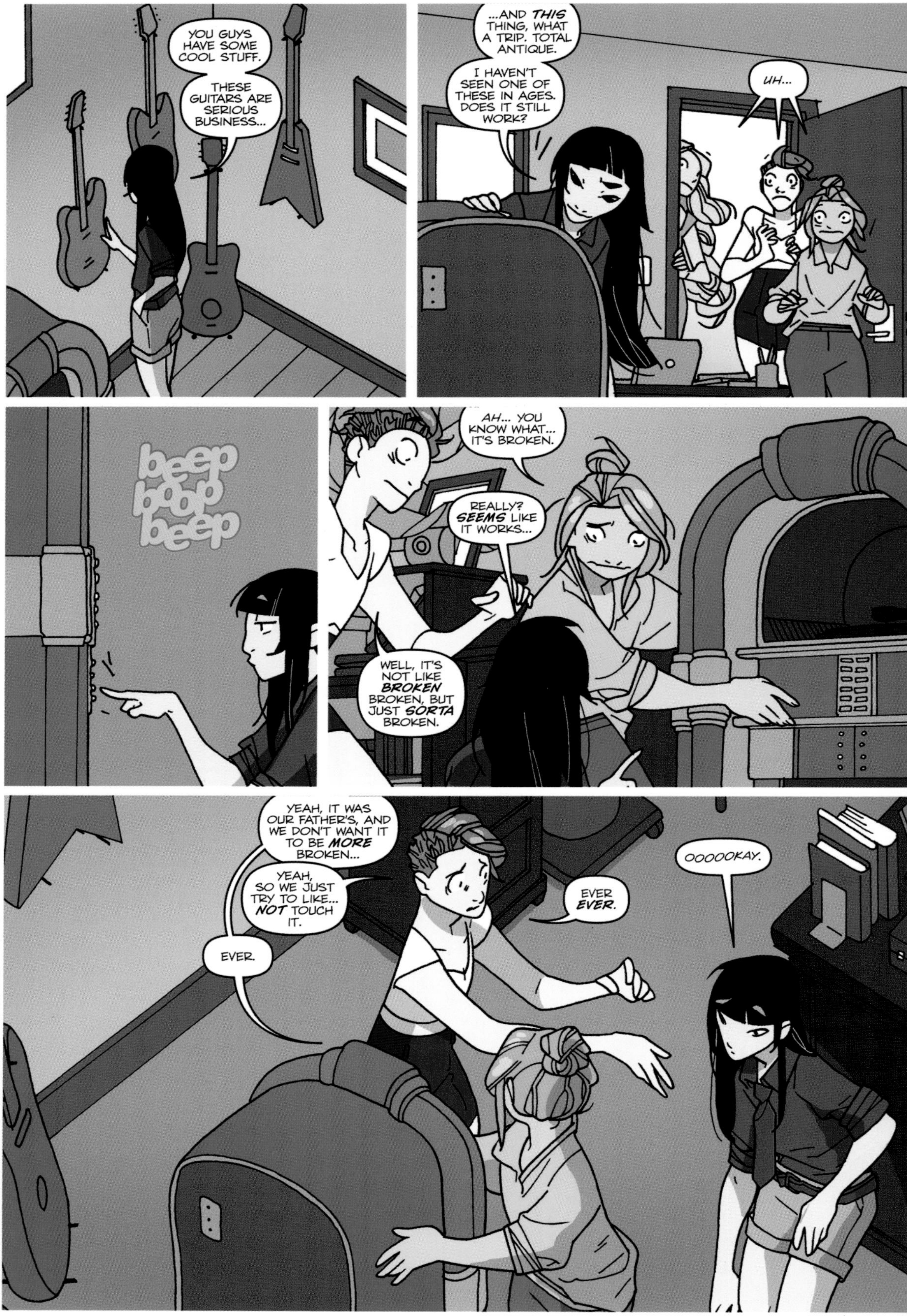
YOU GUYS HAVE SOME COOL STUFF.
THESE GUITARS ARE SERIOUS BUSINESS...
...AND THIS THING, WHAT A TRIP. TOTAL ANTIQUE.
I HAVEN'T SEEN ONE OF THESE IN AGES. DOES IT STILL WORK?
UH...
beep boop beep
AH... YOU KNOW WHAT... IT'S BROKEN.
REALLY? SEEMS LIKE IT WORKS...
WELL, IT'S NOT LIKE BROKEN BROKEN, BUT JUST SORTA BROKEN.
YEAH, IT WAS OUR FATHER'S, AND WE DON'T WANT IT TO BE MORE BROKEN...
YEAH, SO WE JUST TRY TO LIKE... NOT TOUCH IT.
EVER.
EVER EVER.
OOOOOKAY.

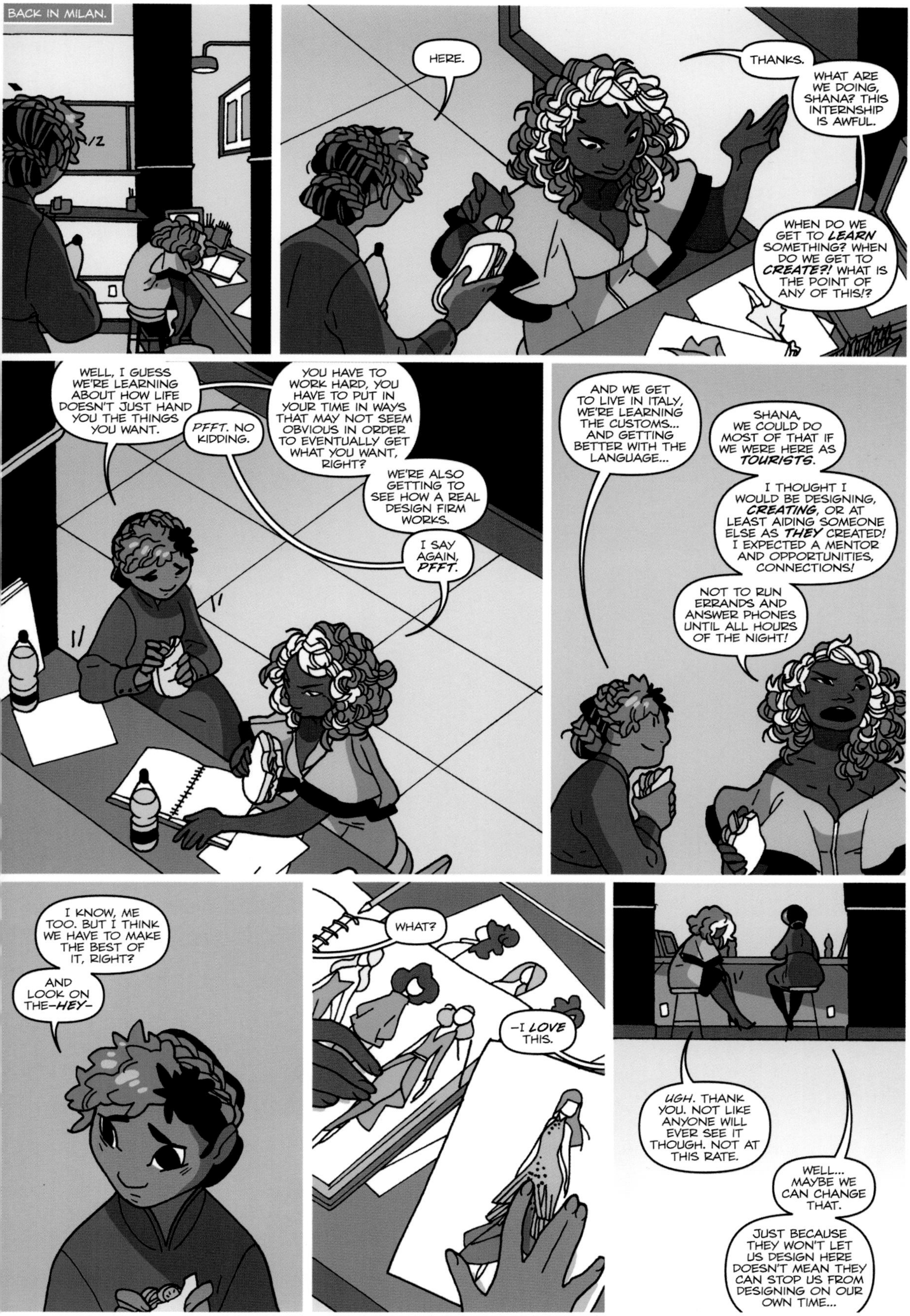
BACK IN MILAN.
/Z
HERE.
THANKS.
WHAT ARE WE DOING, SHANA? THIS INTERNSHIP IS AWFUL.
WHEN DO WE GET TO LEARN SOMETHING? WHEN DO WE GET TO CREATE?! WHAT IS THE POINT OF ANY OF THIS!?
WELL, I GUESS WE'RE LEARNING ABOUT HOW LIFE DOESN'T JUST HAND YOU THE THINGS YOU WANT.
PFFT. NO KIDDING.
YOU HAVE TO WORK HARD, YOU HAVE TO PUT IN YOUR TIME IN WAYS THAT MAY NOT SEEM OBVIOUS IN ORDER TO EVENTUALLY GET WHAT YOU WANT, RIGHT?
WE'RE ALSO GETTING TO SEE HOW A REAL DESIGN FIRM WORKS.
I SAY AGAIN, PFFT.
AND WE GET TO LIVE IN ITALY, WE'RE LEARNING THE CUSTOMS... AND GETTING BETTER WITH THE LANGUAGE...
SHANA, WE COULD DO MOST OF THAT IF WE WERE HERE AS TOURISTS.
I THOUGHT I WOULD BE DESIGNING, CREATING, OR AT LEAST AIDING SOMEONE ELSE AS THEY CREATED! I EXPECTED A MENTOR AND OPPORTUNITIES, CONNECTIONS!
NOT TO RUN ERRANDS AND ANSWER PHONES UNTIL ALL HOURS OF THE NIGHT!
I KNOW, ME TOO. BUT I THINK WE HAVE TO MAKE THE BEST OF IT, RIGHT?
AND LOOK ON THE–HEY–
WHAT?
–I LOVE THIS.
UGH. THANK YOU. NOT LIKE ANYONE WILL EVER SEE IT THOUGH. NOT AT THIS RATE.
WELL... MAYBE WE CAN CHANGE THAT.
JUST BECAUSE THEY WON'T LET US DESIGN HERE DOESN'T MEAN THEY CAN STOP US FROM DESIGNING ON OUR OWN TIME...

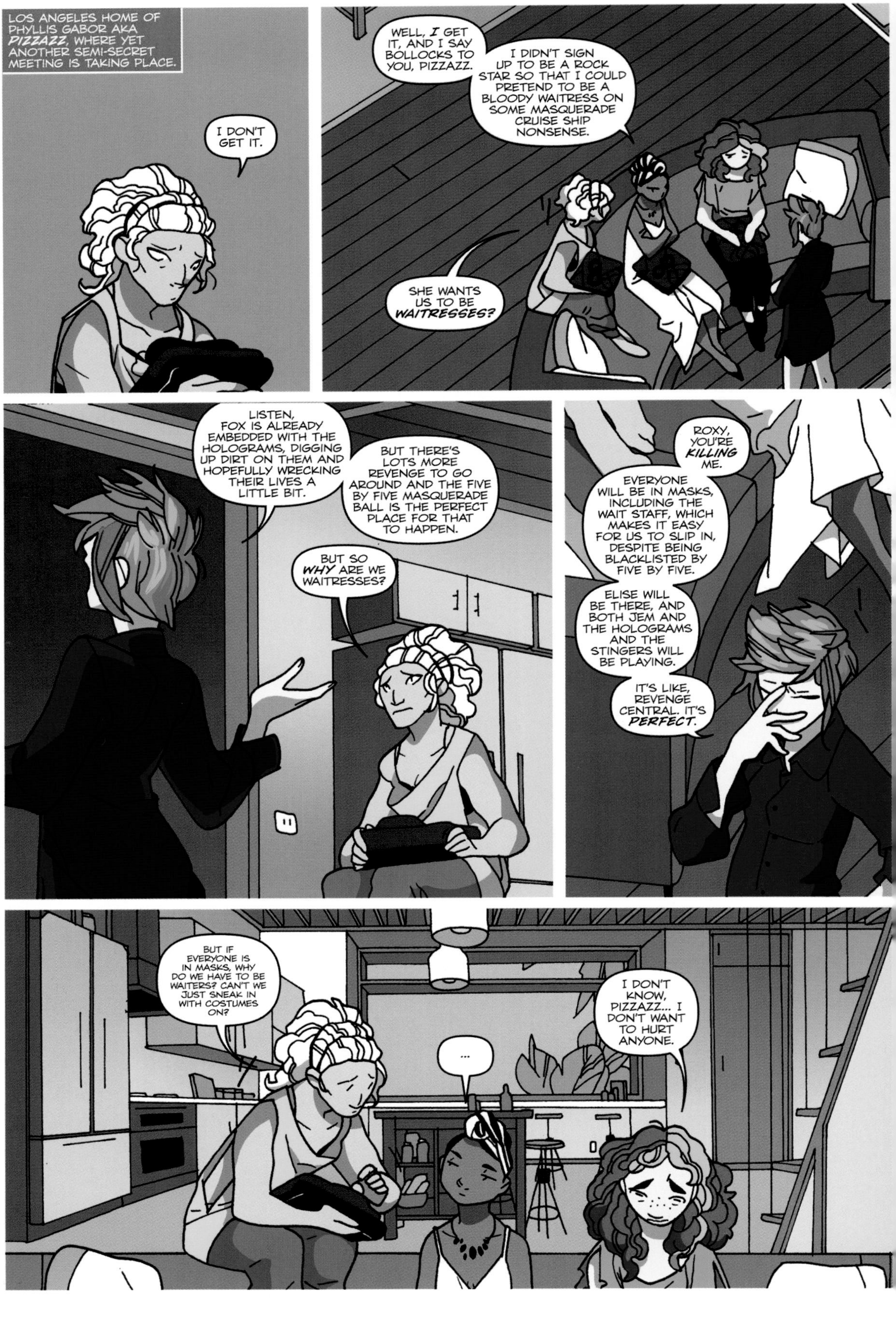
LOS ANGELES HOME OF PHYLLIS GABOR AKA *PIZZAZZ*, WHERE YET ANOTHER SEMI-SECRET MEETING IS TAKING PLACE.
I DON'T GET IT.
WELL, *I* GET IT, AND I SAY BOLLOCKS TO YOU, PIZZAZZ.
I DIDN'T SIGN UP TO BE A ROCK STAR SO THAT I COULD PRETEND TO BE A BLOODY WAITRESS ON SOME MASQUERADE CRUISE SHIP NONSENSE.
SHE WANTS US TO BE *WAITRESSES?*
LISTEN, FOX IS ALREADY EMBEDDED WITH THE HOLOGRAMS, DIGGING UP DIRT ON THEM AND HOPEFULLY WRECKING THEIR LIVES A LITTLE BIT.
BUT THERE'S LOTS MORE REVENGE TO GO AROUND AND THE FIVE BY FIVE MASQUERADE BALL IS THE PERFECT PLACE FOR THAT TO HAPPEN.
BUT SO *WHY* ARE WE WAITRESSES?
ROXY, YOU'RE *KILLING* ME.
EVERYONE WILL BE IN MASKS, INCLUDING THE WAIT STAFF, WHICH MAKES IT EASY FOR US TO SLIP IN, DESPITE BEING BLACKLISTED BY FIVE BY FIVE.
ELISE WILL BE THERE, AND BOTH JEM AND THE HOLOGRAMS AND THE STINGERS WILL BE PLAYING.
IT'S LIKE, REVENGE CENTRAL. IT'S *PERFECT*.
BUT IF EVERYONE IS IN MASKS, WHY DO WE HAVE TO BE WAITERS? CAN'T WE JUST SNEAK IN WITH COSTUMES ON?
...
I DON'T KNOW, PIZZAZZ... I DON'T WANT TO HURT ANYONE.

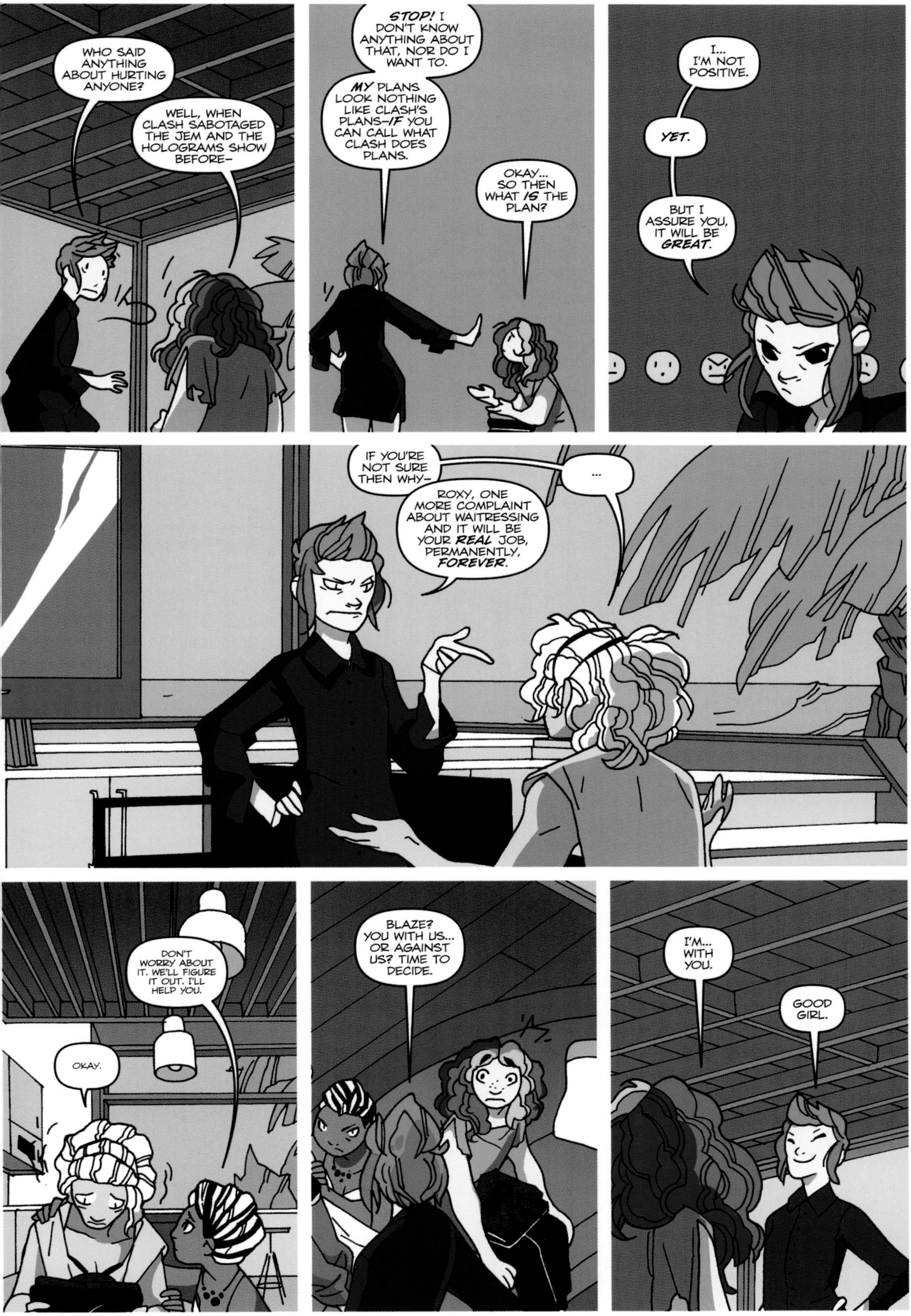
WHO SAID ANYTHING ABOUT HURTING ANYONE?
WELL, WHEN CLASH SABOTAGED THE JEM AND THE HOLOGRAMS SHOW BEFORE–
STOP! I DON'T KNOW ANYTHING ABOUT THAT, NOR DO I WANT TO.
MY PLANS LOOK NOTHING LIKE CLASH'S PLANS–IF YOU CAN CALL WHAT CLASH DOES PLANS.
OKAY... SO THEN WHAT IS THE PLAN?
I... I'M NOT POSITIVE.
YET.
BUT I ASSURE YOU, IT WILL BE GREAT.
IF YOU'RE NOT SURE THEN WHY–
ROXY, ONE MORE COMPLAINT ABOUT WAITRESSING AND IT WILL BE YOUR REAL JOB, PERMANENTLY, FOREVER.
...
DON'T WORRY ABOUT IT. WE'LL FIGURE IT OUT. I'LL HELP YOU.
OKAY.
BLAZE? YOU WITH US... OR AGAINST US? TIME TO DECIDE.
I'M... WITH YOU.
GOOD GIRL.

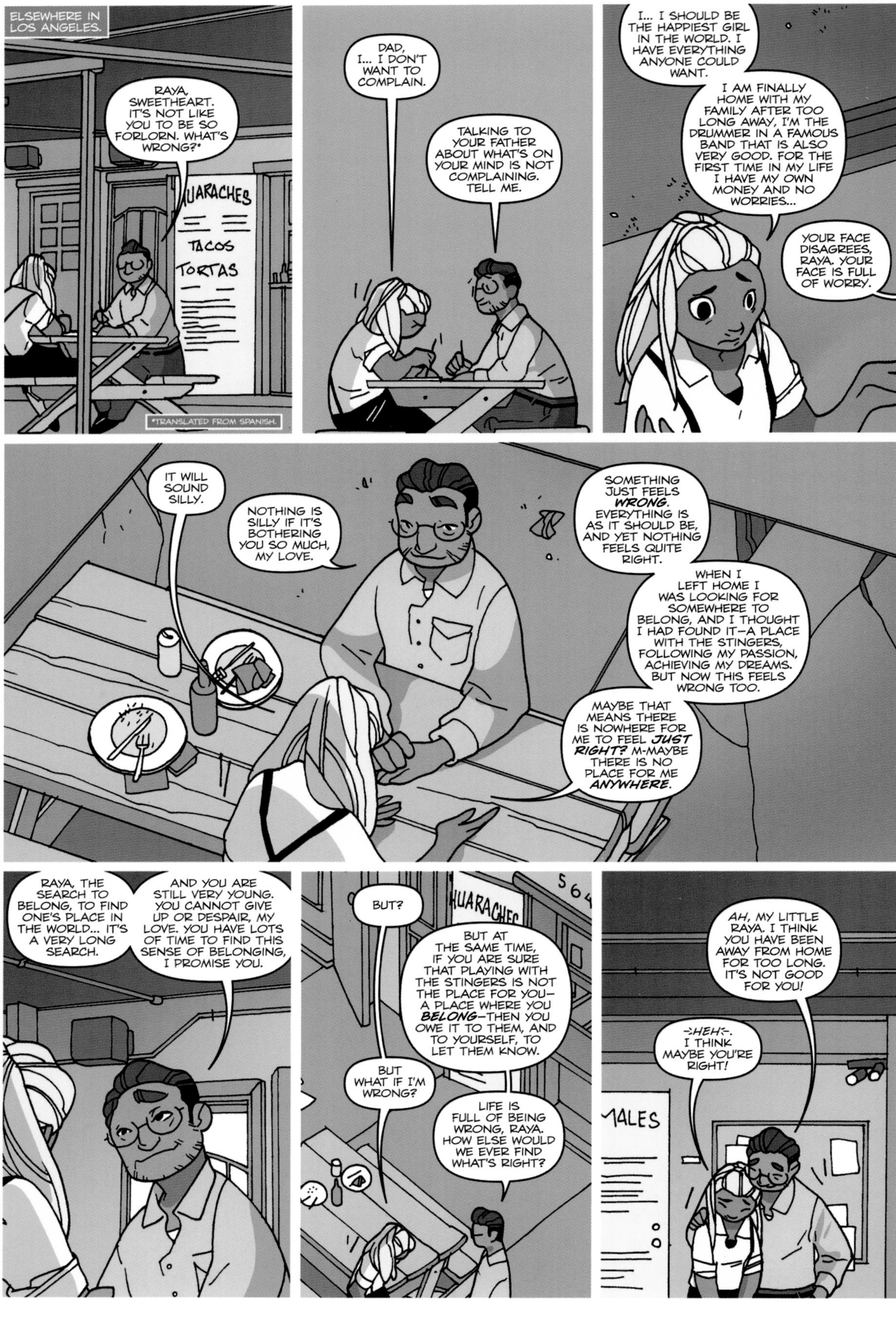
ELSEWHERE IN LOS ANGELES.
RAYA, SWEETHEART. IT'S NOT LIKE YOU TO BE SO FORLORN. WHAT'S WRONG?*
HUARACHES
TACOS
TORTAS
*TRANSLATED FROM SPANISH.
DAD, I... I DON'T WANT TO COMPLAIN.
TALKING TO YOUR FATHER ABOUT WHAT'S ON YOUR MIND IS NOT COMPLAINING. TELL ME.
I... I SHOULD BE THE HAPPIEST GIRL IN THE WORLD. I HAVE EVERYTHING ANYONE COULD WANT.
I AM FINALLY HOME WITH MY FAMILY AFTER TOO LONG AWAY, I'M THE DRUMMER IN A FAMOUS BAND THAT IS ALSO VERY GOOD. FOR THE FIRST TIME IN MY LIFE I HAVE MY OWN MONEY AND NO WORRIES...
YOUR FACE DISAGREES, RAYA. YOUR FACE IS FULL OF WORRY.
IT WILL SOUND SILLY.
NOTHING IS SILLY IF IT'S BOTHERING YOU SO MUCH, MY LOVE.
SOMETHING JUST FEELS ***WRONG***. EVERYTHING IS AS IT SHOULD BE, AND YET NOTHING FEELS QUITE RIGHT.
WHEN I LEFT HOME I WAS LOOKING FOR SOMEWHERE TO BELONG, AND I THOUGHT I HAD FOUND IT—A PLACE WITH THE STINGERS, FOLLOWING MY PASSION, ACHIEVING MY DREAMS. BUT NOW THIS FEELS WRONG TOO.
MAYBE THAT MEANS THERE IS NOWHERE FOR ME TO FEEL ***JUST RIGHT?*** M-MAYBE THERE IS NO PLACE FOR ME ***ANYWHERE***.
RAYA, THE SEARCH TO BELONG, TO FIND ONE'S PLACE IN THE WORLD... IT'S A VERY LONG SEARCH.
AND YOU ARE STILL VERY YOUNG. YOU CANNOT GIVE UP OR DESPAIR, MY LOVE. YOU HAVE LOTS OF TIME TO FIND THIS SENSE OF BELONGING, I PROMISE YOU.
BUT?
HUARACHES
564
BUT AT THE SAME TIME, IF YOU ARE SURE THAT PLAYING WITH THE STINGERS IS NOT THE PLACE FOR YOU—A PLACE WHERE YOU ***BELONG***—THEN YOU OWE IT TO THEM, AND TO YOURSELF, TO LET THEM KNOW.
BUT WHAT IF I'M WRONG?
LIFE IS FULL OF BEING WRONG, RAYA. HOW ELSE WOULD WE EVER FIND WHAT'S RIGHT?
AH, MY LITTLE RAYA. I THINK YOU HAVE BEEN AWAY FROM HOME FOR TOO LONG. IT'S NOT GOOD FOR YOU!
-HEH-. I THINK MAYBE YOU'RE RIGHT!
MALES

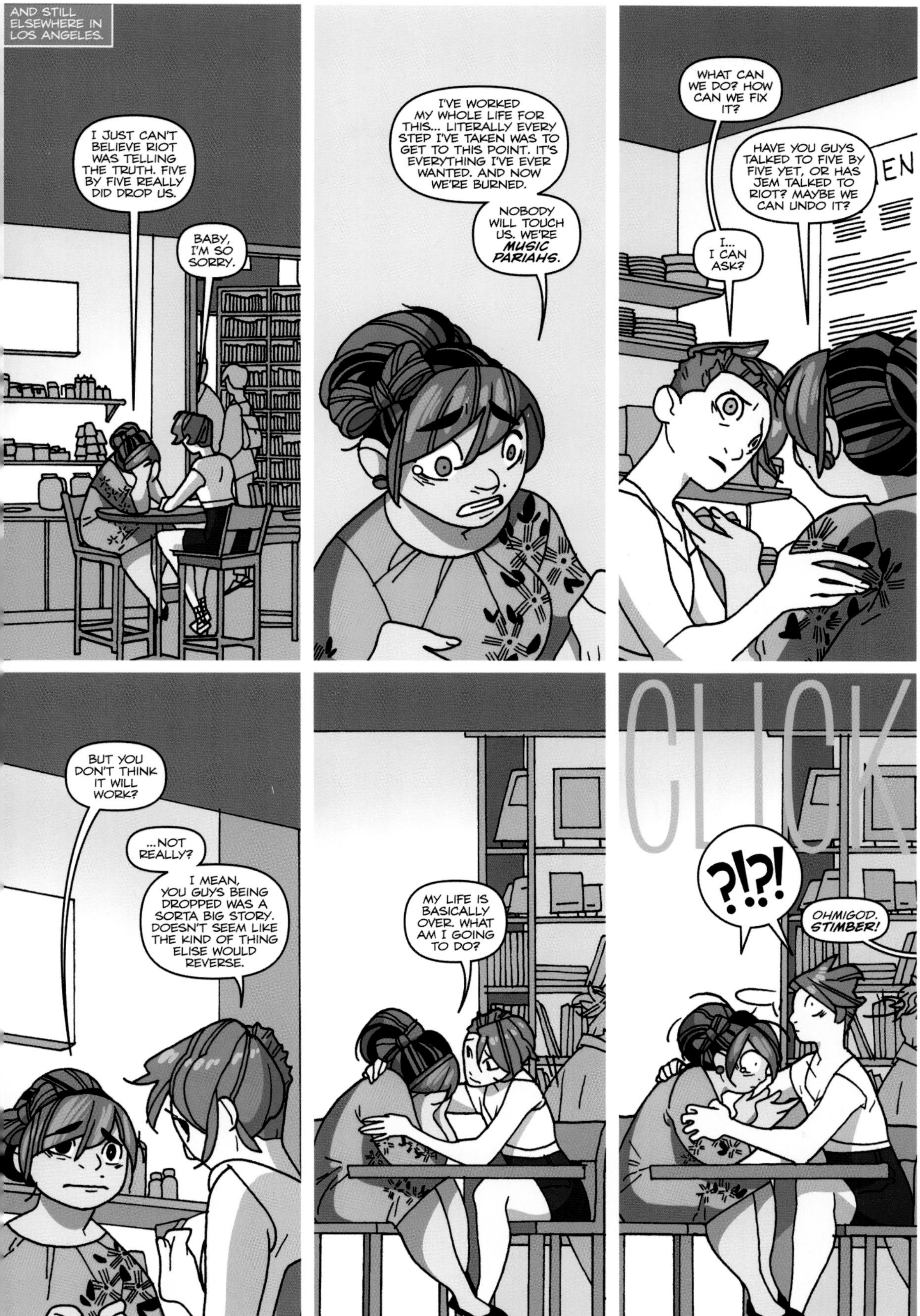
AND STILL ELSEWHERE IN LOS ANGELES.
I JUST CAN'T BELIEVE RIOT WAS TELLING THE TRUTH. FIVE BY FIVE REALLY DID DROP US.
BABY, I'M SO SORRY.
I'VE WORKED MY WHOLE LIFE FOR THIS... LITERALLY EVERY STEP I'VE TAKEN WAS TO GET TO THIS POINT. IT'S EVERYTHING I'VE EVER WANTED. AND NOW WE'RE BURNED.
NOBODY WILL TOUCH US. WE'RE ***MUSIC PARIAHS***.
WHAT CAN WE DO? HOW CAN WE FIX IT?
HAVE YOU GUYS TALKED TO FIVE BY FIVE YET, OR HAS JEM TALKED TO RIOT? MAYBE WE CAN UNDO IT?
I... I CAN ASK?
BUT YOU DON'T THINK IT WILL WORK?
...NOT REALLY?
I MEAN, YOU GUYS BEING DROPPED WAS A SORTA BIG STORY. DOESN'T SEEM LIKE THE KIND OF THING ELISE WOULD REVERSE.
MY LIFE IS BASICALLY OVER. WHAT AM I GOING TO DO?
CLICK
?!?!
OHMIGOD. ***STIMBER!***

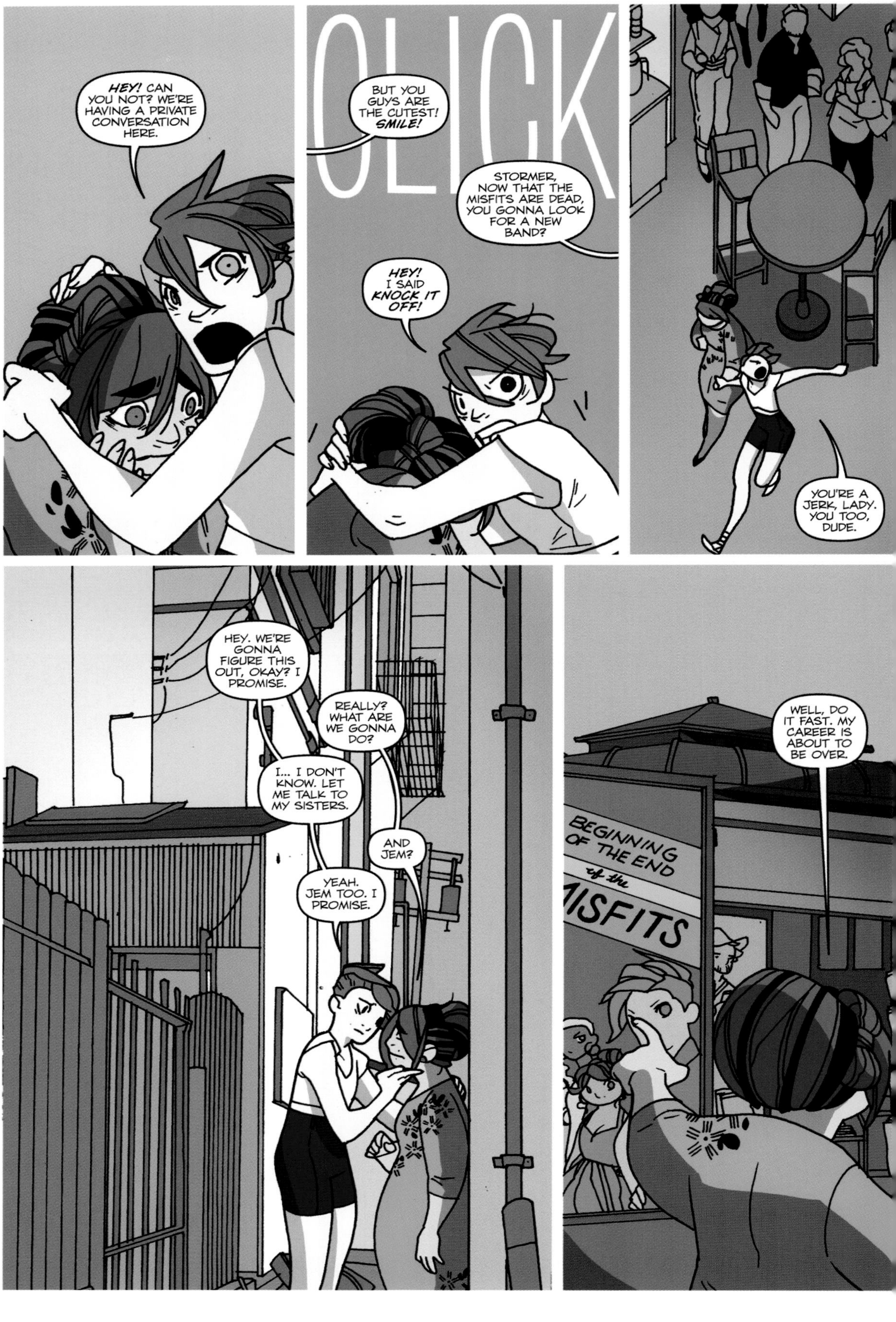
HEY! CAN YOU NOT? WE'RE HAVING A PRIVATE CONVERSATION HERE.
CLICK
BUT YOU GUYS ARE THE CUTEST! SMILE!
STORMER, NOW THAT THE MISFITS ARE DEAD, YOU GONNA LOOK FOR A NEW BAND?
HEY! I SAID KNOCK IT OFF!
YOU'RE A JERK, LADY. YOU TOO, DUDE.
HEY. WE'RE GONNA FIGURE THIS OUT, OKAY? I PROMISE.
REALLY? WHAT ARE WE GONNA DO?
I... I DON'T KNOW. LET ME TALK TO MY SISTERS.
AND JEM?
YEAH. JEM TOO. I PROMISE.
WELL, DO IT FAST. MY CAREER IS ABOUT TO BE OVER.
BEGINNING OF THE END of the MISFITS

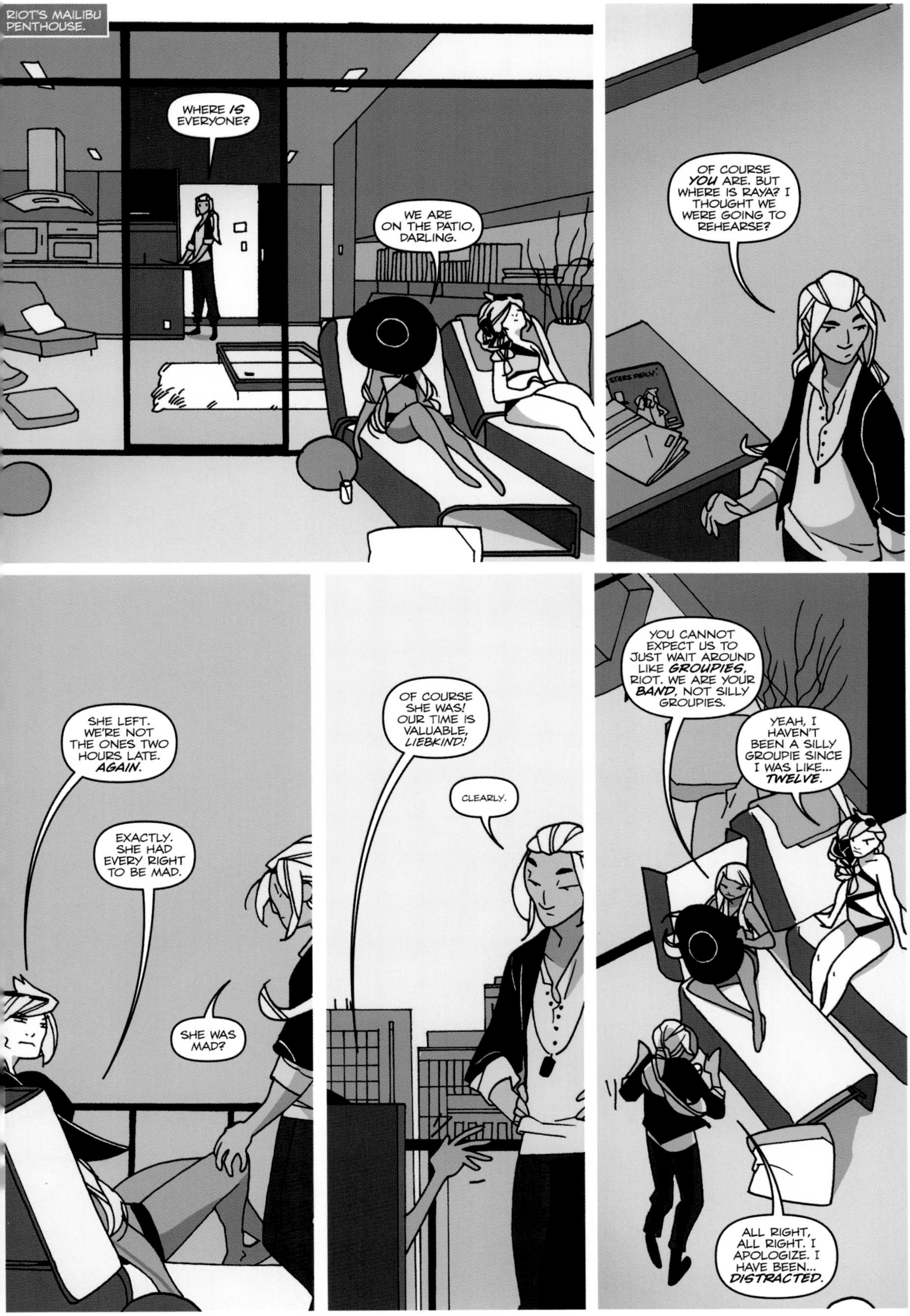
RIOT'S MAILIBU PENTHOUSE.
WHERE *IS* EVERYONE?
WE ARE ON THE PATIO, DARLING.
OF COURSE *YOU* ARE. BUT WHERE IS RAYA? I THOUGHT WE WERE GOING TO REHEARSE?
SHE LEFT. WE'RE NOT THE ONES TWO HOURS LATE. ***AGAIN***.
EXACTLY. SHE HAD EVERY RIGHT TO BE MAD.
SHE WAS MAD?
OF COURSE SHE WAS! OUR TIME IS VALUABLE, *LIEBKIND!*
CLEARLY.
YOU CANNOT EXPECT US TO JUST WAIT AROUND LIKE ***GROUPIES***, RIOT. WE ARE YOUR ***BAND***, NOT SILLY GROUPIES.
YEAH, I HAVEN'T BEEN A SILLY GROUPIE SINCE I WAS LIKE... ***TWELVE***.
ALL RIGHT, ALL RIGHT. I APOLOGIZE. I HAVE BEEN... ***DISTRACTED***.

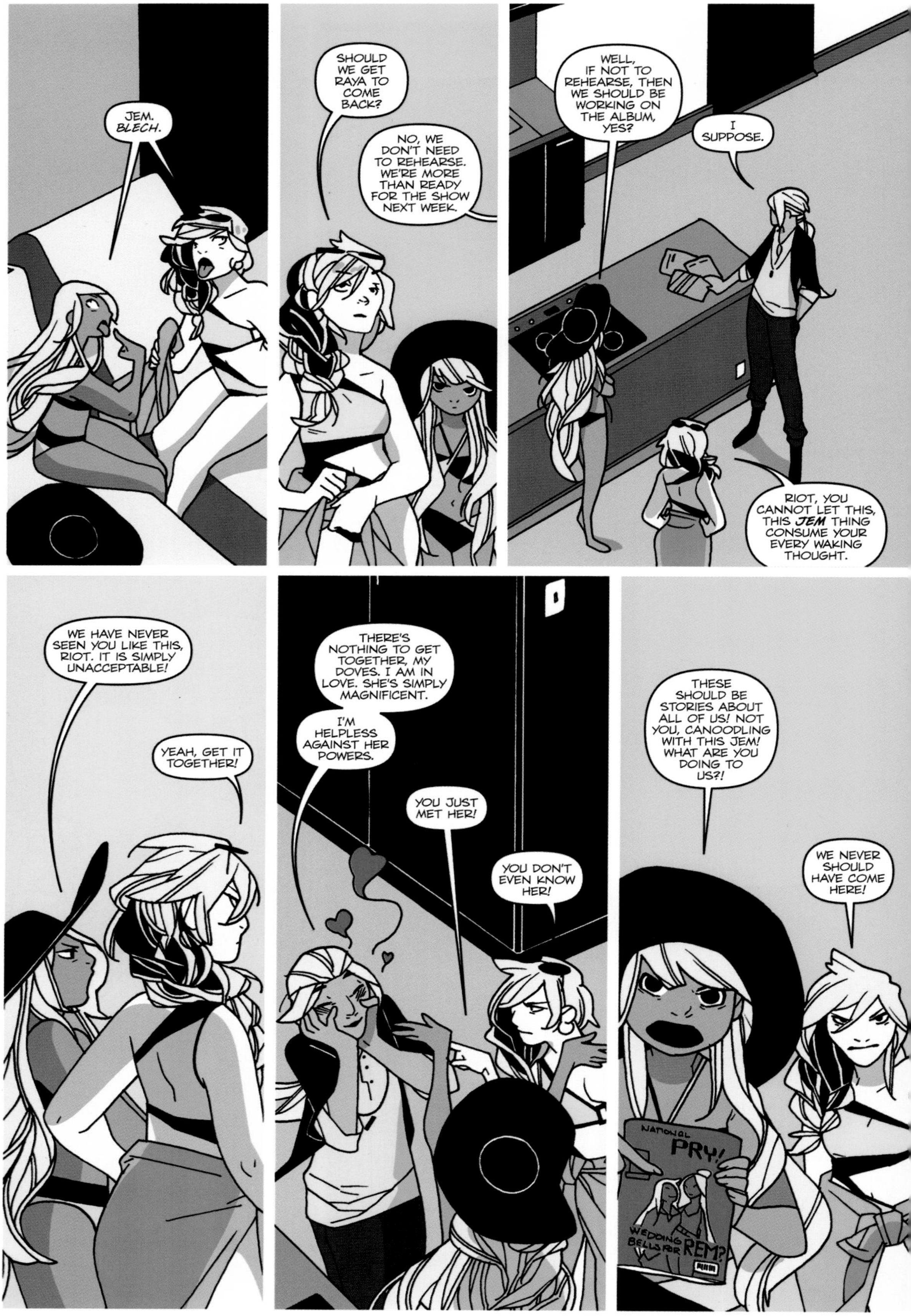
JEM. BLECH.
SHOULD WE GET RAYA TO COME BACK?
NO, WE DON'T NEED TO REHEARSE. WE'RE MORE THAN READY FOR THE SHOW NEXT WEEK.
WELL, IF NOT TO REHEARSE, THEN WE SHOULD BE WORKING ON THE ALBUM, YES?
I SUPPOSE.
RIOT, YOU CANNOT LET THIS, THIS JEM THING CONSUME YOUR EVERY WAKING THOUGHT.
WE HAVE NEVER SEEN YOU LIKE THIS, RIOT. IT IS SIMPLY UNACCEPTABLE!
YEAH, GET IT TOGETHER!
THERE'S NOTHING TO GET TOGETHER, MY DOVES. I AM IN LOVE. SHE'S SIMPLY MAGNIFICENT.
I'M HELPLESS AGAINST HER POWERS.
YOU JUST MET HER!
YOU DON'T EVEN KNOW HER!
THESE SHOULD BE STORIES ABOUT ALL OF US! NOT YOU, CANOODLING WITH THIS JEM! WHAT ARE YOU DOING TO US?!
WE NEVER SHOULD HAVE COME HERE!
NATIONAL PRY!
WEDDING BELLS FOR REM?

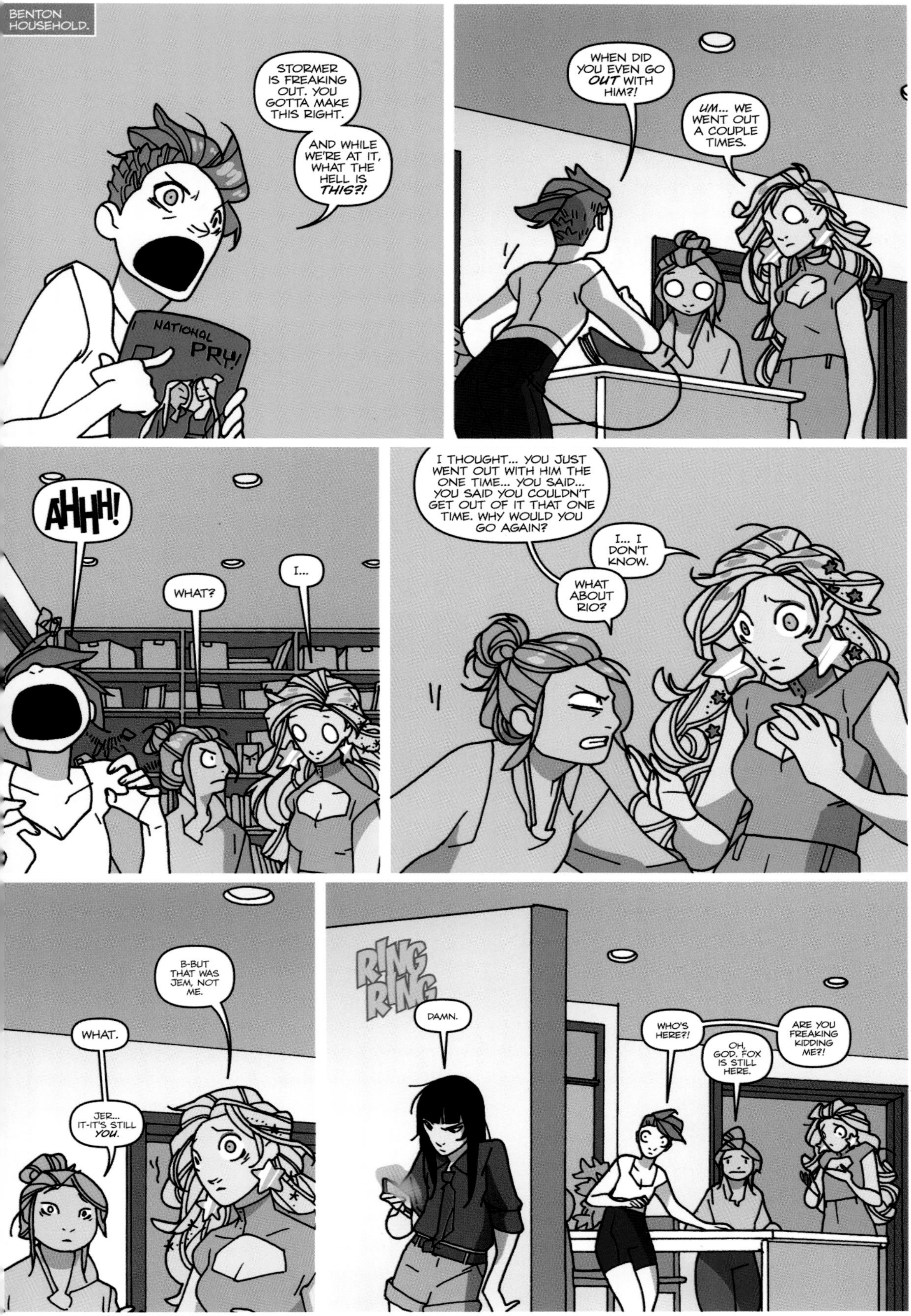

BENTON HOUSEHOLD.
STORMER IS FREAKING OUT. YOU GOTTA MAKE THIS RIGHT.
AND WHILE WE'RE AT IT, WHAT THE HELL IS *THIS?!*
NATIONAL PRY!
WHEN DID YOU EVEN GO *OUT* WITH HIM?!
UM... WE WENT OUT A COUPLE TIMES.
AHHH!
WHAT?
I...
I THOUGHT... YOU JUST WENT OUT WITH HIM THE ONE TIME... YOU SAID... YOU SAID YOU COULDN'T GET OUT OF IT THAT ONE TIME. WHY WOULD YOU GO AGAIN?
I... I DON'T KNOW.
WHAT ABOUT RIO?
B-BUT THAT WAS JEM, NOT ME.
WHAT.
JER... IT-IT'S STILL *YOU*.
RING RING
DAMN.
WHO'S HERE?!
ARE YOU FREAKING KIDDING ME?!
OH, GOD. FOX IS STILL HERE.

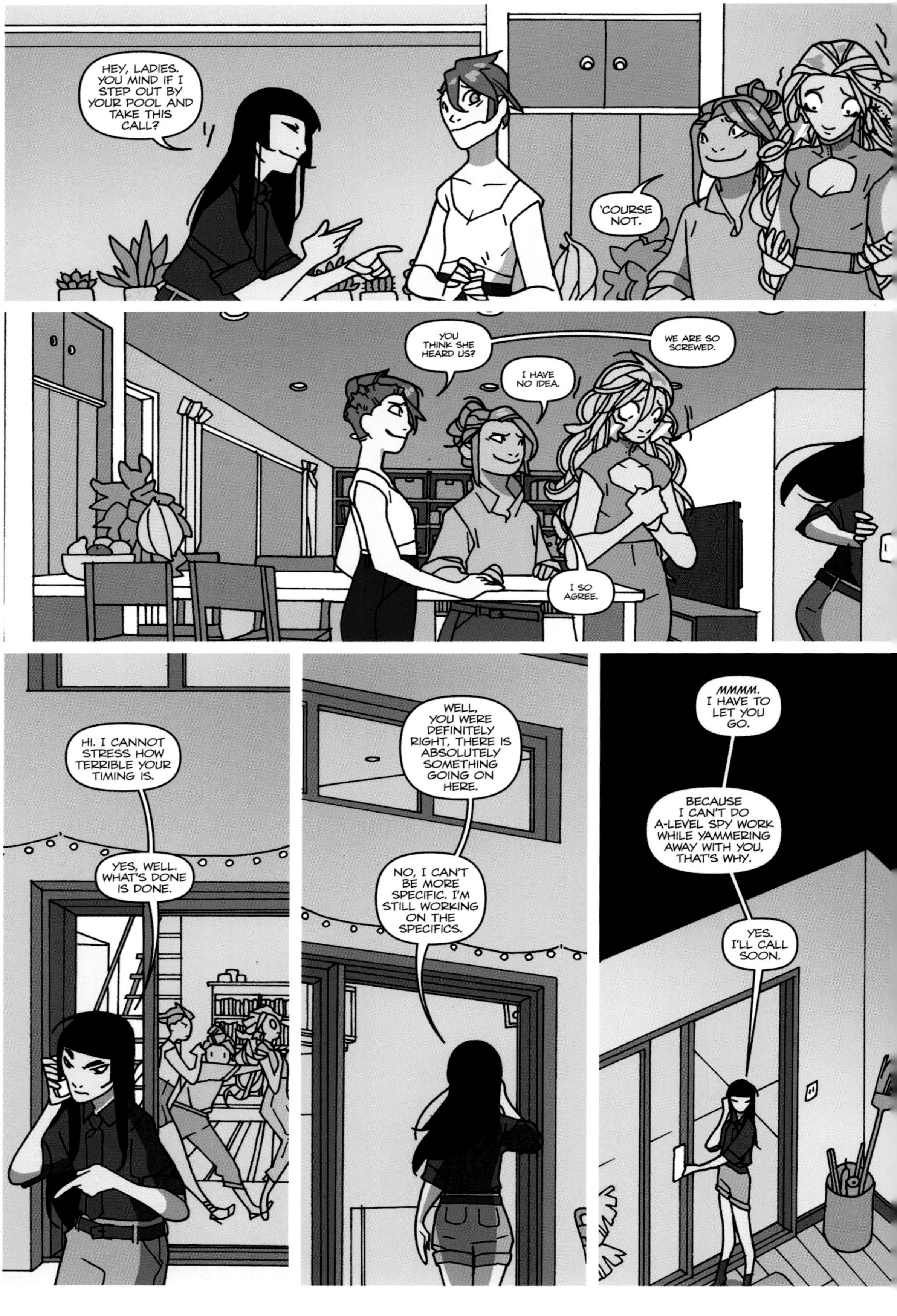
HEY, LADIES. YOU MIND IF I STEP OUT BY YOUR POOL AND TAKE THIS CALL?
'COURSE NOT.
YOU THINK SHE HEARD US?
I HAVE NO IDEA.
WE ARE SO SCREWED.
I SO AGREE.
HI. I CANNOT STRESS HOW TERRIBLE YOUR TIMING IS.
YES, WELL. WHAT'S DONE IS DONE.
WELL, YOU WERE DEFINITELY RIGHT, THERE IS ABSOLUTELY SOMETHING GOING ON HERE.
NO, I CAN'T BE MORE SPECIFIC. I'M STILL WORKING ON THE SPECIFICS.
MMMM. I HAVE TO LET YOU GO.
BECAUSE I CAN'T DO A-LEVEL SPY WORK WHILE YAMMERING AWAY WITH YOU, THAT'S WHY.
YES. I'LL CALL SOON.

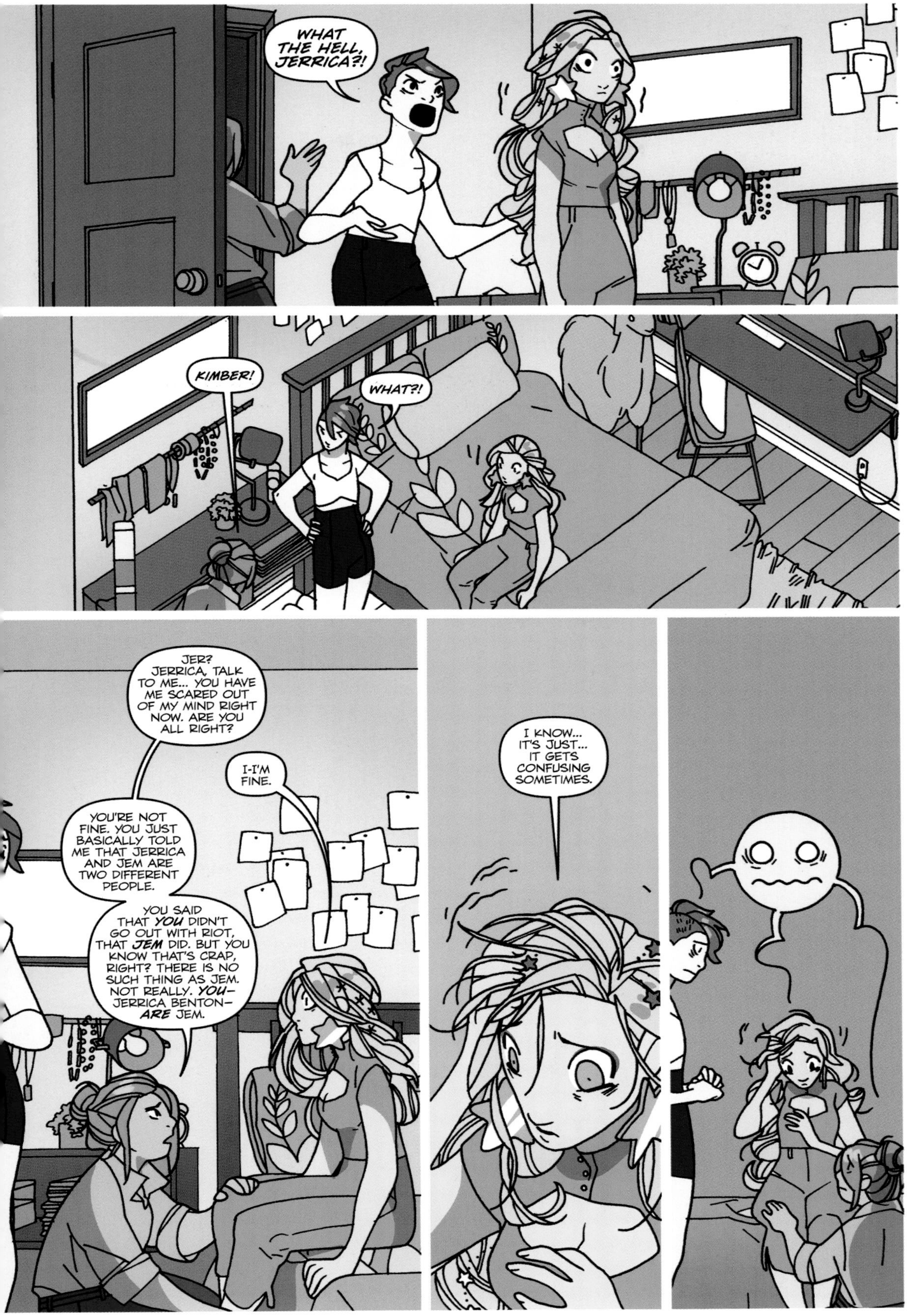
WHAT THE HELL, JERRICA?!
KIMBER!
WHAT?!
JER? JERRICA, TALK TO ME... YOU HAVE ME SCARED OUT OF MY MIND RIGHT NOW. ARE YOU ALL RIGHT?
I-I'M FINE.
YOU'RE NOT FINE. YOU JUST BASICALLY TOLD ME THAT JERRICA AND JEM ARE TWO DIFFERENT PEOPLE.
YOU SAID THAT YOU DIDN'T GO OUT WITH RIOT, THAT JEM DID. BUT YOU KNOW THAT'S CRAP, RIGHT? THERE IS NO SUCH THING AS JEM. NOT REALLY. YOU— JERRICA BENTON— ARE JEM.
I KNOW... IT'S JUST... IT GETS CONFUSING SOMETIMES.

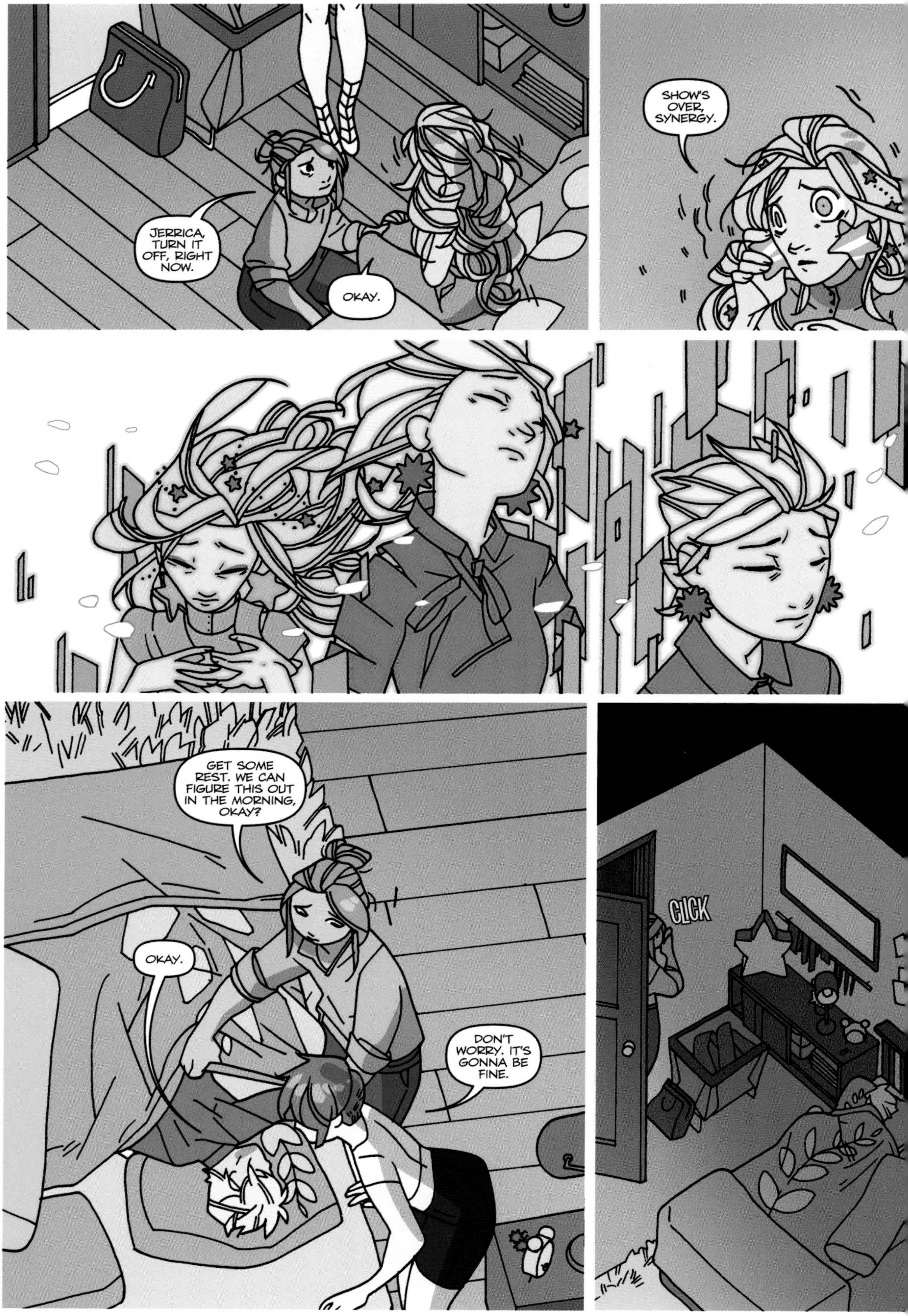
JERRICA, TURN IT OFF, RIGHT NOW.
OKAY.
SHOW'S OVER, SYNERGY.
GET SOME REST. WE CAN FIGURE THIS OUT IN THE MORNING, OKAY?
OKAY.
DON'T WORRY. IT'S GONNA BE FINE.
CLICK

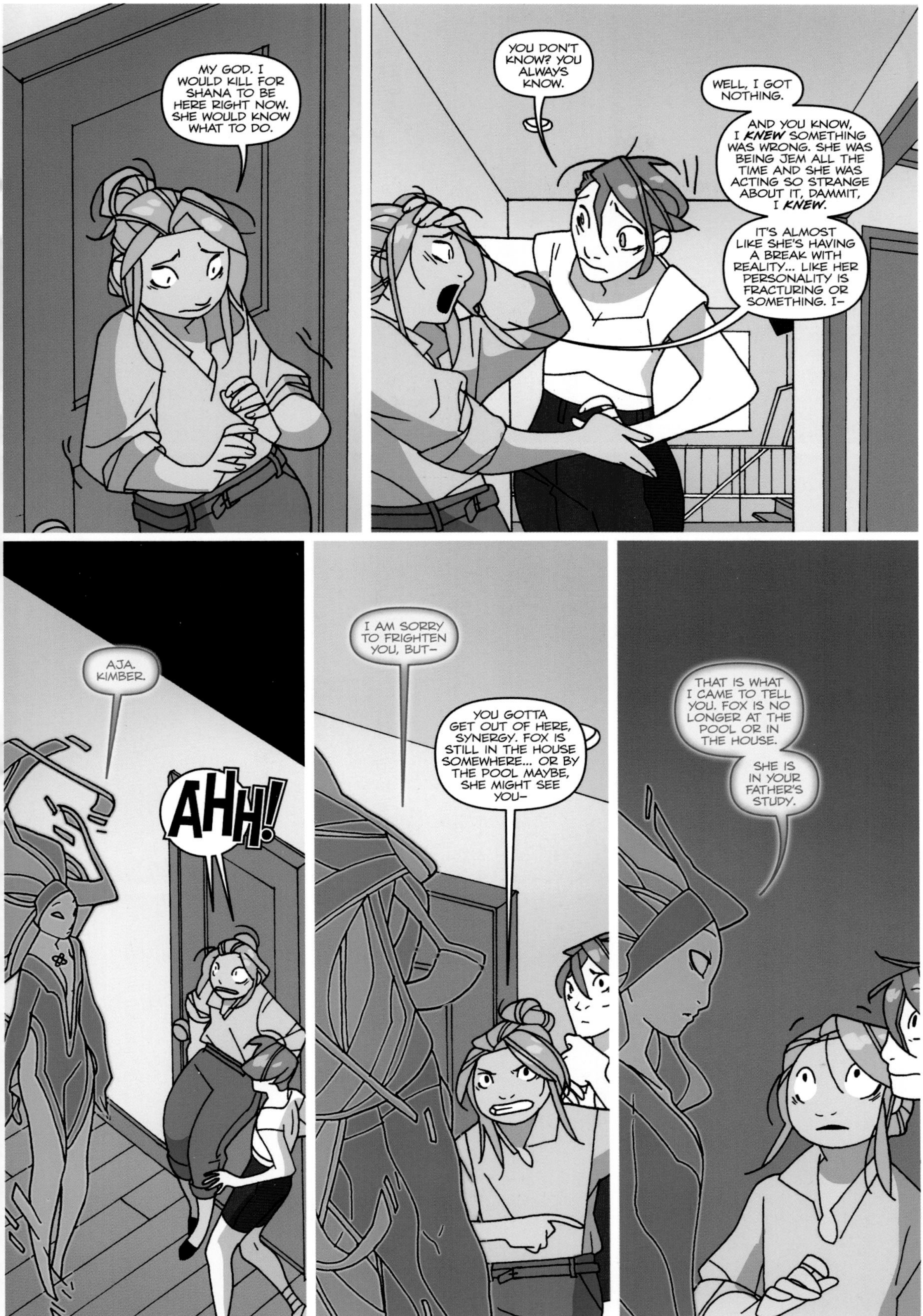
MY GOD. I WOULD KILL FOR SHANA TO BE HERE RIGHT NOW. SHE WOULD KNOW WHAT TO DO.
YOU DON'T KNOW? YOU ALWAYS KNOW.
WELL, I GOT NOTHING.
AND YOU KNOW, I KNEW SOMETHING WAS WRONG. SHE WAS BEING JEM ALL THE TIME AND SHE WAS ACTING SO STRANGE ABOUT IT, DAMMIT, I KNEW.
IT'S ALMOST LIKE SHE'S HAVING A BREAK WITH REALITY... LIKE HER PERSONALITY IS FRACTURING OR SOMETHING. I–
AJA. KIMBER.
AHH!
I AM SORRY TO FRIGHTEN YOU, BUT–
YOU GOTTA GET OUT OF HERE, SYNERGY. FOX IS STILL IN THE HOUSE SOMEWHERE... OR BY THE POOL MAYBE, SHE MIGHT SEE YOU–
THAT IS WHAT I CAME TO TELL YOU. FOX IS NO LONGER AT THE POOL OR IN THE HOUSE.
SHE IS IN YOUR FATHER'S STUDY.

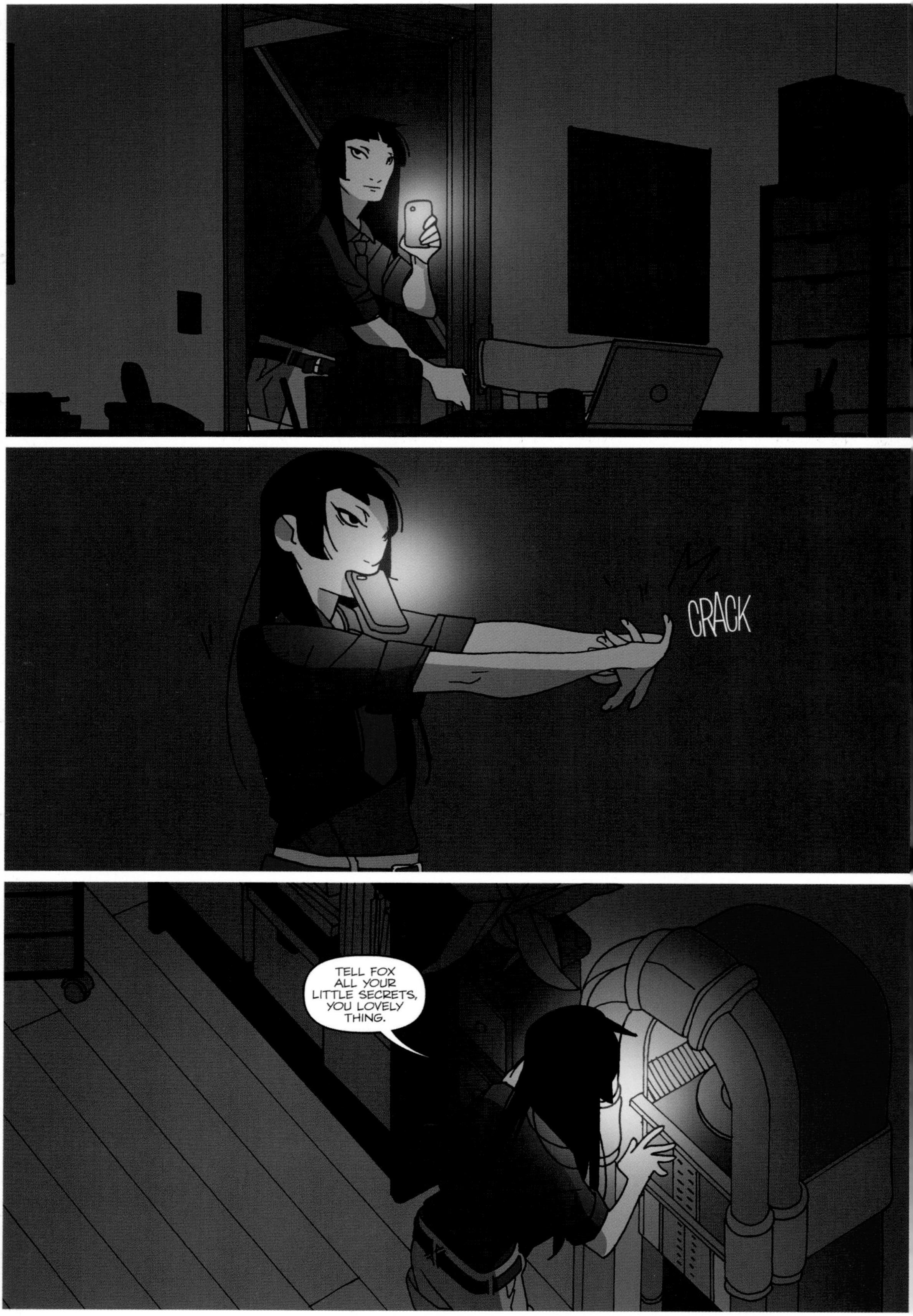
CRACK
TELL FOX ALL YOUR LITTLE SECRETS, YOU LOVELY THING.

COVER ART BY **JEN BARTEL**

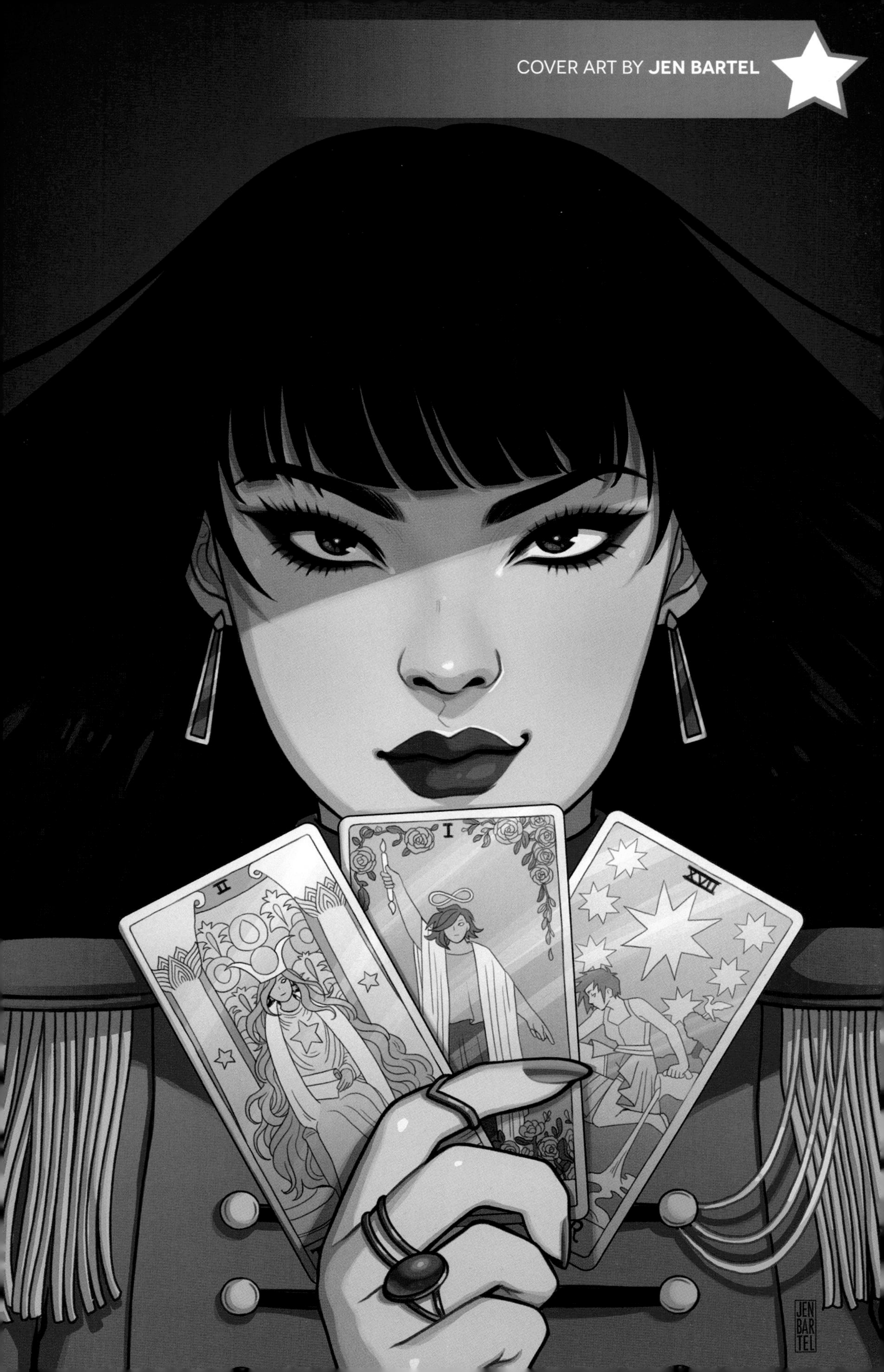
JEN
BAR
TEL

ENTER THE STINGERS PART 4

COVER ART BY **MEREDITH MCCLAREN**

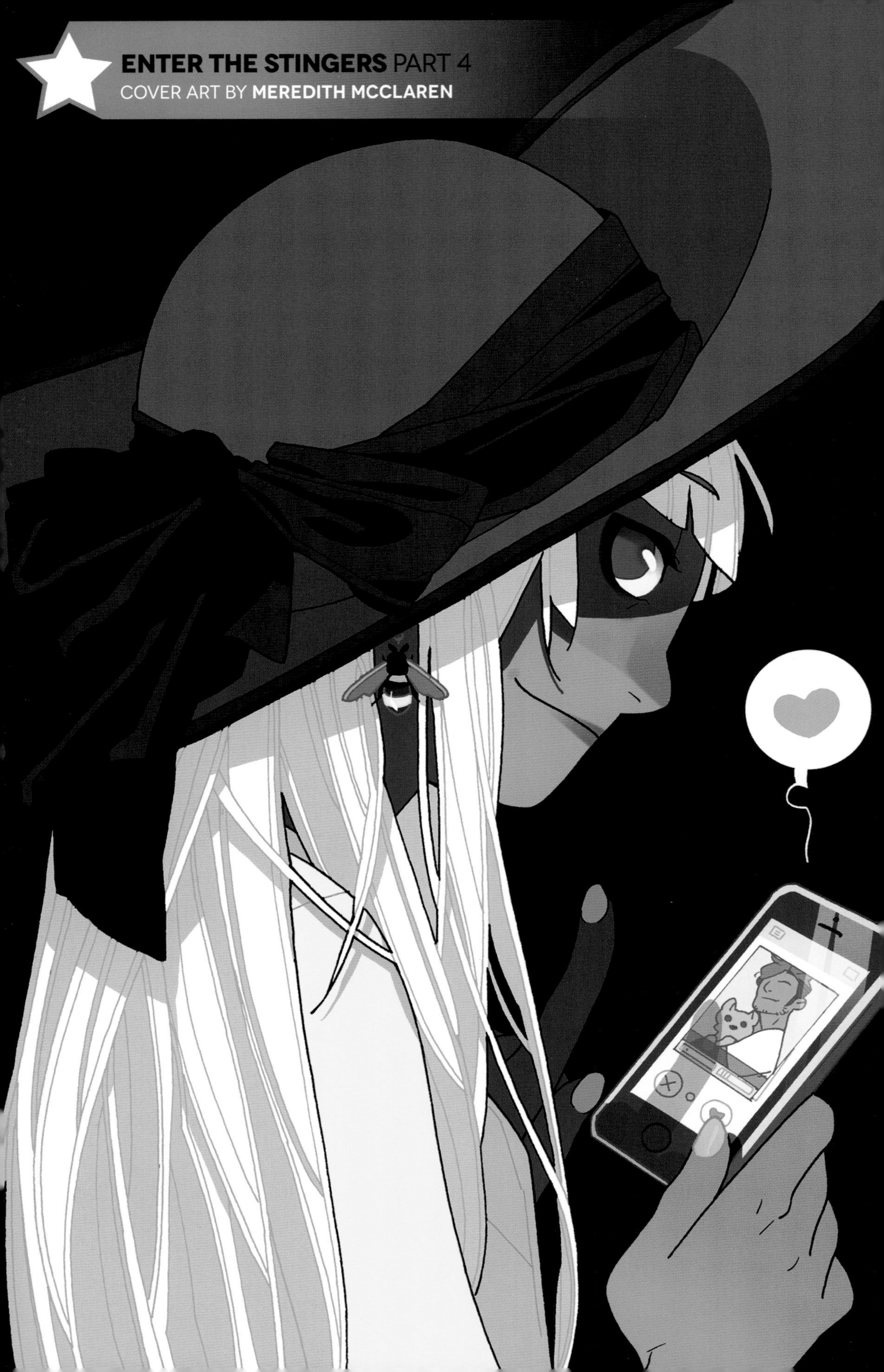

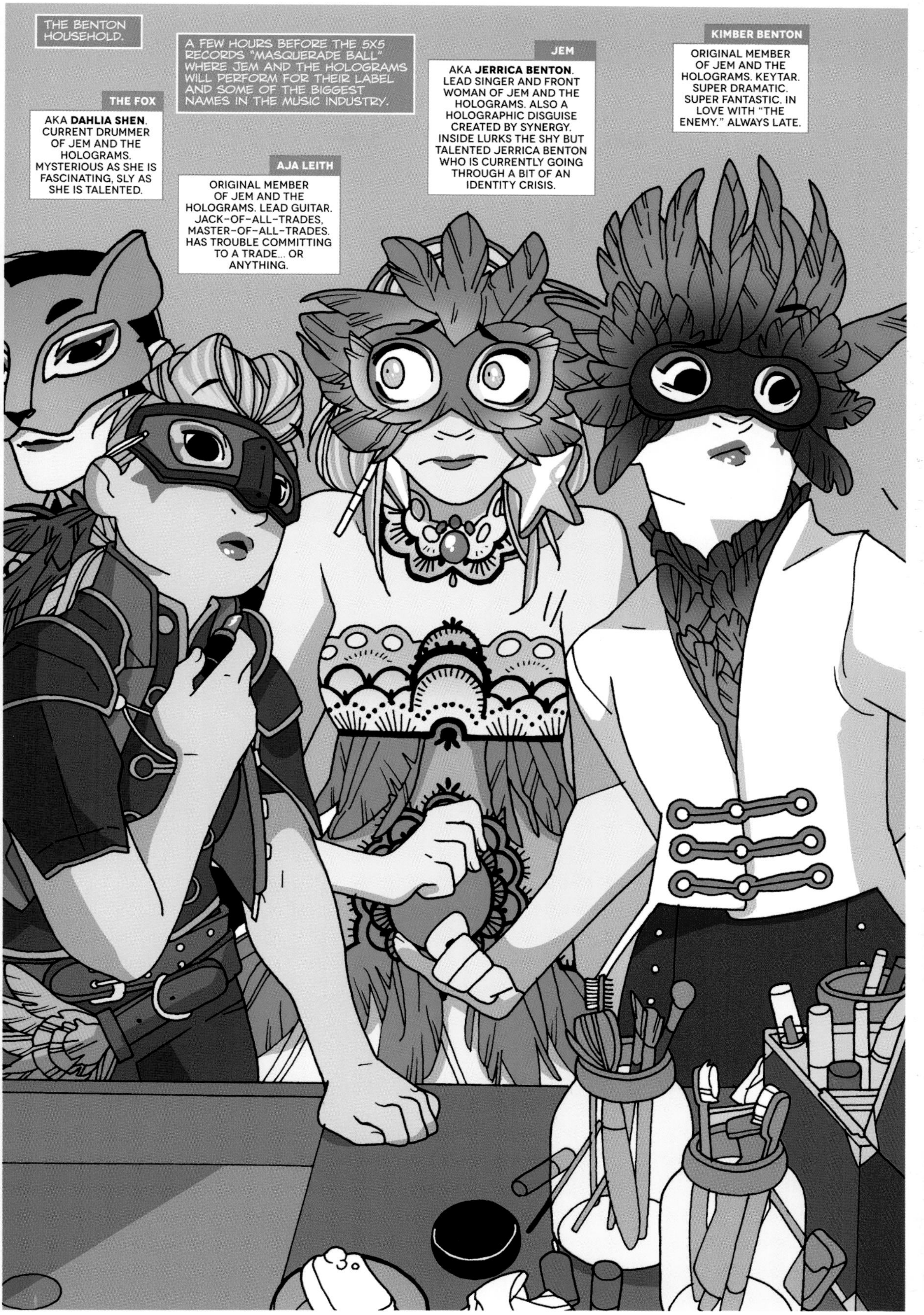
THE BENTON HOUSEHOLD.
A FEW HOURS BEFORE THE 5X5 RECORDS "MASQUERADE BALL" WHERE JEM AND THE HOLOGRAMS WILL PERFORM FOR THEIR LABEL AND SOME OF THE BIGGEST NAMES IN THE MUSIC INDUSTRY.
THE FOX
AKA DAHLIA SHEN. CURRENT DRUMMER OF JEM AND THE HOLOGRAMS. MYSTERIOUS AS SHE IS FASCINATING, SLY AS SHE IS TALENTED.
AJA LEITH
ORIGINAL MEMBER OF JEM AND THE HOLOGRAMS. LEAD GUITAR. JACK-OF-ALL-TRADES, MASTER-OF-ALL-TRADES. HAS TROUBLE COMMITTING TO A TRADE... OR ANYTHING.
JEM
AKA JERRICA BENTON. LEAD SINGER AND FRONT WOMAN OF JEM AND THE HOLOGRAMS. ALSO A HOLOGRAPHIC DISGUISE CREATED BY SYNERGY. INSIDE LURKS THE SHY BUT TALENTED JERRICA BENTON WHO IS CURRENTLY GOING THROUGH A BIT OF AN IDENTITY CRISIS.
KIMBER BENTON
ORIGINAL MEMBER OF JEM AND THE HOLOGRAMS. KEYTAR. SUPER DRAMATIC. SUPER FANTASTIC. IN LOVE WITH "THE ENEMY." ALWAYS LATE.

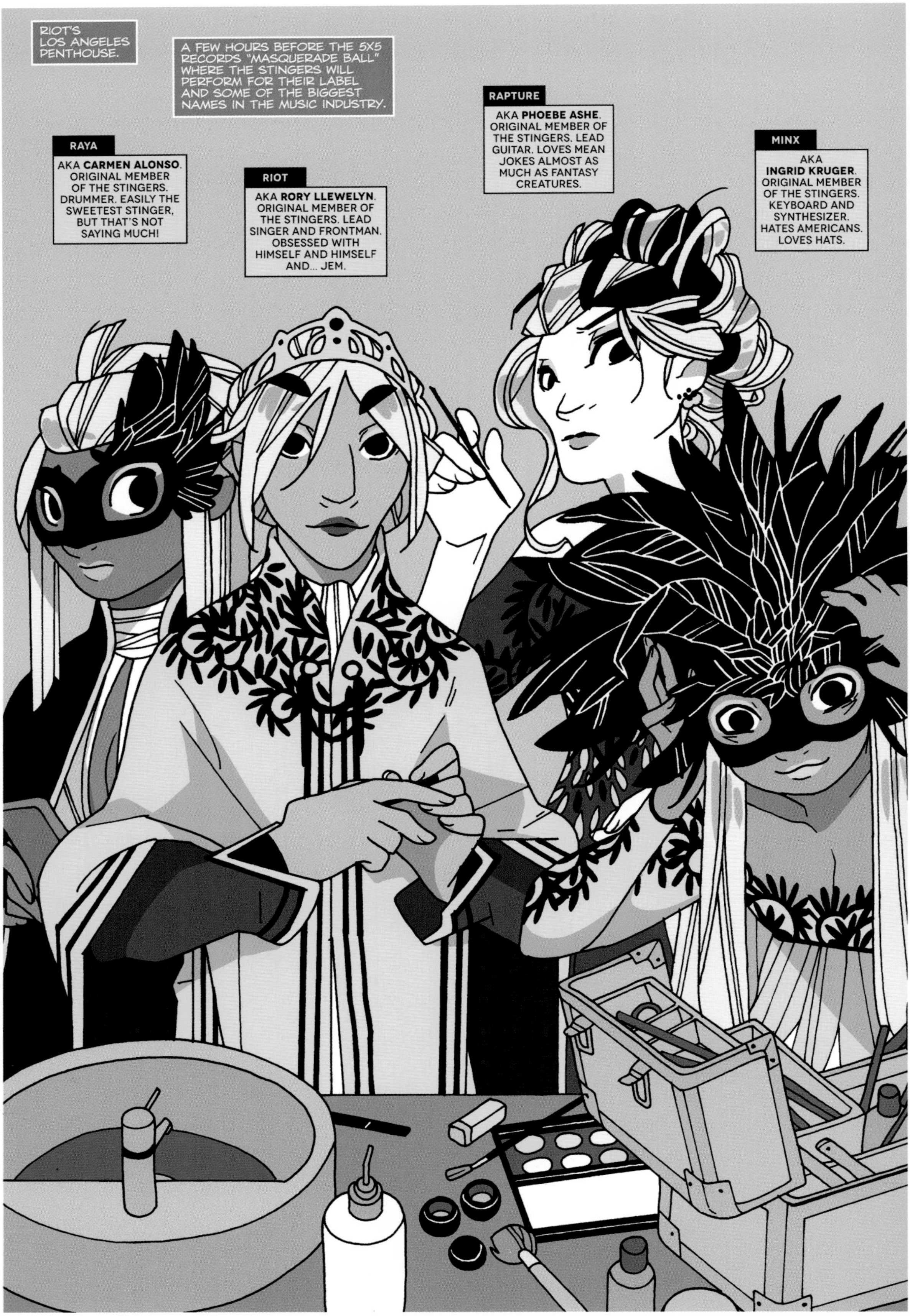
RIOT'S LOS ANGELES PENTHOUSE.
A FEW HOURS BEFORE THE 5X5 RECORDS "MASQUERADE BALL" WHERE THE STINGERS WILL PERFORM FOR THEIR LABEL AND SOME OF THE BIGGEST NAMES IN THE MUSIC INDUSTRY.
RAYA
AKA CARMEN ALONSO. ORIGINAL MEMBER OF THE STINGERS. DRUMMER. EASILY THE SWEETEST STINGER, BUT THAT'S NOT SAYING MUCH!
RIOT
AKA RORY LLEWELYN. ORIGINAL MEMBER OF THE STINGERS. LEAD SINGER AND FRONTMAN. OBSESSED WITH HIMSELF AND HIMSELF AND... JEM.
RAPTURE
AKA PHOEBE ASHE. ORIGINAL MEMBER OF THE STINGERS. LEAD GUITAR. LOVES MEAN JOKES ALMOST AS MUCH AS FANTASY CREATURES.
MINX
AKA INGRID KRUGER. ORIGINAL MEMBER OF THE STINGERS. KEYBOARD AND SYNTHESIZER. HATES AMERICANS. LOVES HATS.

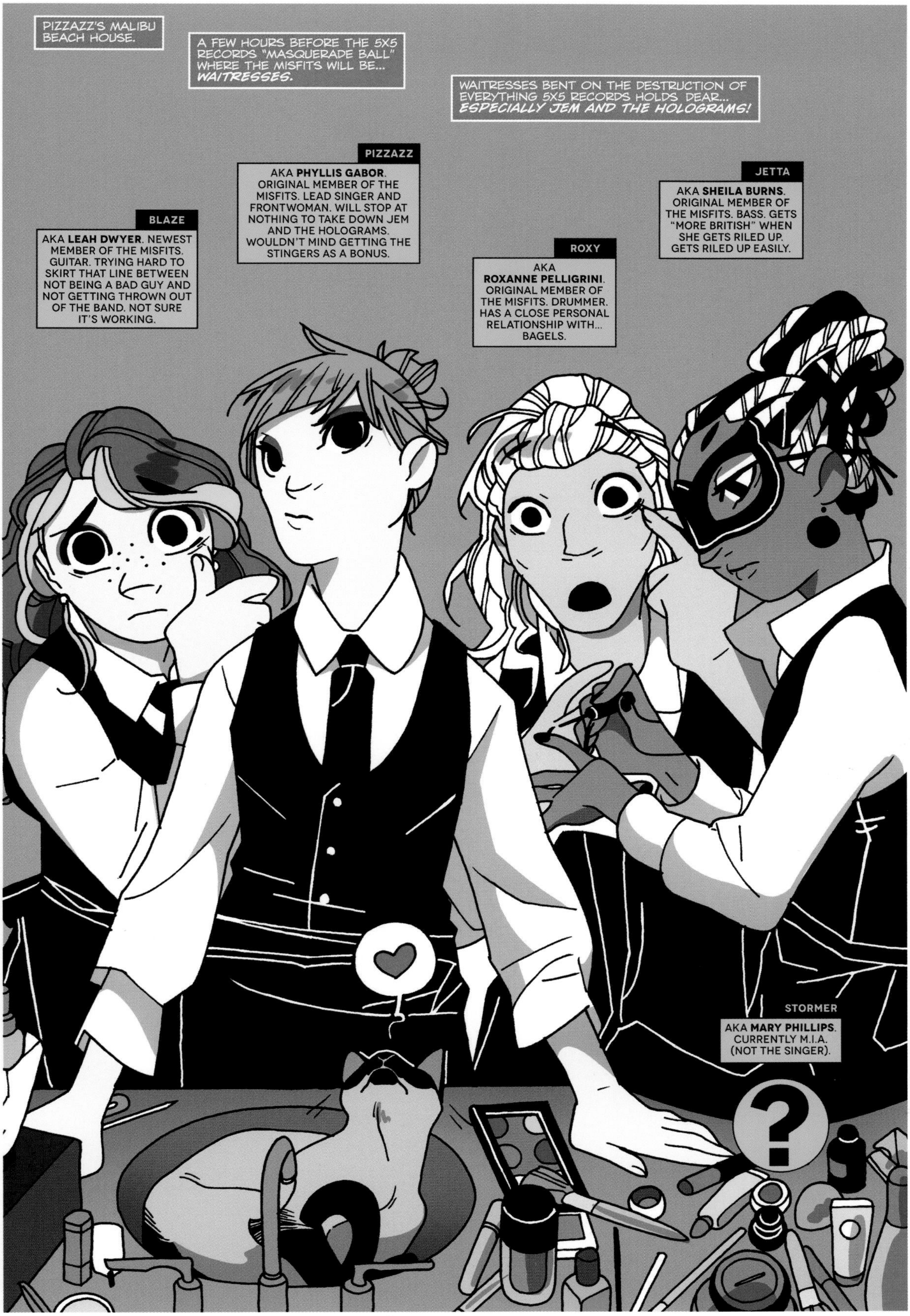

PIZZAZZ'S MALIBU BEACH HOUSE.
A FEW HOURS BEFORE THE 5X5 RECORDS "MASQUERADE BALL" WHERE THE MISFITS WILL BE... WAITRESSES.
WAITRESSES BENT ON THE DESTRUCTION OF EVERYTHING 5X5 RECORDS HOLDS DEAR... ESPECIALLY JEM AND THE HOLOGRAMS!
BLAZE
AKA LEAH DWYER. NEWEST MEMBER OF THE MISFITS. GUITAR. TRYING HARD TO SKIRT THAT LINE BETWEEN NOT BEING A BAD GUY AND NOT GETTING THROWN OUT OF THE BAND. NOT SURE IT'S WORKING.
PIZZAZZ
AKA PHYLLIS GABOR. ORIGINAL MEMBER OF THE MISFITS. LEAD SINGER AND FRONTWOMAN. WILL STOP AT NOTHING TO TAKE DOWN JEM AND THE HOLOGRAMS. WOULDN'T MIND GETTING THE STINGERS AS A BONUS.
ROXY
AKA ROXANNE PELLIGRINI. ORIGINAL MEMBER OF THE MISFITS. DRUMMER. HAS A CLOSE PERSONAL RELATIONSHIP WITH... BAGELS.
JETTA
AKA SHEILA BURNS. ORIGINAL MEMBER OF THE MISFITS. BASS. GETS "MORE BRITISH" WHEN SHE GETS RILED UP. GETS RILED UP EASILY.
STORMER
AKA MARY PHILLIPS. CURRENTLY M.I.A. (NOT THE SINGER).
?

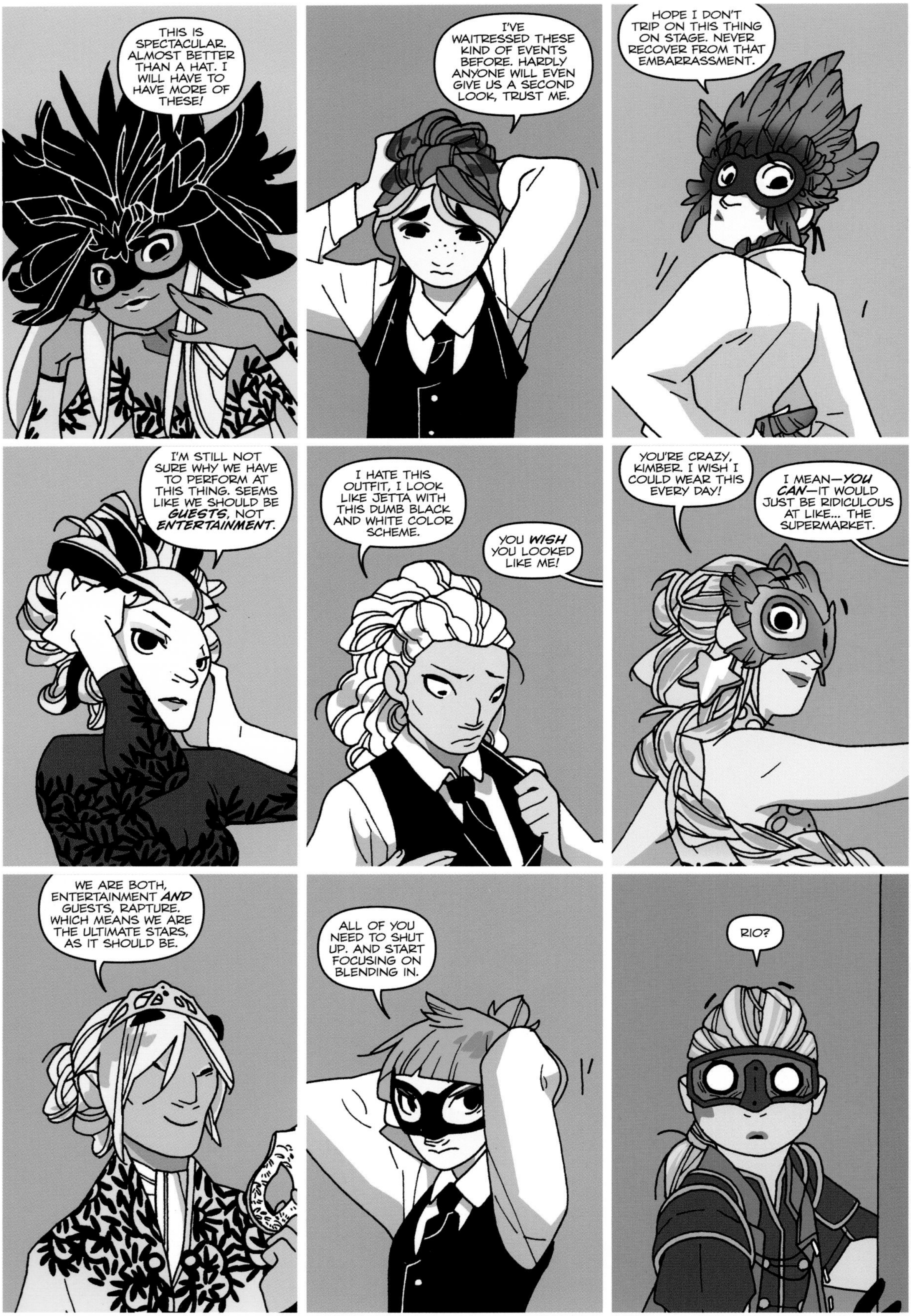
THIS IS SPECTACULAR. ALMOST BETTER THAN A HAT. I WILL HAVE TO HAVE MORE OF THESE!
I'VE WAITRESSED THESE KIND OF EVENTS BEFORE. HARDLY ANYONE WILL EVEN GIVE US A SECOND LOOK, TRUST ME.
HOPE I DON'T TRIP ON THIS THING ON STAGE. NEVER RECOVER FROM THAT EMBARRASSMENT.
I'M STILL NOT SURE WHY WE HAVE TO PERFORM AT THIS THING. SEEMS LIKE WE SHOULD BE GUESTS, NOT ENTERTAINMENT.
I HATE THIS OUTFIT, I LOOK LIKE JETTA WITH THIS DUMB BLACK AND WHITE COLOR SCHEME.
YOU WISH YOU LOOKED LIKE ME!
YOU'RE CRAZY, KIMBER. I WISH I COULD WEAR THIS EVERY DAY!
I MEAN—YOU CAN—IT WOULD JUST BE RIDICULOUS AT LIKE... THE SUPERMARKET.
WE ARE BOTH, ENTERTAINMENT AND GUESTS, RAPTURE. WHICH MEANS WE ARE THE ULTIMATE STARS, AS IT SHOULD BE.
ALL OF YOU NEED TO SHUT UP. AND START FOCUSING ON BLENDING IN.
RIO?

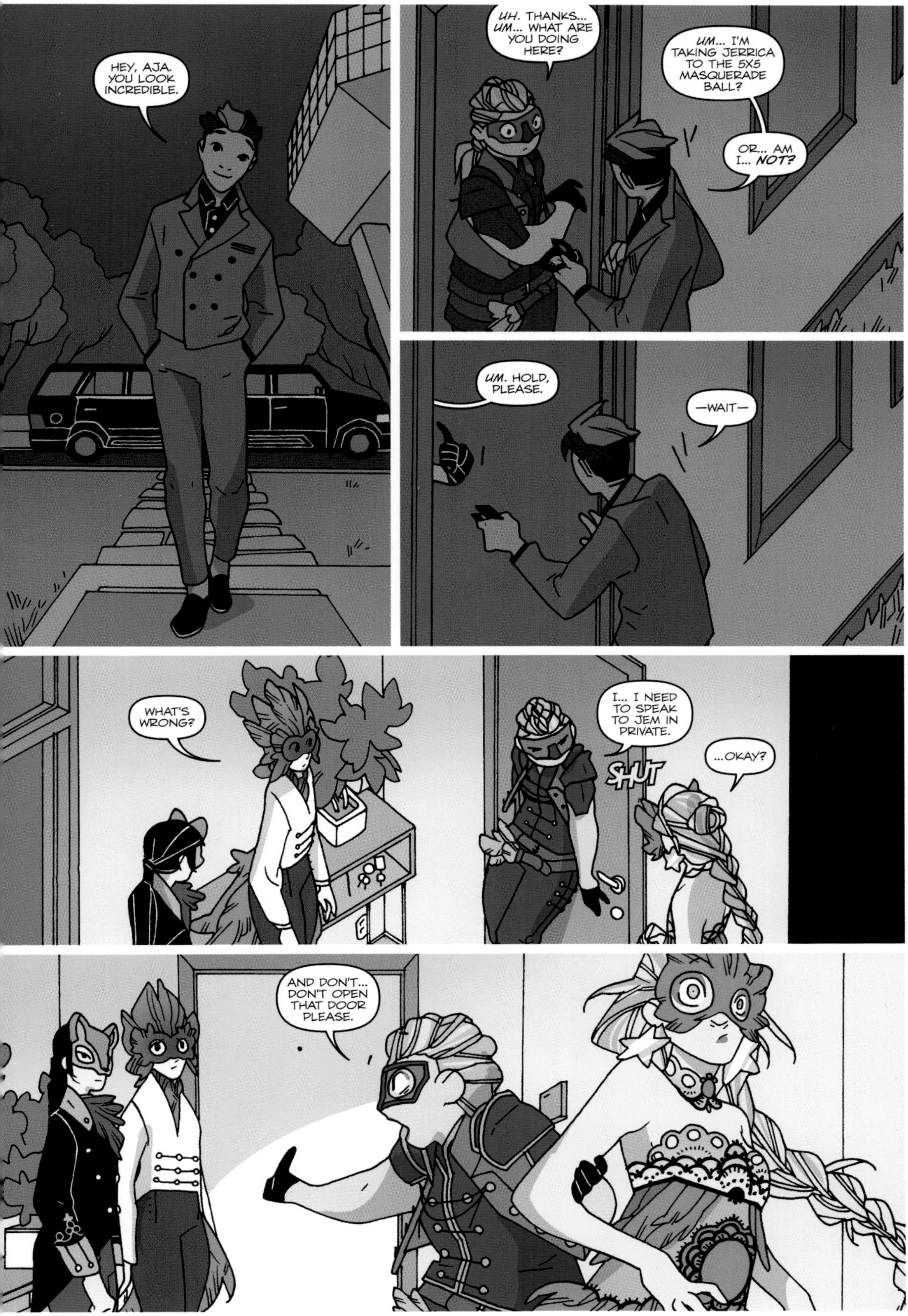
HEY, AJA. YOU LOOK INCREDIBLE.
UH. THANKS... UM... WHAT ARE YOU DOING HERE?
UM... I'M TAKING JERRICA TO THE 5X5 MASQUERADE BALL?
OR... AM I... NOT?
UM. HOLD, PLEASE.
—WAIT—
WHAT'S WRONG?
I... I NEED TO SPEAK TO JEM IN PRIVATE.
SHUT
...OKAY?
AND DON'T... DON'T OPEN THAT DOOR PLEASE.

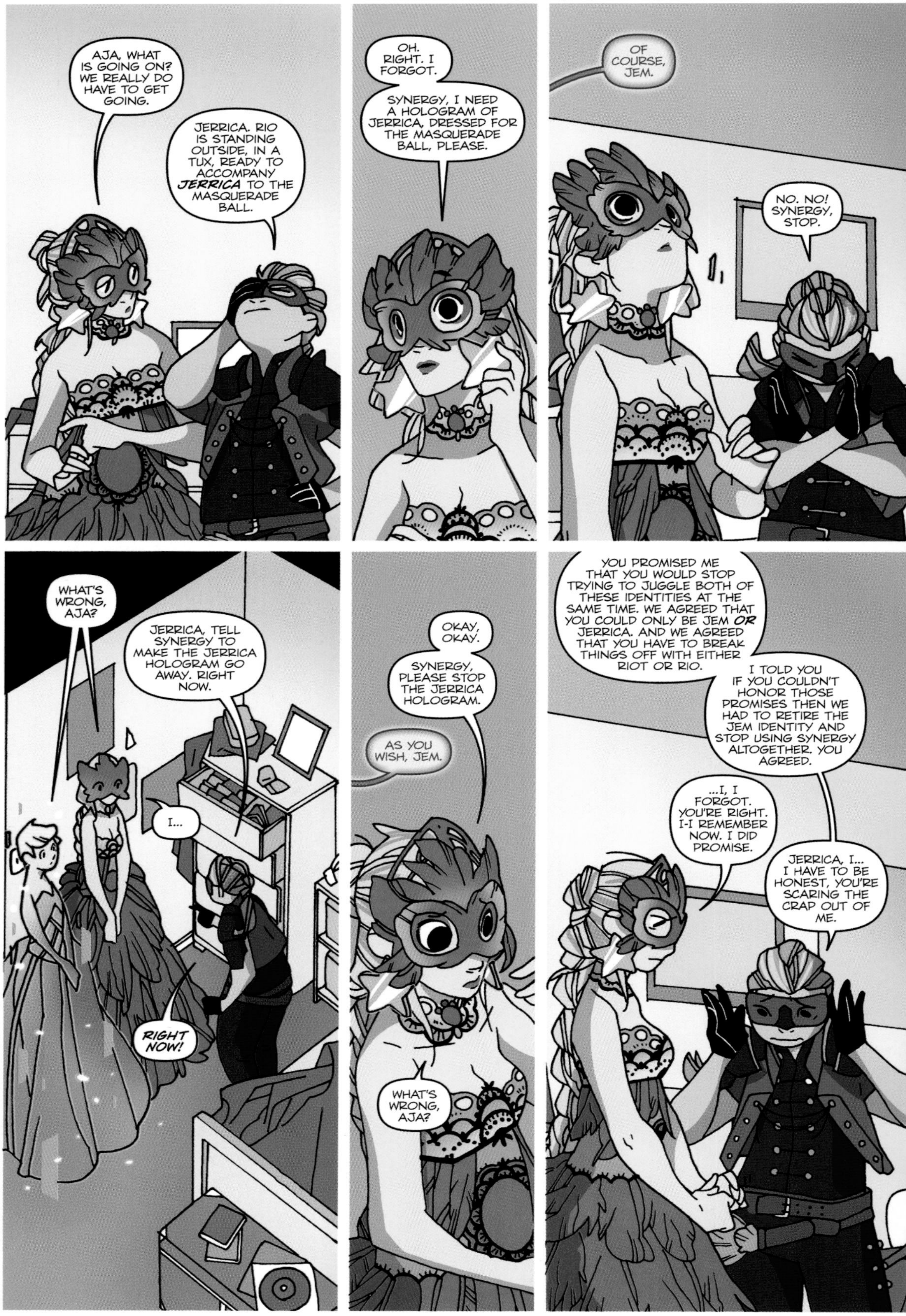
AJA, WHAT IS GOING ON? WE REALLY DO HAVE TO GET GOING.
JERRICA. RIO IS STANDING OUTSIDE, IN A TUX, READY TO ACCOMPANY *JERRICA* TO THE MASQUERADE BALL.
OH. RIGHT. I FORGOT.
SYNERGY, I NEED A HOLOGRAM OF JERRICA, DRESSED FOR THE MASQUERADE BALL, PLEASE.
OF COURSE, JEM.
NO. NO! SYNERGY, STOP.
WHAT'S WRONG, AJA?
JERRICA, TELL SYNERGY TO MAKE THE JERRICA HOLOGRAM GO AWAY. RIGHT NOW.
I...
RIGHT NOW!
OKAY, OKAY.
SYNERGY, PLEASE STOP THE JERRICA HOLOGRAM.
AS YOU WISH, JEM.
WHAT'S WRONG, AJA?
YOU PROMISED ME THAT YOU WOULD STOP TRYING TO JUGGLE BOTH OF THESE IDENTITIES AT THE SAME TIME. WE AGREED THAT YOU COULD ONLY BE JEM *OR* JERRICA. AND WE AGREED THAT YOU HAVE TO BREAK THINGS OFF WITH EITHER RIOT OR RIO.
I TOLD YOU IF YOU COULDN'T HONOR THOSE PROMISES THEN WE HAD TO RETIRE THE JEM IDENTITY AND STOP USING SYNERGY ALTOGETHER. YOU AGREED.
...I, I FORGOT. YOU'RE RIGHT. I-I REMEMBER NOW. I DID PROMISE.
JERRICA, I... I HAVE TO BE HONEST, YOU'RE SCARING THE CRAP OUT OF ME.

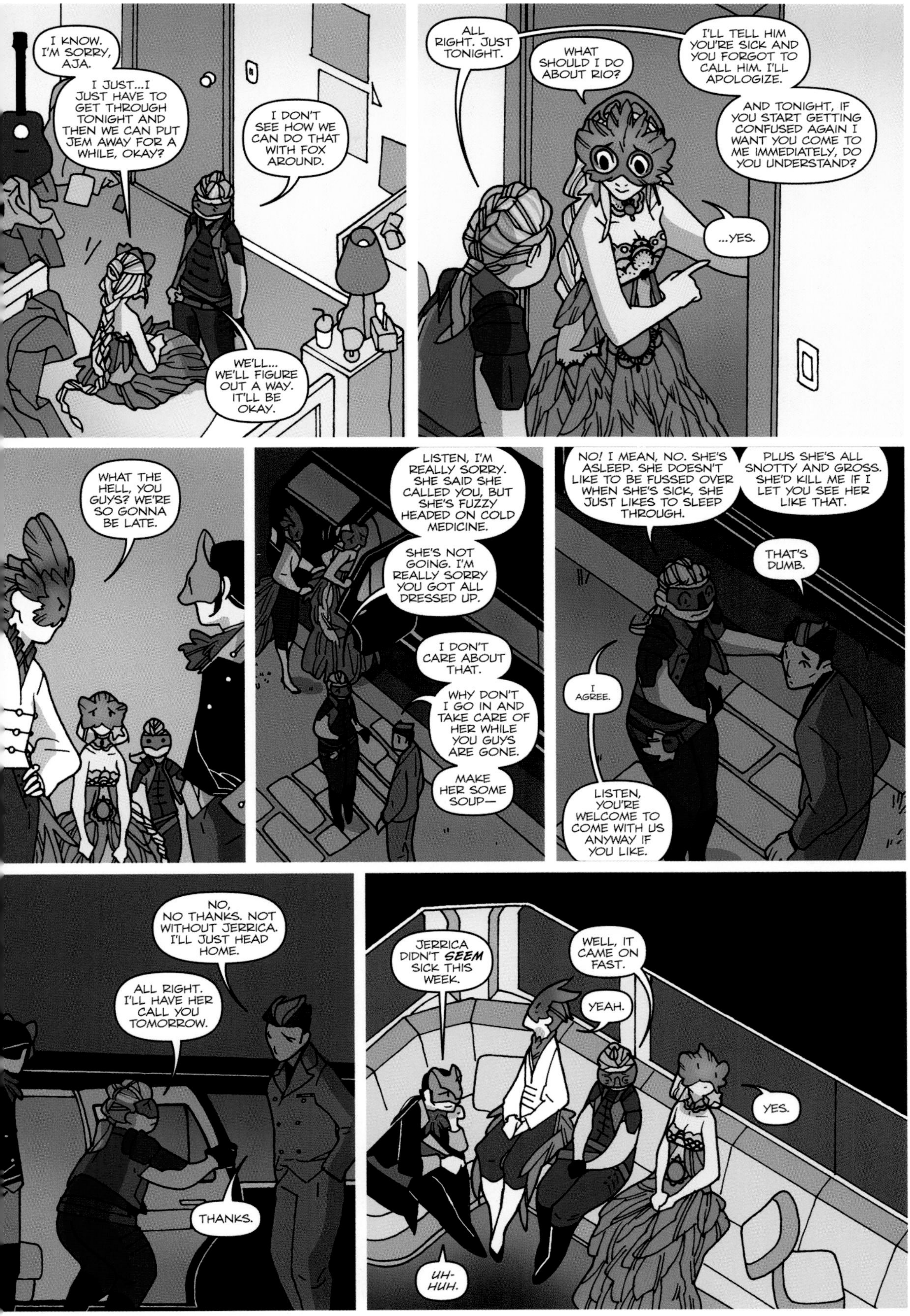
I KNOW. I'M SORRY, AJA.
I JUST...I JUST HAVE TO GET THROUGH TONIGHT AND THEN WE CAN PUT JEM AWAY FOR A WHILE, OKAY?
I DON'T SEE HOW WE CAN DO THAT WITH FOX AROUND.
WE'LL... WE'LL FIGURE OUT A WAY. IT'LL BE OKAY.
ALL RIGHT. JUST TONIGHT.
WHAT SHOULD I DO ABOUT RIO?
I'LL TELL HIM YOU'RE SICK AND YOU FORGOT TO CALL HIM. I'LL APOLOGIZE.
AND TONIGHT, IF YOU START GETTING CONFUSED AGAIN I WANT YOU COME TO ME IMMEDIATELY, DO YOU UNDERSTAND?
...YES.
WHAT THE HELL, YOU GUYS? WE'RE SO GONNA BE LATE.
LISTEN, I'M REALLY SORRY. SHE SAID SHE CALLED YOU, BUT SHE'S FUZZY HEADED ON COLD MEDICINE.
SHE'S NOT GOING. I'M REALLY SORRY YOU GOT ALL DRESSED UP.
I DON'T CARE ABOUT THAT.
WHY DON'T I GO IN AND TAKE CARE OF HER WHILE YOU GUYS ARE GONE.
MAKE HER SOME SOUP—
NO! I MEAN, NO. SHE'S ASLEEP. SHE DOESN'T LIKE TO BE FUSSED OVER WHEN SHE'S SICK, SHE JUST LIKES TO SLEEP THROUGH.
PLUS SHE'S ALL SNOTTY AND GROSS. SHE'D KILL ME IF I LET YOU SEE HER LIKE THAT.
THAT'S DUMB.
I AGREE.
LISTEN, YOU'RE WELCOME TO COME WITH US ANYWAY IF YOU LIKE.
NO, NO THANKS. NOT WITHOUT JERRICA. I'LL JUST HEAD HOME.
ALL RIGHT. I'LL HAVE HER CALL YOU TOMORROW.
THANKS.
JERRICA DIDN'T *SEEM* SICK THIS WEEK.
WELL, IT CAME ON FAST.
YEAH.
YES.
UH-HUH.

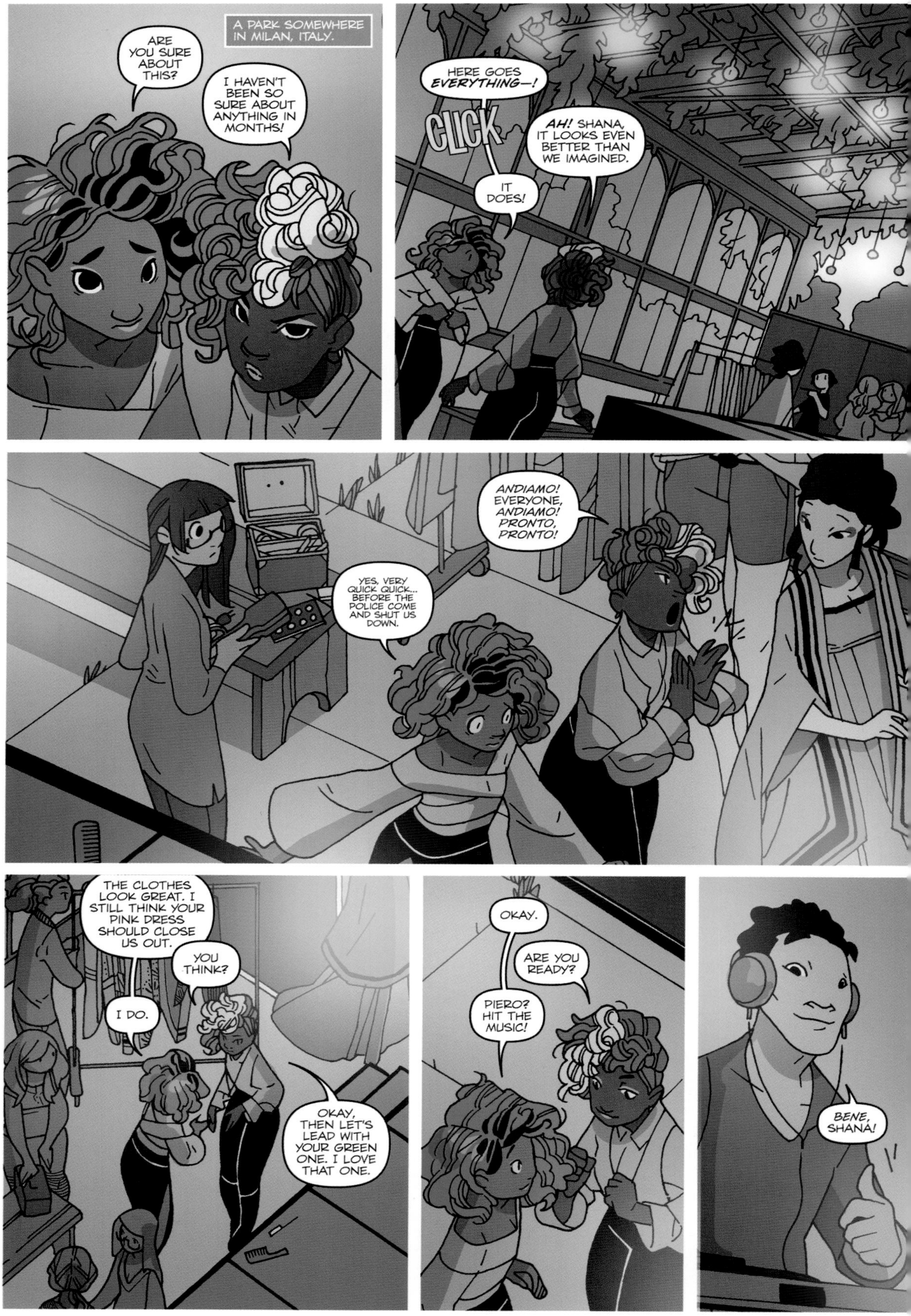
A PARK SOMEWHERE IN MILAN, ITALY.
ARE YOU SURE ABOUT THIS?
I HAVEN'T BEEN SO SURE ABOUT ANYTHING IN MONTHS!
HERE GOES EVERYTHING—!
CLICK
IT DOES!
AH! SHANA, IT LOOKS EVEN BETTER THAN WE IMAGINED.
ANDIAMO! EVERYONE, ANDIAMO! PRONTO, PRONTO!
YES, VERY QUICK QUICK... BEFORE THE POLICE COME AND SHUT US DOWN.
THE CLOTHES LOOK GREAT. I STILL THINK YOUR PINK DRESS SHOULD CLOSE US OUT.
YOU THINK?
I DO.
OKAY, THEN LET'S LEAD WITH YOUR GREEN ONE. I LOVE THAT ONE.
OKAY.
ARE YOU READY?
PIERO? HIT THE MUSIC!
BENE, SHANA!

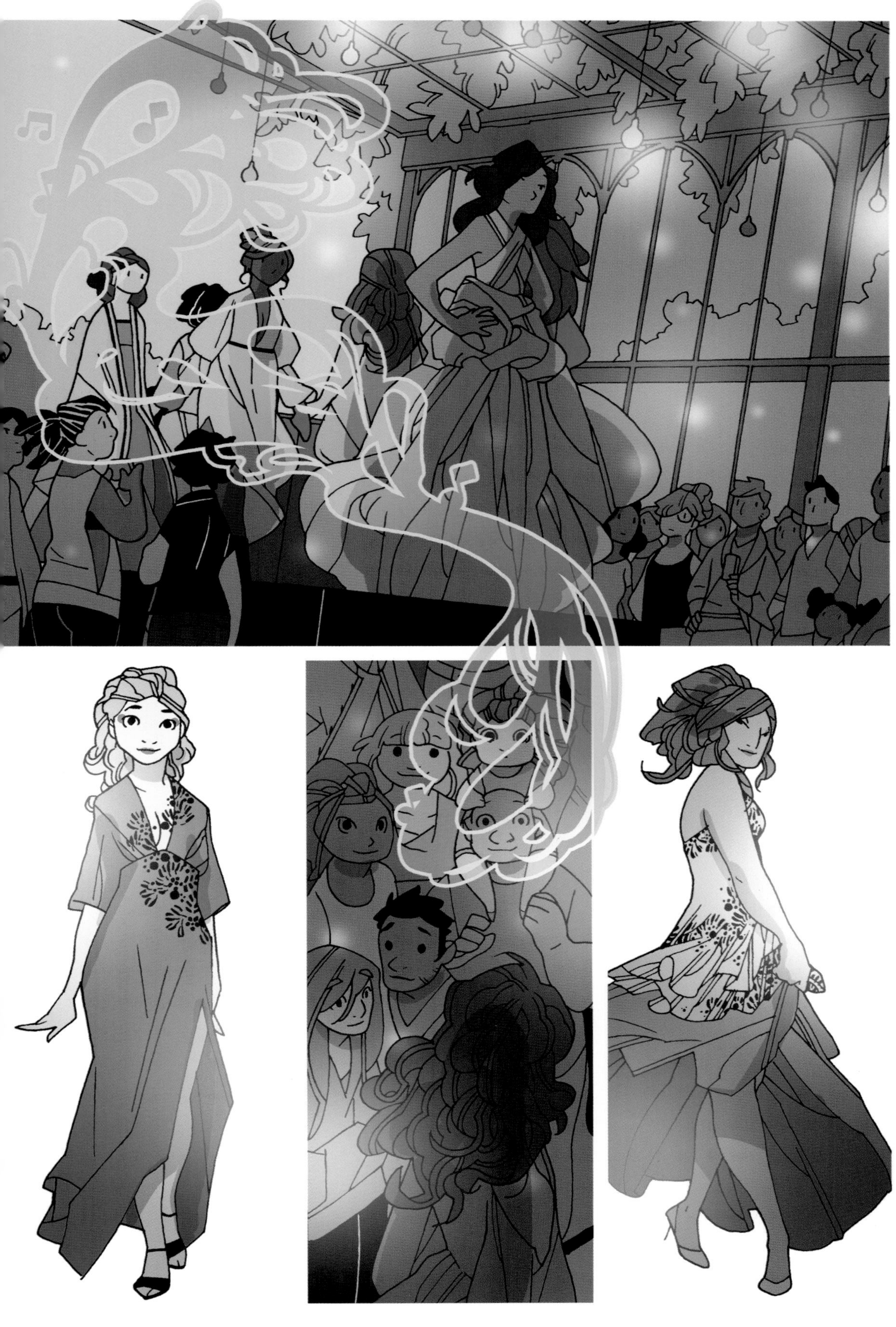

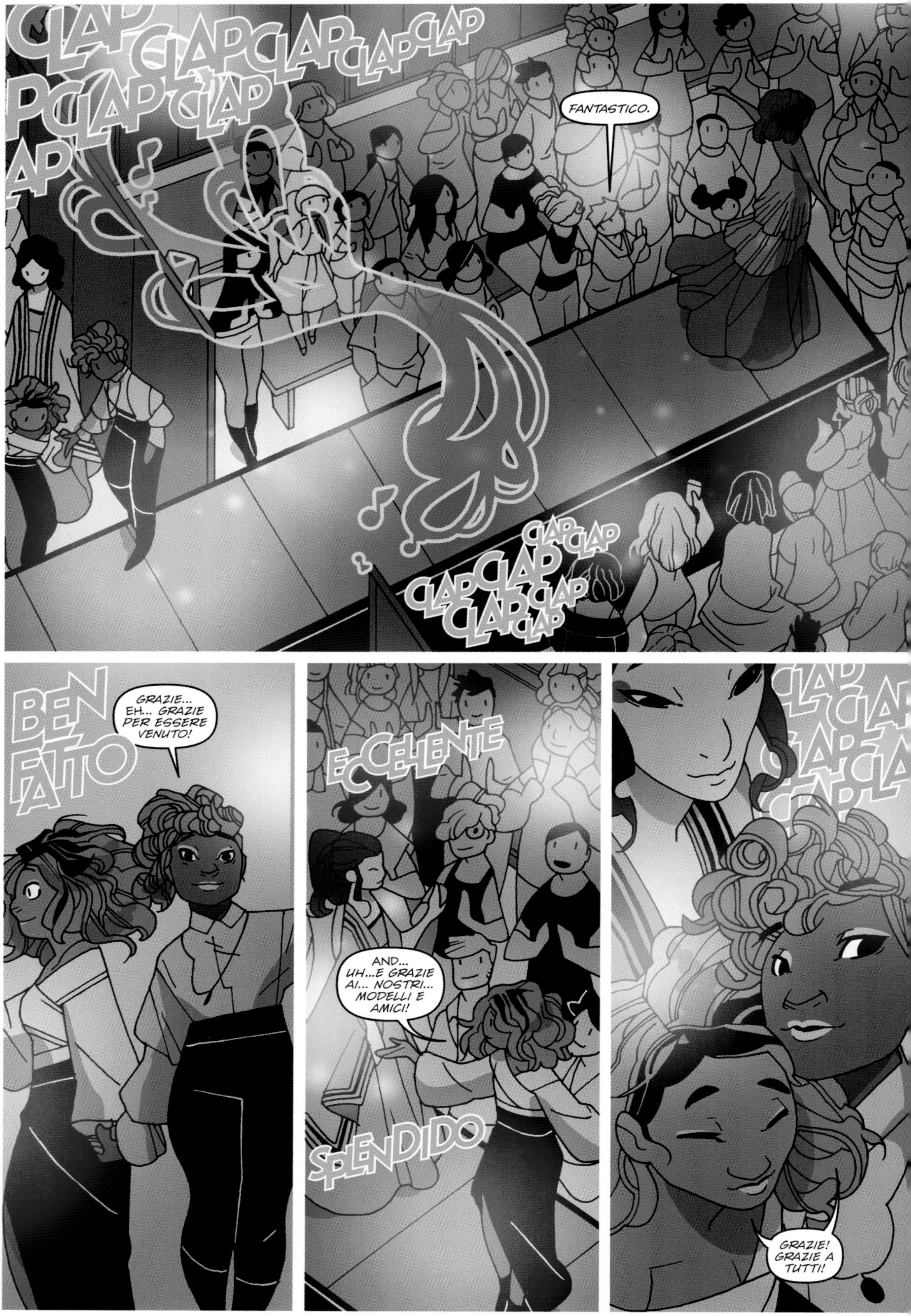
CLAP CLAP CLAP CLAP CLAP
PCLAP CLAP
AP
FANTASTICO.
CLAP CLAP
CLAP CLAP CLAP
CLAP CLAP
BEN FATTO
GRAZIE... EH... GRAZIE PER ESSERE VENUTO!
ECCELLENTE
AND... UH...E GRAZIE AI... NOSTRI... MODELLI E AMICI!
SPLENDIDO
CLAP CLAP CLAP CLAP
GRAZIE! GRAZIE A TUTTI!

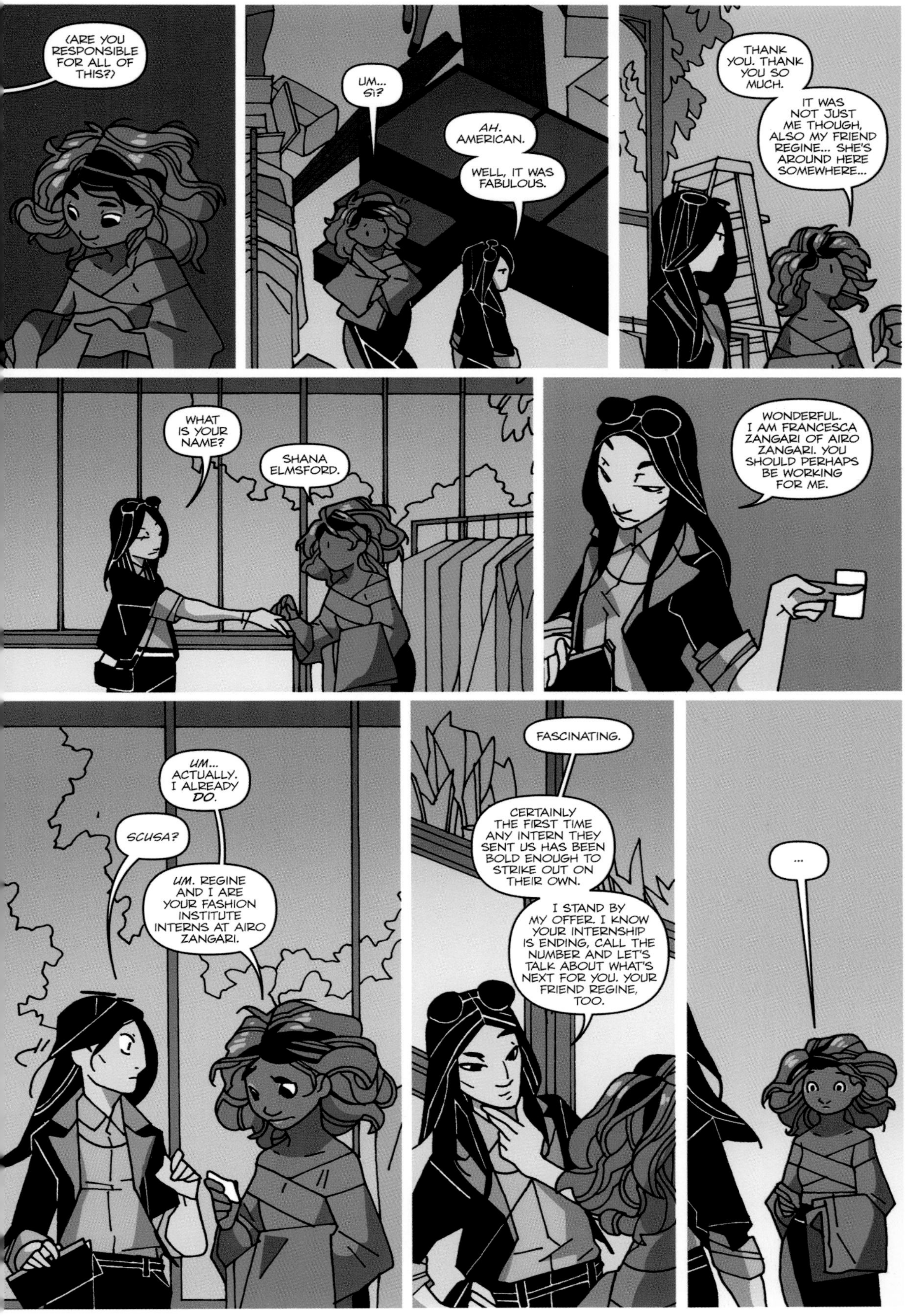

(ARE YOU RESPONSIBLE FOR ALL OF THIS?)
UM... SI?
AH. AMERICAN.
WELL, IT WAS FABULOUS.
THANK YOU. THANK YOU SO MUCH.
IT WAS NOT JUST ME THOUGH, ALSO MY FRIEND REGINE... SHE'S AROUND HERE SOMEWHERE...
WHAT IS YOUR NAME?
SHANA ELMSFORD.
WONDERFUL. I AM FRANCESCA ZANGARI OF AIRO ZANGARI. YOU SHOULD PERHAPS BE WORKING FOR ME.
UM... ACTUALLY. I ALREADY DO.
SCUSA?
UM. REGINE AND I ARE YOUR FASHION INSTITUTE INTERNS AT AIRO ZANGARI.
FASCINATING.
CERTAINLY THE FIRST TIME ANY INTERN THEY SENT US HAS BEEN BOLD ENOUGH TO STRIKE OUT ON THEIR OWN.
I STAND BY MY OFFER. I KNOW YOUR INTERNSHIP IS ENDING, CALL THE NUMBER AND LET'S TALK ABOUT WHAT'S NEXT FOR YOU. YOUR FRIEND REGINE, TOO.
...

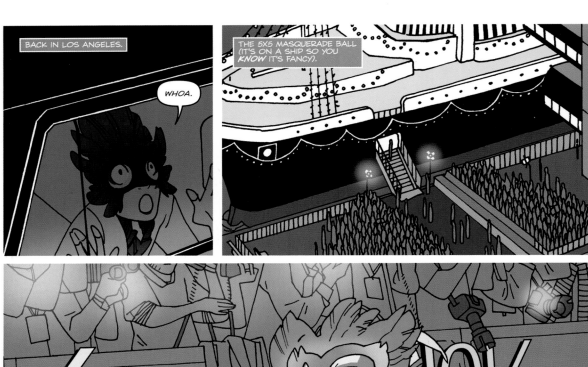

BACK IN LOS ANGELES.

WHOA.

THE 5X5 MASQUERADE BALL (IT'S ON A SHIP SO YOU *KNOW* IT'S FANCY).

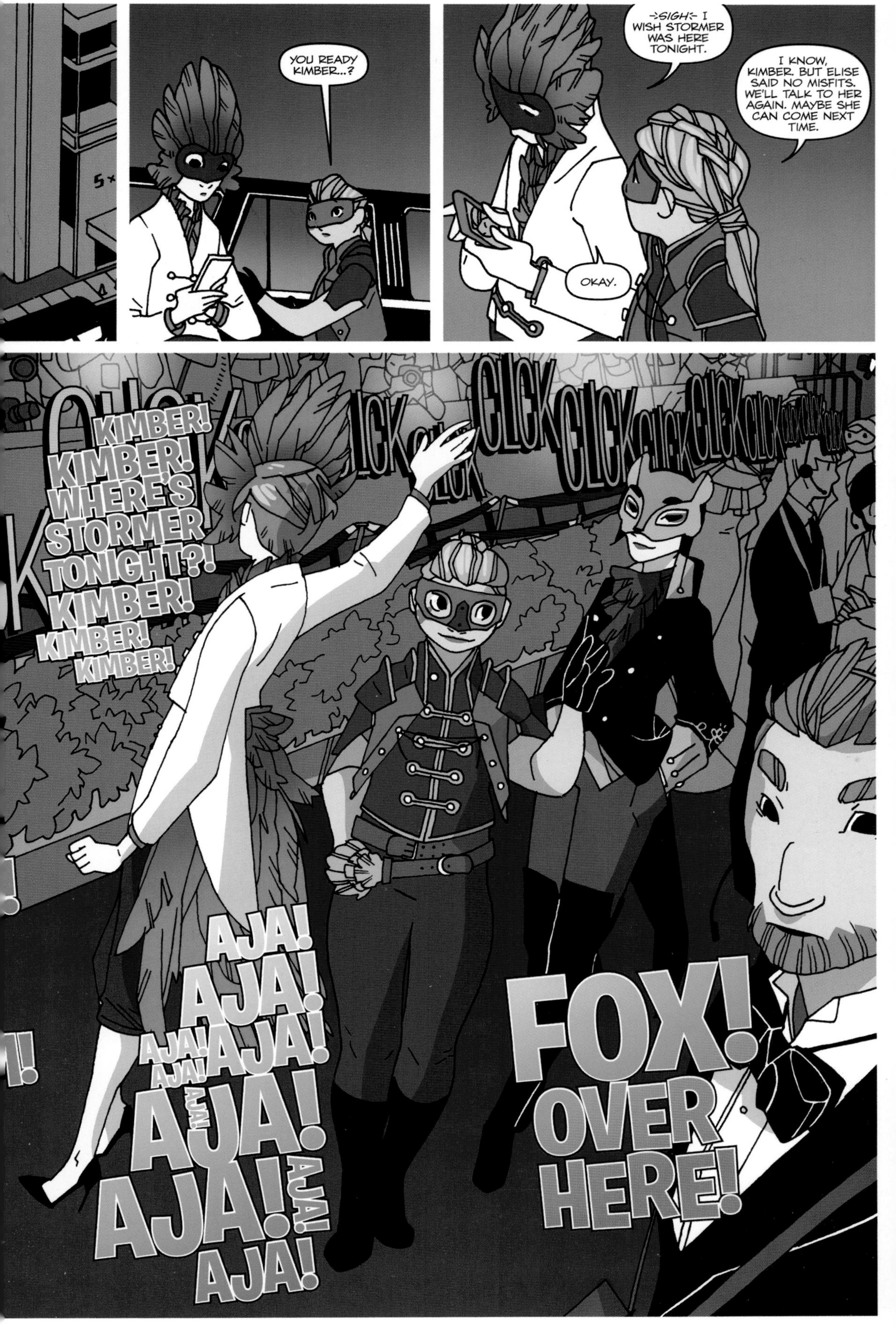

YOU READY KIMBER...?
-SIGH- I WISH STORMER WAS HERE TONIGHT.
I KNOW, KIMBER. BUT ELISE SAID NO MISFITS. WE'LL TALK TO HER AGAIN. MAYBE SHE CAN COME NEXT TIME.
OKAY.
CLICK CLICK CLICK CLICK CLICK CLICK CLICK CLICK
KIMBER! KIMBER! WHERE'S STORMER TONIGHT?! KIMBER! KIMBER! KIMBER!
AJA! AJA! AJA! AJA! AJA! AJA! AJA! AJA! AJA! AJA!
FOX! OVER HERE!

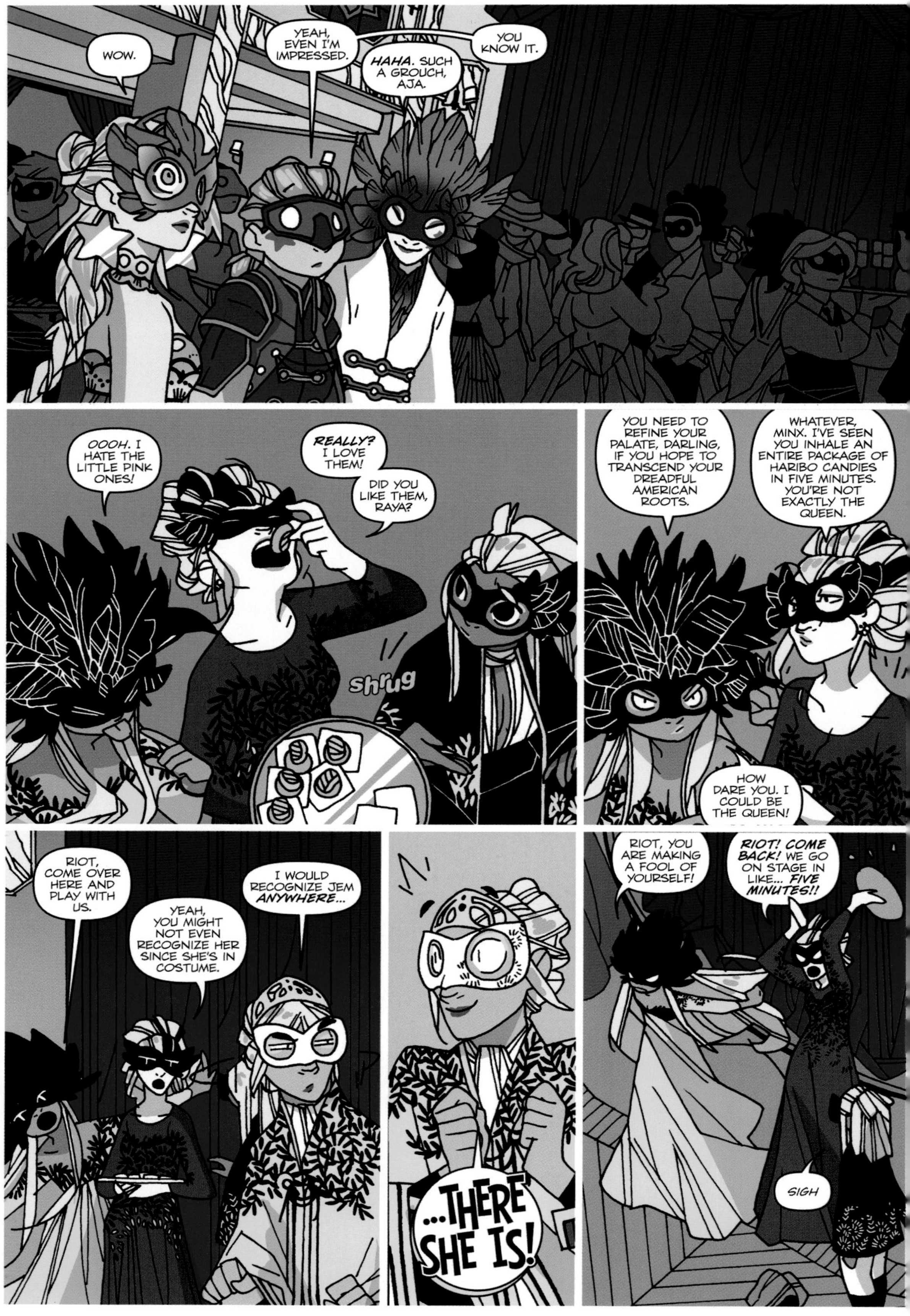
WOW.
YEAH, EVEN I'M IMPRESSED.
YOU KNOW IT.
HAHA. SUCH A GROUCH, AJA.
OOOH. I HATE THE LITTLE PINK ONES!
REALLY? I LOVE THEM!
DID YOU LIKE THEM, RAYA?
SHRUG
YOU NEED TO REFINE YOUR PALATE, DARLING, IF YOU HOPE TO TRANSCEND YOUR DREADFUL AMERICAN ROOTS.
WHATEVER, MINX. I'VE SEEN YOU INHALE AN ENTIRE PACKAGE OF HARIBO CANDIES IN FIVE MINUTES. YOU'RE NOT EXACTLY THE QUEEN.
HOW DARE YOU. I COULD BE THE QUEEN!
RIOT, COME OVER HERE AND PLAY WITH US.
YEAH, YOU MIGHT NOT EVEN RECOGNIZE HER SINCE SHE'S IN COSTUME.
I WOULD RECOGNIZE JEM ANYWHERE...
...THERE SHE IS!
RIOT, YOU ARE MAKING A FOOL OF YOURSELF!
RIOT! COME BACK! WE GO ON STAGE IN LIKE... FIVE MINUTES!!
SIGH

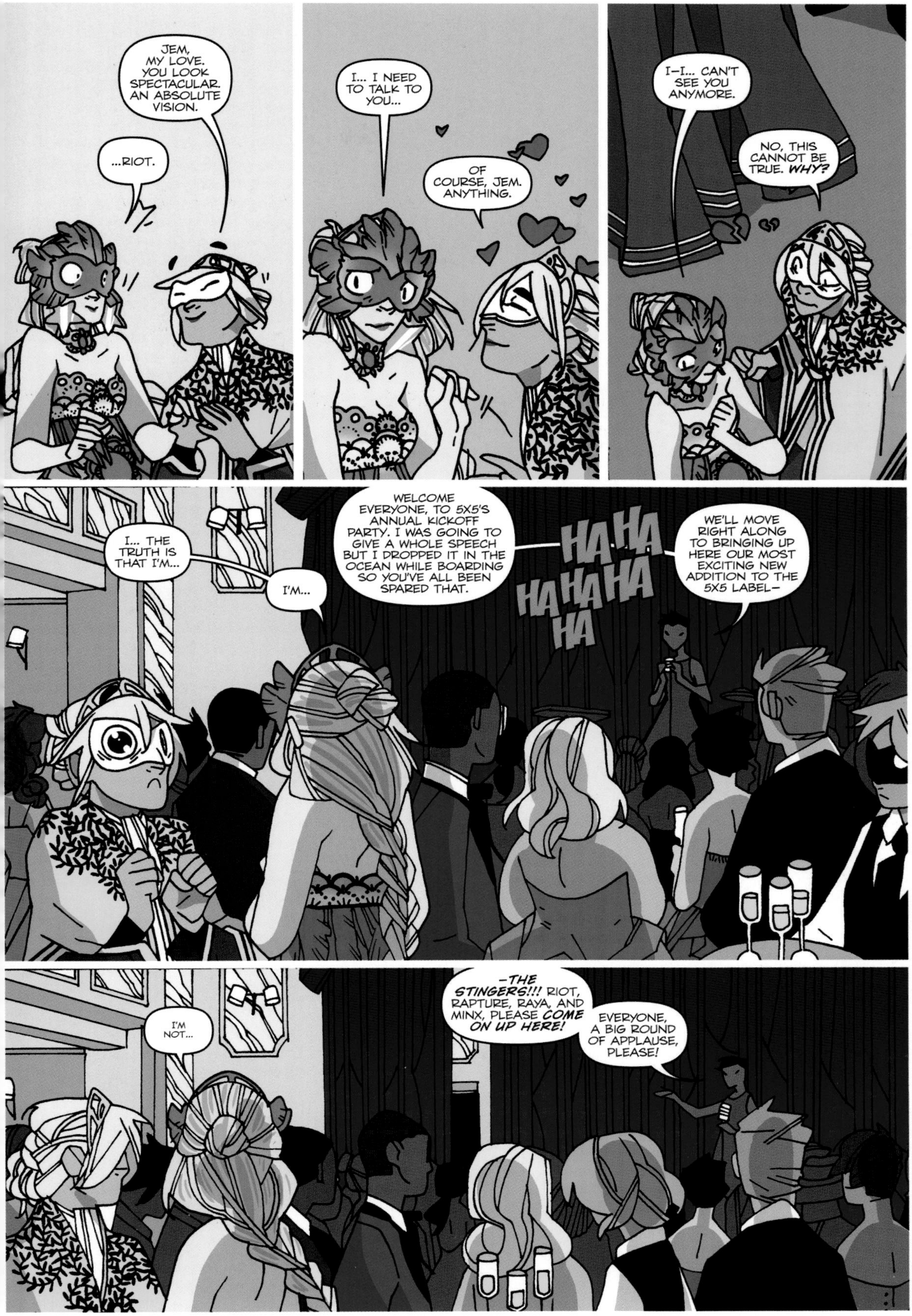
...RIOT.
JEM, MY LOVE. YOU LOOK SPECTACULAR. AN ABSOLUTE VISION.
I... I NEED TO TALK TO YOU...
OF COURSE, JEM. ANYTHING.
I—I... CAN'T SEE YOU ANYMORE.
NO, THIS CANNOT BE TRUE. WHY?
I... THE TRUTH IS THAT I'M...
I'M...
WELCOME EVERYONE, TO 5X5'S ANNUAL KICKOFF PARTY. I WAS GOING TO GIVE A WHOLE SPEECH BUT I DROPPED IT IN THE OCEAN WHILE BOARDING SO YOU'VE ALL BEEN SPARED THAT.
HA HA HA HA HA HA
WE'LL MOVE RIGHT ALONG TO BRINGING UP HERE OUR MOST EXCITING NEW ADDITION TO THE 5X5 LABEL—
I'M NOT...
—THE STINGERS!!! RIOT, RAPTURE, RAYA, AND MINX, PLEASE COME ON UP HERE!
EVERYONE, A BIG ROUND OF APPLAUSE, PLEASE!

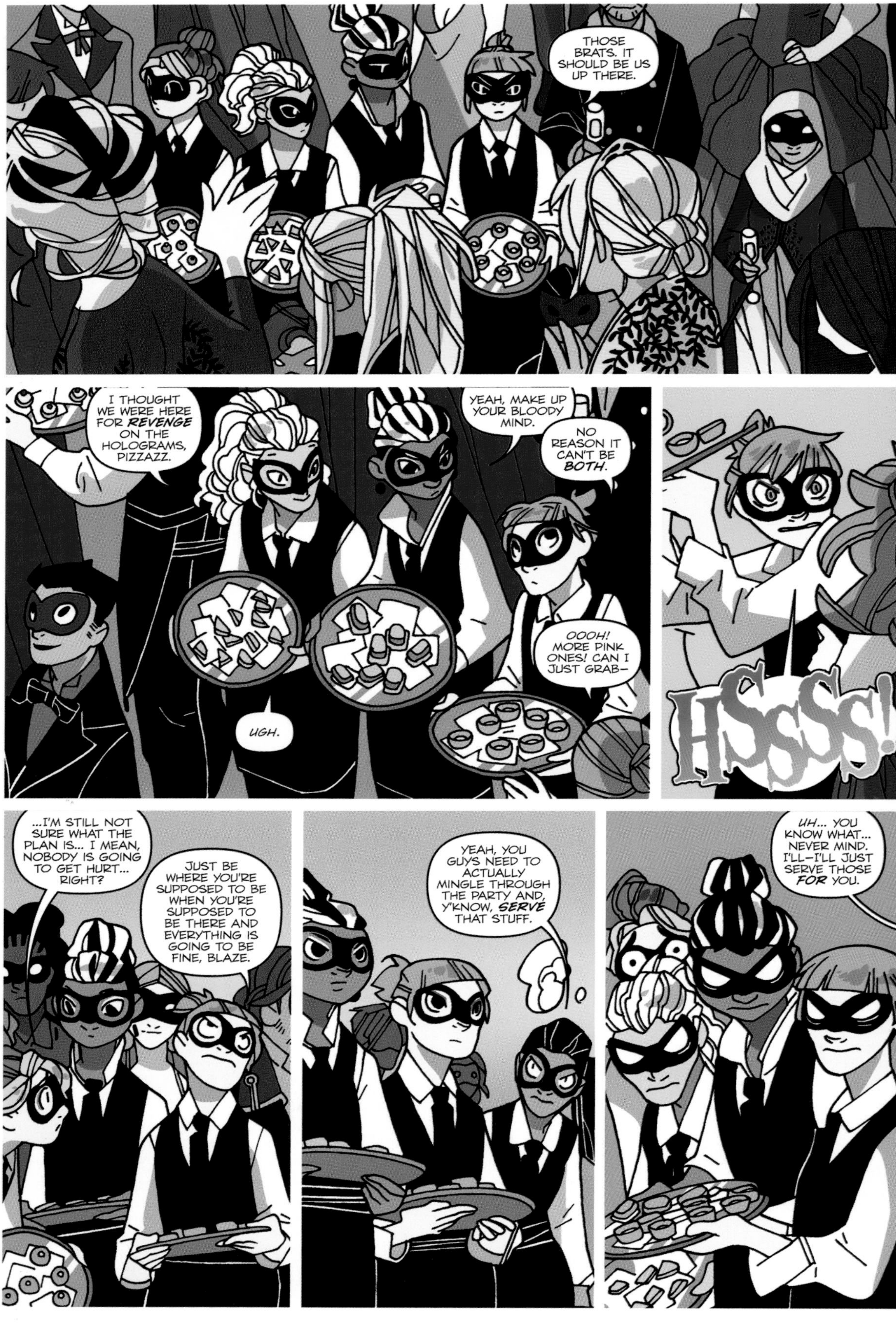

THOSE BRATS. IT SHOULD BE US UP THERE.
I THOUGHT WE WERE HERE FOR *REVENGE* ON THE HOLOGRAMS, PIZZAZZ.
YEAH, MAKE UP YOUR BLOODY MIND.
NO REASON IT CAN'T BE *BOTH*.
OOOH! MORE PINK ONES! CAN I JUST GRAB–
UGH.
HSSSS!
...I'M STILL NOT SURE WHAT THE PLAN IS... I MEAN, NOBODY IS GOING TO GET HURT... RIGHT?
JUST BE WHERE YOU'RE SUPPOSED TO BE WHEN YOU'RE SUPPOSED TO BE THERE AND EVERYTHING IS GOING TO BE FINE, BLAZE.
YEAH, YOU GUYS NEED TO ACTUALLY MINGLE THROUGH THE PARTY AND, Y'KNOW, *SERVE* THAT STUFF.
UH... YOU KNOW WHAT... NEVER MIND. I'LL–I'LL JUST SERVE THOSE *FOR* YOU.

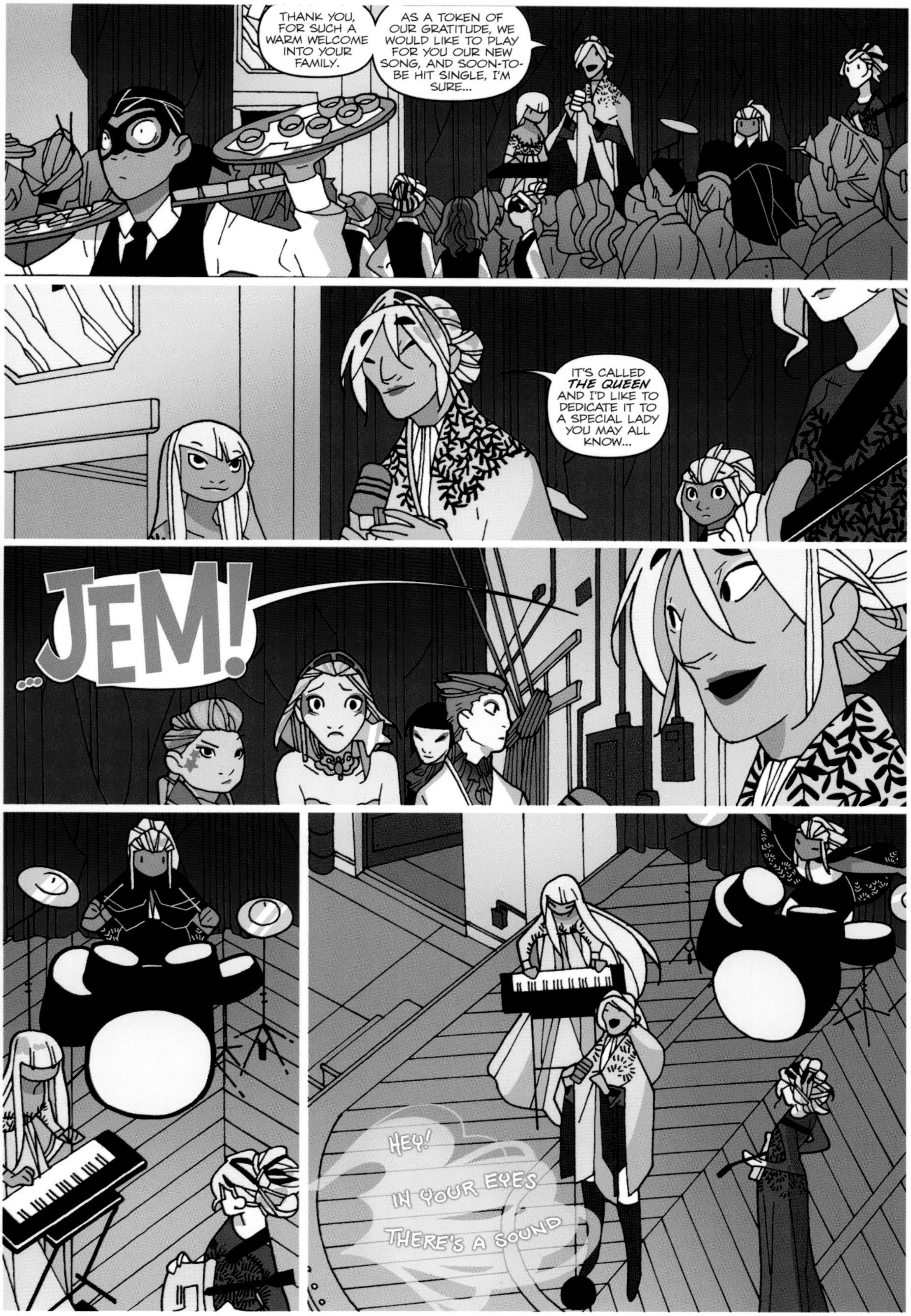
THANK YOU, FOR SUCH A WARM WELCOME INTO YOUR FAMILY.
AS A TOKEN OF OUR GRATITUDE, WE WOULD LIKE TO PLAY FOR YOU OUR NEW SONG, AND SOON-TO-BE HIT SINGLE, I'M SURE...
IT'S CALLED THE QUEEN AND I'D LIKE TO DEDICATE IT TO A SPECIAL LADY YOU MAY ALL KNOW...
JEM!
...
HEY!
IN YOUR EYES
THERE'S A SOUND

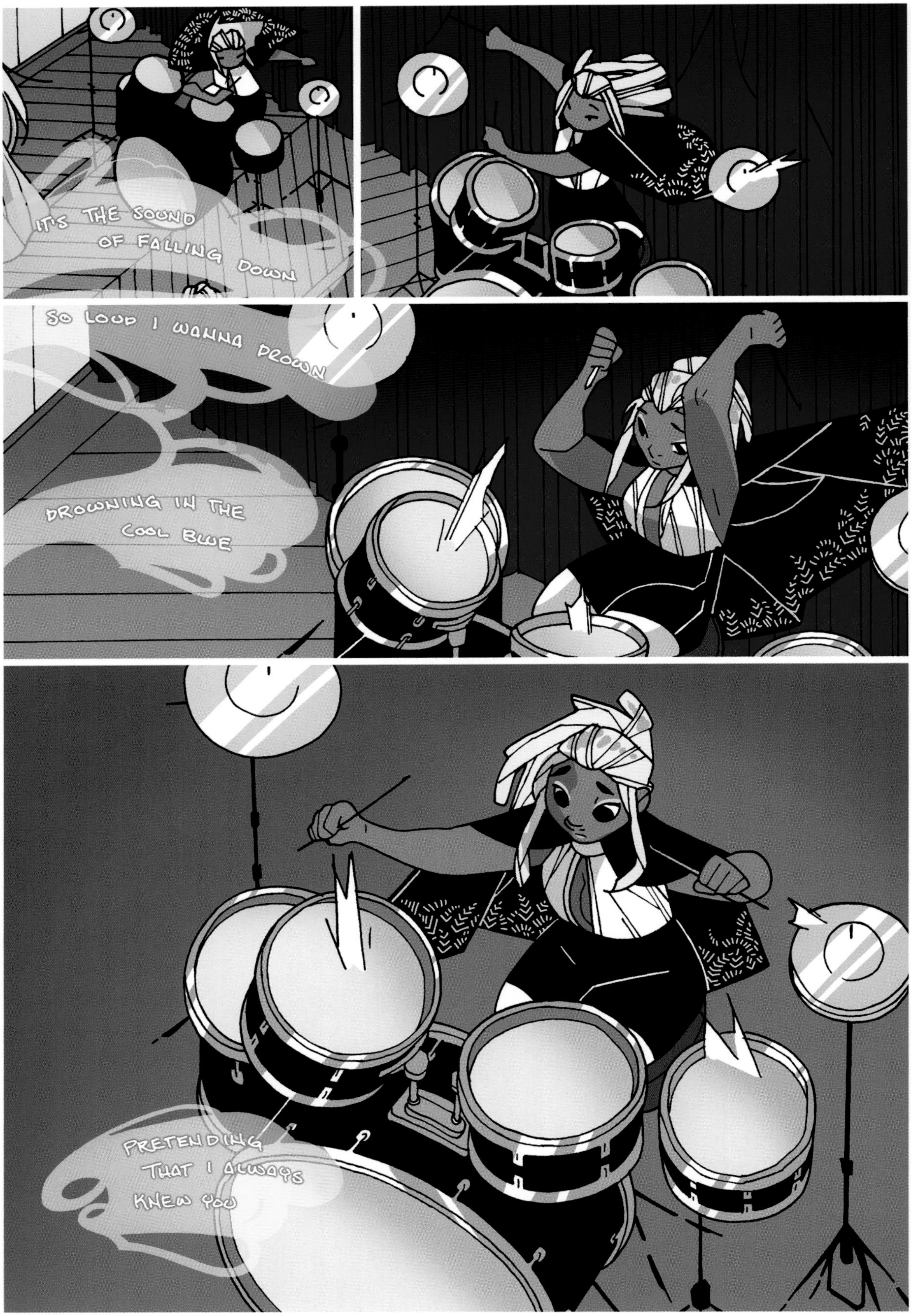
IT'S THE SOUND
OF FALLING DOWN
SO LOUD I WANNA DROWN
DROWNING IN THE
COOL BLUE
PRETENDING
THAT I ALWAYS
KNEW YOU

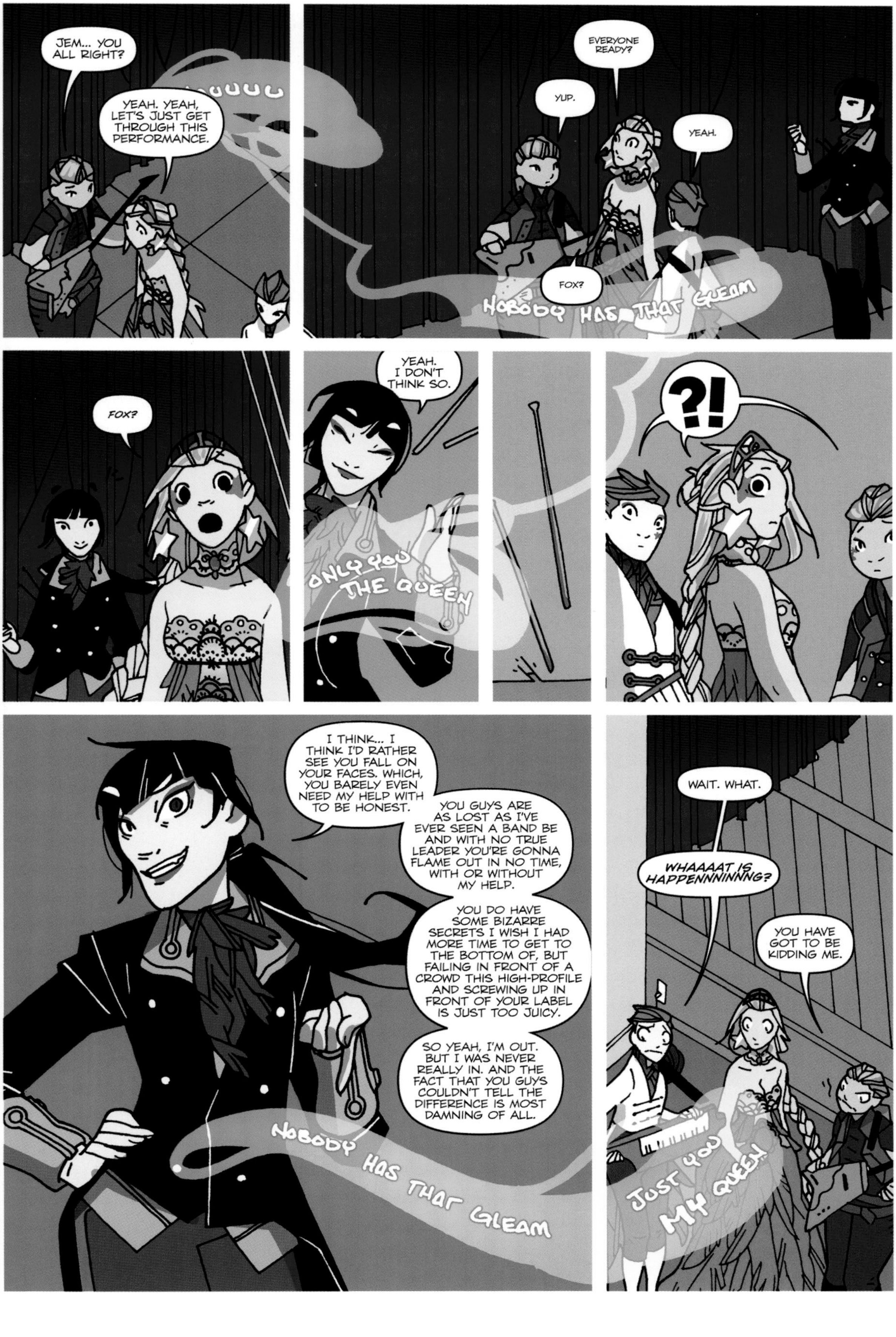
JEM... YOU ALL RIGHT?
YEAH. YEAH, LET'S JUST GET THROUGH THIS PERFORMANCE.
EVERYONE READY?
YUP.
YEAH.
FOX?
NOBODY HAS THAT GLEAM
FOX?
YEAH. I DON'T THINK SO.
ONLY YOU THE QUEEN
?!
I THINK... I THINK I'D RATHER SEE YOU FALL ON YOUR FACES. WHICH, YOU BARELY EVEN NEED MY HELP WITH TO BE HONEST.
YOU GUYS ARE AS LOST AS I'VE EVER SEEN A BAND BE AND WITH NO TRUE LEADER YOU'RE GONNA FLAME OUT IN NO TIME, WITH OR WITHOUT MY HELP.
YOU DO HAVE SOME BIZARRE SECRETS I WISH I HAD MORE TIME TO GET TO THE BOTTOM OF, BUT FAILING IN FRONT OF A CROWD THIS HIGH-PROFILE AND SCREWING UP IN FRONT OF YOUR LABEL IS JUST TOO JUICY.
SO YEAH, I'M OUT. BUT I WAS NEVER REALLY IN. AND THE FACT THAT YOU GUYS COULDN'T TELL THE DIFFERENCE IS MOST DAMNING OF ALL.
NOBODY HAS THAT GLEAM
WAIT. WHAT.
WHAAAAT IS HAPPENNNINNNG?
YOU HAVE GOT TO BE KIDDING ME.
JUST YOU MY QUEEN

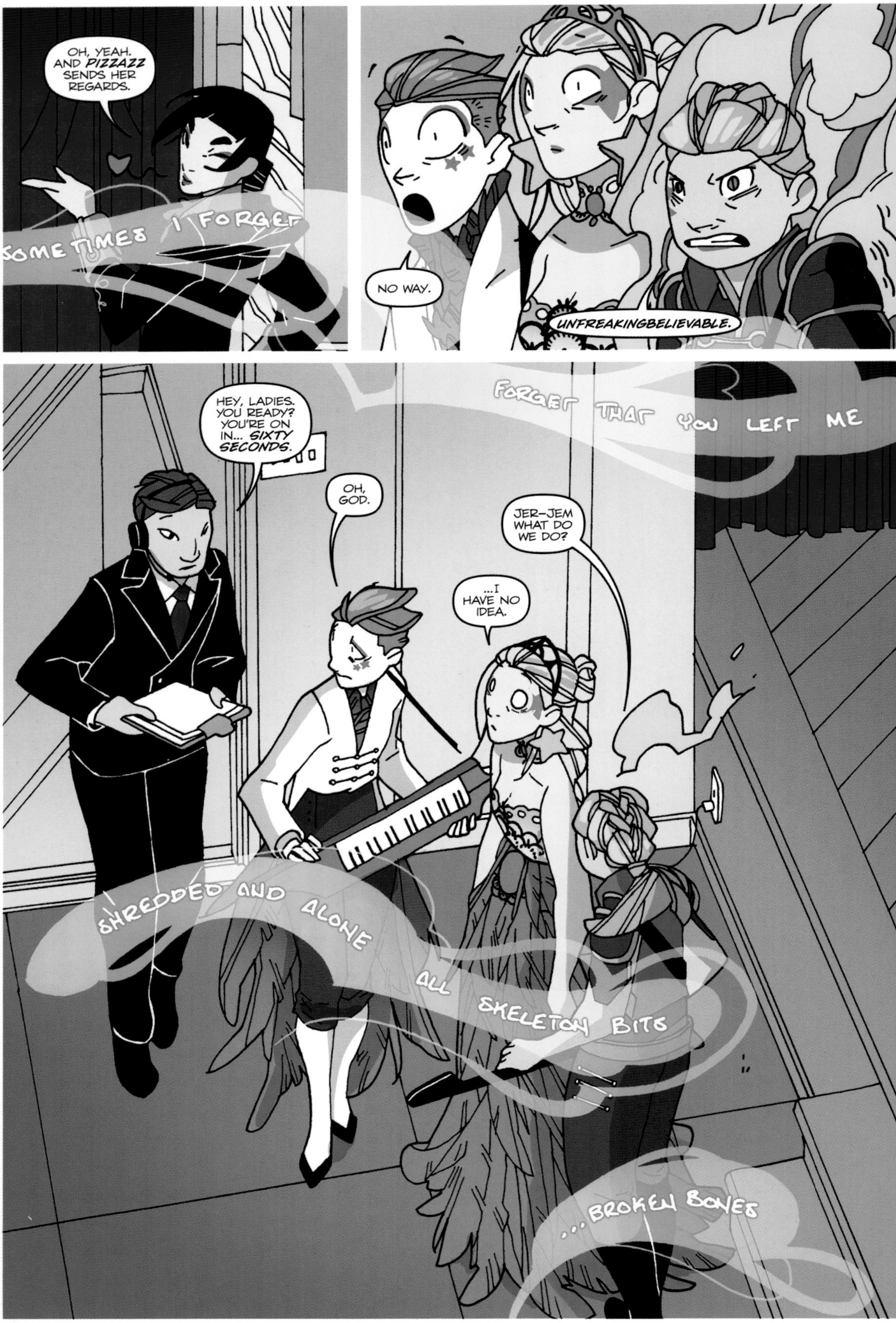
OH, YEAH. AND PIZZAZZ SENDS HER REGARDS.
SOMETIMES I FORGET
NO WAY.
UNFREAKINGBELIEVABLE.
FORGET THAT YOU LEFT ME
HEY, LADIES. YOU READY? YOU'RE ON IN... SIXTY SECONDS.
OH, GOD.
JER-JEM WHAT DO WE DO?
...I HAVE NO IDEA.
SHREDDED AND ALONE
ALL SKELETON BITS
...BROKEN BONES

COVER ART BY **JEN BARTEL**

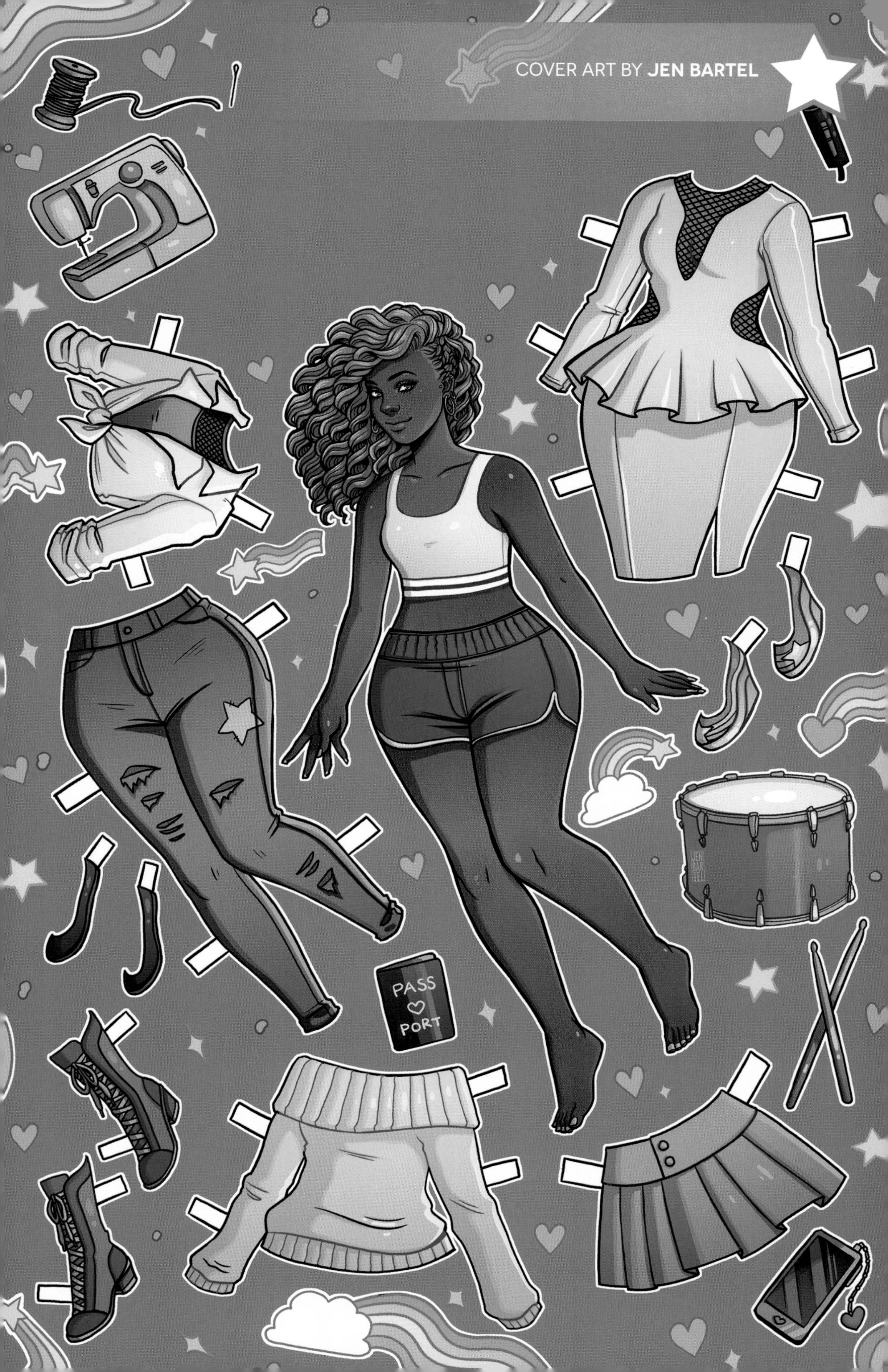
PASS
PORT
JEN
BAR
TEL

ENTER THE STINGERS PART 5

COVER ART BY **MEREDITH MCCLAREN**

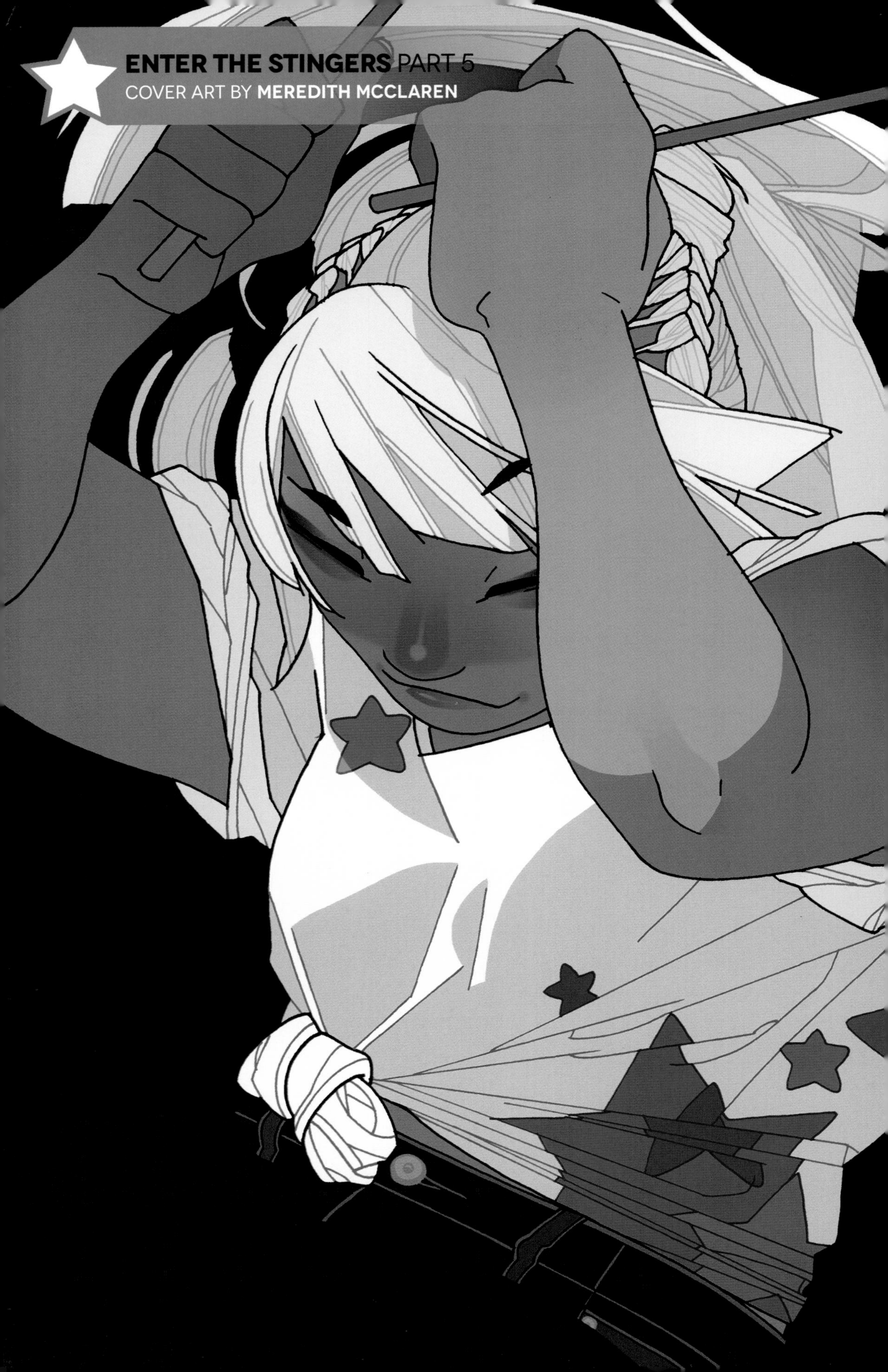

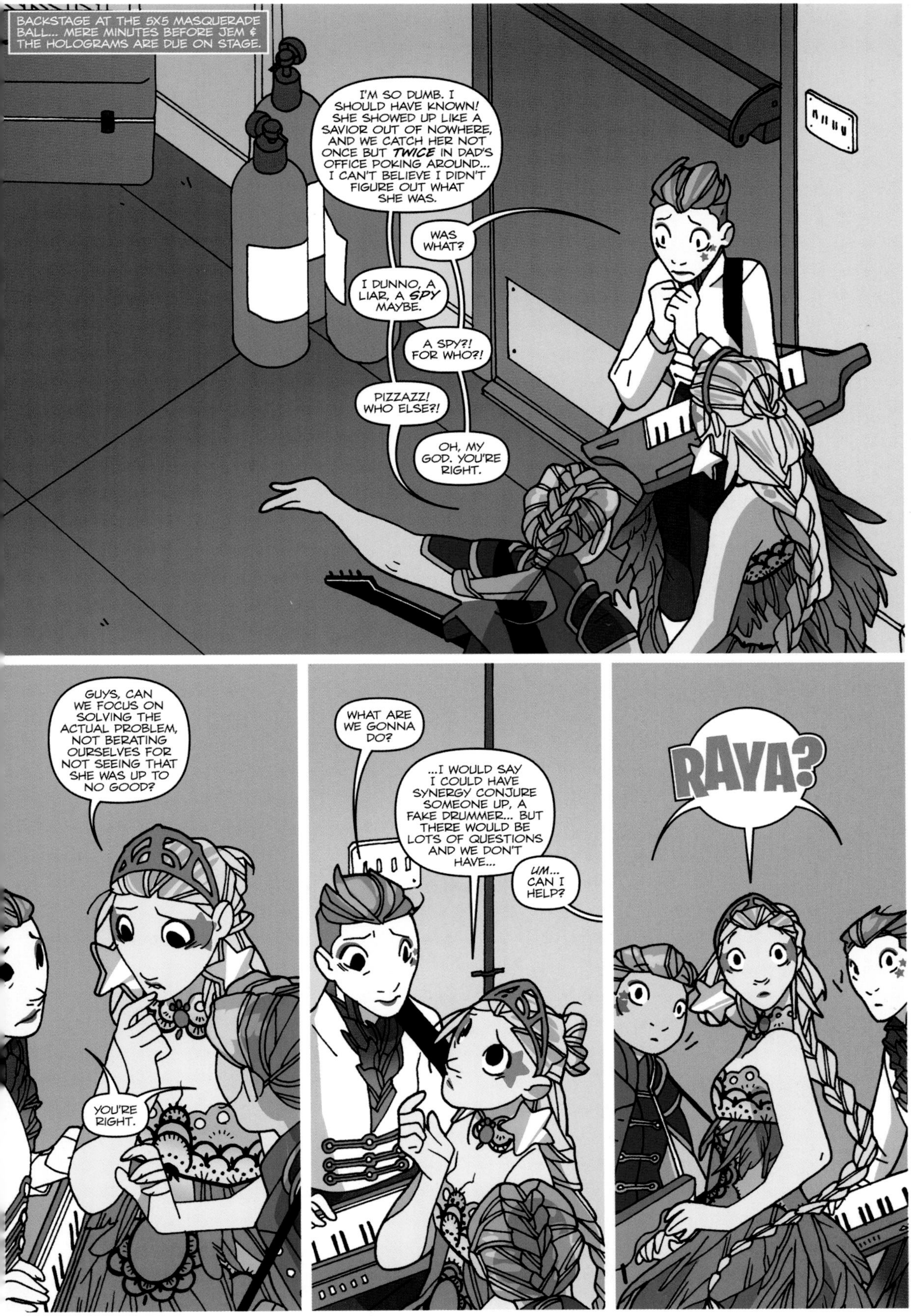

BACKSTAGE AT THE 5X5 MASQUERADE BALL... MERE MINUTES BEFORE JEM & THE HOLOGRAMS ARE DUE ON STAGE.
I'M SO DUMB. I SHOULD HAVE KNOWN! SHE SHOWED UP LIKE A SAVIOR OUT OF NOWHERE, AND WE CATCH HER NOT ONCE BUT TWICE IN DAD'S OFFICE POKING AROUND... I CAN'T BELIEVE I DIDN'T FIGURE OUT WHAT SHE WAS.
WAS WHAT?
I DUNNO, A LIAR, A SPY MAYBE.
A SPY?! FOR WHO?!
PIZZAZZ! WHO ELSE?!
OH, MY GOD. YOU'RE RIGHT.
GUYS, CAN WE FOCUS ON SOLVING THE ACTUAL PROBLEM, NOT BERATING OURSELVES FOR NOT SEEING THAT SHE WAS UP TO NO GOOD?
YOU'RE RIGHT.
WHAT ARE WE GONNA DO?
...I WOULD SAY I COULD HAVE SYNERGY CONJURE SOMEONE UP, A FAKE DRUMMER... BUT THERE WOULD BE LOTS OF QUESTIONS AND WE DON'T HAVE...
UM... CAN I HELP?
RAYA?

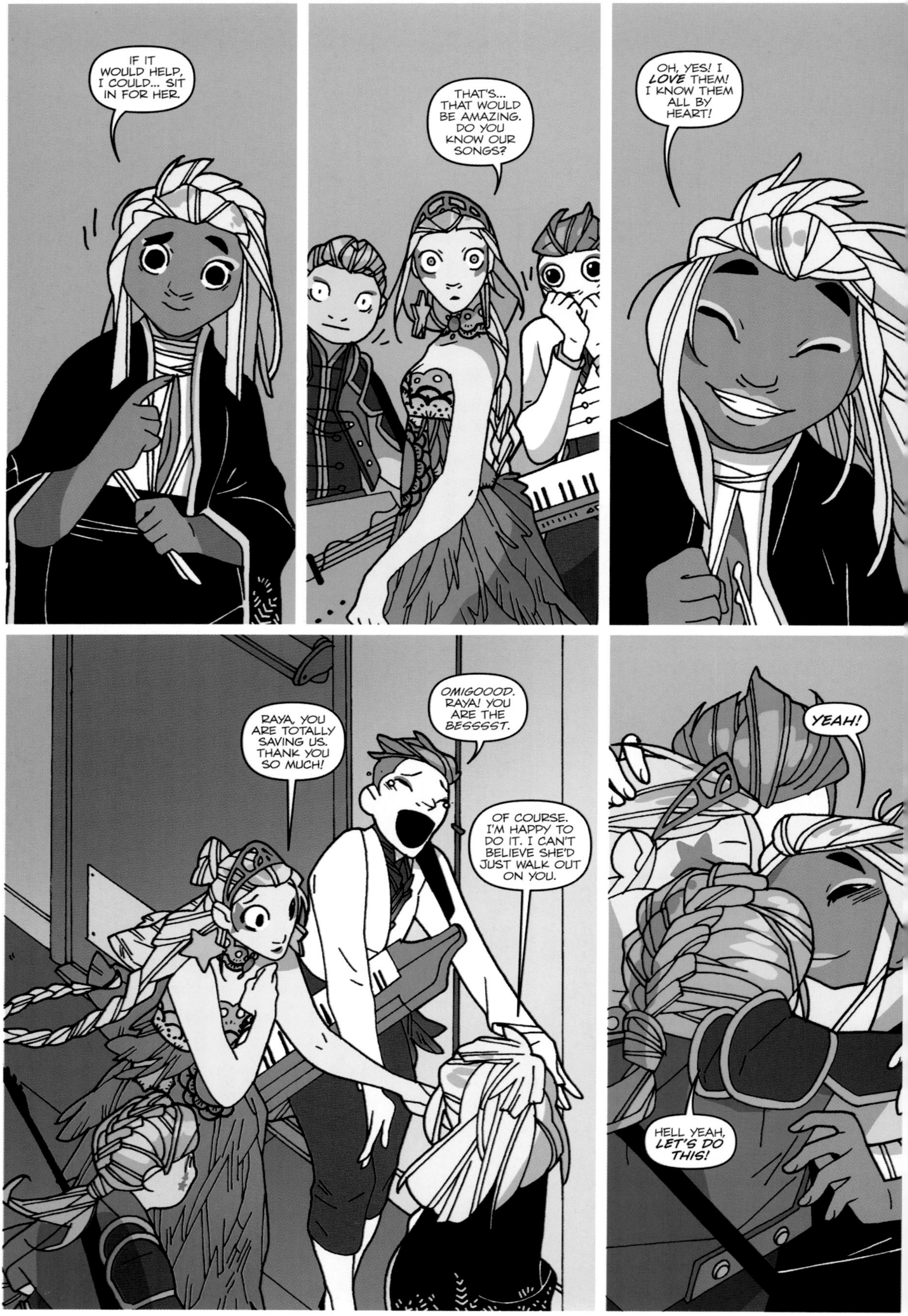
IF IT WOULD HELP, I COULD... SIT IN FOR HER.
THAT'S... THAT WOULD BE AMAZING. DO YOU KNOW OUR SONGS?
OH, YES! I *LOVE* THEM! I KNOW THEM ALL BY HEART!
RAYA, YOU ARE TOTALLY SAVING US. THANK YOU SO MUCH!
OMIGOOOD. RAYA! YOU ARE THE BESSSST.
OF COURSE. I'M HAPPY TO DO IT. I CAN'T BELIEVE SHE'D JUST WALK OUT ON YOU.
YEAH!
HELL YEAH, *LET'S DO THIS!*

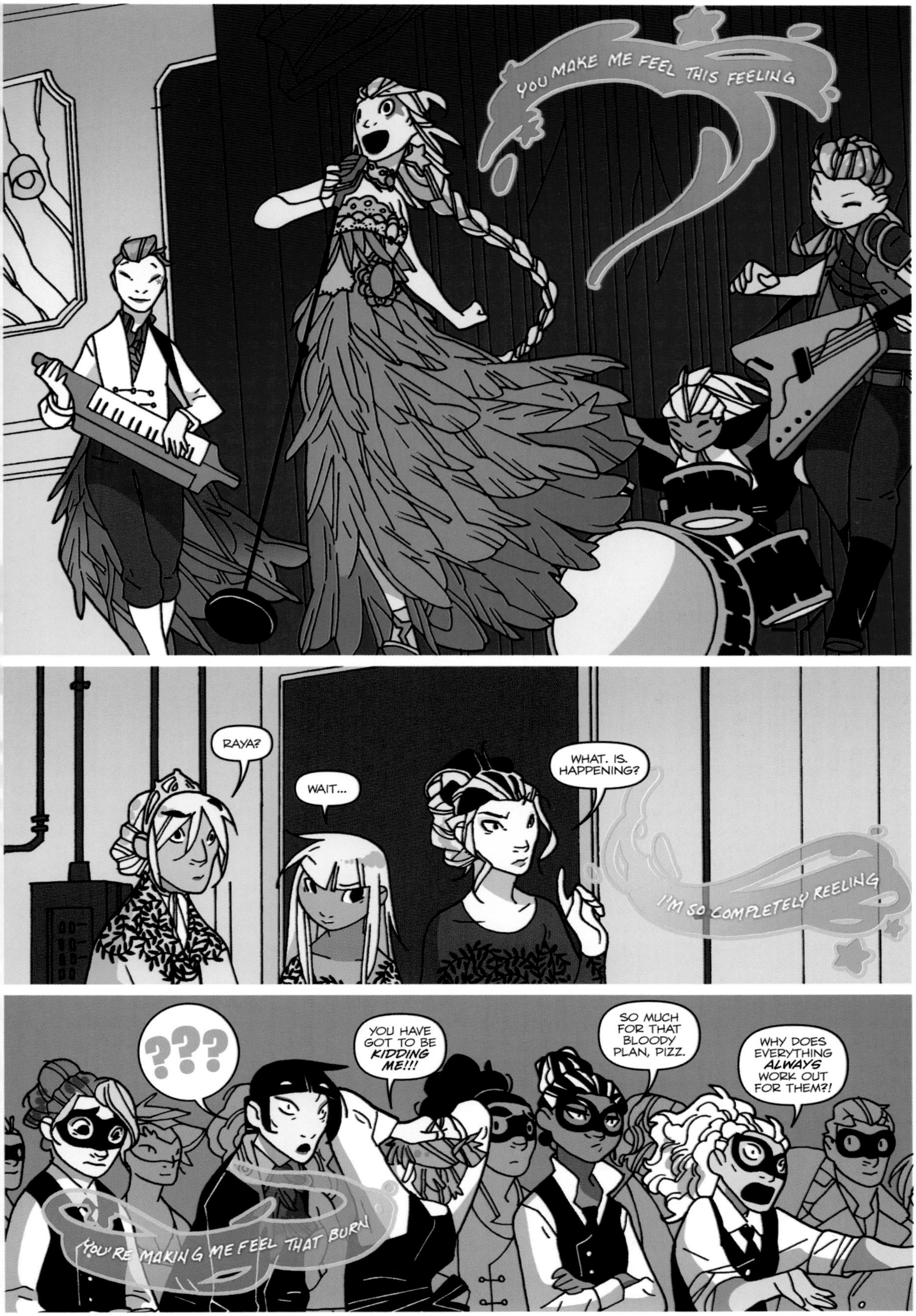
YOU MAKE ME FEEL THIS FEELING
RAYA?
WAIT...
WHAT. IS. HAPPENING?
I'M SO COMPLETELY REELING
???
YOU HAVE GOT TO BE *KIDDING ME!!!*
SO MUCH FOR THAT BLOODY PLAN, PIZZ.
WHY DOES EVERYTHING *ALWAYS* WORK OUT FOR THEM?!
YOU'RE MAKING ME FEEL THAT BURN

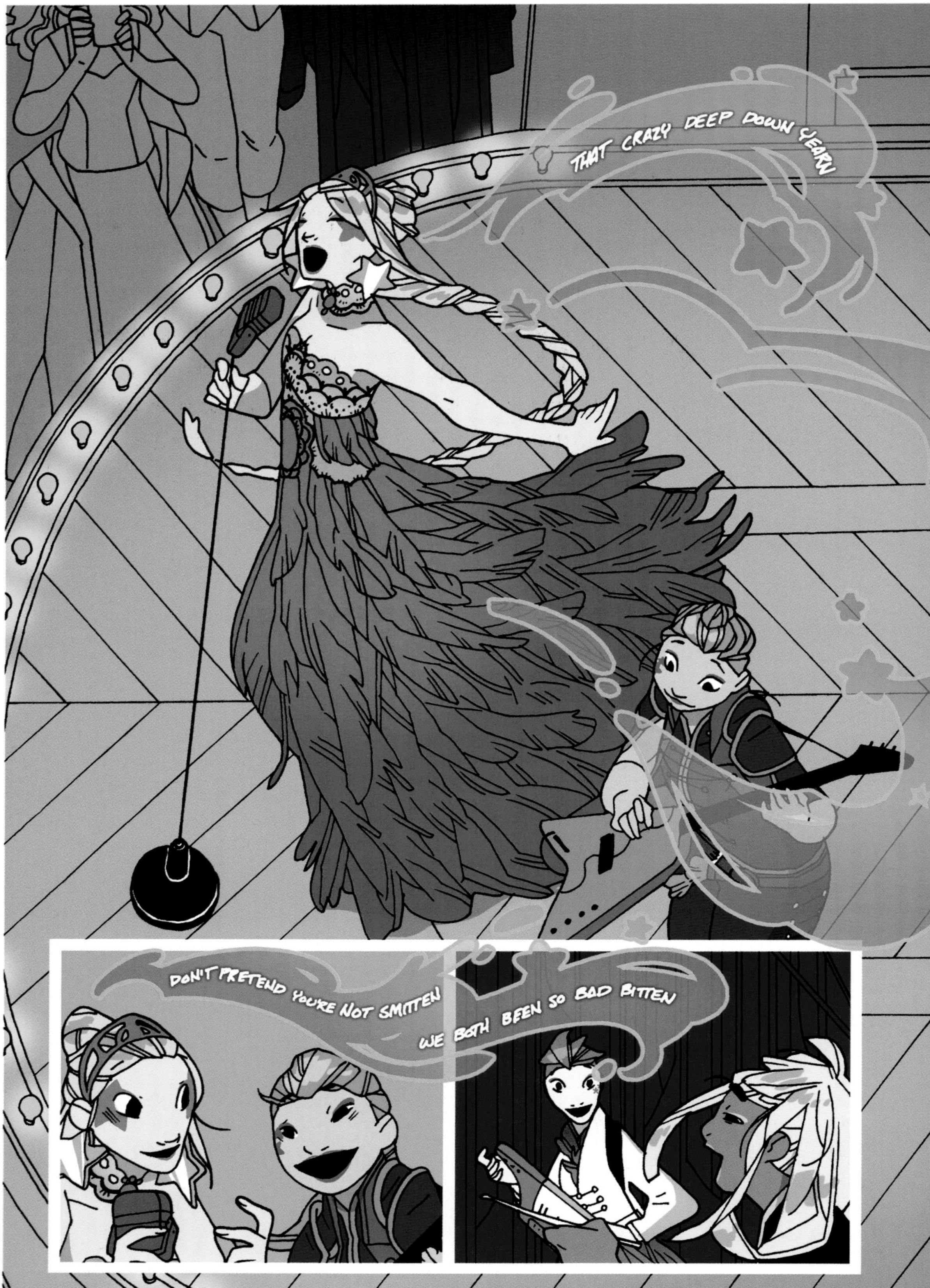
THAT CRAZY DEEP DOWN YEARN
DON'T PRETEND YOU'RE NOT SMITTEN
WE BOTH BEEN SO BAD BITTEN

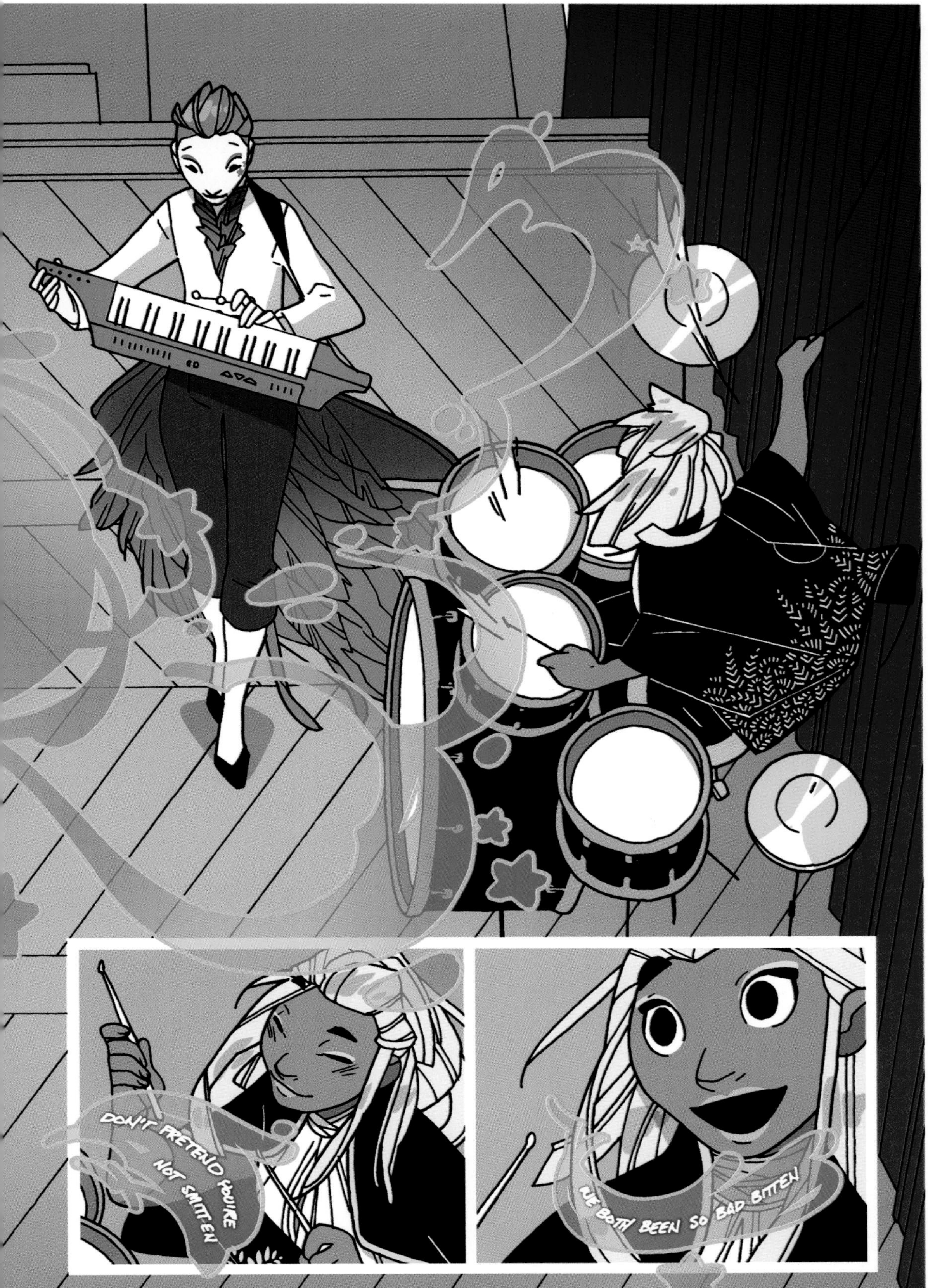
DON'T PRETEND YOU'RE NOT SMITTEN
WE BOTH BEEN SO BAD BITTEN

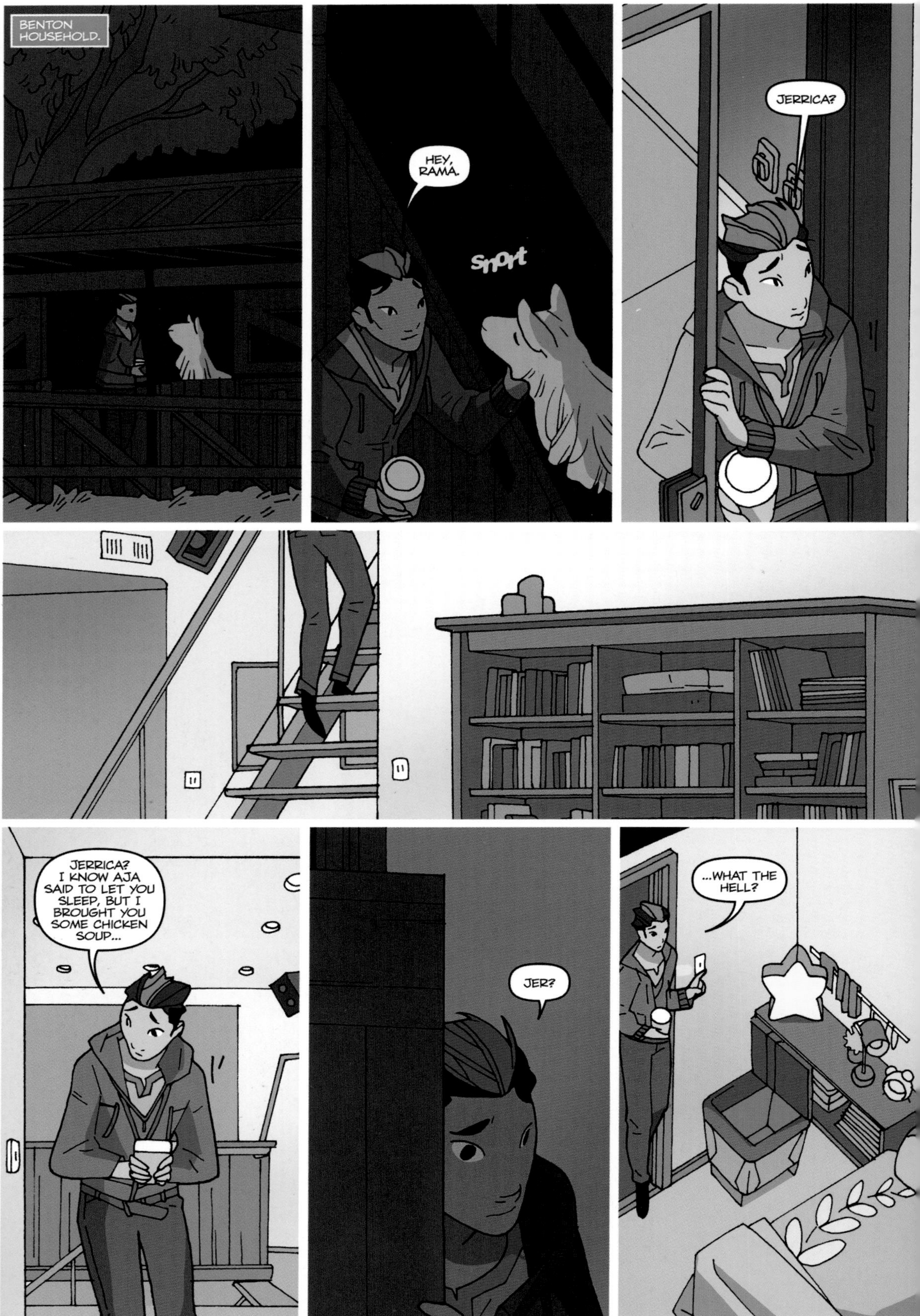
BENTON HOUSEHOLD.
HEY, RAMA.
SNORT
JERRICA?
JERRICA? I KNOW AJA SAID TO LET YOU SLEEP, BUT I BROUGHT YOU SOME CHICKEN SOUP...
JER?
...WHAT THE HELL?

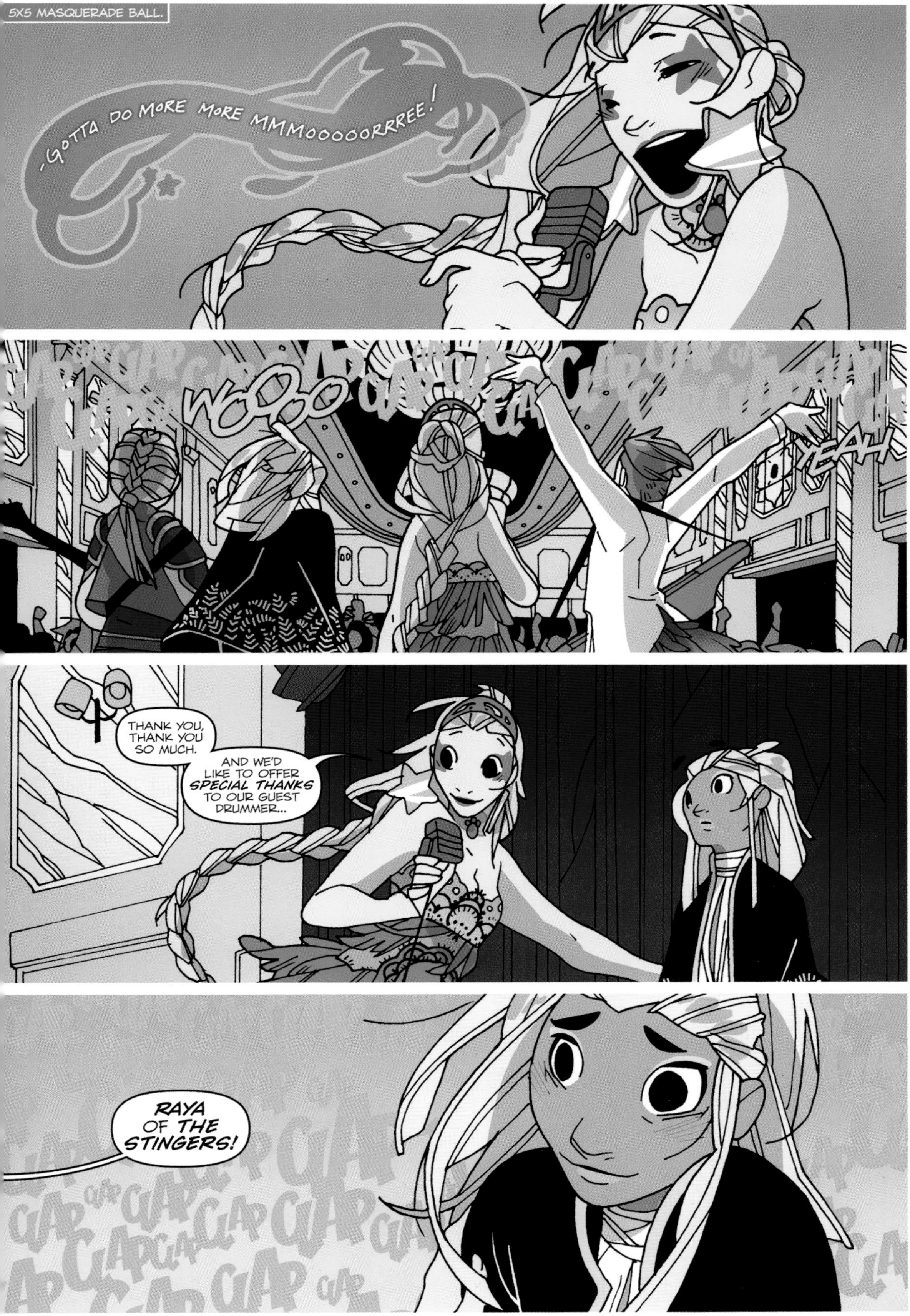
5X5 MASQUERADE BALL.
-GOTTA DO MORE MORE MMMOOOOORRREE!
CLAP CLAP CLAP WOOOO CLAP CLAP CLAP
YEAH
THANK YOU, THANK YOU SO MUCH.
AND WE'D LIKE TO OFFER *SPECIAL THANKS* TO OUR GUEST DRUMMER...
RAYA OF *THE STINGERS!*
CLAP CLAP CLAP CLAP CLAP CLAP

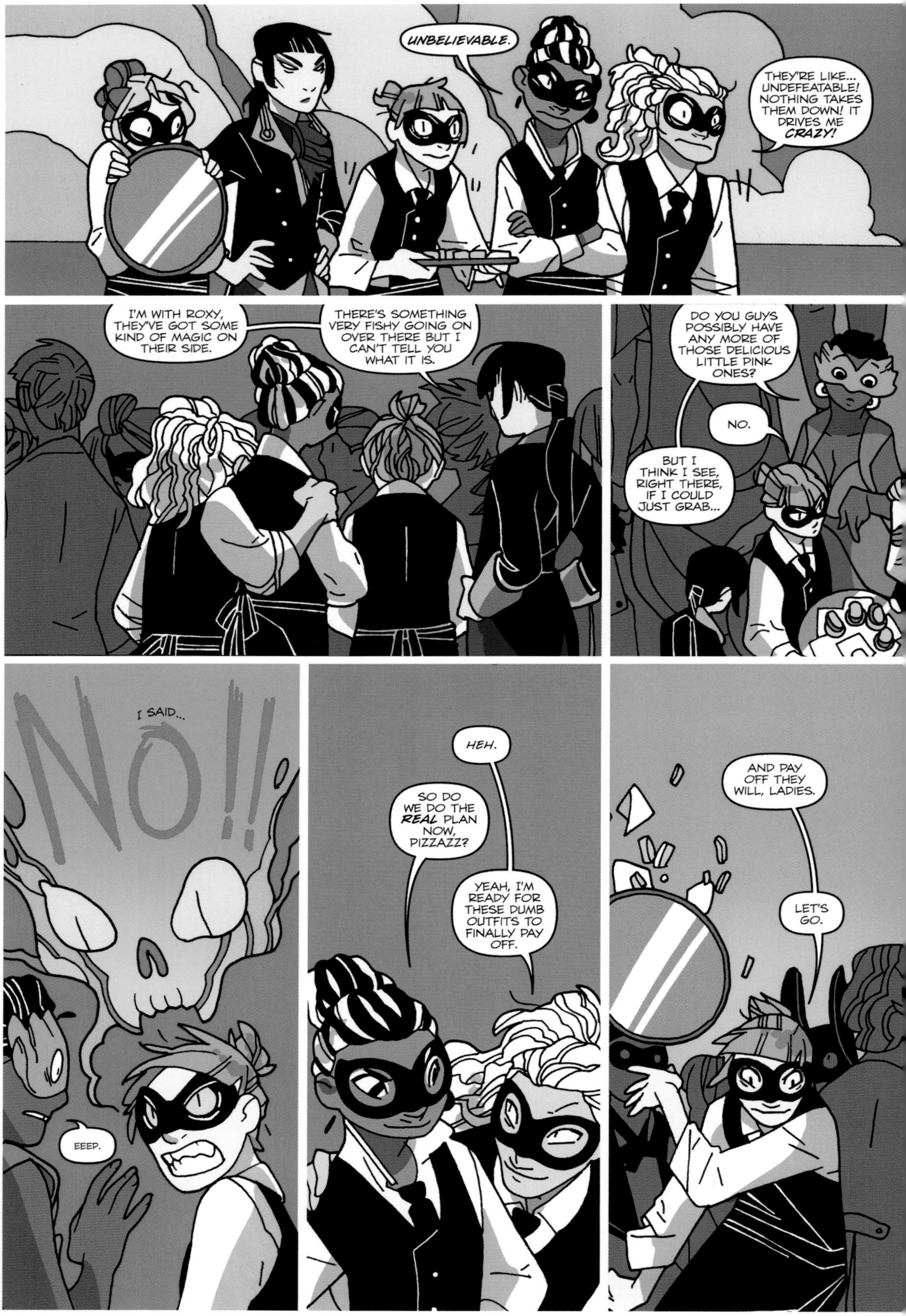
UNBELIEVABLE.
THEY'RE LIKE... UNDEFEATABLE! NOTHING TAKES THEM DOWN! IT DRIVES ME CRAZY!
I'M WITH ROXY, THEY'VE GOT SOME KIND OF MAGIC ON THEIR SIDE.
THERE'S SOMETHING VERY FISHY GOING ON OVER THERE BUT I CAN'T TELL YOU WHAT IT IS.
DO YOU GUYS POSSIBLY HAVE ANY MORE OF THOSE DELICIOUS LITTLE PINK ONES?
NO.
BUT I THINK I SEE, RIGHT THERE, IF I COULD JUST GRAB...
I SAID...
NO!!
EEEP.
HEH.
SO DO WE DO THE REAL PLAN NOW, PIZZAZZ?
YEAH, I'M READY FOR THESE DUMB OUTFITS TO FINALLY PAY OFF.
AND PAY OFF THEY WILL, LADIES.
LET'S GO.

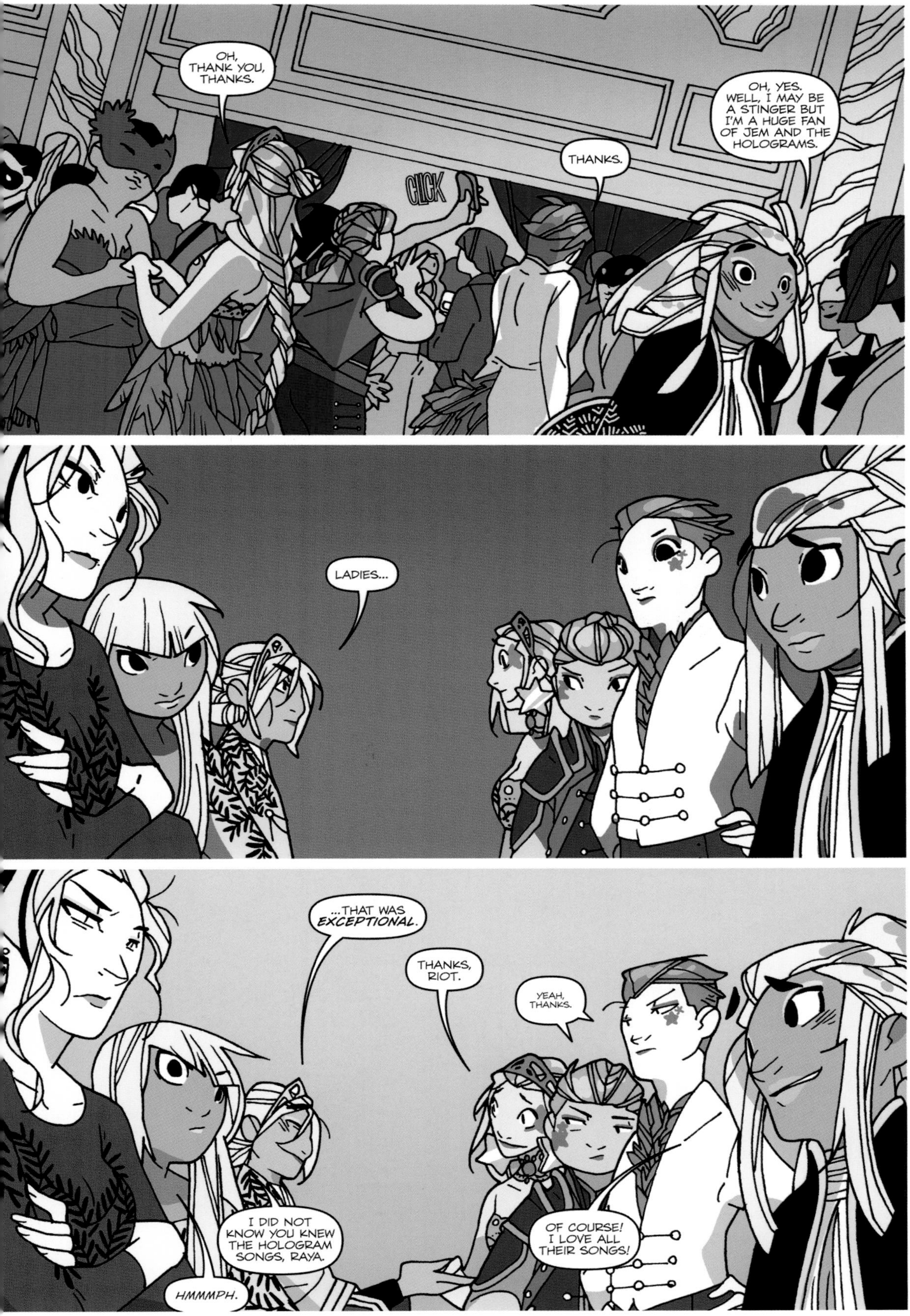
OH, THANK YOU, THANKS.
CLICK
THANKS.
OH, YES. WELL, I MAY BE A STINGER BUT I'M A HUGE FAN OF JEM AND THE HOLOGRAMS.
LADIES...
...THAT WAS *EXCEPTIONAL*.
THANKS, RIOT.
YEAH, THANKS.
I DID NOT KNOW YOU KNEW THE HOLOGRAM SONGS, RAYA.
HMMMPH.
OF COURSE! I LOVE ALL THEIR SONGS!

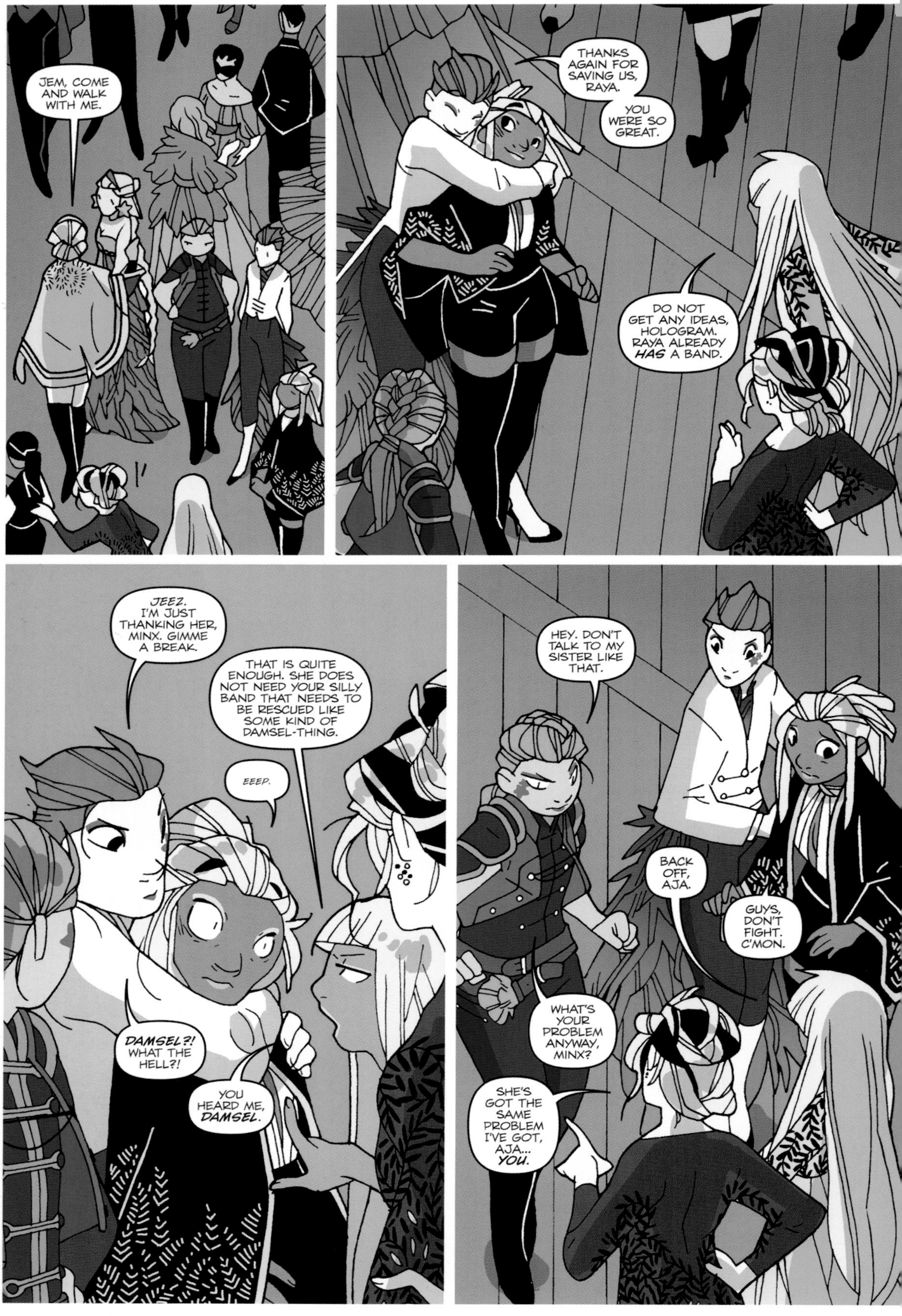
JEM, COME AND WALK WITH ME.
THANKS AGAIN FOR SAVING US, RAYA.
YOU WERE SO GREAT.
DO NOT GET ANY IDEAS, HOLOGRAM. RAYA ALREADY *HAS* A BAND.
JEEZ. I'M JUST THANKING HER, MINX. GIMME A BREAK.
THAT IS QUITE ENOUGH. SHE DOES NOT NEED YOUR SILLY BAND THAT NEEDS TO BE RESCUED LIKE SOME KIND OF DAMSEL-THING.
EEEP.
DAMSEL?! WHAT THE HELL?!
YOU HEARD ME, *DAMSEL*.
HEY. DON'T TALK TO MY SISTER LIKE THAT.
BACK OFF, AJA.
GUYS, DON'T FIGHT. C'MON.
WHAT'S YOUR PROBLEM ANYWAY, MINX?
SHE'S GOT THE SAME PROBLEM I'VE GOT, AJA... *YOU*.

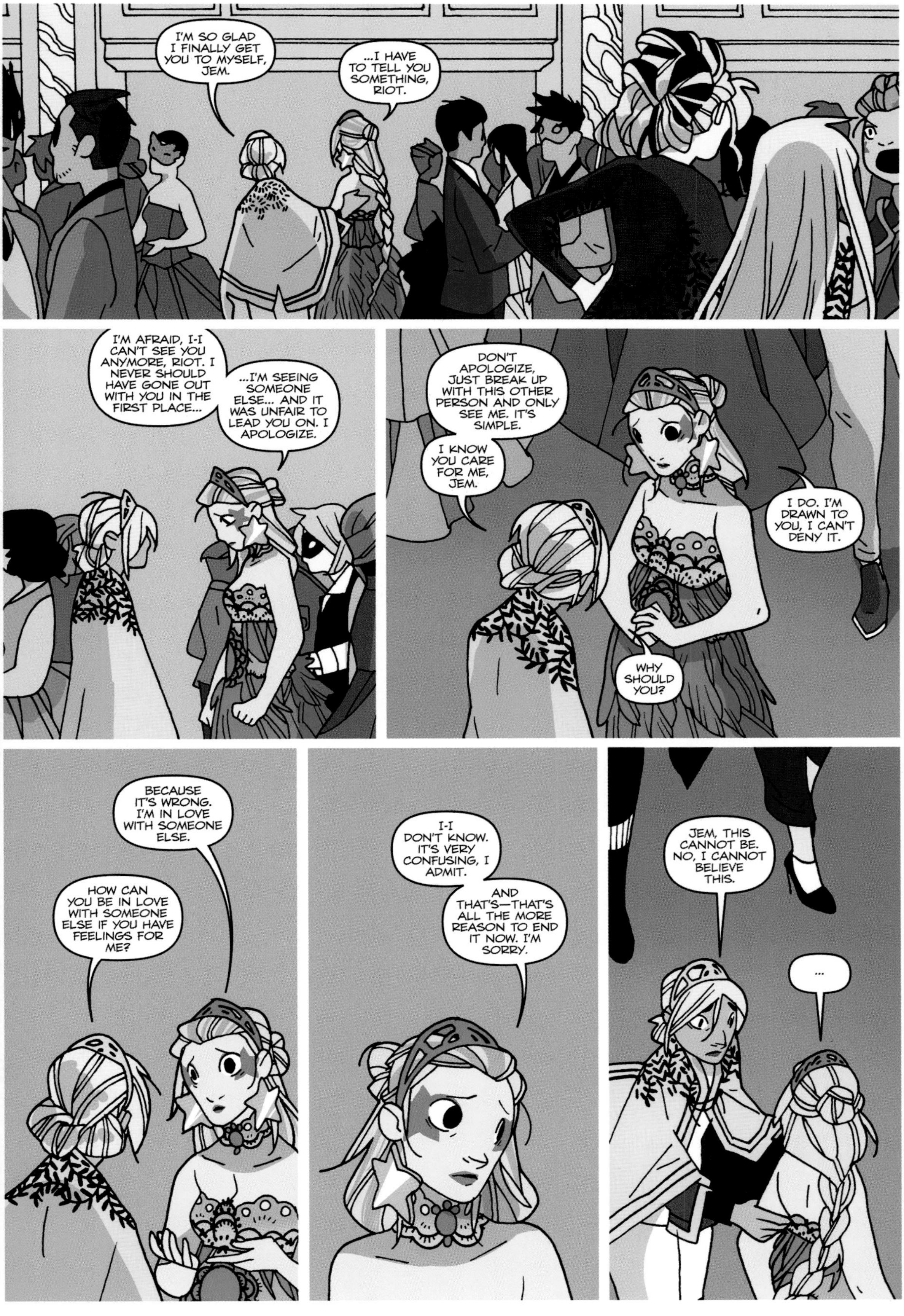
I'M SO GLAD I FINALLY GET YOU TO MYSELF, JEM.
...I HAVE TO TELL YOU SOMETHING, RIOT.
I'M AFRAID, I-I CAN'T SEE YOU ANYMORE, RIOT. I NEVER SHOULD HAVE GONE OUT WITH YOU IN THE FIRST PLACE...
...I'M SEEING SOMEONE ELSE... AND IT WAS UNFAIR TO LEAD YOU ON. I APOLOGIZE.
DON'T APOLOGIZE, JUST BREAK UP WITH THIS OTHER PERSON AND ONLY SEE ME. IT'S SIMPLE.
I KNOW YOU CARE FOR ME, JEM.
I DO. I'M DRAWN TO YOU, I CAN'T DENY IT.
WHY SHOULD YOU?
BECAUSE IT'S WRONG. I'M IN LOVE WITH SOMEONE ELSE.
HOW CAN YOU BE IN LOVE WITH SOMEONE ELSE IF YOU HAVE FEELINGS FOR ME?
I-I DON'T KNOW. IT'S VERY CONFUSING, I ADMIT.
AND THAT'S—THAT'S ALL THE MORE REASON TO END IT NOW. I'M SORRY.
JEM, THIS CANNOT BE. NO, I CANNOT BELIEVE THIS.
...

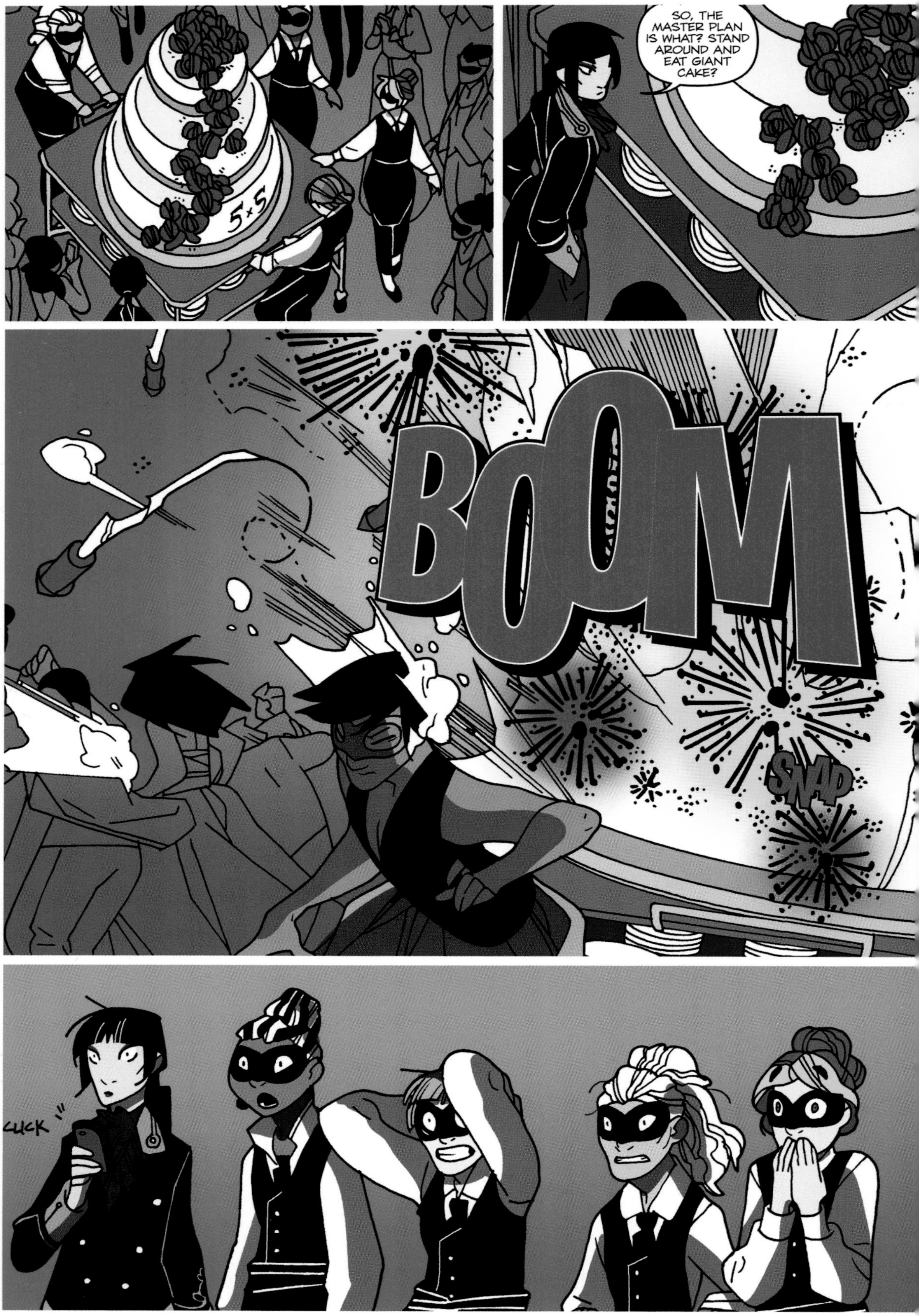
SO, THE MASTER PLAN IS WHAT? STAND AROUND AND EAT GIANT CAKE?
BOOM
SNAP
CLICK

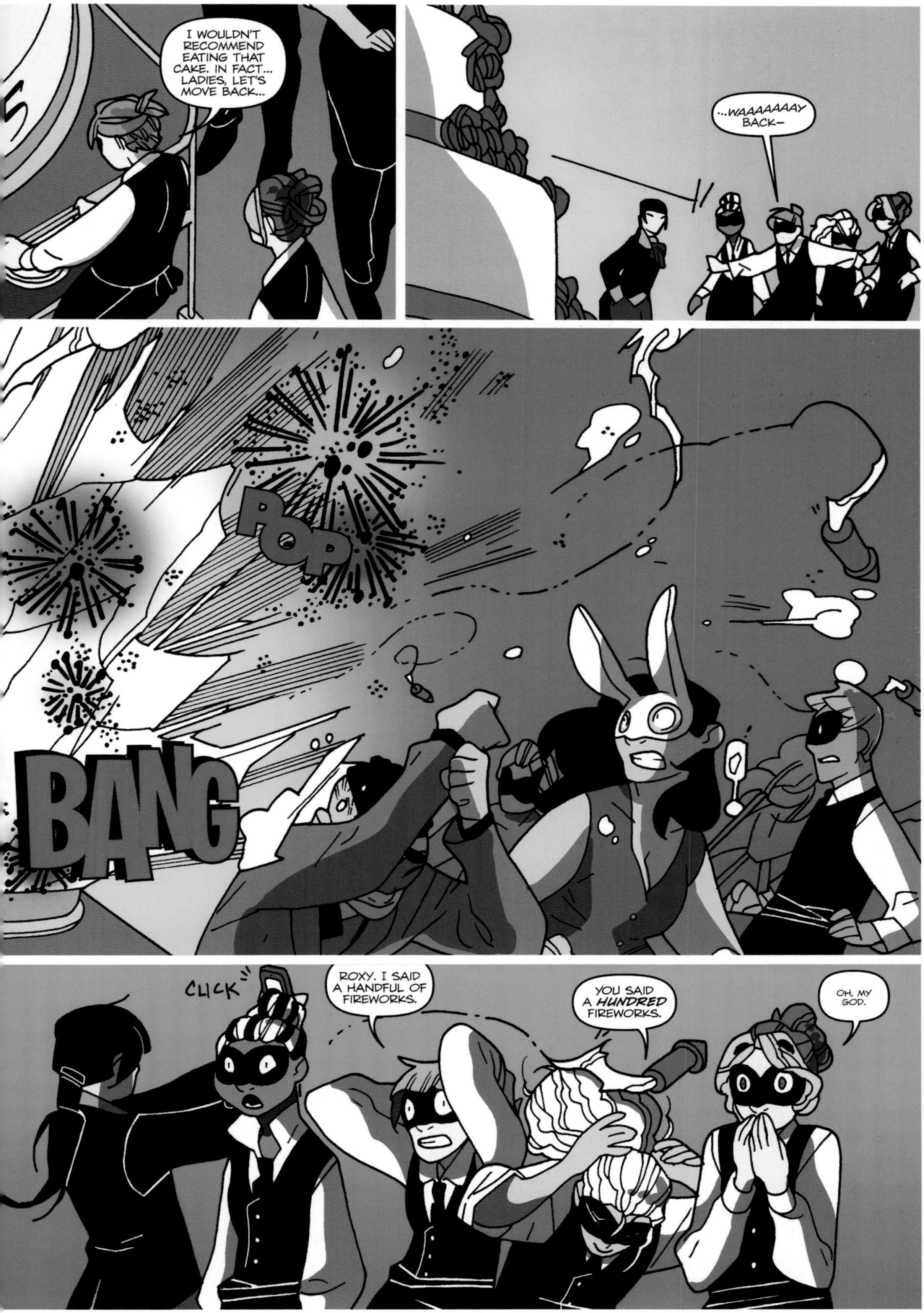
I WOULDN'T RECOMMEND EATING THAT CAKE. IN FACT... LADIES, LET'S MOVE BACK...
...WAAAAAAAY BACK—
POP
BANG
CLICK
ROXY. I SAID A HANDFUL OF FIREWORKS.
YOU SAID A *HUNDRED* FIREWORKS.
OH, MY GOD.

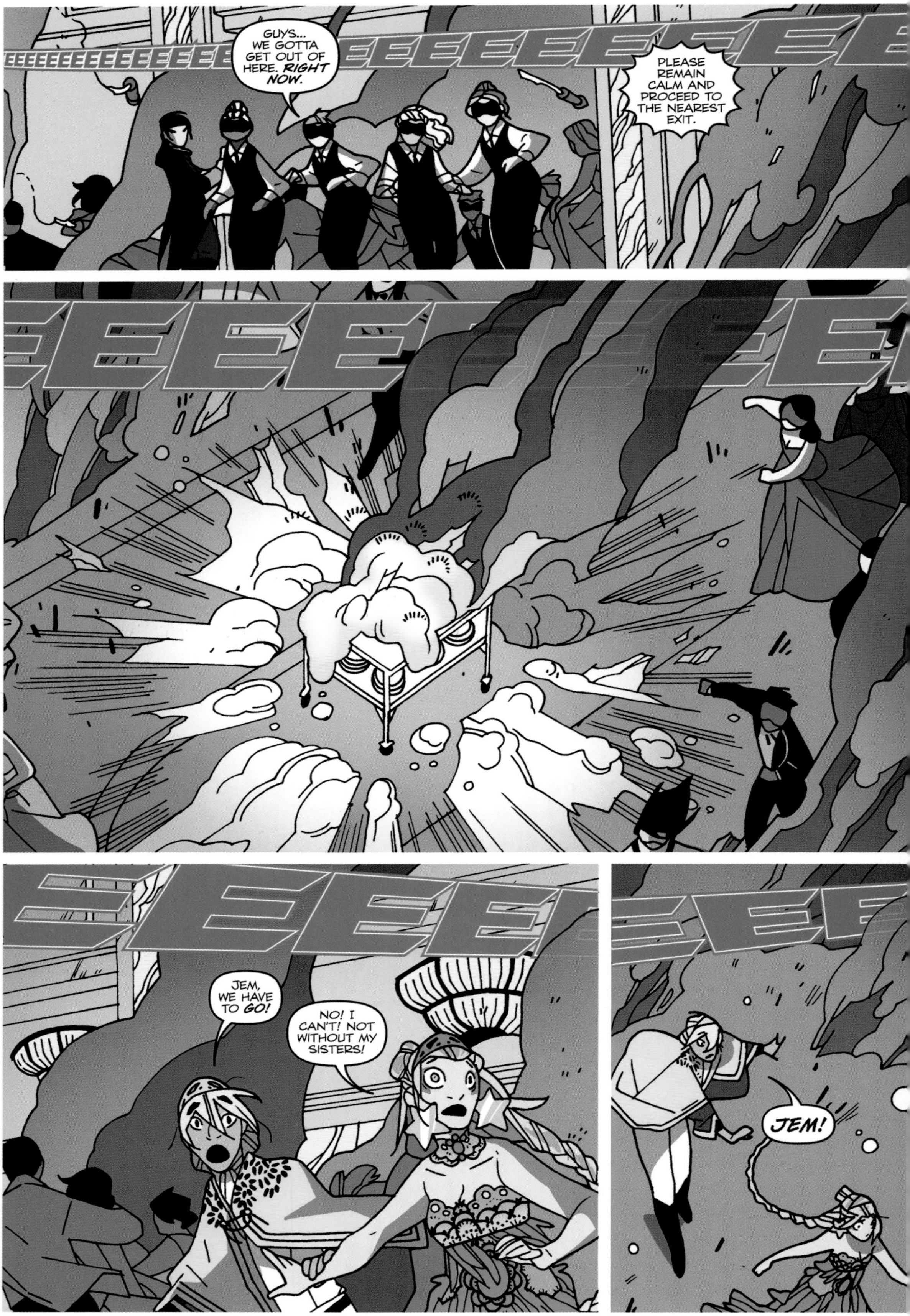
EEEEEEEEEEEEEEEEEEEEEEEEEEE
GUYS... WE GOTTA GET OUT OF HERE. RIGHT NOW.
PLEASE REMAIN CALM AND PROCEED TO THE NEAREST EXIT.
JEM, WE HAVE TO GO!
NO! I CAN'T! NOT WITHOUT MY SISTERS!
JEM!

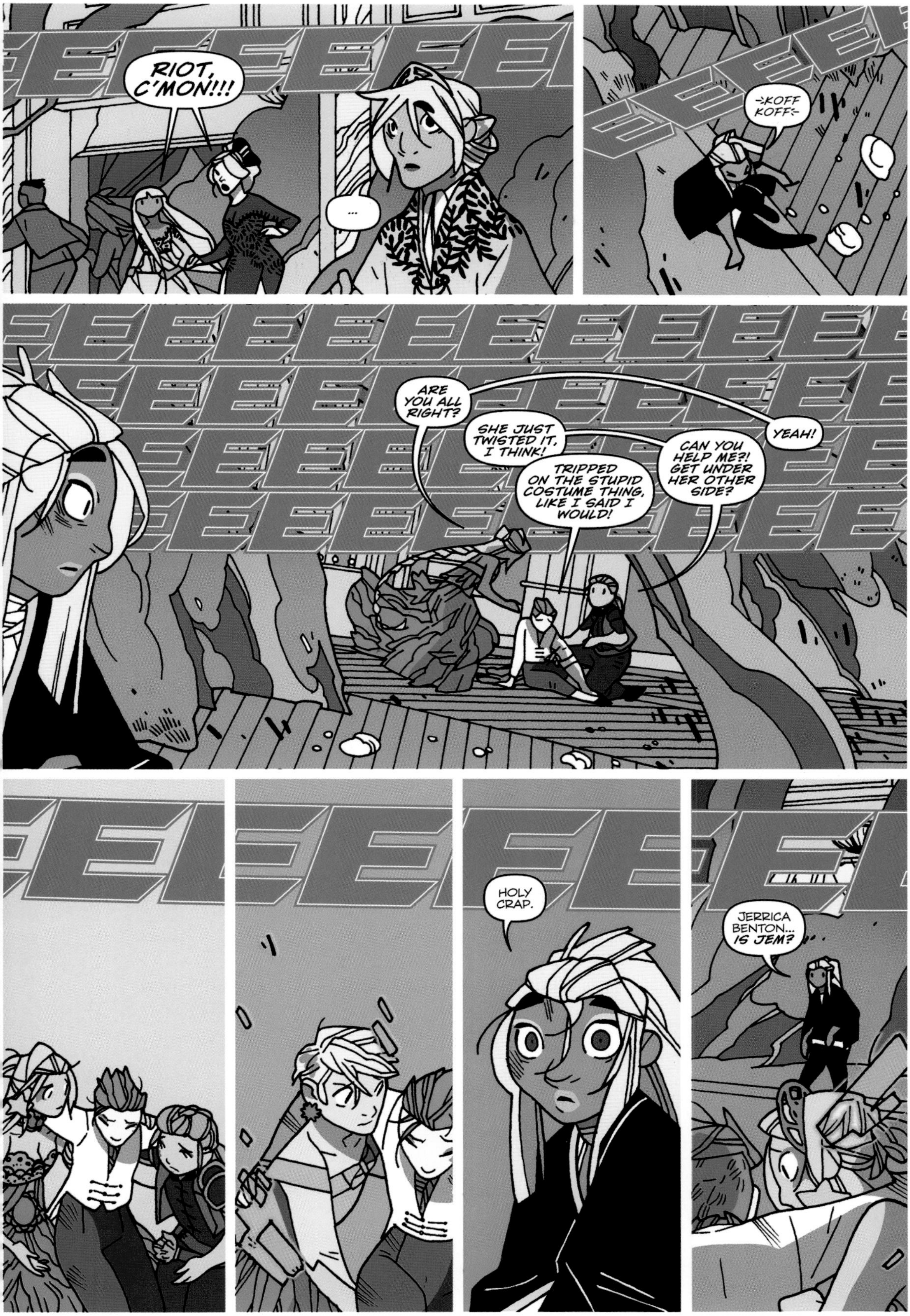
RIOT, C'MON!!!
...
KOFF KOFF
ARE YOU ALL RIGHT?
YEAH!
SHE JUST TWISTED IT, I THINK!
TRIPPED ON THE STUPID COSTUME THING, LIKE I SAID I WOULD!
CAN YOU HELP ME?! GET UNDER HER OTHER SIDE?
HOLY CRAP.
JERRICA BENTON... IS JEM?

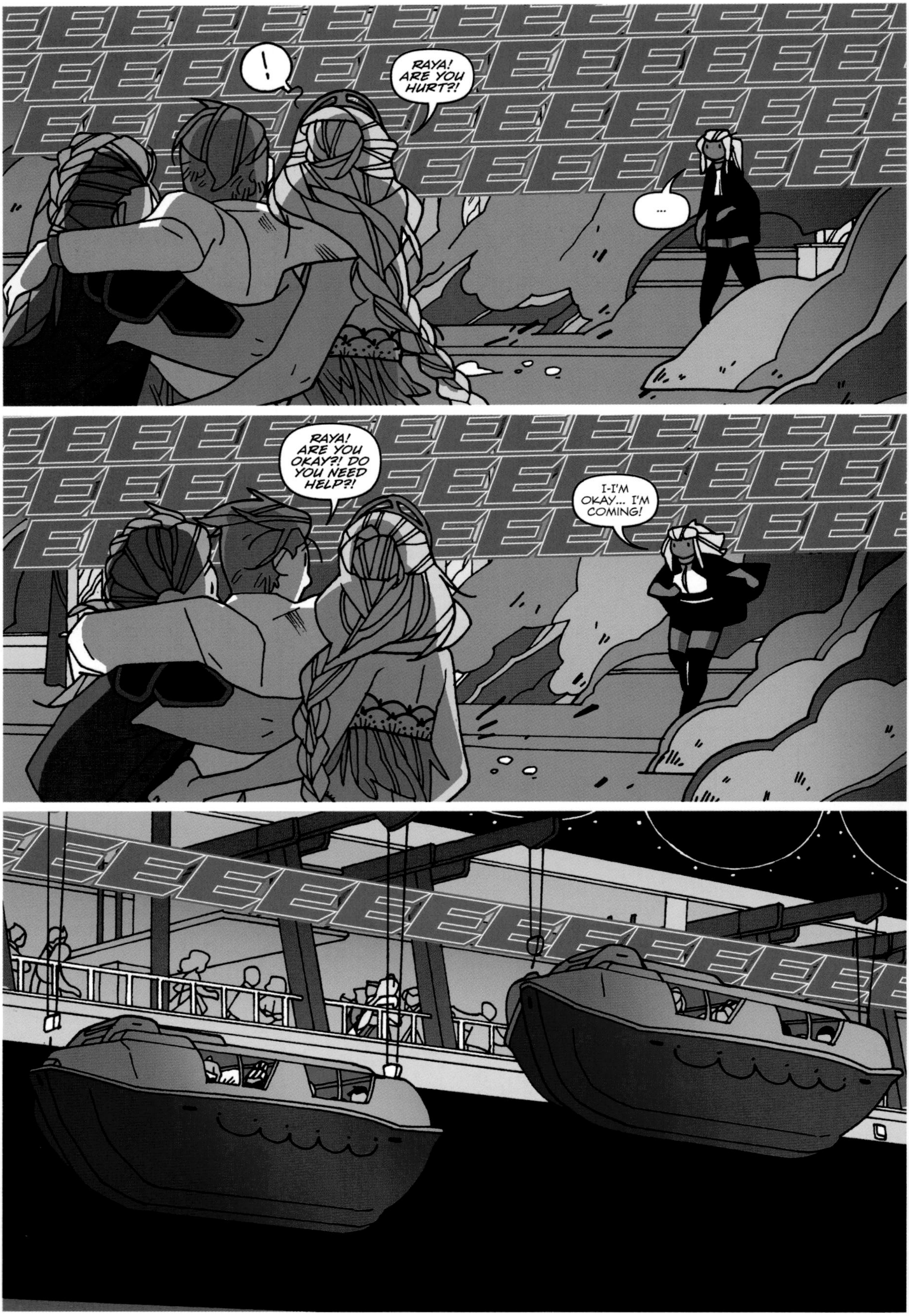
!
RAYA! ARE YOU HURT?!
...
RAYA! ARE YOU OKAY?! DO YOU NEED HELP?!
I-I'M OKAY... I'M COMING!

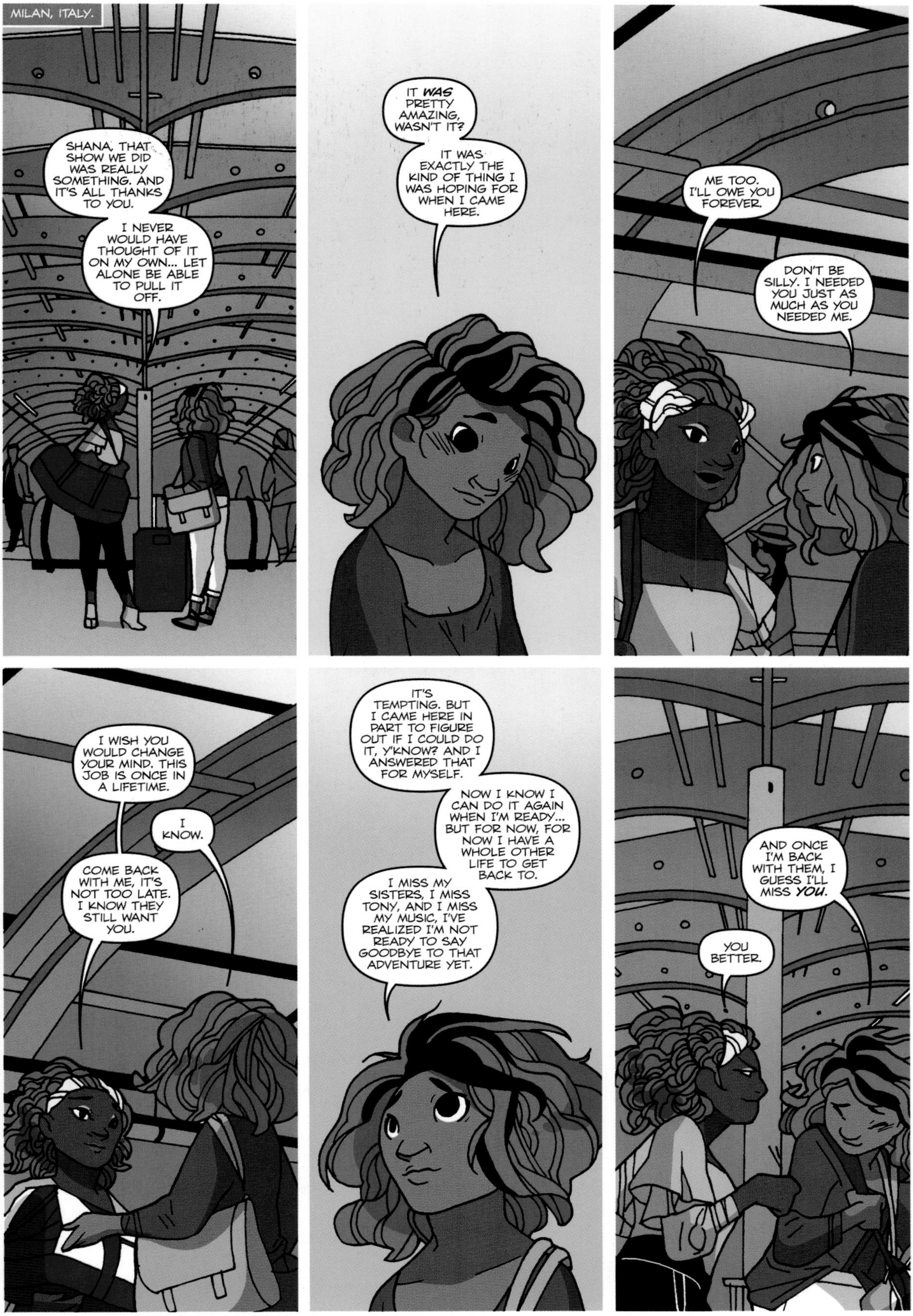
MILAN, ITALY.
SHANA, THAT SHOW WE DID WAS REALLY SOMETHING. AND IT'S ALL THANKS TO YOU.
I NEVER WOULD HAVE THOUGHT OF IT ON MY OWN... LET ALONE BE ABLE TO PULL IT OFF.
IT *WAS* PRETTY AMAZING, WASN'T IT?
IT WAS EXACTLY THE KIND OF THING I WAS HOPING FOR WHEN I CAME HERE.
ME TOO. I'LL OWE YOU FOREVER.
DON'T BE SILLY. I NEEDED YOU JUST AS MUCH AS YOU NEEDED ME.
I WISH YOU WOULD CHANGE YOUR MIND. THIS JOB IS ONCE IN A LIFETIME.
I KNOW.
COME BACK WITH ME, IT'S NOT TOO LATE. I KNOW THEY STILL WANT YOU.
IT'S TEMPTING. BUT I CAME HERE IN PART TO FIGURE OUT IF I COULD DO IT, Y'KNOW? AND I ANSWERED THAT FOR MYSELF.
NOW I KNOW I CAN DO IT AGAIN WHEN I'M READY... BUT FOR NOW, FOR NOW I HAVE A WHOLE OTHER LIFE TO GET BACK TO.
I MISS MY SISTERS, I MISS TONY, AND I MISS MY MUSIC, I'VE REALIZED I'M NOT READY TO SAY GOODBYE TO THAT ADVENTURE YET.
AND ONCE I'M BACK WITH THEM, I GUESS I'LL MISS *YOU*.
YOU BETTER.

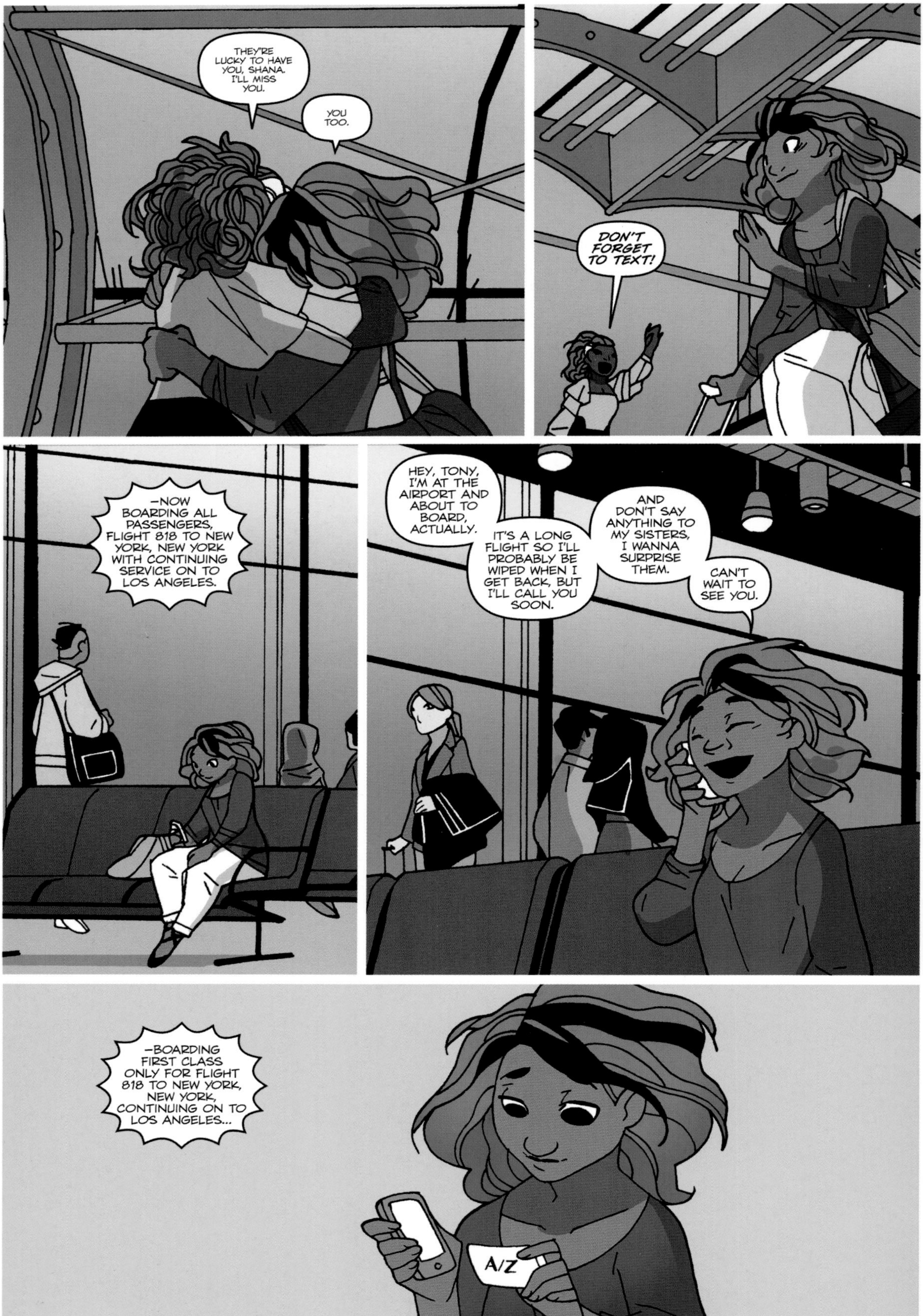
THEY'RE LUCKY TO HAVE YOU, SHANA. I'LL MISS YOU.
YOU TOO.
DON'T FORGET TO TEXT!
—NOW BOARDING ALL PASSENGERS, FLIGHT 818 TO NEW YORK, NEW YORK WITH CONTINUING SERVICE ON TO LOS ANGELES.
HEY, TONY, I'M AT THE AIRPORT AND ABOUT TO BOARD, ACTUALLY.
IT'S A LONG FLIGHT SO I'LL PROBABLY BE WIPED WHEN I GET BACK, BUT I'LL CALL YOU SOON.
AND DON'T SAY ANYTHING TO MY SISTERS, I WANNA SURPRISE THEM.
CAN'T WAIT TO SEE YOU.
—BOARDING FIRST CLASS ONLY FOR FLIGHT 818 TO NEW YORK, NEW YORK, CONTINUING ON TO LOS ANGELES...
A/Z

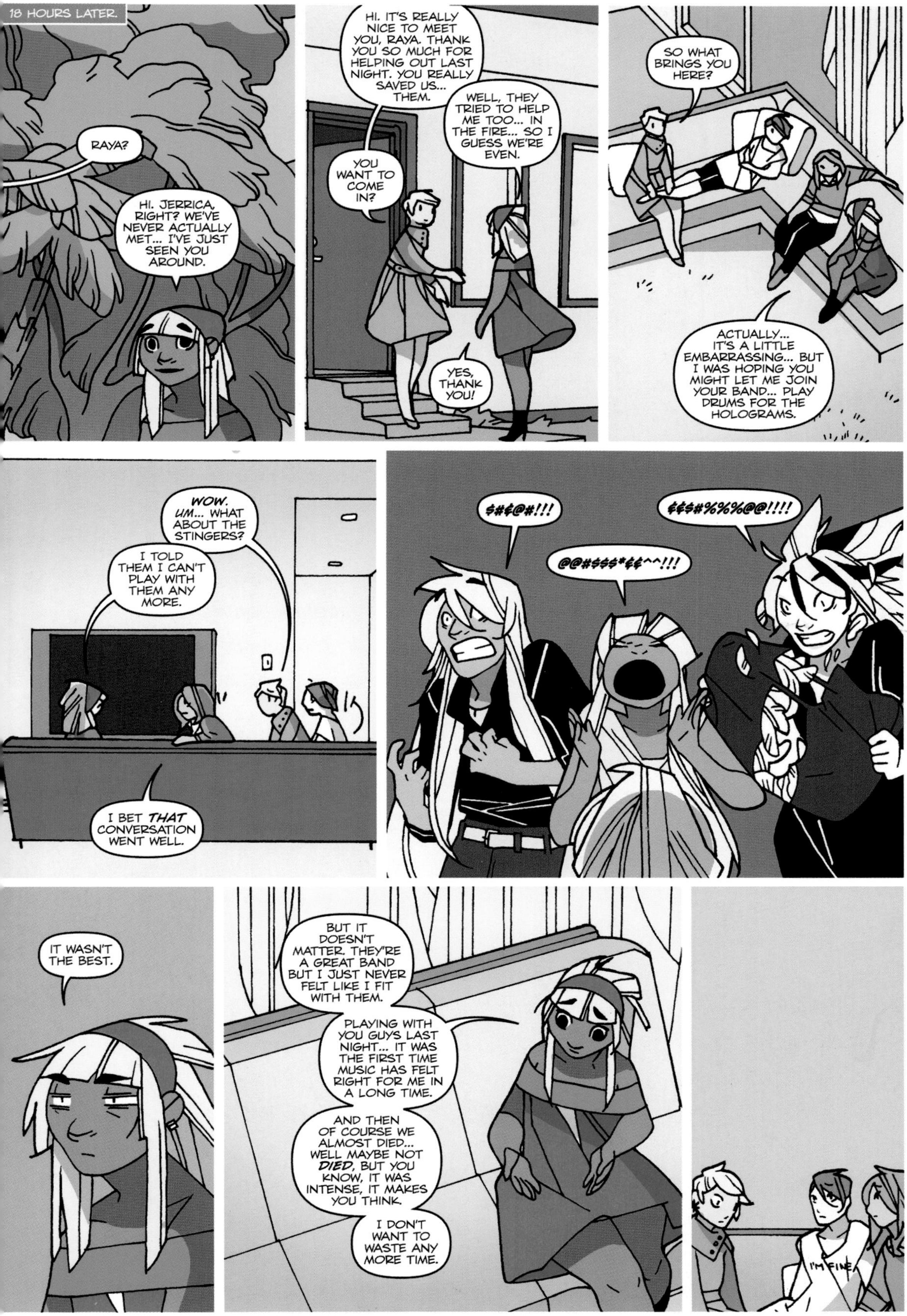

18 HOURS LATER.
RAYA?
HI. JERRICA, RIGHT? WE'VE NEVER ACTUALLY MET... I'VE JUST SEEN YOU AROUND.
HI. IT'S REALLY NICE TO MEET YOU, RAYA. THANK YOU SO MUCH FOR HELPING OUT LAST NIGHT. YOU REALLY SAVED US... THEM.
WELL, THEY TRIED TO HELP ME TOO... IN THE FIRE... SO I GUESS WE'RE EVEN.
YOU WANT TO COME IN?
YES, THANK YOU!
SO WHAT BRINGS YOU HERE?
ACTUALLY... IT'S A LITTLE EMBARRASSING... BUT I WAS HOPING YOU MIGHT LET ME JOIN YOUR BAND... PLAY DRUMS FOR THE HOLOGRAMS.
WOW. UM... WHAT ABOUT THE STINGERS?
I TOLD THEM I CAN'T PLAY WITH THEM ANY MORE.
I BET THAT CONVERSATION WENT WELL.
$#¢@#!!!
@@#$$$*¢¢^^!!!
¢¢$#%%%@@!!!!
IT WASN'T THE BEST.
BUT IT DOESN'T MATTER. THEY'RE A GREAT BAND BUT I JUST NEVER FELT LIKE I FIT WITH THEM.
PLAYING WITH YOU GUYS LAST NIGHT... IT WAS THE FIRST TIME MUSIC HAS FELT RIGHT FOR ME IN A LONG TIME.
AND THEN OF COURSE WE ALMOST DIED... WELL MAYBE NOT DIED, BUT YOU KNOW, IT WAS INTENSE, IT MAKES YOU THINK.
I DON'T WANT TO WASTE ANY MORE TIME.
I'M FINE

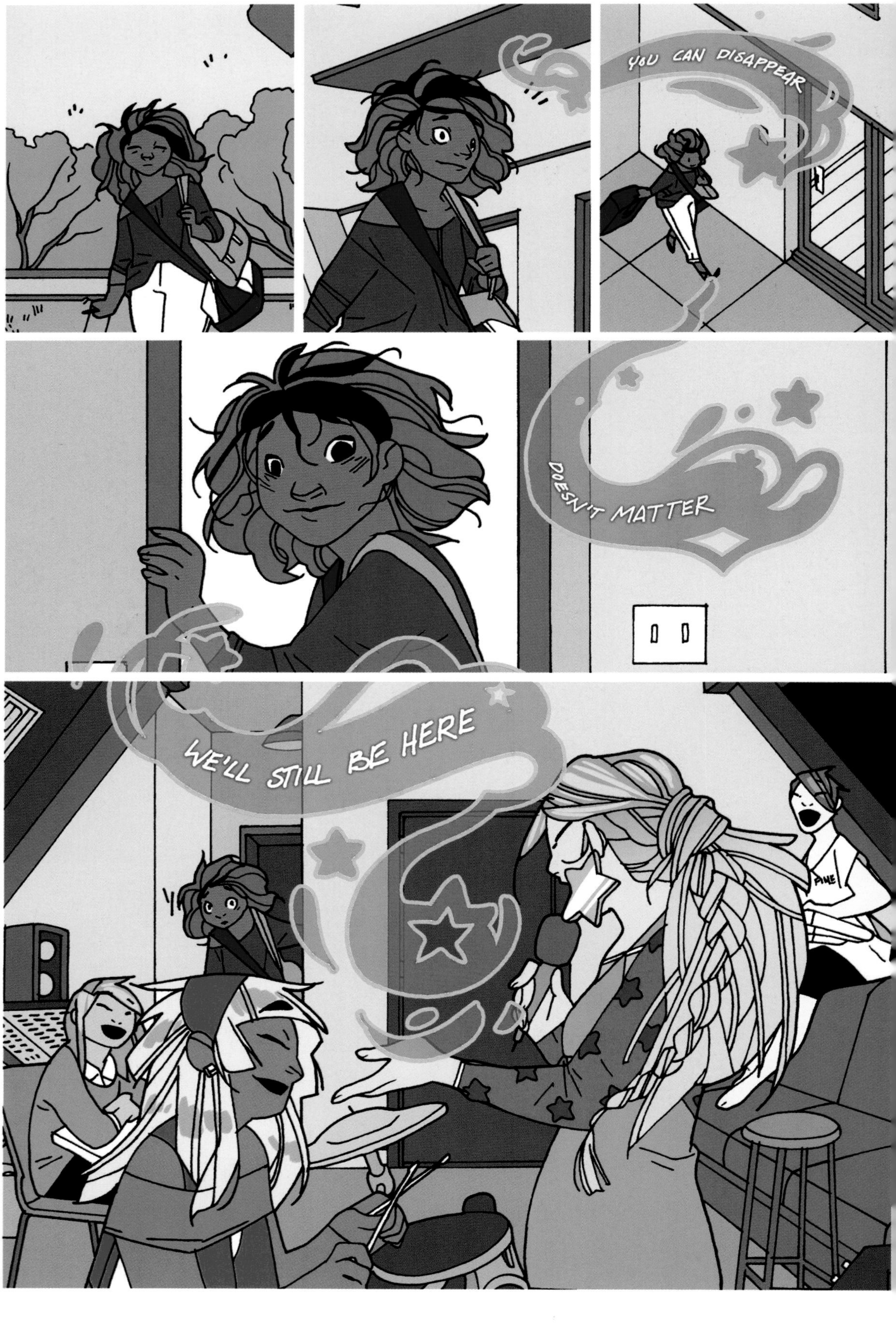
YOU CAN DISAPPEAR
DOESN'T MATTER
WE'LL STILL BE HERE

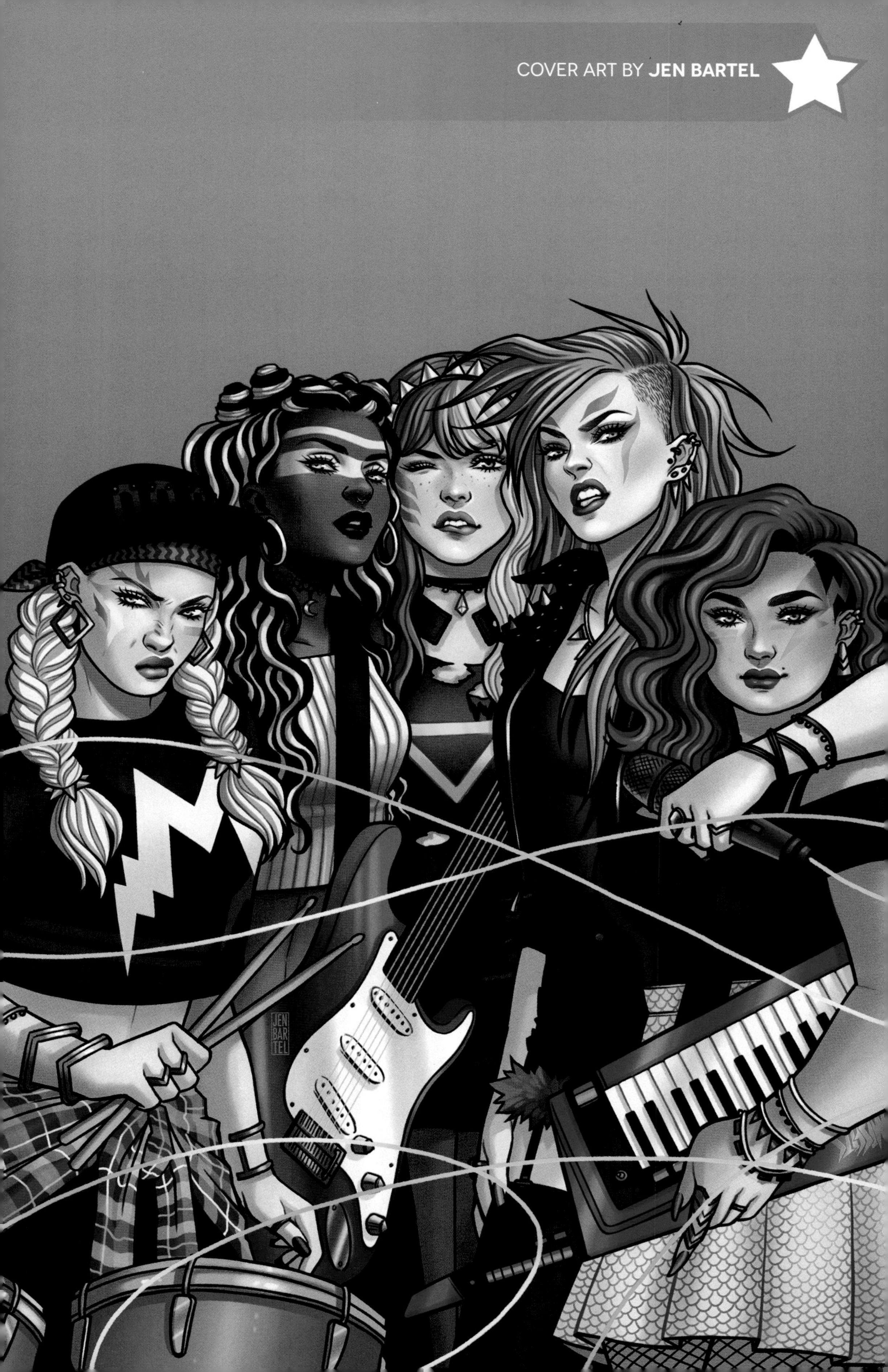
JEN BARTEL
COVER ART BY **JEN BARTEL**

ART BY **ANDREW GRIFFITH**

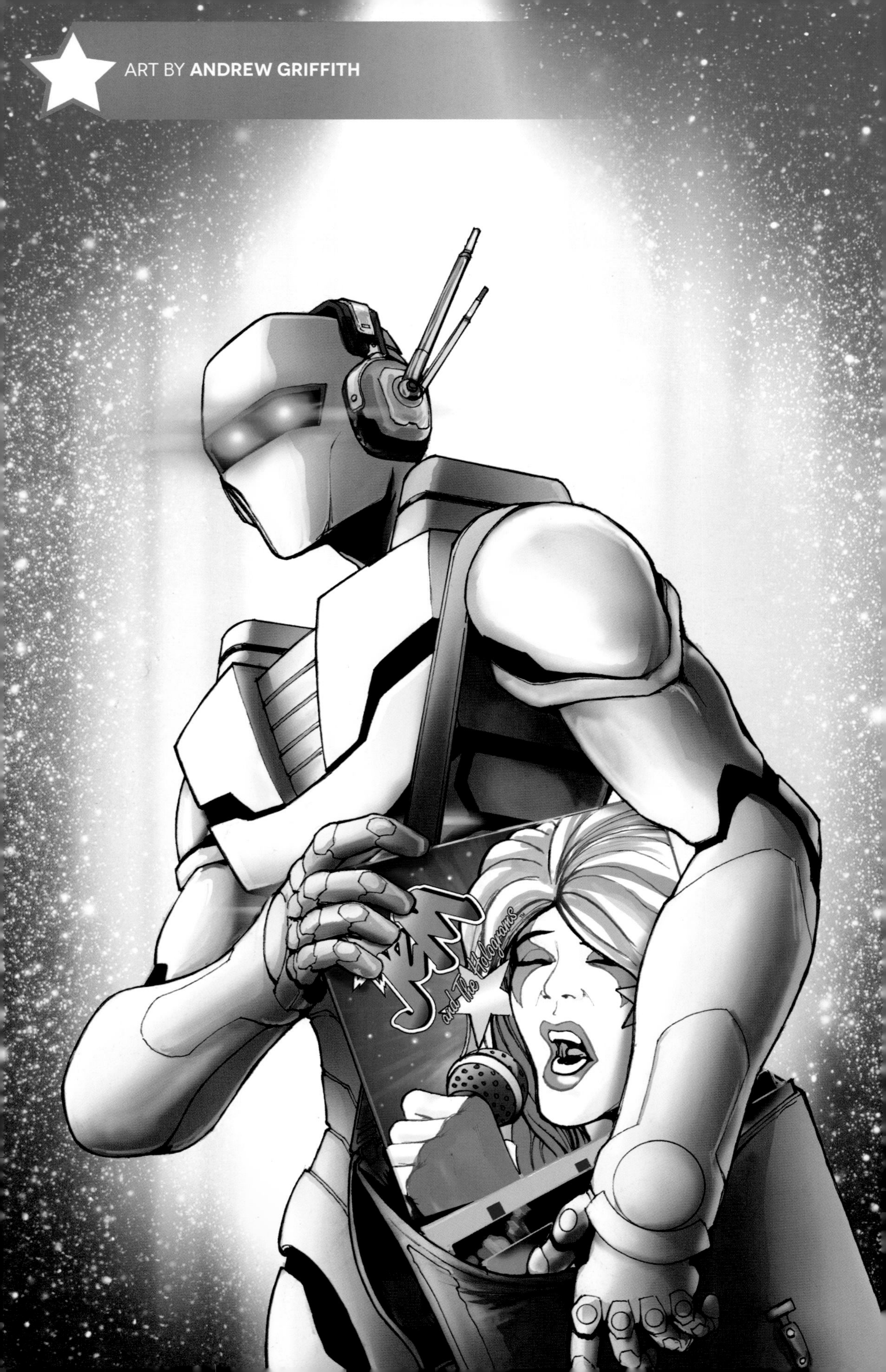

ART BY **GISELE LAGACE**
COLORS BY **JASON MILLET**

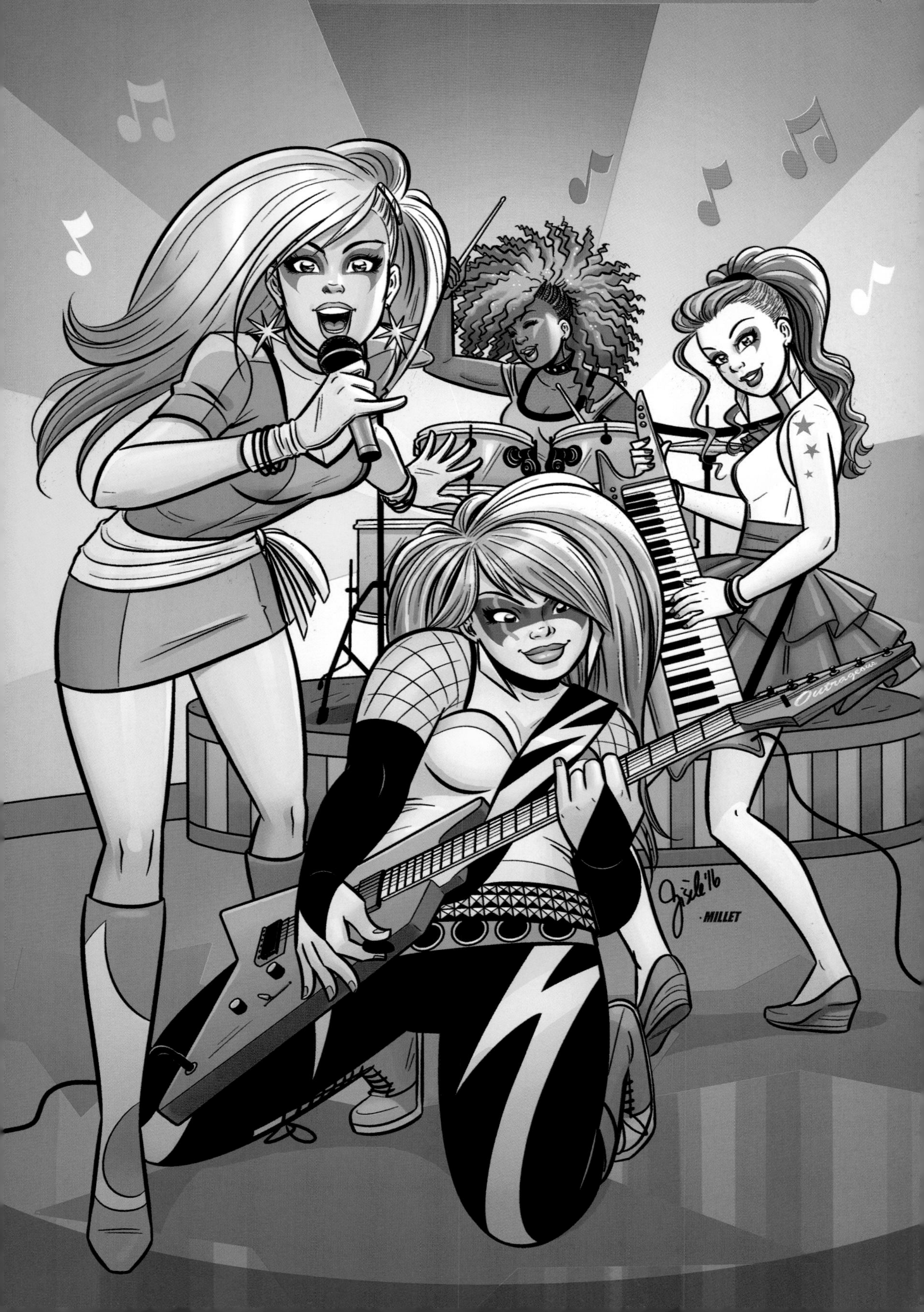
Outrageous
Gisele '16
MILLET

ART BY **GISELE LAGACE**
COLORS BY **JASON MILLET**

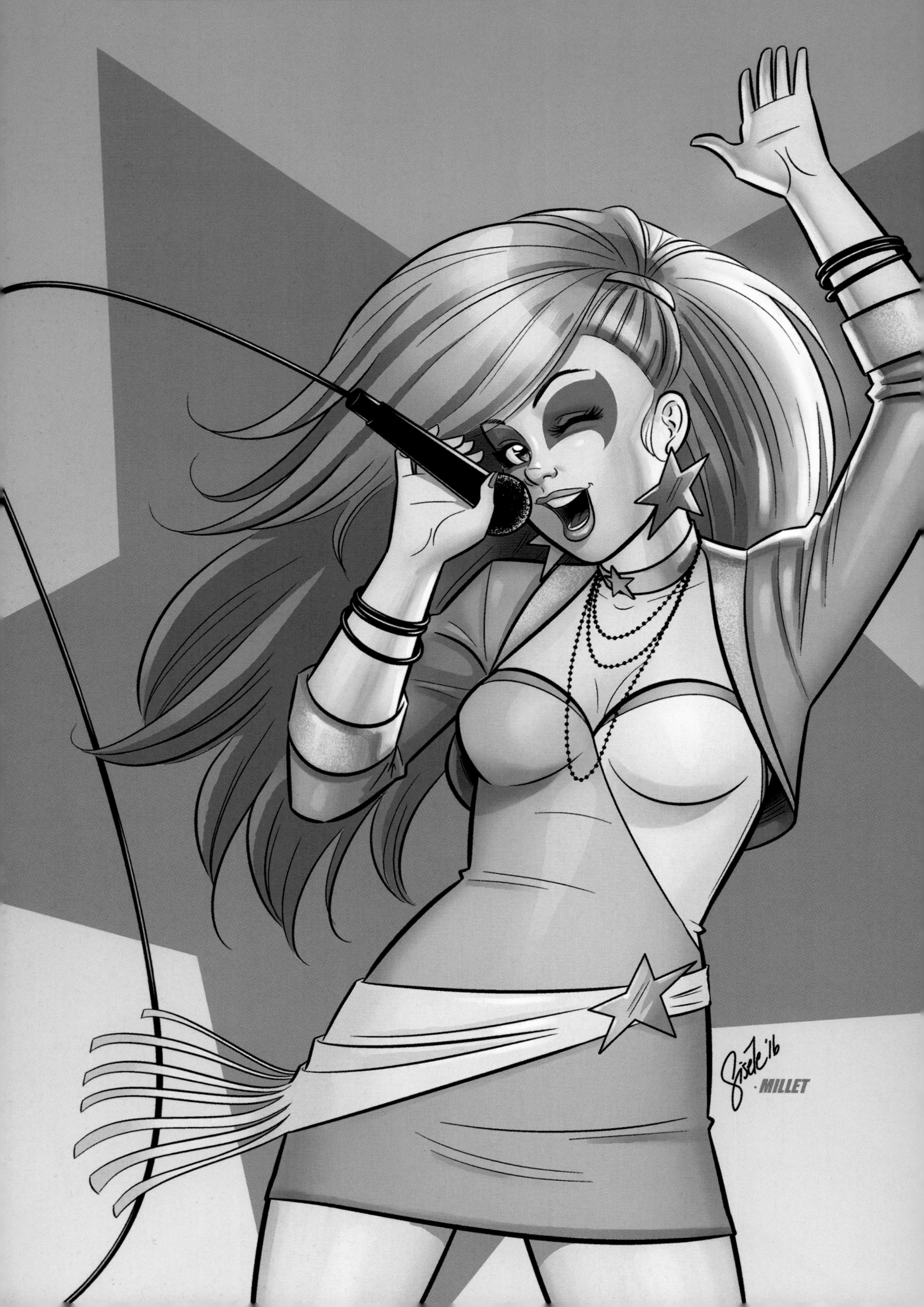
Gisele '16
MILLET

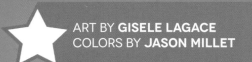

ART BY **GISELE LAGACE**
COLORS BY **JASON MILLET**

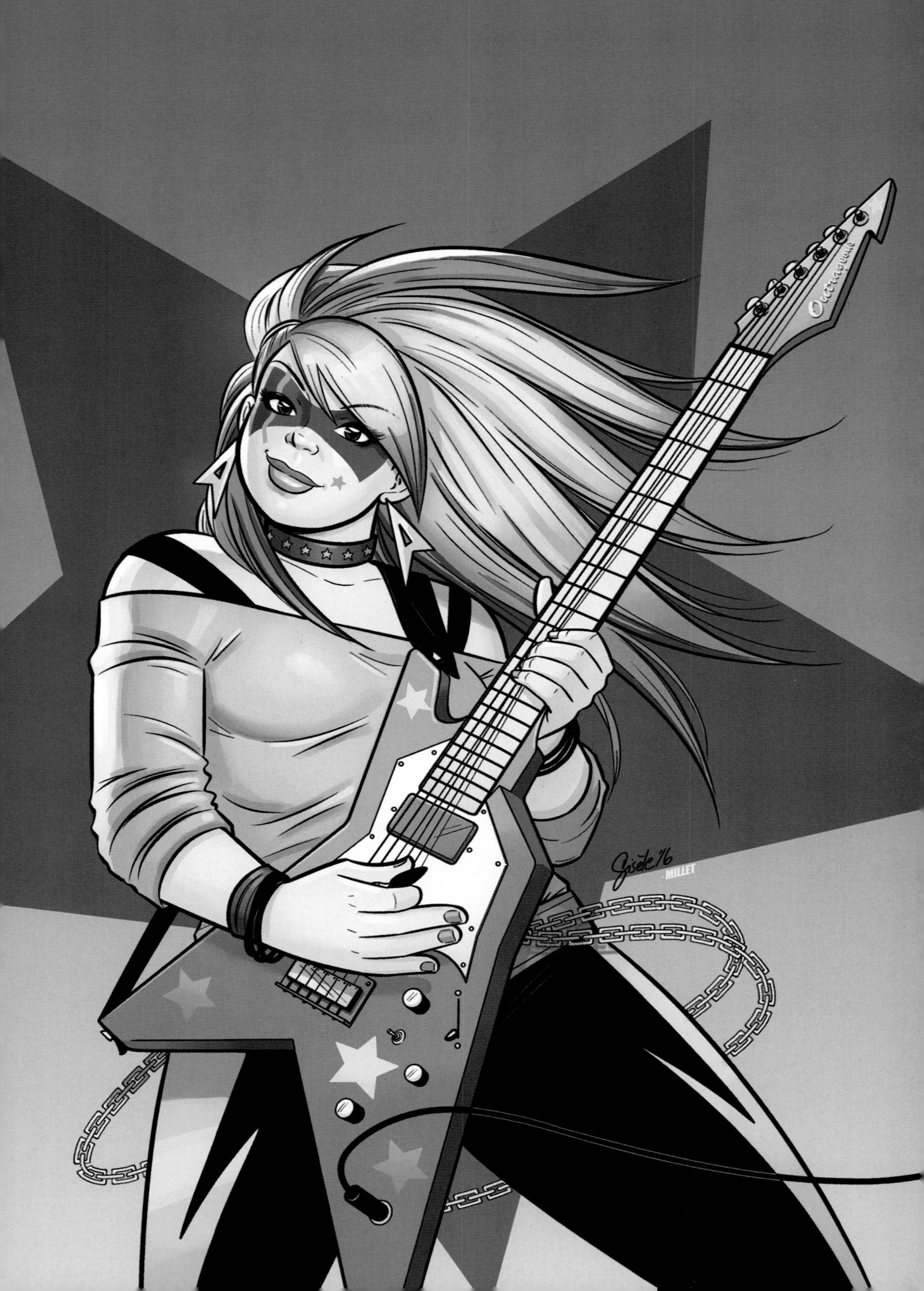

ART BY **GISELE LAGACE**
COLORS BY **JASON MILLET**

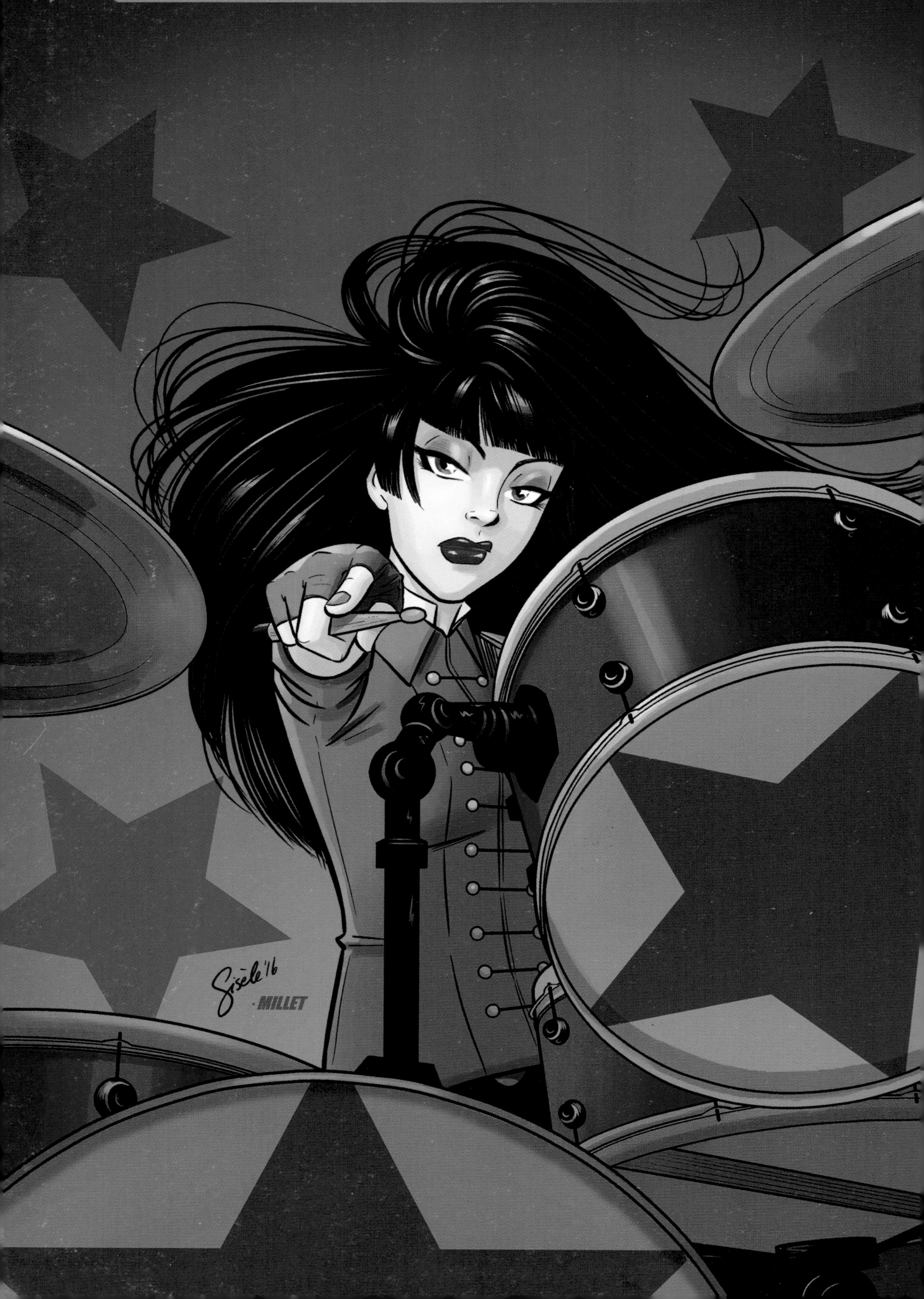
Gisèle '16
MILLET